SECOND EDITION

Women and Power in American History: Volume I to 1880

Edited by
Kathryn Kish Sklar
and
Thomas Dublin

Prentice
Hall

Upper Saddle River, New Jersey 07458

Library of Congress Cataloging-in-Publication Data

Women and power in American history / edited by Kathryn Kish Sklar and
Thomas Dublin.—[2nd ed.].
    p. cm.
    Includes bibliographical references and index.
    Contents: v. 1. To 1880 — v. 2. From 1870.
    ISBN 0-13-041570-7 (vol. 1) —ISBN 0-13-041581-2 (vol. 2)
    1. Women—United States—History. 2. Women—United States—Social conditions. I.
Sklar, Kathryn Kish. II. Dublin, Thomas

HQ1410 .W643 2002
305.4'0973—dc21

2001036624

VP, Editorial Director: Charlyce Jones-Owen
Senior Acquisitions Editor: Charles Cavaliere
Editorial Assistant: Adrienne Paul
Senior Managing Editor: Jan Stephan
Production Liaison: Fran Russello
Editorial/Production Supervision: Marianne Hutchinson (Pine Tree Composition, Inc.)
Prepress and Manufacturing Buyer: Tricia Kenny
Art Director: Jayne Conte
Cover Design: Kiwi Design
Cover art: Lucille Chabot (American, born 1908), "Gabriel Weathervane" © 1939, watercolor on
    paper, .362 × .524 (14 1/4 × 20 5/8) Board of Trustees, National Gallery of Art, Washington, D.C.
Director, Image Resource Center: Melinda Lee Reo
Manager, Rights & Permissions: Key Dellosa
Image Specialist: Beth Boyd
Photo Researcher: Teri Stratford
Marketing Manager: Claire Rehwinkel

For permission to use copyrighted material, grateful acknowledgment is made to the copyright
holders on page 285, which are hereby made part of this copyright page.

This book was set in 10/12 New Baskerville by Pine Tree Composition, Inc.,
and was printed and bound by RR Donnelley & Sons Company.
The cover was printed by The Lehigh Press, Inc.

©2002, 1991 by Pearson Education, Inc.
Upper Saddle River, New Jersey 07458

Printed in the United States of America
10 9 8 7 6 5 4 3 2 1

ISBN 0-13-041570-7

Pearson Education Ltd., *London*
Pearson Education Australia Pte. Limited, *Sydney*
Pearson Education Singapore, Pte. Ltd.
Pearson Education North Asia Ltd., *Hong Kong*
Pearson Education Canada, Ltd., *Toronto*
Pearson Educatión de Mexico, S.A. de C.V.
Pearson Education—Japan, *Tokyo*
Pearson Education Malaysia, Pte. Ltd.
Pearson Education, Upper Saddle River, *New Jersey*

Contents

Preface to the Second Edition

When we completed the first edition of *Women and Power in American History: A Reader* in 1991, we commented on the way the two volumes demonstrated the phenomenal growth of the field of U.S. women's history over the previous twenty years. A decade later the growing institutionalization of the field has become even more visible. Two major journals, the *Journal of Women's History* and *Gender and History,* are now both more than ten years old, as is a major dissertation prize, the Lerner-Scott Award. The number of graduate programs in U.S. Women's History has expanded as universities have responded to the growing demand for faculty in the field. While initially a department of history typically had a faculty member in U.S. Women's History and perhaps another in European Women's History, today it is increasingly common to find several faculty members in a department in each of these fields, as well as other colleagues with interests in women or gender in Asia, Africa, or Latin America.

These developments have prompted us to gather a second edition. Our goal remains the same as in 1991: to bring together a coherent group of articles related to the unifying theme of power in women's lives over time. This focus helped us to consider new selections as we sorted through voluminous recent additions to scholarship in American Women's History. Fourteen of the 38 articles that we employ in this second edition are new to the reader, reflecting the changing perspectives that have emerged in the field as it has matured. In addition, we have thoroughly reworked the selected bibliography and have also added a new section to each volume, focusing on resource materials in U.S. Women's History on the World Wide Web. The emergence of the World Wide Web has been one of the most dramatic changes in the academic world in the past decade, and in history as well as in other disciplines, it offers rich new possibilities for research and teaching. We have both used the Web extensively in our teaching; collaboratively we have joined this revolution as codirectors of "Women and Social Movements in the United States," (http://womhist.binghamton.edu), a major source of primary documents for teaching in U.S. Women's History.

U.S. Women's History emerged as a specialized field of historical study partly in response to the rebirth of the organized women's movement beginning in the 1960s. In that movement, women attacked gender inequalities in the broader society and struggled against barriers to women's full participation in American society. To us, as scholars and activists, it seems particularly appropriate to focus our readings in U.S. Women's History on questions of women and power in American History. A greater understanding of how power inequalities are organized along gender lines can help us work toward a more egalitarian and just society. Because the work of the women's movement is far from complete, our need for a fuller historical understanding of gender relations and women remains as great as ever. We trust this new reader will contribute to greater understanding and continuing change in women's and men's lives.

Our thanks to Professors Nancy Page Fernandez, California State University, Northridge, and Anya Jabour, University of Montana, for their thoughtful reviews of the first edition of this reader, and to Melissa Doak of the State University of New York at Binghamton for consistent support as this project evolved.

Kathryn Kish Sklar
Thomas Dublin

Contributors

Mary H. Blewett writes on the social history of industrialization in the nineteenth and early twentieth centuries, specializing in gender, ethnic, and class analysis. Her most recent book is *Constant Turmoil: The Politics of Industrial Life in Nineteenth-Century New England* (2000).

Janet Farrell Brodie is Professor of History at Claremont Graduate University and the author of *Contraception and Abortion in Nineteenth-Century America.*

Kathleen M. Brown is Associate Professor of History at the University of Pennsylvania, where she teaches the history of women and gender and early American history. She is currently working on a history of cleanliness in the United States before the Civil War.

Lois Green Carr is Historian at the Historic St. Mary's (Maryland) City Commission. She has authored numerous articles on Chesapeake history and is coauthor of *Robert Cole's World: Agriculture and Society in Early Maryland.*

Lucie Cheng is Professor of Sociology and Urban Planning at the University of California, Los Angeles. She is the author or editor of more than thirty books and articles on women, ethnic relations, migration, and development.

Lyle Koehler was an independent scholar in Las Cruces, New Mexico, and the author of *A Search for Power: The "Weaker Sex" in Seventeenth-Century New England.*

Allan Kulikoff is the Abraham Baldwin Professor of the Humanities at the University of Georgia. His current work concerns the development of the yeoman classes in early America and he has recently published *From British Peasants to Colonial American Farmers.*

Carol Lasser is Professor of History at Oberlin College. She works in nineteenth-century American history and is currently researching the interracial history of Oberlin, Ohio.

Glenda Riley is the Alexander M. Bracken Professor of History at Ball State University and a past president of the Western History Association. Her latest books are *Women and Nature: Saving the "Wild" West* and the third edition of her textbook, *Inventing the American Woman: An Inclusive History.*

Caroll Smith-Rosenberg is the Alice Freeman Palmer Professor of History and teaches in both the American Culture Program and the Women's Studies Program at the University of Michigan. She is the author of *Disorderly*

Conduct: Visions of Gender in Victorian America and the forthcoming *Federalist Capers: Constituting the New American.*

Laurel Thatcher Ulrich is Phillips Professor of Early American History at Harvard University. Her most recent book, *The Age of Homespun,* looks at textile production in New England from the early colonial period to the 1830s.

Lorena S. Walsh is Historian at Colonial Williamsburg, author of numerous articles on Chesapeake history, and author of *From Calabar to Carter's Grove: The History of a Virginia Slave Community.*

Deborah Gray White is Chair of the Department of History at Rutgers University. She is the author of *Ar'n't I A Woman?: Female Slaves in the Plantation South, Too Heavy a Load: Black Women in Defense of Themselves,* and *Let My People Go: African Americans, 1804–1860.*

Introduction: Power as a Theme in Women's History

One of the biggest challenges facing historians of American women is the task of identifying the causes and consequences of long-term changes in women's lives. That task looms large not only because it is central to the historian's chief calling—analyzing change over time—but also because the turning points of historical change for women differ from those that have mattered most for men. When history is seen from the perspective of women's experience, new categories of analysis are clearly needed, since wars and other political events that have marked the standard historical divisions have usually been less important in the lives of average women than changes in family relationships, social movements, or the organization of the paid labor force. Thus, during the first thirty years of its existence as an academic discipline, the field of U.S. women's history has focused more attention on women's family lives, their working lives, and their community activism than on the themes of power that pervade male-centered treatments of American history.

Yet the need to analyze change over time in U.S. women's history has grown more urgent as the field itself has grown. Its abundant diversity, embracing women of all classes, ethnicities, races, religions, sexual orientations, and regions, poses serious challenges as to how this diversity can be meaningfully synthesized into a coherent whole. In their search for unifying themes, historians of American women have found new uses for the most fundamental category of analysis known in the discipline of history—the study of social power, its components, causes, and consequences.

Power is a very useful means of depicting change in women's lives over time. First, it is a theme capable of linking changes in the three fundamental dimensions of women's lives—family, work, and community experiences. We know that changes in these three arenas of women's experience overlap and influence one another, but to understand that process we need tools of analysis that cut across all three. Themes relating to power do that effectively because they embrace personal relations of the sort found in family life as well as collective identities located in community activities and the workplace.

Second, power is a valuable theme for connecting women's history with other dimensions of American history. The field's effectiveness as an illuminator of all American history hinges on its use of a Promethean new category of historical analysis: gender as a principle of social organization. Since women can never be studied totally in isolation from men, gender relations are central to women's history, bringing with them the experience of men and their relations with women. In this context, power is a key category of analysis because it illuminates the relationships between men and women.

Third, power is a helpful vehicle for understanding relations among women of different social standing. Most differences among women are socially constructed. Differences of class, race, ethnicity, religion, sexual orientation, or region are generated by social structures. Although they might appear to be natural, they are created by social values and social institutions that reinforce social hierarchies and distribute power unevenly. Women's history needs to take account of differences among women and how social disparities translate into differences of power.

For these and other reasons, historians of women are increasingly using power as a leading category of analysis. This collection of writings in American women's history is the first to focus centrally on themes of power in women's lives. It seeks to convey the diverse perspectives from which this theme can fruitfully be viewed, as well as the wide variety of female experiences the theme can integrate.

What do historians of women mean by "power?" The newness of the term's application to women can be seen in historians' tendency to leave the term undefined. Many dictionaries define power as the "possession of control, authority, or influence over others,"* yet an important aspect of women's power has been expressed in their ability to exercise control over their own bodies, to limit men's access to their sexuality, and to control their own reproductive lives. Therefore, from the perspective of women's history, a more suitable definition of power is the ability to control the distribution of social resources. Women's power has often rested in their ability to control the distribution of things or services rather than persons. Put another way, the essence of women's power has historically rested in their control of goods or services through which they frequently, albeit indirectly, have controlled persons. Women's power has often been expressed through withdrawal of their services. For example, Anne Hutchinson and her supporters created an uproar in the 1630s by withdrawing their support from Boston's chief minister, John Wilson. In the first half of the nineteenth century, the power of northern women increased substantially when they assumed greater control over their bodies and their sexual relationships with suitors and husbands.

Short introductions to each article in this collection provide a guide to how each historian analyzes themes of power. Less evident are the ways that women's power has changed over time. It is useful to identify four principles of change that shaped the period between 1636 and 1869—that is, the years between Anne Hutchinson's expression of discontent with women's

---

* *Webster's Ninth New Collegiate Dictionary* (Springfield, Mass.: Merriam-Webster, 1989).

subordination in the Puritan church and the creation of institutions devoted explicitly and exclusively to women's rights.

The first principle concerns the interconnectedness of the major arenas of women's activities—family, work, and community life. Changes in one of these dimensions have invariably been linked to changes in the others. Thus, for example, changes in the working lives of New England women who constituted the first industrial workforce at textile mills in Lowell, Massachusetts, in the 1830s were closely related to changes in women's family lives, in which young women experienced a period of independence from family life while living together in boardinghouses in Lowell, and changes in community life, in which Lowell women formed peer communities that supported their decision to strike in protest against reduced wages. How the causal arrows point within the triad of family, work, and community life depends upon the circumstances at any given moment, but those connections have been central to women's experience of change over time.

Another important principle is that change in female experience is often excruciatingly slow. Perhaps because gender constitutes one of the most fundamental forms of social organization—one upon which others are often built—changes in gender relations involve a multitude of other categories of change, and these, in turn, require their own set of causes, many of which are long in the making. The best example of such slow processes is the "demographic transition" between 1800 and 1940 from high birth and death rates to low birth and death rates (see Figure 1). This long-term decline was caused by factors so complex and pervasive that they continue to elude historical analysis today. Women in all races, classes, and regions experienced this dramatic decline in birth rates between 1800 and 1940, which reduced from seven to two the average number of children born to women who survived to the age of fifty. Two-thirds of this decline occurred before 1880, before widespread use of artificial contraceptive techniques. The proportion of women who never married rose between 1870 and 1910 to a level only equaled in the 1990s. Relying mostly on withdrawal and sexual abstinence to lengthen the intervals between births, couples were aided by Victorian sexual values, which discouraged the expression of sexual desire and granted women unprecedented control over their own bodies. These values also exaggerated the differences between the sexes and treated women as morally superior to men. In this context, many women—married and unmarried—formed what historians have come to call "homosocial" relationships with other women.

Historians used to attribute the long-term decline in birth rates to industrialization and urbanization. However, recent research has shown that rural Americans accounted for most of that decline during its most intensive decades—the 1840s and 1850s. Historians also found that since birth rates began to decline before significant reduction in infant mortality (the chief contributor to high death rates), the decline in birth rates cannot be explained as due to declining death rates. Recently, historians have turned to even larger

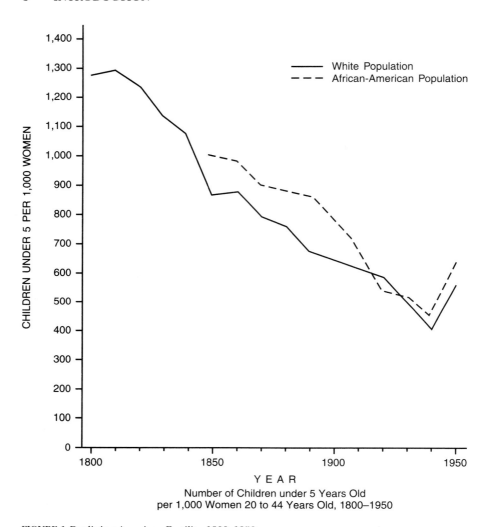

FIGURE 1 Declining American Fertility, 1800–1950
Source: Bureau of the Census, *Historical Statistics of the United States: Colonial Times to 1957* (Washington, D.C.: Government Printing Office, 1960), Series B37–68, p. 24.

and more elusive causes, such as the growth of the market economy and its mirror image, the decline of subsistence agriculture. Historians now believe that the new valuation placed on each individual child was also important, along with religious beliefs that made human agency the cause of salvation. Since each of these and other components of fertility decline had its own chain of causes, fertility decline rested upon a pyramid of other historical changes. Taken together, they constituted an almost total transformation in American life, a transformation that took more than one hundred years to achieve.

Other, less complicated changes in women's lives also need to be measured by decades rather than years. For example, the women's rights movement—born during a speaking tour by Angelina and Sarah Grimké in Massachusetts in 1837, codified in Seneca Falls, New York, in 1848, and advocated by the National Woman Suffrage Association and American Woman Suffrage Association after 1869—took more than seventy years to achieve its goal of woman suffrage in 1920, making it the longest continuous social movement in U.S. history.

This does not mean that women's history lacks turning points or that it forms one long progression of achievement. Rather, it shows us that when turning points do occur, they usually involve multiple causes that have deep social roots and extend across more than one generation.

Another key principle of change over time in women's history involves differences among women. The social construction of dissimilarities among women may change, reflecting changing social, economic, or political structures. For example, the Virginia slave codes for the 1660s and 1670s created new inequalities among women when they defined slavery as a status derived from the mother: children of slave women thereby became slaves, while children of free women remained free. Conversely, changing social, political, or economic realities have also eroded differences among women. For example, heightened gender consciousness among northern white women in the early nineteenth century created new bonds among them that transcended differences of age, religious affiliation, and education. Differences and similarities among women are therefore constantly changing, reflecting, and influencing changes in the larger society, polity, and economy.

Finally, and perhaps most importantly, women's agency—that is, their ability to influence changes in their lives and in their society—commands our attention as a crucial principle in the interpretation of change over time in women's history. No one proposition is more widely held in the field of women's history than the view that women have not been merely passive victims, but have played a part in shaping their historical destiny. No women were totally lacking in agency; even slave women made choices that enhanced their ability to control their life circumstances.

The extent to which women have been able to shape the circumstances of their lives has itself changed over time, offering us one of the most fruitful avenues of historical inquiry. For example, by comparing the ability of Ann Hutchinson and her contemporaries to affect social change in the 1630s with that of women in the American Female Moral Reform Society in the 1830s, we are struck by the expansion of women's agency in the latter period.

By viewing changes in women's agency over time we gain a clearer understanding of the other principles of change evident in women's history: the interrelationships among family, work, and community life; the tendency for changes in women's lives to reflect long-term, deeply rooted transformations; and the shifting relationships between different groups of women. For example, the empowerment that women generated within evangelical religion in the first half of the nineteenth century buttressed an expansion of women's agency in family life, and, as Catharine Beecher's career showed, in women's ability to work outside the home as teachers. Dramatic fertility decline in the mid-nineteenth century, which occurred prior to effective contraceptive use, was due in part to women's choice of abortion as a means of controlling their reproductive lives. Finally, white women enhanced their ability to survive in the often hostile environment of the frontier by befriending Indian women, turning the difference between the two races into an asset.

The history of American women is a history of struggle. We can understand that struggle better by viewing the changing dimensions of power in women's lives.

*   *   *

The selections included in this volume demonstrate the centrality of domestic institutions to women's lives in the seventeenth, eighteenth, and nineteenth centuries. Changes in those institutions dramatically altered female experiences among Native Americans, European Americans, African Americans, and Chinese Americans.

Relations between Native Americans and the first British settlers of North America were shaped by the differing domestic gender relations in each culture, as Kathleen M. Brown has shown for colonial Virginia. Women in the Powhatan confederacy held greater responsibilities in Indian agriculture than was the case in English seventeenth-century society, and their economic importance was reflected in women's greater power through the matrilineal transmission of wealth and in community decision making. The English perception of Indian society as feminized contributed to their sense of superiority in relation to Native Americans, but Brown shows that they nevertheless incorporated elements of Indian gender systems in their own practices in the New World.

Changing family relations contributed to significant change in the lives of European-American women over time. By the 1830s, alterations long under way in American family and economic life matured to produce a fundamental transformation in the power of white American women by assigning to mothers rather than fathers primary responsibility for shaping the character of children. This marked the beginning of the end of patriarchal family relations and a crucial turning point in the history of middle-class women. Other changes, such as those associated with evangelical religion and continental expansion, combined with these shifts in family relationships to redefine domestic life as the basis for women's claim to a voice in public affairs and their unprecedented participation in secular social movements. Thus while women's domestic status could and did serve to limit their access to the larger world, it also launched them into that world and justified their assumption of special responsibilities in it.

Family life was just as critical to the historical experience of African-American women. Because tobacco, the chief commercial crop of the southern colonies before 1800, utilized the labor of women and children all year round, almost as many women as men were imported slaves. This produced a relatively equal "sex ratio"—the number of men per one hundred women—and encouraged family formation in the decades immediately before and after 1700, but it placed a double burden on slave women. Since most plantations were relatively small, most slave marriages occurred across plantations, and mothers and children often did not live in the same household as their husbands and fathers. Thus, in addition to their work in tobacco, women carried the main responsibility for the welfare of their children. Nevertheless, slave families became a major source of resistance to the oppressions of slavery. Newspaper ads placed for runaway slaves before 1700 indicate that owners expected to find errant slaves in the woods; after 1700, runaways were thought to be harbored by family members on other plantations.

Chinese-American women reflected their community's difficulties in forging family ties during an era when the vast majority of Chinese immigrants were men who entered the country as contract laborers expecting to postpone family life until they returned to China. The small numbers of Chinese women and the high sex ratio reflected the limited occupations available to women, prostitution being among the most prominent.

Differences among women in the first two and a half centuries of American history were easily measured by differences in their working lives. The production of goods for market flourished among women in the northeast, where a diversified agricultural economy encouraged exchange at the local level. Spinning bees in the 1770s lent a political meaning to northern women's household productivity. However, household production among southern white women was constricted by the dominance of tobacco as a cash crop. Tobacco profits discouraged female employment in the production of eggs, poultry, or butter, when their time could be more profitably employed in the production of tobacco. This created opportunities for African-American women, slave and free, who produced those and other goods for sale and exchange. After the Civil War and the abolition of slavery, African-American women spent less time in the fields working crops for commercial exchange and concentrated on gardening and other forms of household production.

In the early nineteenth century, the emergence of factory employment for women in textiles and shoemaking in the New England and Middle Atlantic states opened up a major division among women of different social classes. Increasing numbers of rural women left the countryside for urban employment, where they were joined by recent immigrants and daughters of immigrants as the century progressed. Factory employment had a decidedly contradictory impact on working women in these decades. It offered greater social and economic independence to some young, single women, while binding others firmly within the limits of an emerging family wage economy.

The interconnections of the family, work, and community lives of women were nowhere so evident as in domestic service, the occupation that remained the single largest source of employment for women between 1800 and 1940. Offering ready employment to generations of urban immigrant women, but isolating them in individual homes where class differences between employer and employee were dramatically evident, domestic service was shunned by those whose class, race, or skills gave them access to other work. Still, as Carol Lasser has demonstrated, even Irish domestic servants in Boston in the mid-nineteenth century had a measure of bargaining power in relation to their Yankee employers.

Between 1630 and 1870, community life tested the relative power of women and men. By the 1740s, in the Puritan-dominated colonies of the northeast, patriarchal values were gradually undermined by the numerical predominance of women in Puritan churches, but male authority and privilege grew in secular legal and political institutions, especially in courts. By comparing religious and secular proceedings arising from a case of fornication in the 1740s, we see that the secular courts that sustained male privilege had the last word. However, with the separation of church and state after 1800 and the end of public support for ministerial salaries, religious revivals and new optimistic theologies reinvigorated the independent cultural power of churches and their laity. Since the majority of the laity were women, many ministers developed new respect for them, and encouraged women to seek greater social influence. Women's empowerment within revitalized Protestantism fueled their participation in two social movements—one directed against slavery, one against prostitution—and fostered the birth of the woman suffrage movement at a conference held at Seneca Falls, New York, in 1848.

Among Protestant African Americans a contrary current developed. Women gave way to male leadership within the African-American community when, after 1800, evangelical religion became an avenue of male advancement at the same time that it captured the hearts and minds of the community. Itinerant women preachers managed to sustain limited power within their own ministries, but almost none rose to social prominence, and male ministers energetically opposed their power. Among the female laity, race took precedence over gender as the key component in understanding oppression.

Viewed from the perspective of American history as a whole, these essays reveal the history of women as an integral part of that national drama. They support the notion that women's power has evolved in a complex process of interaction within their families, their work, and their communities. We can see that different groups of women held different degrees of power and those differences have played critical roles in the broader development of American history. Yet they also show that important aspects of women's experience resonate across the differences among women.

1

The Anglo-Algonquian Gender Frontier

Kathleen M. Brown

Recent scholarship on first European contact and settlement in North America has illuminated the cultural differences between and mutual influences of European Americans and Native Americans. Offering a case study of English–Indian relations along the Chesapeake Bay in the seventeenth century, Kathleen M. Brown shows in this essay how gender differences were an important element in those early interactions. As Brown writes, "The gendering of Anglo–Indian relations in English writing was not without contest and contradiction . . . nor did it lead inevitably to easy conclusions of English dominance." Ultimately, she demonstrates the ways that the gender beliefs and structures of each group influenced their interaction and how, in turn, that interaction influenced each group's gender perspectives.

Recent scholarship has improved our understanding of the relationship between English settlers and Indians during the early seventeenth century. We know, for instance, that English expectations about American Indians were conditioned by Spanish conquest literature, their own contact with the Gaelic Irish, elite perceptions of the lower classes, and obligations to bring Christianity to those they believed to be in darkness.[1]

Largely unacknowledged by historians, gender roles and identities also played an important role in shaping English and Indian interactions. Accompanied by few English women, English male adventurers to Roanoake and Jamestown island confronted Indian men and women in their native land. In this cultural encounter, the gender ways, or what some feminist theorists might call the "performances," of Virginia Algonquians challenged English gentlemen's assumptions about the naturalness of their own gender identities. This interaction brought exchanges, new cultural forms, created sites of commonality, painful deceptions, bitter misunderstandings, and bloody conflicts.[2]

Identities as English or Indian were only partially formed at the beginning of this meeting of cultures; it required the daily presence of an "other" to crystallize self-conscious articulations of group identity. In contrast, maleness and femaleness within each culture provided explicit and deep-rooted foundations for individual identity and the organization of social relations. In both Indian and English societies, differences between men and women were critical to social order. Ethnic identities formed along this "gender frontier," the site of creative and destructive processes resulting from the confrontations of culturally-specific manhoods and womanhoods. In the emerging Anglo-Indian struggle, gender symbols and social relations signified claims to power. Never an absolute barrier, however, the gender frontier also produced sources for new identities and social practices.[3]

In this essay, I explore in two ways the gender frontier that evolved between English settlers and the indigenous peoples of Virginia's tidewater. First, I assess how differences in gender roles shaped the perceptions and interactions of both groups. Second, I analyze the "gendering" of the emerging Anglo–Indian power struggle. While the English depicted themselves as warriors dominating a feminized native population, Indian women and men initially refused to acknowledge claims to military supremacy, treating the foreigners as they would subject peoples, cowards, or servants. When English warrior discourse became unavoidable, however, Indian women and men attempted to exploit what they saw as the warrior's obvious dependence upon others for the agricultural and reproductive services that ensured group survival.

The indigenous peoples who engaged in this struggle were residents of Virginia's coastal plain, a region of fields, forests, and winding rivers that extended from the shores of the Chesapeake Bay to the mountains and waterfalls near present-day Richmond. Many were affiliated with Powhatan, the *werowance* who had consolidated several distinct groups under his influence at the time of contact with the English.[4] . . . Although culturally diverse, tidewater inhabitants shared certain features of social organization, commonalities that may have become more pronounced with Powhatan's ambitious chiefdom-building and the arrival of the English.

*   *   *

Of the various relationships constituting social order in England, those between men and women were among the most contested at the time the English set sail for Virginia in 1607. Accompanied by few women before 1620, male settlers left behind a pamphlet debate about the nature of the sexes and a rising concern about the activities of disorderly women. The gender hierarchy the English viewed as "natural" and "God-given" was in fact fraying at the edges. Male pamphleteers argued vigorously for male dominance over women as crucial to maintaining orderly households and communities. . . . By the late sixteenth century, as English attempts to subdue Ireland became increasingly violent and as hopes for a profitable West African trade dimmed, gender figured increasingly in English colonial discourses.[5]

English gender differences manifested themselves in primary responsibilities and arenas of activity, relationships to property, ideals for conduct, and social identities. Using plow agriculture, rural Englishmen cultivated grain while women oversaw household production, including gardening, dairying, brewing, and spinning. Women also constituted a flexible reserve labor force, performing agricultural work when demand for labor was high, as at harvest time. While Englishmen's property ownership formed the basis of their political existence and identity, most women did not own property until they were no longer subject to a father or husband.[6]

By the early seventeenth century, advice-book authors enjoined English women to concern themselves with the conservation of estates rather than with production. Women were also advised to maintain a modest demeanor. Publicly punishing shrewish and sexually aggressive women, communities enforced this standard of wifely submission as ideal and of wifely domination as intolerable.[7] The sexual activity of poor and unmarried women proved particularly threatening to community order; these "nasty wenches" provided pamphleteers with a foil for the "good wives" female readers were urged to emulate.[8]

How did one know an English good wife when one saw one? Her body and head would be modestly covered. The tools of her work, such as the skimming ladle used in dairying, the distaff of the spinning wheel, and the butter churn reflected her domestic production. When affixed to a man, as in community-initiated shaming rituals, these gender symbols communicated his fall from "natural" dominance and his wife's unnatural authority over him.[9]

Advice-book authors described man's "natural" domain as one of authority derived from his primary economic role. A man's economic assertiveness, mirrored in his authority over wife, child and servant, was emblematized by the plow's penetration of the earth, the master craftsman's ability to shape his raw materials, and the rider's ability to subdue his horse. Although hunting and fishing supplemented the incomes of many Englishmen, formal group hunts—occasions in which associations with manual labor and economic gain had been carefully erased—remained the preserve of the aristocracy and upper gentry.

The divide between men's and women's activities described by sixteenth- and seventeenth-century authors did not capture the flexibility of gender relations in most English communities. Beliefs in male authority over women and in the primacy of men's economic activities sustained a perception of social order even as women marketed butter, cheese, and ale and cuckolded unlucky husbands.

* * *

Gender roles and identities were also important to the Algonquian speakers whom the English encountered along the three major tributaries of the Chesapeake Bay. Like indigenous peoples throughout the Americas, Virginia Algonquians invoked a divine division of labor to explain and justify differences between men's and women's roles on earth. A virile warrior god and a congenial female hostess provided divine examples for the work appropriate to human men and women.[10] Indian women's labor centered on cultivating and processing corn, which provided up to seventy-five percent of the calories consumed by residents of the coastal plain.[11] Women also grew squash, peas, and beans, fashioned bedding, baskets, and domestic tools, and turned animal skins into clothing and household items. They may even have built the houses of semi-permanent summer villages and itinerant winter camps. Bearing and raising children and mourning the dead rounded out the range of female duties. All were spiritually united by life-giving and its association with earth and agricultural production, sexuality and reproduction. Lineage wealth and political power passed through the female line, perhaps because of women's crucial role in producing and maintaining property. Among certain peoples, women may also have had the power to determine the fate of captives, the nugget of truth in the much-embellished tale of Pocahontas's intervention on behalf of Captain John Smith.[12]

Indian women were responsible not only for reproducing the traditional features of their culture, but for much of its adaptive capacity as well. As agriculturalists, women must have had great influence over decisions to move to new grounds, to leave old grounds fallow, and to initiate planting. As producers and consumers of vital household goods and implements, women may have been among the first to feel the impact of new technologies, commodities, and trade. And as accumulators of lineage property, Indian women may have been forced to change strategies as subsistence opportunities shifted.

Indian men assumed a range of responsibilities that complemented those of women. Men cleared new planting grounds by cutting trees and burning stumps. They fished and hunted for game, providing highly valued protein. After the last corn harvest, whole villages traveled with their hunters to provide support services throughout the winter. Men's pursuit of game shaped the rhythms of village life during these cold months, just as women's cultivation of crops determined feasts and the allocation of labor during the late spring and summer. By ritually separating themselves from women through sexual abstinence, hunters periodically became warriors, taking revenge for killings or initiating their own raids. This adult leave-taking rearticulated the *huskanaw,* the coming of age ritual in which young boys left their mothers' homes to become men.[13]

Men's hunting and fighting roles were associated with life-taking, with its ironic relationship to the life-sustaining acts of procreation, protection, and provision. Earth and corn symbolized women, but the weapons of the hunt, the trophies taken from the hunted, and the predators of the animal world represented men. The ritual use of *pocones,* a red dye, also reflected this gender division. Women anointed their bodies with *pocones* before sexual encounters and ceremonies celebrating the harvest, while men wore it during hunting, warfare, or at the ritual celebrations of successes in these endeavors.[14]

The exigencies of the winter hunt, the value placed on meat, and intermittent warfare among native peoples may have been the foundation of male dominance in politics and religious matters. Women were not without their bases of power in Algonquian society, however; their important roles as agriculturalists, reproducers of Indian culture, and caretakers of lineage property kept gender relations in rough balance. . . . By no means equal to men, whose political and religious decisions directed village life, Indian women were perhaps more powerful in their subordination than English women.[15]

Even before the English sailed up the river they renamed the James, however, Indian women's power may have been waning, eroded by Powhatan's chiefdom-building tactics. During the last quarter of the sixteenth century, perhaps as a consequence of early Spanish forays into the region, he began to add to his inherited chiefdom, coercing and manipulating other coastal residents into economic and military alliances. . . . With the arrival of the English, the value of male warfare and the symbolism of corn as tribute only intensified, further strengthening the patriarchal tendencies of Powhatan's people.[16]

*   *   *

Almost every writer described the land west and south of Chesapeake Bay as an unspoiled "New World."[17] Small plots of cultivated land, burned forest undergrowth, and seasonal residence patterns often escaped the notice of English travelers habituated to landscapes shaped by plow agriculture and permanent settlement. . . .

Conquest seemed justifiable to many English because Native Americans had failed to tame the wilderness according to English standards. Writers claimed they found "only an idle, improvident, scattered people . . . carelesse of anything but from hand to mouth."[18] . . . The seasonal migration of native groups and the corresponding shift in diet indicated to the English a lack of mastery over the environment, reminding them of animals.

The English derision of Indian dependence on the environment and the comparison to animals . . . also contained implicit gender meanings. Women's bodies, for example, showed great alteration during pregnancy from fat to lean, strong to weak. English authors often compared female sexual appetites and insubordination to those of wild animals in need of taming. Implicit in all these commentaries was a critique of indigenous men for failing to fulfill the responsibility of economic provision with which the English believed all men to be charged. Lacking private property in the English sense, Indian men, like the Gaelic Irish before them, appeared to the English to be feminine and not yet civilized to manliness.[19]

For many English observers, natives' "failure" to develop an agricultural economy or dense population was rooted in their gender division of labor. Women's primary responsibility for agriculture merely confirmed the abdication by men of their proper role and explained the "inferiority" of native economies in a land of plenty. Smith commented that "the land is not populous, for the men be fewe; their far greater number is of women and children," a pattern he attributed to inadequate cultivation.[20] . . .

English commentators reacted with disapproval to seeing women perform work relegated to laboring men in England while Indian men pursued activities associated with the English aristocracy. Indian women, George Percy claimed, "doe all their drugerie. The men takes their pleasure in hunting and their warres, which they are in continually."[21] . . .

The English were both fascinated and disturbed by other aspects of Native American society through which gender identities were communicated, including hairstyle, dress and make-up. The native male fashion of going clean-shaven, for example, clashed with English associations of beards with male maturity, perhaps diminishing Indian men's claims to manhood in the eyes of the English. . . . It probably did not enhance English respect for Indian manhood that female barbers sheared men's facial hair.[22]

Most English writers found it difficult to distinguish between the sexual behavior of Chesapeake dwellers and what they viewed as sexual potency conveyed through dress and ritual. English male explorers were particularly fascinated by indigenous women's attire, which seemed scanty and immodest compared to English women's multiple layers and wraps. John Smith described an entertainment arranged for him in which "30 young women came naked out of the woods (only covered behind and before with a few greene leaves), their bodies al painted."[23] . . .

For most English writers, Indian manners and customs reinforced an impression of sexual passion. Hospitality that included sexual privileges, for instance, sending "a woman fresh painted red with *Pocones* and oile" to be the "bedfellow" of a guest, may have confirmed in the minds of English men the reading of Indian folkways as sexually provocative. Smith's experience with the thirty women, clad in leaves, body paint, and buck's horns and emitting, "hellish cries and shouts," undoubtedly strengthened the English association of Indian culture with unbridled passion. . . . These and other Indian gender ways left the English with a vivid impression of unconstrained sexuality that in their own culture could mean only promiscuity.

The stark contrast between Indian military techniques and formal European land stratagems reinforced English judgements that indigenous peoples were animalistic by nature.[24] George Percy's description of one skirmish invoked a comparison to the movement of animals: "At night, when we were going aboard, there came the Savages creeping upon all foure, from the Hills, like Beares, with their Bowes in their mouthes."[25] While writers regaled English readers with tales of Indian men in hasty retreat from English guns, thus reconfirming for the reader the female vulnerability of Indians and the superior weaponry of the English, they also recounted terrifying battle scenes such as the mock war staged for the entertainment of John Smith, which included "horrible shouts and screeches, as though so many infernall helhounds could not have made them more terrible."[26]

Although the dominant strand of English discourse about Indian men denounced them for being savage and failed providers, not all Englishmen shared these assessments of the meaning of cultural differences. Throughout the early years of settlement, male laborers deserted military compounds to escape puny rations, disease and harsh discipline, preferring to take their chances with local Indians whom they knew had food aplenty. . . . a lurking and disquieting suspicion that Indian men were like the English disrupted discourses about natural savagery and inferiority. John Smith often explained Indian complexions and resistance to the elements as a result of conditioning and daily practice rather than of nature.[27] Despite the flamboyant rhetoric about savage warriors lurking in the forests like animals, Smith soon had Englishmen learning to fight in the woods.[28] He clearly thought his manly English, many of whom could barely shoot a gun, had much to learn from their Indian opponents.

Most English did not dwell on these areas of similarity and exchange, however, but emphasized the "wild" and animalistic qualities of tidewater peoples. English claims to dominance and superiority rested upon constructions of Indian behavior as barbaric. . . . Through depictions of feminized male "naturalls," Englishmen reworked Anglo–Indian relations to fit the "natural" dominance of men in gender relations. In the process, they contributed to an emerging male colonial identity that was deeply rooted in English gender discourses.

The gendering of Anglo–Indian relations in English writing was not without contest and contradiction, however, nor did it lead inevitably to easy conclusions of English dominance. Englishmen incorporated Indian ways into their diets and military tactics, and Indian women into their sexual lives. Some formed close bonds with Indian companions, while others lived to father their own "naturall" progeny. As John Rolfe's anguish over his marriage to Pocahontas attested, colonial domination was a complex process involving sexual intimacy, cultural incorporation and self-scrutiny.[29]

*   *   *

The Englishmen who landed on the shores of Chesapeake Bay and the James River were not the first European men that Virginia Algonquians had seen. During the 1570s, Spanish Jesuits established a short-lived mission near the James River tributary that folded with the murder of the clerics. The Spaniards who revenged the Jesuit deaths left an unfavorable impression upon local Chickahominy, Paspegh, and Kecoughtan Indians. . . .

The maleness of English explorers' parties and early settlements un-doubtedly raised Indian suspicions of bellicose motives. Interrogating Smith at their first meeting about the purpose of the English voyage, Powhatan was apparently satisfied with Smith's answer that the English presence was tempo-rary. Smith claimed his men sought passage to "the backe Sea," the ever–elusive water route to India which they believed lay beyond the falls of the Chesapeake river system. . . .

Frequent English military drills in the woods and the construction of a fort at Jamestown, however, may have aroused his suspicions that the English strangers planned a longer and more violent stay.[30]

Equipped with impressive blasting guns, the English may have found it easy to perpetuate the warrior image from afar; up close was a different mat-ter, however. English men were pale, hairy, and awkward compared to Indian men. They also had the dirty habit of letting facial hair grow so that it ob-scured the bottom part of their faces where it collected food and other de-bris. Their clumsy stomping through the woods announced their presence to friends, enemies, and wildlife alike and they were forced, on at least one very public occasion, to ask for Indian assistance when their boats became mired in river ooze. Perhaps worst of all from the perspective of Indian people who valued a warrior's stoicism in the face of death, the Englishmen they captured and killed died screaming and whimpering. William Strachey recorded the mocking song sung by Indian men sometime in 1611, in which they ridiculed "what lamentation our people made when they kild him, namely saying how they [the Englishmen] would cry whe, whe."[31]

Indian assumptions about masculinity may have led Powhatan to overes-timate the vulnerability of Smith's men. The gentlemen and artisans who were the first to arrive in Virginia proved to be dismal farmers, remaining wholly dependent upon native corn stores during their first three years and partially dependent thereafter. They tried, futilely, to persuade Indians to grow more corn to meet their needs, but their requests were greeted with scorn by Indian men who found no glory in the "woman-like exercise" of farming. . . .

When Powhatan and other Indian peoples reminded Smith of his de-pendence upon Indian food supplies, Smith reacted with anger. In his first account of Virginia, he recalled with bitterness the scorn of the Kecoughtan Indians for "a famished man": they "would in derision offer him a handfull of Corne, a peece of bread."[32] Such treatment signified both indigence and fe-male vulnerability to the English, made worse by the fact that the crops they needed were grown by women. At Kecoughtan, Smith responded by "let[ting] fly his muskets" to provoke a Kecoughtan retreat and then killing several men at close range. . . . The English thus used their superior weaponry to transform themselves from scorned men into respected warriors and to re-cast the relationship: humble agriculturists became duty-bound to produce for those who spared their lives.[33]

Powhatan's interactions with Englishmen may also have been guided by his assessment of the gender imbalance among them. His provision of women to entertain English male guests was a political gesture whose message seems to have been misunderstood as sexual license by the English.[34] Smith, for example, believed the generosity stemmed from Powhatan's having "as many women as he will," and thereby growing occasionally "weary of his women."[35] By voluntarily sharing his wealth in women and thus communicating his benign intent, Powhatan invoked what he may have believed to be a transcendent male political bond, defined by men's common relationship to women.[36] Powhatan may also have believed that by encouraging English warriors' sexual activity, he might diminish their military potency. It was the fear of this loss of power, after all, that motivated Indian warriors' ritual abstinence before combat. Ultimately, Powhatan may have hoped that intimacy between native women and English men would lead to an integration of the foreigners and a diffusion of the threat they presented. Lacking women with whom to reciprocate and unfettered by matrilineage ties, the English, Powhatan may have reasoned, might be rapidly brought into alliance. Powhatan's gesture, however, only reinforced the English rationale for subjugating the "uncivilized" and offered English men an opportunity to express the Anglo–Indian power relationship sexually with native women.[37]

Indian women were often more successful than Powhatan in manipulating Englishmen's desires for sexual intimacy. At the James River village of Appocant in late 1607, the unfortunate George Cawson met his death when village women "enticed [him] up from the barge into their howses."[38] Oppossunoquonuske, a clever *werowansqua* of another village, similarly led fourteen Englishmen to their demise. Inviting the unwary men to come "up into her Towne, to feast and make Merry," she convinced them to "leave their Armes in their boat, because they said how their women would be afrayd ells of their pieces."[39]

Although both of these accounts are cautionary tales that represent Indians literally as feminine seducers capable of entrapping Englishmen in the web of their own sexual desires, the incidents suggest Indian women's canny assessment of the men who would be colonial conquerors. Exploiting Englishmen's hopes for colonial pleasures, Indian women dangled before them the opportunity for sexual intimacy, turning a female tradition of sexual hospitality into a weapon of war. . . .

Feigned sexual interest in Englishmen was not the only tactic available to Indian women. Some women clearly wanted nothing to do with the English strangers and avoided all contact with them. When John Smith traveled to Tappahannock in late 1607, for example, Indian women fled their homes in fear.[40] Other Indian women treated the English not as revered guests, to be gently wooed into Indian ways or seduced into fatal traps, but as lowly servants. . . .

In addition to violence and manipulations of economic dependence and sexual desire, Algonquians tried to maneuver the English into positions of political subordination. Smith's account of his captivity, near-execution, and rescue by Pocahontas was undoubtedly part of an adoption ritual in which Powhatan defined his relationship to Smith as one of patriarchal dominance. Smith became Powhatan's prisoner after warriors easily slew his English companions and then "missed" with nearly all of the twenty or thirty arrows they aimed at Smith himself. Clearly, Powhatan wanted Smith brought to him alive. Smith reported that during his captivity he was offered "life, libertie, land and women," prizes Powhatan must have believed to be very attractive to Englishmen, in exchange for information about how best to capture Jamestown.[41] After ceremonies and consultations with priests, Powhatan brought Smith before an assembly where, according to Smith, Pocahontas risked her own life to prevent him from being clubbed to death by executioners. It seems that Smith understood neither the ritual adoption taking place nor the significance of Powhatan's promise to make him a *werowance* and to "for ever esteeme him as [he did] his son Nantaquoud."[42]

*   *   *

Over the next weeks and months the two men wrangled over the construction of their short-lived alliance and the meaning of Powhatan's promises to supply the English with corn. . . . Smith and Powhatan continued to do a subtle two-step over the meaning of the corn. Was it tribute coerced by the militarily superior English? Or was it a sign of a father's compassion for a subordinate *werowance* and his hungry people? Powhatan made clear to Smith that he understood the extent of the English dependence upon his people for corn. . . . He also appreciated the degree to which the English could make him miserable if they did not get what they wanted. . . .

Ultimately, Powhatan attempted to represent his conflict with Smith as the clash of an older, wiser authority with a young upstart. "I knowe the difference of peace and warre, better then any in my Countrie," he reminded Smith, his paternal self-depiction contrasting sharply with what he labeled Smith's youthful and "rash unadvisednesse." Displeased with this rendering of their relationship with its suggestion of childish inexperience, Smith reasserted the English warrior personae with a vengeance. He informed Powhatan that "for your sake only, wee have curbed our thirsting desire of revenge," reminding him that the "advantage we have by our armes" would have allowed the English easily to overpower Powhatan's men "had wee intended you anie hurt."[43]

*   *   *

Although we can never know with any certainty what the all-male band of English settlers signified to indigenous peoples, their own organization of gender roles seems to have shaped their responses to the English. Using sexual hospitality to "disarm" the strangers and exploiting English needs for food, Algonquians were drawn into a female role as suppliers of English sexual and subsistence needs. Although Indian women were occasionally successful in manipulating English desires for sexual intimacy and dominance, the English cast these triumphs as the consequence of female seduction, an interpretation that only reinforced discourses about feminized Algonquians. Dependence upon indigenous peoples for corn was potentially emasculating for the English; they thus redefined corn as tribute or booty resulting from English military dominance.

The encounter of English and Indian peoples wrought changes in the gender relations of both societies. Contact bred trade, political reshuffling, sexual intimacy and warfare. On both sides, male roles intensified in ways that appear to have reinforced the patriarchal tendencies of each culture. The very process of confrontation between two groups with male-dominated political and religious systems may initially have strengthened the value of patriarchy for each.

The rapid change in Indian life and culture had a particularly devastating impact upon women. Many women, whose office it was to bury and mourn the dead, may have been relegated to perpetual grieving. Corn was also uniquely the provenance of women; economically it was the source of female authority, and religiously and symbolically they were identified with it. The wanton burning and pillaging of corn supplies, through which the English transformed their dependence into domination, may have represented to tidewater residents an egregious violation of women. Maneuvering to retain patriarchal dominance over the English and invoking cultural roles in which women exercised power, Algonquian Indians may have presented their best defense against the "feminization" of their relationship to the English. But as in Indian society itself, warriors ultimately had the upper hand over agriculturists.[44]

English dominance in the region ultimately led to the decline of the native population and its way of life. As a consequence of war, nutritional deprivation, and disease, Virginia Indians were reduced in numbers from the approximately 14,000 inhabitants of the Chesapeake Bay and tidewater in 1607 to less than 3,000 by the early eighteenth century. White settlement forced tidewater dwellers further west, rupturing the connections between ritual activity, lineage, and geographic place. Priests lost credibility as traditional medicines failed to cure new diseases while confederacies such as Powhatan's declined and disappeared. Uprooted tidewater peoples also encountered opposition from piedmont inhabitants upon whose territory they encroached. The erosion of traditionally male-dominated Indian political institutions eventually created new opportunities for individual women to assume positions of leadership over tribal remnants.[45]

The English, meanwhile, emerged from these early years of settlement with gender roles more explicitly defined in English, Christian, and "middling order" terms. This core of English identity proved remarkably resilient, persisting through seventy years of wars with neighboring Indians and contin-

uing to evolve as English settlers imported Africans to work the colony's tobacco fields. Initially serving to legitimate the destruction of traditional Indian ways of life, this concept of Englishness ultimately constituted one of the
most powerful legacies of the Anglo–Indian gender frontier.

NOTES

1. Spanish literature divided "barbaric" populations into two main categories: one of obedi-
ent and child-like laborers, and the other of evil, conniving and dangerous cannibals. The En-
glish similarly typed both Gaelic Irish and American Indians. See Anthony Pagden, *The Fall of
Natural Man* (Cambridge: Cambridge University Press, 1986); Nicholas P. Canny, *The Elizabethan
Conquest of Ireland: A Pattern Established 1565–76* (New York: Barnes and Noble, 1976), 160; Loren
E. Pennington, "The Amerindian in English Promotional Literature 1575–1625" in *The Westward
Enterprise: English Activities in Ireland, the Atlantic, and America, 1480–1650,* ed. K.R. Andrews,
Nicholas P. Canny, and P.E.H. Hair (Detroit: Wayne State University Press, 1979), 184, 188; Anne
Laurence, "The Cradle to the Grave: English Observation of Irish Social Customs in the Seven-
teenth Century," *The Seventeenth Century,* 3 (Spring 1988): 63–84; Nicholas P. Canny, "The Ideology of English Colonization: From Ireland to America," *William and Mary Quarterly,* 3rd ser., 30
(October 1973): 597 (hereafter cited as *WMQ*).
2. For a useful discussion of the performative nature of identity that is especially applicable
to the early modern period and the encounter of cultures in the Americas, see Judith Butler,
"Gender Trouble," in *Feminism/Postmodernism,* ed. Linda J. Nicholson (New York: Routledge, 1990),
336–339.
3. For the by-now classic account of gender as a means of communicating power, see Joan
Scott, "Gender: A Useful Category of Historical Analysis," *American Historical Review,* 91 (December 1986): 1053–1075. For analyses of economic, linguistic, and religious "frontiers," see James
Merrell, "'The Customes of Our Country': Indians and Colonists in Early America," in *Strangers
Within the Realm: Cultural Margins of the First British Empire,* ed. Bernard Bailyn and Phillip D. Morgan (Chapel Hill: University of North Carolina Press, 1991), 117–156. In no way separate or distinct, the gender frontier infiltrated other frontiers we usually describe as economic, social, or
cultural; for further elaboration see Kathleen M. Brown, "Brave New Worlds: Women's and Gender History," *WMQ,* 3rd ser., 50 (April 1993): 311–328.
4. On Powhatan's influence over neighboring Algonquian-speaking peoples, see Nancy
Lurie, "Indian Cultural Adjustment to European Civilization," in *Seventeenth-Century America,* ed.
James Morton Smith (Westport, Ct.: Greenwood Press, 1980), 40–42. Lurie uses the term "Confederacy" to refer to these peoples, although she distinguishes between the "influence"
Powhatan wielded and the "undisputed control" he never fully realized. Helen Rountree, *Pocahontas's People* (Norman, Ok.: University of Oklahoma Press, 1990), 3, argues that "Confederacy"
is inaccurate, preferring to describe it as a "sophisticated government."
5. For examples of gendered discourses of difference in the Irish context, see Laurence,
"Cradle to the Grave"; for a classic early English account of Africans, see Richard Jobson, *The
Golden Trade* [London, 1623].
6. Among the most useful accounts of English agriculture are Joan Thirsk, ed., *The Agrarian
History of England and Wales,* 6 vols. (Cambridge: Cambridge University Press, 1967) vol. 4;
K.D.M. Snell, *Annals of the Laboring Poor: Social Change and Agrarian England, 1660–1900* (Cambridge: Cambridge University Press, 1985); D.E. Underdown, "Taming of the Scold: the Enforce-
ment of Patriarchal Authority in Early Modern England," in Fletcher and Stevenson, *Order and
Disorder in Early Modern England,* 116–136; Ann Kussmaul, *Servants in Husbandry in Early Modern
England* (Cambridge: Cambridge University Press, 1981).
7. Cahn, *Industry of Devotion,* 80–90, 158; Amussen. *Ordered Society;* William Gouge, *Domesti-
call Duties* (London, 1622); Richard Brathwait, *The English Gentlewoman* (London, 1631); Gervase
Markham, *Country Contentments or the English Housewife* (London, 1623).
8. For the terms "good wives" and "nasty wenches," see John Hammond, *Leah and Rachel, or
the Two Fruitfull Sisters* (London, 1656).

9. Martin Ingram, "Ridings, Rough Music, and the 'Reform of Popular Culture,' in Early Modern England," *Past and Present*, 105 (November 1984): 79–113; Underdown. "The Taming of the Scold."

10. Ramon Gutierrez, *When Jesus Came the Corn Mothers Went Away* (Stanford, Ca.: Stanford University Press, 1991), 3–7; Hudson, *Southeastern Indians*, 148–159; Helen Rountree, *The Powhatan Indians of Virginia: Their Traditional Culture* (Norman, Ok: University of Oklahoma Press, 1989), 135–138; William Strachey; *The Historie of Travell into Virginia Britania* [London, 1612], 89, 103.

11. Edwin Randolph Turner, "An Archaeological and Ethnohistorical Study on the Evolution of Rank Societies in the Virginia Coastal Plain" (Ph.D. diss., The Pennsylvania State University, 1976), 182–187; Rountree, *Powhatan Indians*, 45, finds Turner's estimates perhaps too high.

12. Herndon, "Indian Agriculture in the Southern Colonies," 288, 292–296, especially the reference on 292 to "She-Corn." Hudson, *Southeastern Indians*, 151–156, 259–260; Wright, *Only Land They Knew*, 8–14; Silver, *New Face on the Countryside*, 39–41, 44–52; Colonel Henry Norwood, "A Voyage to Virginia" [London, 1649] in *Tracts and Other Papers, relating principally to the Origin, Settlement and Progress of the North American Colonies*, ed. Peter Force, 4 vols. (New York, 1836; rpt., Cambridge, Mass., Peter Smith, 1947), 3: 36–37. John Smith often rendered invisible or insignificant the work of women; see Kupperman, *John Smith*, 138–139. See also Kupperman, *John Smith*, 151, 156, for Smith's description of women's role as mourners and the passage of property and political power through women.

13. Wright, *Only Land They Knew*, 8–14; Hudson, *Southeastern Indians*, 148–156, 258–260; Kupperman, *John Smith*, 105, 144, 153; Henry Spelman, "Relation of Virginia," in *Travels and Works of Captain John Smith*, ed. Edward Arber and A. G. Bradley, 2 vols. (Edinburgh: John Grant, 1910), 1: cvi.

14. Hudson, *Southeastern Indians*, 259; Kupperman, *John Smith*, 61, 163.

15. Strachey, *Historie*, 83, 74.

16. For Powhatan's clever manipulation of gender customs and symbols of power, see Strachey, *Historie*, 40, 44, 62, 65–69, and Spelman, "Relation," cxiv.

17. For a survey of changing English attitudes toward Indians in the South, see Gary B. Nash, "The Image of the Indian in the Southern Colonial Mind," *WMQ*, 3rd ser., 29 (April 1972): 197–230. See also George Percy, "Observations by Master George Percy, 1607," [London, 1607], in Tyler, *Narratives*, 17–18, and Thomas Hariot, *A Briefe and True Report of the New Found Land of Virginia* (London, 1588; rpt. New York, 1903).

18. Smith, *Proceedings of the English Colonies*, in Tyler, *Narratives*, 178, John Smith, "Description of Virginia," [London, 1612], in Tyler, *Narratives*, 83; Pennington, "The Amerindians in English Promotional Literature," 189, for her summation of the argument in Robert Gray, *A Good Speed to Virginia* [London, 1609]. For Smith's recognition of native concepts of property, see Kupperman, *John Smith*, 140. Most early English commentators also noted the potential of New World abundance for exploitation by agriculturists and hunters: see, for example, Percy, "Observations" in Tyler, *Narratives*, 17–18; Hariot, *A Briefe and True Report*.

19. V.G. Kieman, "Private Property in History," in *Family and Inheritance: Rural Society in Western Europe, 1200–1800*, ed. Jack Goody, Joan Thirsk, and E. P. Thompson (Cambridge: Cambridge University Press, 1976), 361–398: see also E. P. Thompson, *Whigs and Hunters: The Origin of the Black Act* (New York: Random House, 1975). James Axtell, *The European and the Indian: Essays in the Ethnohistory of Colonial North America* (New York: Oxford University Press, 1981), discusses the English view of "civilizing" Indians as a process of making men out of children. Although most voyagers wrote critically of Indian men, others compared them favorably to English men whose overly cultured and effeminate ways had made them weak in character and resolve; Hariot, *A Briefe and True Report*. For a critique of English effeminacy, see *Haec Vir* [London, 1620] in Henderson and MacManus, *Half Humankind;* Richard Brathwait, *The English Gentleman* (London, 1631). Strachey, *Historie*, 18, 24, 25, equated civility with manliness.

20. Kupperman, *John Smith*, 158. Smith, "Description of Virginia," in Tyler, *Narratives*, 98–99.

21. Percy, "Observations," in Tyler, *Narratives*, 18. For an extended discussion of this theme for Virginia and elsewhere, see David D. Smits, "The Squaw Drudge: A Prime Index of Savagism," *Ethnohistory* 29 (1982): 281–306.

22. See Axtell, *The European and the Indian*, 45, 47–55, 57–60, for the deeper reverberations of different clothing and naming practices: Kupperman, *John Smith*, 100; Strachey, *Historie*, 73.

23. Smith, *Proceedings of the English Colonies*, in Tyler, *Narratives*, 153–154.

24. Hariot, *A Briefe and True Report*.

25. Percy, "Observations," in Tyler, *Narratives*, 10.
26. Smith, "Description," in Tyler, *Narratives*, 106. Percy, "Observations," in Tyler, *Narratives*, 6.
27. Smith, "Description," in Tyler, *Narratives*, 99; Strachey, *Historie*, 70.
28. Smith, *True Relation*, in Barbour, *Complete Works*, 1: 85.
29. "Letter of John Rolfe, 1614," in Tyler, *Narratives*, 241.
30. Smith, *True Relation*, in Barbour, *Complete Works*, 1: 39, 91.
31. Axtell, *Beyond 1492*, 101; Strachey, *Historie*, 85. See also *Ibid 66*, for an account of Warroskoyack Indians mocking the English when an Indian hostage escaped from an English ship.
32. Kupperman, *John Smith*, 174, for Powhatan's speech to Smith. For a Chickahominy orator's similar comments to Smith, see Kupperman, *John Smith*, 190. See also Kupperman, *John Smith*, 185, for Smith's admission of the English dependence on native corn supplies. For Smith's description of the engagement with the Kecoughtan, see Smith, *General Historie*, in Barbour, *Complete Works*, 2: 144.
33. Kupperman, *John Smith*, 175.
34. These sexual diplomats may well be the same women Smith claimed "were common whores by profession"; see Kupperman, *John Smith*, 156, 157.
35. Smith, "Description," in Tyler, *Narratives*, 114–115.
36. The provision of women to foreign men was a fairly common Indian diplomatic practice throughout the South as well as in Central and South America; see for example, Gutierrez, *Corn Mothers*, 16–20. This was a highly politicized form of sexual hospitality which stood in sharp contrast to the violent reaction when native women were kidnapped by foreign warriors: see Kupperman, *John Smith*, 100.
37. Axtell, *Beyond 1492*, 39, 45, 102; my interpretation is compatible with Axtell, *Beyond 1492*, 31–33, in which he claims that while Europeans stressed sharp distinctions between Europeans and non-Europeans. Indians stressed the similarities. William Strachey believed that assimilation was Powhatan's strategy for mediating English relations with other Indians outside the paramount chiefdom; see Strachey, *Historie*, 107.
38. Strachey, *Historie*, 60.
39. Strachey, *Historie*, 63; Smith, *True Relation*, in Barbour, *Complete Works*, 1: 71, for a similar tactic by Powhatan.
40. Smith, *True Relation*, in Barbour, *Complete Works*, 1:39.
41. Kupperman, *John Smith*, 62, 65.
42. J.A. Leo Lemay, *Did Pocahontas Save Captain John Smith?* (Athens, Ga.: University of Georgia Press, 1992) is the most recent interpretation of this event. An ardent believer in Smith's veracity, Lemay fails to explore the degree to which Smith may have misunderstood the meaning of the near-death ritual. For prior accounts of the events, see Smith, *True Relation*, in Barbour, *Complete Works*, 1: 45; Smith, *General Historie*, in Kupperman, *John Smith*, 64–65.
43. Kupperman, *John Smith*, 175.
44. Stephen R. Potter, "Early English Effects on Virginia Algonquian Exchange and Tribute," in Wood, *Powhatan's Mantle*, 151–172, especially 151, 160; Martha McCartney, "Cockacoeske, Queen of the Pamunkey: Diplomat and Suzeraine," in Wood, *Powhatan's Mantle*, 173–195; Merrell, "Customes of Our Country," 122–123; Robert Beverley, *The History and Present State of Virginia [1705]*, ed. Louis V. Wright (Chapel Hill, 1947), 232–233.
45. For analyses of the devastation wrought by contact, see Hudson, *Southeastern Indians*, chap. 8; Silver, *New Face on the Countryside*, 74–83, 88, 102; Crosby, *Ecological Imperialism*, chap. 9; Merrell, "The Customes of Our Country," 122–126. Powhatan himself commented upon the devastation he had witnessed in the course of three generations; see Kupperman, *John Smith*, 174. See also Wright, *The Only Land They Knew*, 24–26; Peter Wood, "The Changing Population of the Colonial South: An Overview by Race and Region, 1685–1790," in Wood, *Powhatan's Mantle*, 38, 40–42; Silver, *New Face on the Countryside*, 72, 81, 87–88, 91; Potter, "Early English Effects on Virginia Algonquian Exchange and Tribute," Robert Steven Grumet, "Sunksquaws, Shamans, and Tradeswomen: Middle Atlantic Coastal Algonkian Women during the 17th and 18th Centuries" in *Women and Colonization: Anthropological Perspectives*, ed. Mona Etienne and Eleanor Leacock (New York: Praeger, 1980), 43–62.

2

The Weaker Sex as Religious Rebel

Lyle Koehler

Lyle Koehler's article shows us that New England Puritanism embraced two fundamentally contradictory notions about women's social power. By placing a great deal of spiritual power within the individual, Puritanism cultivated women's autonomous spiritual and intellectual development. Yet New England society was organized around family units that were profoundly patriarchal. Anne Hutchinson's struggle with male authorities in early Massachusetts illuminates both the potential for women's power in that society and the institutional curbs that constrained it.

As might be expected in a particularly religious century, many women's searches for power—for control over their own lives and for impact upon others—had important religious components. Like their Puritan contemporaries, the Antinomians, Gortonists, Anabaptists, and Quakers tied themselves to the absolute power of God and interpreted the Bible in accordance with their own needs. Both Puritans and heretics used religion to order their realities in some coherent, comprehensive way. The relatively powerless Calvinists of Old England and the heretics of New England tied themselves to theologies which became sounding boards for grievances about society. Religion justified unorthodox behavior. It offered the powerless a link with God, the incarnation of power; it solidified conviction and provided the security of knowing that one's deeply felt needs were permissible.

Women, in particular, were susceptible to the lure of heresy. Cotton Mather related, "It is the mark of [religious] seducers that they lead captive silly women" into sin because the " 'weaker sex' is more easily gained by the devil." "Indeed," he wrote, "a poyson does never insinuate so quickly, nor operate so strongly, as when women's milk is the vehicle wherein 'tis given."[1] Female weakness served as an easy explanation of why there were so many woman heretics, and Mather did not (*could* not) look at some of the broader reasons for their participation in the century's various religious "movements." However, the modern researcher, unfettered by seventeenth-century expectations, can do so.

Excerpted from "The Weaker Sex as Religious Rebel," Chapter 8 of *A Search for Power: The "Weaker Sex" in Seventeenth-Century New England* by Lyle Koehler (Urbana: University of Illinois Press, 1980).

Mrs. Elizabeth Freake and Baby Mary, c. 1671–74. Worcester Art Museum, Worcester, Mass.

FROM WILLIAMS TO HUTCHINSON

New England's first influential religious rebel was Roger Williams, the Salem minister who infuriated Massachusetts authorities by preaching that the civil magistrate ought to stay out of church affairs, that Indians were the rightful owners of the New World land, that more humility was needed in Puritan churches, that forced worship "stinks in God's nostrils," and that each person ought to be allowed the liberty to believe as conscience dictated.[2] Williams developed some following at Salem, especially among the devout, church-going women, several of whom separated from the church there. Jane Verin, Mary Oliver, Margery Reeves, and maidservant Margery Holliman refused to worship with the congregation from 1635 to 1638, and the latter two women denied that the churches of the Bay Colony were true churches.[3]

Why these women adopted Williams's theology is a matter for speculation, since none of his female followers left records explaining his appeal, and Williams himself felt that women were by nature unfit for preaching, governing, or other "Manly Actions and Employments."[4] However, we can infer that this theology offered women certain privileges and compensations. Williams's belief that Puritans ought to humble themselves before God in sackcloth and ashes had, theoretically, special meaning for women. An emphasis on humility celebrated and raised to a position of some "power" that which was the female sex's "natural" condition. Reducing men to such a level of visually apparent humility eased the power gap between men and women; furthermore, it served as practical testimony of the equality of the sexes before God. Women could also interpret Williams's constant defense of liberty of conscience to mean that choice of a belief system was their individual prerogative—an act of intellectual and spiritual freedom. In a world where female freedom was carefully curbed, where women were to ask their husbands and fathers for religious guidance, liberty of conscience had revolutionary implications. To be free to believe was the first step in becoming free to do as one wished. . . .

At the time of Williams's abrupt departure in January, 1636, the Bay Colony women had not expressed any discontent about Puritanism or their stereotyped sex-role conditioning. That situation soon changed, however, and with the marked increase of Antinomian sentiment in Boston and Anne Hutchinson's powerful example of resistance, the distressed females of Massachusetts discovered how to channel their deeply felt frustrations into a viable theological form and to rebel openly against the spiritual and secular status quo. Since they had only a rudimentary consciousness of what they were doing, Antinomian women could embrace a belief system which actually minimized the importance of individual action, for Antinomians felt that salvation could be demonstrated only by the individual experiencing God's grace within.[5]

The issue of the relative importance of good works (i.e., individual effort) and grace (i.e., God's effort) in preparing man for salvation nagged English Calvinists from their earliest origins and engendered a sizable amount of theological debate. In New England, John Cotton, the teacher of the Boston Church, opened a Pandora's box when "he warned his listeners away from the specious comfort of preparation [through good works] and reemphasized the covenant of grace as something in which God acted alone and unassisted."[6] When Cotton directed his congregation "not to be afraid of the word Revelation," the elders of the Bay Colony feared that "Revelation" might be dangerously construed to invalidate biblical law.[7]

The elders' fears were justified in that respect, because Bostonians of every rank, age, and sex enthusiastically supported the notion of personal revelation and solicited converts to an emerging, loosely knit ideology which the divines pejoratively called Antinomianism, Opinionism, or Familism.[8] The authorities were shocked to hear Antinomian principles defended at military trainings, in town meetings, and before the various courts. They complained that all of society's institutions—church, state, and family—were being "turned upside down among us."[9] That such turmoil should result from a turning to revelation was only natural, for many individuals and groups were hungry for power in Puritan New England. It was easy for each potential rebel to perceive the operation of God's grace upon his or her own soul, and to use that perception to consecrate a personal rebellion against contemporary authorities and institutions. Women in particular used a feeling of the inward-dwelling Holy Spirit to castigate various authorities: magistrates as guardians of the state, ministers as guardians of the church, and their husbands as guardians of the home. As the most outspoken of these female rebels, Anne Hutchinson spread her opinions among all social classes through contacts made in the course of her midwifery, and in biweekly teaching sessions at her home. Thomas Weld believed her lectures responsible for distributing "the venome of these [Antinomian] opinions into the very veines and vitalls of the People in the Country." Indeed, she was soon called "the leader" and "the prime seducer of the whole faction."[10]

A WOMEN'S REBELLION

Many women identified with Anne Hutchinson's rebellious intellectual stance and aggressive spirit. Edward Johnson wrote that "the weaker sex" set her up as "a Priest" and "thronged" after her. . . . Weld charged the Antinomians with using the yielding, flexible, and tender women as "an Eve, to catch their husbands also." One anonymous English pamphleteer found in Antinomianism a movement "somewhat like the Trojan horse for rarity" because "it was covered with womens aprons, and bolstered out with the judgement and deep discerning of the godly and reverent."[11]

From late 1636 to early 1637 the expression of female discontent ascended to a higher pitch in the Boston church. At one point, when pastor John Wilson rose to preach, Hutchinson left the congregation; many women followed her out of the meetinghouse. Because these women "pretended many excuses for their going out," it was impossible for the authorities to convict them of contempt for Wilson. Other rebels did, however, challenge the pastor's words as he spoke them, causing Weld to comment, "Now the faithfull Ministers of Christ must have dung cast on their faces and be no better than Legall Preachers, Baals Priests, Popish Factors, Scribes, Pharisees, and Opposers of Christ himselfe."[12]

Included among these church rebels were two particularly active women, Jane Hawkins and Mary Dyer, both of whom [Governor John] Winthrop found obnoxious. The governor considered the youthful wife of William Dyer to be "of a very proud spirit," "much addicted to revelations," and "notoriously infected with Mrs. Hutchinson's errors."[13] The other was no more agreeable: Winthrop denounced Hawkins as being "notorious for familiarity with the devill" because, in her capacity as a midwife, she dispensed fertility potions to barren women and occasionally fell into a trancelike state in which she spoke Latin. The General Court, sharing the governor's apprehension, on March 12, 1638, forbade Hawkins to question "matters of religion" or "to meddle" in "surgery, or phisick, drinks, plaisters or oyles." She apparently disobeyed that order, for three years later the deputies banished her from the colony under the penalty of a severe whipping or such other punishment as the judges thought fit.[14]

Other women, both rich and poor, involved themselves in the Antinomian struggle. William Coddington's spouse, like her merchant husband, was "taken with the familistical opinions." Mary Dummer, wife of the wealthy landowner and Assistant Richard Dummer, convinced her husband to move from Newbury to Boston so that she might be closer to Hutchinson.[15] Mary Oliver, a poor Salem calenderer's wife, and onetime supporter of Williams, reportedly exceeded Anne "for ability of speech, and appearance of zeal and devotion." According to Winthrop, Mary Oliver might "have done hurt, but that she was poor and had little acquaintance [with theology]." This Salem rebel held the "dangerous" opinions that the church was managed by the "heads of the people, both magistrates and ministers, met together" instead of by the people themselves, and that anyone professing faith in Christ ought to be admitted to the church and the sacraments. Between 1638 and 1650 she appeared before the magistrates six times for making remarks contemptuous of ministerial and magisterial authority; for these offenses she experienced the stocks, the lash, the placement of a cleft stick on her tongue, and imprisonment. One Salem magistrate became so frustrated with Oliver's refusal to respect his authority that he put her in the stocks without a trial. She sued him for false arrest, collecting a minimal ten shillings in damages. Her victory was short lived, however, and before she left the Bay Colony in 1650 she had managed to secure herself some reputation as a witch.[16]

Mary Oliver and the other female rebels could easily identify with the Antinomian ideology, because its theological emphasis on the individual's inability to achieve salvation echoed women's inability to achieve recognition on a socio-political level. As a woman realized that she could receive wealth, power, and status only through a man—her father or her husband—so the Antinomian realized that he or she could receive grace only through God's beneficence. However, Antinomianism's accentuated condition of dependency was also its great appeal, because in the "new" theology *both* men and women were relegated, vis-á-vis God, to the status that women occupied in Puritan society vis-á-vis men: that is, to the status of malleable inferiors in the hands of a higher being. All power emanated from God, respecting no sex, rather than from male authority figures striving to interpret the Divine Word. Fortified by a consciousness of the Holy Spirit's inward dwelling, the Antinomians could rest secure and self-confident in the belief that they were mystically experiencing the transcendent power of the Almighty, a power far beyond anything mere magistrates and ministers could muster. Antinomianism could not secure for women such practical earthly items as sizable estates, professional success, and participation in the church and civil government, but it provided compensation by reducing the significance of these powers for men. Viewed from this perspective, Antinomianism accomplished what Williams's theology had strongly hinted at, extending the feminine experience of humility to both sexes (although not through the vehicle of sackcloth and ashes). That, in turn, paradoxically created the possibility of feminine pride, as Anne Hutchinson's dynamic example amply demonstrates.

ONE WOMAN BEFORE THE JUDGES

Anne Hutchinson's example caused the divines much frustration. They were chagrined to find that she was not content simply to repeat to the "simple Weomen"[17] the sermons of John Wilson; rather, she chose to interpret and even question the content of those sermons. When she charged that the Bay Colony ministers did not teach a covenant of grace as "clearly" as Cotton and her brother-in-law John Wheelwright, she was summoned in 1636 to appear before a convocation of the clergy. At this convocation, and in succeeding examinations, the ministers found particularly galling her implicit assertion that she was intellectually able to judge the biblical truth of their theology. Such an assertion threatened their collective self-image as the community's intellectual leaders and as the spokesmen for a male-dominated society. The ministers and magistrates therefore sharply criticized her for not fulfilling her ordained womanly role. In September 1637, a synod of elders resolved that women might meet "to pray and edify one another"; however, when one woman "in a prophetical way" resolved questions of doctrine and expounded Scripture, the meeting was "disorderly." At Hutchinson's examination on November 7 and 8, Winthrop began by charging that she criticized the ministers and maintained a "meeting and an assembly in your house that hath been condemned by the general assembly as a thing not tolerable nor comely in the sight of God nor fitting for your sex." Later in the interrogation Winthrop accused her of disobeying her "parents," the magistrates, in violation of the Fifth Commandment, and paternalistically told her, "We do not mean to discourse with those of your sex." Hugh Peter, the Salem Pastor, also indicated that she was not fulfilling the properly submissive, non-intellectual feminine role. He ridiculed her choice of a female preacher of the Isle of Ely as a model for her own behavior and told her to consider "that you have stept out of your place, *you have rather bine a Husband than a Wife and a preacher than a Hearer; and a Magistrate than a Subject.*"[18]

When attacked for behavior inappropriate to her sex, Anne Hutchinson demonstrated (sometimes coyly, sometimes pointedly) that she was the intellectual equal of her accusers. She tried to trap Winthrop when he charged her with dishonoring her "parents": "But put the case Sir that I do fear the Lord and my parents, may not I entertain them that fear the Lord because my parents will not give me leave?" To provide a biblical justification for her teaching activities, she cited Titus' rule (2:3–4) "that the elder women should instruct the younger." Winthrop ordered her to take that rule "in the sense that elder women must instruct the younger about their [women's] business, and to love their husbands." But Anne disagreed with this interpretation, saying, "I do not conceive but that it is meant for some publick times." Winthrop rejoined, "We must . . . restrain you from maintaining this course," and she qualified, "If you have a rule for it from God's word you may." Her resistance infuriated the governor, who exclaimed, "We are your judges, and not you ours." When Winthrop tried to lure her into admitting that she taught men, in violation of Paul's proscription (I Timothy 2:11–2),[19] she replied that she thought herself justified in teaching a man who asked her for instruction, and added sarcastically, "Do you think it not lawful for me to teach women . . . [then] why do you call me to teach the court?"[20]

Hutchinson soon realized that sarcastic remarks would not persuade the court of the legitimacy of her theological claims. Alternatively, therefore, she affected a modest style to cozen the authorities. But, at the same time, she expressed a kind of primitive feminism through double-entendre statements, and by attacking the legitimacy of Paul's idea of the nonspeaking, nonintellectual female church member. When the court charged her with "prophesying," she responded, "The men of Berea are commended for examining *Pauls* Doctrine; wee do no more [in our meetings] but read the notes of our teachers Sermons, and then reason of them by searching the Scriptures."[21] Such a statement was, on one level, an "innocent" plea to the divines that the women were only following biblical prescription. On another level it was an attack on the ministers for presuming to have the final word on biblical interpretation. On yet a third level, since she focused on "Paul's Doctrine" and reminded "men" that they should take another look at that teaching, her statement suggested that ministerial attitudes toward the "place" of women ought to be reexamined.

At another point, Hutchinson responded to Winthrop's criticism with another statement which had meaning on three levels. The governor had accused her of traducing the ministers and magistrates and, when summoned to answer this charge, of saying that "the fear of man was a snare and therefore she would not be affeared of them." She replied, "They say I said the fear of man is a snare, why should I be afraid? When I came unto them, they urging many things unto me and I being backward to answer at first, at length this scripture came into my mind 29th Prov. 15. The fear of man bringeth a snare, but who putteth his trust in the Lord shall be safe."[22] Again her response was phrased as an "innocent" plea to God to assuage her fears, while at the same time it implied that God was on her side, in opposition to the ministers and magistrates. Her statement also assured women that, if they trusted in God and relied on his grace for support, they need not fear men, for such fear trapped them into being "backward" about reacting in confrontations with men.

Although she was aware of the "backwardness" of women as a group, Anne did not view intensified group activity as a remedy for woman's downtrodden status. Her feminism consisted essentially of the recognition of her own strength and gifts, and the apparent belief that other women could come to the same recognition. A strong, heroic example of female self–assertiveness was necessary for one to develop this recognition of her own personal strength; as Hutchinson was a strong example for the other discontented women of Massachusetts, so she had chosen a woman preacher on the Isle of Ely as her own particular heroic model. She did, Hugh Peter chided, "exceedingly magnifie" that preacher "to be a Womane of 1000 hardly any like to her." Anne Hutchinson could thus dissociate herself from the "divers worthy and godly Weomen" of the Bay Colony and confidently deride them as being no better than "soe many Jewes," unconverted by the light of Christ.[23] Other Massachusetts women who wished to reach beyond the conventional, stereotypic behavior of "worthy and godly Weomen" attached themselves to Hutchinson's emphatic example, and to God's ultimate power, in order to resist the constraints which they felt as Puritan women.

Fearful that other women might imitate Hutchinson, the divines wished to catch her in a major theological error and subject her to public punishment. Their efforts were not immediately successful. Throughout her 1637 examination she managed to parry the verbal thrusts of the ministers and magistrates by replying to their many questions with queries of her own, forcing them to justify their positions from the Bible, pointing out their logical inconsistencies, and using innuendo to cast aspersions upon their authoritarianism. With crucial assistance from the sympathetic John Cotton, she left the ministers with no charge to level against her. Female intellectuality was not a prosecutable offense, and she was winning the debate when, in an apparently incautious moment, she gave the authorities the kind of declaration for which they had been hoping. Raising herself to the position of judge over her accusers, she asserted, "I know that for this you goe about to doe to me, God will ruine you and your posterity, and this whole State." Asked how she knew this, she explained, "By an immediate revelation."[24] That was too much for the ministers. They were convinced of her heresy and took steps to expose her in excommunication proceedings before the Boston church, hoping thereby to expel a heretic from their midst, to reestablish support for the Puritan way, to prevent unrest in the state and the family, and, in the process, to shore up their own anxious egos.

The ministers' predisposition to defame Hutchinson before the congregation caused them to ignore what she was actually saying in her excommunication trial. Although she did describe a relationship with Christ which was closer than anything Cotton had envisioned, she did not believe she had experienced Christ's Second Coming in her own life. Such a claim would have denied the resurrection of the body at the Last Judgment, and would have clearly stamped her as a Familist.[25] Hutchinson's accusers, ignoring Thomas Leverett's reminder that she had expressed belief in the resurrection, argued that, if the resurrection did not exist, biblical law would have no validity and the marriage covenant would lack all legal or utilitarian value. The result would be a kind of world which no Puritan could tolerate, a world where the basest desires would be fulfilled and "foule, groce, filthye and abominable" sexual promiscuity would run rampant. Cotton, smarting from a psychological slap Hutchinson had given him earlier in the excommunication proceedings[26] and in danger of losing the respect of the other ministers, admonished her with these words: "though I have not herd, nayther do I thinke, you have bine unfaythfull to your Husband in his Marriage Covenant, *yet that will follow upon it*." By referring to "his" marriage covenant, Cotton did not even accord her equal participation in the making of that covenant. The Boston teacher concluded his admonition with a criticism of his protégée's pride: "I have often feared the highth of your Spirit and being puft up with your owne parts."[27]

Cotton believed the woman who thought for herself would not choose to respect her husband's power over her, or his right to the exclusive use of her body. Many women used adultery as a way to get back at their husbands; so Cotton apparently feared that indiscriminate sexual relations would be the necessary consequence of the extension of freedom to the female sex. Such an imputation in all likelihood shocked Anne Hutchinson, who enjoyed a close relationship with her own husband, William, and had borne fifteen children by him.

The introduction of the sexual issue into the trial, and Cotton's denunciation of Hutchinson, must have curbed dissent from the congregation. Few Puritans would want to defend her in public when such a defense could be construed as supporting promiscuity and adultery. Since Cotton had earlier been sympathetic to the Antinomian cause, and had tried to save Hutchinson at her 1637 examination, his vigorous condemnation of her probably confused her followers. Cotton even went so far as to exempt male Antinomians from any real blame for the controversy when he characterized Antinomianism as a women's delusion. He urged that women be watched, like children; he reproved Hutchinson's sons for not controlling her theological ventures; and he called those sons "Vipers . . . [who] Eate through the very Bowells of your Mother, to her Ruine." Cotton warned the Boston women "to looke to your selves and to take heed that you reaceve nothinge for Truth which hath not the stamp of the Word of God [as interpreted by the ministers] . . . for you see she [Anne] is but a Woman and many unsound and dayngerous principles are held by her." Thomas Shepard, the Cambridge minister, agreed that intellectual activity did not suit women and warned the congregation that Hutchinson was likely "to seduce and draw away many. Espetially simple Weomen of her owne sex."[28]

Because of Paul's injunction against women speaking in church, the female church members, who would have had good reason to resent the clergy's castigation of Hutchinson and themselves, could not legitimately object to the excommunication proceedings. They had been spoken to as if they were children, but, lacking a clearly defined feminist consciousness and filled with "backward" fear, the women could not ignore that injunction. Their heroic model had been presented by the clergy as the epitome of despicableness, a woman of simple intellect and a liar, puffed up with pride and verging on sexual promiscuity. Although five men rose to defend her, their objections were dismissed as arising out of self-interest or misguided affection for her.[29]

In Anne Hutchinson's excommunication proceedings the ministers demonstrated that they had found the means to deal effectively with a rebellious woman and a somewhat hostile congregation. At her examination and her excommunication trial, she attempted to place the ministers on the defensive by questioning them and forcing them to justify their positions, while she herself explained little. She achieved some success in the 1637 trial, but before her fellow church members a few months later she found it difficult to counteract the misrepresentation of her beliefs and the attack on her character. Perhaps fearing the banishment which had been so quickly imposed on her associate John Wheelwright, she recanted, but even then she did not totally compromise her position. She expressed sorrow for her errors of expression, but admitted no errors in judgment and assumed no appearance of humiliation. When Wilson commanded her "as a Leper to withdraw your selfe out of the Congregation," Anne rose, walked to the meetinghouse door, accepted Mary Dyer's offered hand, and turned to impugn her accusers' power: "The Lord judgeth not as man judgeth, better to be cast out of the Church then [*sic*] to deny Christ."[30] . . .

The Massachusetts magistrates [took] special care to ensure that Antinomianism would be rooted out of the Bay Colony. The threat of a humiliating courtroom appearance and a possible whipping was designed to keep Antinomians quiet. When Anne Hutchinson's son-in-law William Collins and son Francis reviled the churches and the ministers while on a journey to Boston in 1641, they were assessed record fines, a fact which helped clamp the lid on dissent.[31] New ministers were carefully scrutinized, lest they deliver "some points savoring of familism,"[32] and several publications were prepared to justify the emergent orthodox position. Of these publications, which were directed at audiences in both New and old England, Cotton's

Singing of Psalmes a Gospel-Ordinance most significantly asserted the need for women to behave submissively. Apparently keeping Anne Hutchinson in mind, the Boston teacher told his readers that "the woman is more subject to error than a man." Cotton continued, "It is not permitted to a woman to speak in the Church by way of propounding questions though under pretence of desire to learn for her own satisfaction; but rather it is required she should ask her husband at home. For under pretence of questioning for learning sake, she might so propound her question as to teach her teachers; or if not so, yet to open a door to some of her own weak and erroneous apprehensions, or at least soon exceed the bounds of womanly modesty." A woman could speak in church only when she wished to confess a sin or participate in hymn-singing.[33]

The effort to discredit the Antinomians and Antinomian sentiment in the Bay Colony was ultimately quite successful. By the mid-1640s Antinomianism was no longer threatening in a practical sense. The ministers had been returned to a position of public respect, and fewer people dared to challenge the authority of the magistrates. A number of sermons and publications had reaffirmed the appropriateness of female submission.

NOTES

1. C. Mather, *Magnalia*, II, 446.

2. Polishook, ed., *Williams, Cotton, & Rel. Freedom*, pp. 1–35.

3. Winthrop, *Journal*, I, 162, 168; Felt, *Annals of Salem*, II, 573, 576; C. Pope, *Pioneers of Maine & N. Hamp.*, p. 382.

4. R. Williams, *Geo. Fox Digg'd*, p. 16; appendix, pp. 26–27.

5. Much of the information throughout the rest of this chapter closely parallels or duplicates that appearing in Koehler, "Case of Am. Jezebels," and in "Letter."

6. E. Morgan, *Puritan Dilemma*, p. 137, Michael McGiffert's introduction to Thomas Shepard's autobiography and journal contains a discussion of the Puritans' problems with assurance of salvation. See [T. Shephard,] *God's Plot*. Puritan attitudes toward the preparation process are treated comprehensively and perceptively in Pettit, *Heart Prepared*.

7. John Cotton, *Treatise of Covenant of Grace*, p. 177. Cotton's subsequent debate with the other ministers appears in Hall, ed., *Antinomian Controversy*, pp. 24–151.

8. The Familists or Family of Love, a sect which originated in Holland about 1540 and spread to England, gained a largely undeserved reputation for practicing promiscuity. Antinomianism was associated in the Puritan mind with the licentious orgies that accompanied the enthusiasm of John Agricola in sixteenth-century Germany. "Opinionism" was a term often used for any theology that the divines disliked (Hastings, ed., *Encyc. of Rel. & Ethics*, I, 581–82; V, 319; IX, 102).

9. Winthrop, *Short Story of Rise of Antinomians*, pp. 203, 208–9, 253.

10. *Ibid.*, pp. 207, 262; C. Mather, *Magnalia*, II, 446.

11. E. Johnson, *Wonder-Working Prov.*, p. 132; *Good News from N. Eng.*, p. 206.

12. John Cotton, *Way of Cong. Churches Cleared*, pt. 1, p. 61; Winthrop, *Short Story of Rise of Antinomians*, p. 209.

13. Winthrop, *Journal*, I, 266; *Short Story of Rise of Antinomians*, p. 281.

14. E. Johnson, *Wonder-Working Prov.*, pp. 132, 134; Winthrop, *Short Story of Rise of Antinomians*, p. 281; Shurtleff, ed., *Mass. Rec.*, I, 224, 329.

15. Winthrop, *Journal*, I, 270; "The Rev. John Eliot's Record of the Church Members, Roxbury, Massachusetts," in Boston Rec. Cmrs., *Rep. Containing Roxbury Rec.*, p. 77.

16. Winthrop, *Journal*, I, 285–86; G. Dow, ed., *Essex Ct. Rec.*, I, 12, 138, 180, 182–83, 186; Noble & Cronin, eds., *Rec. of Mass. Assts.*, II, 80; Perley, *Hist. of Salem*, II, 50; T. Hutchinson, *Witchcraft Delusion*, p. 6.

17. "Rep. of Trial of A. Hutchinson before Boston Church," p. 365.

18. Winthrop, *Journal*, I, 234; "Examination of A. Hutchinson at Newton Ct.," pp. 312–14, 318; "Rep. of Trial of A. Hutchinson before Boston Church," pp. 380, 382–83.

19. Paul told woman that she was to hold her tongue in church and be careful not "to teach, nor usurp authority over the man, but to be in silence."

20. "Examination of A. Hutchinson at Newtown Ct.," pp. 313–16.

21. Winthrop, *Short Story of Rise of Antinomians*, p. 268.

22. "Examination of A. Hutchinson at Newtown Ct.," p. 330.

23. "Rep. of Trial of A. Hutchinson before Boston Church," p. 380. That Hutchinson chose a woman preacher as a model for her own rebellious behavior, instead of selecting the more popular "Spirit-mystic" and "apostle of Ely" William Sedgwick, indicated her level of feminist self-awareness and suggested that she was not greatly in need of that male guidance which the historian Emery Battis has maintained she really desired. (See Battis, *Saints & Sectaries*, pp. 51–52.) Cotton expressed the view that she was far from satisfied with his guidance: "Mistris Hutchinson seldome resorted to mee, and when she did come to me, it was seldome or never (that I can tell of) that she tarried long. I rather think, she was loath to resort much to me, or, to conferre long with me, lest she might seeme to learne somewhat from me" (Cotton, *Way of Cong. Churches Cleared*, pt. 1, p. 89). Of course, Cotton's testimony may not be completely accurate, since he was writing to wash the Antinomian stain off his own hands.

Little is known about Anne Hutchinson's role model, the woman of Ely. Thomas Edwards, an English Puritan divine, remarked "that there are also some women preachers in our times, who keep constant lectures, preaching weekly to many men and women. In Lincolnshire, in Holland and those parts [i.e., the parts about Holland in Lincolnshire] there is a woman preacher who preaches (it's certain), and it's reported also she baptizeth, but that's not so certain. *In the Isle of Ely (that land of errors and sectaries) is a woman preacher also*" (Edwards, *Gangraena*... [London, 1646], pt. 2, p. 29, quoted in Battis, *Saints & Sectaries*, p. 43n).

24. Winthrop, *Short Story of Rise of Antinomians*, p. 273; "Examination of A. Hutchinson at Newtown Court," p. 337.

25. A good discussion of the theological issues surrounding resurrection is provided in Rosenmeier, "N. Eng.'s Perfection." Rosenmeier, however, describes Hutchinson too explicitly as a Familist, without supplying sufficient evidence of the same.

26. Hutchinson had responded to an argument of Cotton's with the rejoinder, "I desire to hear God speak this and not man" ("Rep. of Trial of A. Hutchinson before Boston Church," pp. 358, 362, 355).

27. *Ibid.*, p. 372.

28. *Ibid.*, pp. 369–70, 365.

29. *Ibid.*, pp. 385–87, 366–68.

30. *Ibid.*, pp. 378, 388; Winthrop, *Short Story of Rise of Antinomians*, p. 307.

31. William Collins was sentenced to pay £100 for charging the Massachusetts churches and ministers with being anti-Christian and calling the king of England the king of Babylon. Francis Hutchinson objected to the popular rumor that he would not sit at the same table with his excommunicated mother; feeling that the Boston Church was to blame, he called that body "a strumpet"—a statement for which he was fined £40. The Assistants fined only one man, Captain John Stone, an amount equal to that assessed Collins. Stone had assaulted Assistant Roger Ludlow and called him a "just ass." Only one other man was fined more than young Hutchinson; Robert Anderson was penalized with a £50 fine for "contempt" (Noble & Cronin, eds., *Rec. of Mass. Assts.*, II, 35, 66, 109; Winthrop, *Journal*, II, 38–40; John Cotton, "Letter," p. 186).

32. In 1639 the authorities criticized the Reverend Hanserd Knowles for holding "some of Mrs. Hutchinson's opinions," and two years later they forced the Reverend Jonathan Burr to renounce certain errors which, wrote Winthrop, "savor[ed] of familism" (Winthrop, *Journal*, I. 295; II, 22–23).

33. John Cotton, "Psalm-Singing a Godly Exercise," p. 266.

3

The Planter's Wife: The Experience of White Women in Seventeenth-Century Maryland

Lois Green Carr and Lorena S. Walsh

Economic and demographic conditions in the seventeenth-century Chesapeake colonies were strikingly different from those in New England. Lois Green Carr and Lorena S. Walsh explore the consequences of these differences for power relations between white men and women in the colony of Maryland. Most female colonists came to Maryland as indentured servants, obligated to work for terms of four or five years in exchange for the cost of their transportation and food, clothing, and shelter during their period of service. Carr and Walsh describe conditions for women in servitude and the transition to the role of planter's wife that awaited those who survived servitude and married. They found that Maryland women married late, bore relatively few children, and were commonly widowed. They tended to remarry, but the evidence suggests they often had some control over the property brought from their first marriages.

Carr and Walsh note a relative decline in the position of women with the transition from the immigrant to the native-born generation. Earlier marriage, greater life expectancy, and declining sex ratios all promoted greater male authority within the family.

Four facts were basic to all human experience in seventeenth-century Maryland. First, for most of the period the great majority of inhabitants had been born in what we now call Britain. Population increase in Maryland did not result primarily from births in the colony before the late 1680s and did not produce a predominantly native population of adults before the first decade of the eighteenth century. Second, immigrant men could not expect to live beyond age forty-three, and 70 percent would die before age fifty. Women may have had even shorter lives. Third, perhaps 85 percent of the immigrants, and practically all the unmarried immigrant women, arrived as indentured servants and consequently married late. Family groups were never predominant in the immigration to Maryland and were a significant part for only a brief time at mid-century. Fourth, many more men than women immigrated during the whole period.[1] These facts—immigrant predominance, early death, late marriage, and sexual imbalance—created circumstances of social and demographic disruption that deeply affected family and community life.

Excerpted from "The Planter's Wife: The Experience of White Women in Seventeenth–Century Maryland," by Lois Green Carr and Lorena S. Walsh in *In Search of Early America: The William & Mary Quarterly, 1943–1993* (Williamsburg, Va.: Institute of Early American History and Culture, 1993).

We need to assess the effects of this disruption on the experience of women in seventeenth-century Maryland. Were women degraded by the hazards of servitude in a society in which everyone had left community and kin behind and in which women were in short supply? Were traditional restraints on social conduct weakened? If so, were women more exploited or more independent and powerful than women who remained in England? Did any differences from English experience which we can observe in the experience of Maryland women survive the transformation from an immigrant to a predominantly native-born society with its own kinship networks and community traditions? The tentative argument put forward here is that the answer to all these questions is Yes. There were degrading aspects of servitude, although these probably did not characterize the lot of most women; there were fewer restraints on social conduct, especially in courtship, than in England; women were less protected but also more powerful than those who remained at home; and at least some of these changes survived the appearance in Maryland of New World creole communities. However, these issues are far from settled, and we shall offer some suggestions as to how they might be further pursued.

Maryland was settled in 1634, but in 1650 there were probably no more than six hundred persons and fewer than two hundred adult women in the province. After that time population growth was steady; in 1704 a census listed 30,437 white persons, of whom 7,163 were adult women.[2] Thus, in discussing the experience of white women in seventeenth-century Maryland, we are dealing basically with the second half of the century.

Marylanders of that period did not leave letters and diaries to record their New World experience or their relationships to one another. Nevertheless, they left trails in the public records that give us clues. Immigrant lists kept in England and documents of the Maryland courts offer quantifiable evidence about the kinds of people who came and some of the problems they faced in making a new life. Especially valuable are the probate court records. Estate inventories reveal the kinds of activities carried on in the house and on the farm, and wills, which are usually the only personal statements that remain for any man or woman, show something of personal attitudes. This essay relies on the most useful of the immigrant lists and all surviving Maryland court records, but concentrates especially on the surviving records of the lower Western Shore, an early-settled area highly suitable for tobacco. . . .

Because immigrants predominated, who they were determined much about the character of Maryland society. The best information so far available comes from lists of indentured servants who left the ports of London, Bristol, and Liverpool.[3]

Servants who arrived under indenture included yeomen, husbandmen, farm laborers, artisans, and small tradesmen, as well as many untrained to any special skill. They were young: over half of the men on the London lists of 1683–1684 were aged eighteen to twenty-two. They were seldom under seventeen or over twenty-eight. The women were a little older; the great majority were between eighteen and twenty-five, and half were aged twenty to twenty-two. Most servants contracted for four or five years service, although those under fifteen were to serve at least seven years.[4] These youthful immigrants represented a wide range of English society. All were seeking opportunities they had not found at home. . . .

Whatever their status, one fact about immigrant women is certain: many fewer came than men. Immigrant lists, headright lists, and itemizations of servants in inventories show severe imbalance. On a London immigrant list of 1634–1635 men outnumbered women six to one. From the 1650s at least until the 1680s most sources show a ratio of three to one. From then on, all sources show some, but not great, improvement. Among immigrants from Liverpool over the years 1697–1707 the ratio was just under two and one half to one.[5]

Why did not more women come? Presumably, fewer wished to leave family and community to venture into a wilderness. But perhaps more important, women were not as desirable as men to merchants and planters who were making fortunes raising and marketing tobacco, a crop that requires large amounts of labor. The gradual improvement in the sex ratio among servants toward the end of the century may have been the result of a change in recruiting the needed labor. In the late 1660s the supply of young men willing to emigrate stopped increasing sufficiently to meet the labor demands of a growing Chesapeake population. Merchants who recruited servants for planters turned to other sources, and among these sources were women. They did not crowd the ships arriving in the Chesapeake, but their numbers did increase.[6]

To ask the question another way, why did women come? Doubtless, most came to get a husband, an objective virtually certain of success in a land where women were so far outnumbered. The promotional literature, furthermore, painted bright pictures of the life that awaited men and women once out of their time; and various studies suggest that for a while, at least, the promoters were not being entirely fanciful. Until the 1660s, and to a less degree the 1680s, the expanding economy of Maryland and Virginia offered opportunities well beyond those available in England to men without capital and to the women who became their wives.[7]

Nevertheless, the hazards were also great, and the greatest was untimely death. Newcomers promptly became ill, probably with malaria, and many died. . . . The majority of women who survived seasoning paid their transportation costs by working for a four or five-year term of service. The kind of work depended on the status of the family they served. A female servant of a small planter—who through about the 1670s might have had a servant[8]— probably worked at the hoe. Such a man could not afford to buy labor that would not help with the cash crop. In wealthy families women probably were household servants, although some are occasionally listed in inventories of well-to-do planters as living on the quarters—that is, on plantations other than the dwelling plantation. Such women saved men the jobs of preparing food and washing linen but doubtless also worked in the fields.[9] In middling households, experience must have varied. Where the number of people to feed and wash for was large, female servants would have had little time to tend the crops. . . .

An additional risk for the woman who came as a servant was the possibility of bearing a bastard. At least 20 percent of the female servants who came to Charles County between 1658 and 1705 were presented to the county court for this cause.[10] A servant woman could not marry unless someone was willing to pay her master for the term she had left to serve.[11] If a man made her pregnant, she could not marry him unless he could buy her time. Once a woman became free, however, marriage was clearly the usual solution. Only a handful of free women were presented in Charles County for bastardy between 1658 and 1705. Since few free women remained either single or widowed for long, not many were subject to the risk. The hazard of bearing a bastard was a hazard of being a servant.[12]

This high rate of illegitimate pregnancies among servants raises lurid questions. Did men import women for sexual exploitation?. . . In our opinion, the answer is clearly No. Servants were economic investments on the part of planters who needed labor. . . . The servant woman was in the household to work—to help feed and clothe the family and make tobacco. She was not primarily a concubine.

This point could be established more firmly if we knew more about the fathers of the bastards. Often the culprits were fellow servants or men recently freed but too poor to purchase the woman's remaining time. Sometimes the master was clearly at fault. But often the father is not identified. Some masters surely did exploit their female servants sexually. Nevertheless, masters were infrequently accused of fathering their servants' bastards, and those found guilty were punished as severely as were other men. Community mores did not sanction their misconduct.[13]

A female servant paid dearly for the fault of unmarried pregnancy. She was heavily fined, and if no one would pay her fine, she was whipped. Furthermore, she served an extra twelve to twenty-four months to repay her master for the "trouble of his house," and labor lost, and the fathers often did not share in this payment of damages. On top of all, she might lose the child after weaning unless by then she had become free, for the courts bound out bastard children at very early ages.[14] . . .

Some women escaped all or part of their servitude because prospective husbands purchased the remainder of their time. At least one promotional pamphlet published in the 1660s described such purchases as likely, but how often they actually occurred is difficult to determine.[15] Suggestive is a 20 percent difference between the sex ratios found in a Maryland headright sample, 1658–1681, and among servants listed in lower Western Shore inventories for

1658–1679.[16] Some of the discrepancy must reflect the fact that male servants were younger than female servants and therefore served longer terms; hence they had a greater chance of appearing in an inventory. But part of the discrepancy doubtless follows from the purchase of women for wives. Before 1660, when sex ratios were even more unbalanced and the expanding economy enabled men to establish themselves more quickly, even more women may have married before their terms were finished.[17]. . .

If a woman's time was not purchased by a prospective husband, she was virtually certain to find a husband once she was free. Those famous spinsters, Margaret and Mary Brent, were probably almost unique in seventeenth–century Maryland. In the four counties of the lower Western Shore only two of the women who left a probate inventory before the eighteenth century are known to have died single.[18] Comely or homely, strong or weak, any young woman was too valuable to be overlooked, and most could find a man with prospects.

The woman who immigrated to Maryland, survived seasoning and service, and gained her freedom became a planter's wife. She had considerable liberty in making her choice. There were men aplenty, and no fathers or brothers were hovering to monitor her behavior or disapprove her preference. . . . . There is some evidence that the absence of kin and the pressures of the sex ratio created conditions of sexual freedom in courtship that were not customary in England. A register of marriages and births for seventeenth-century Somerset County shows that about one-third of the immigrant women whose marriages are recorded were pregnant at the time of the ceremony—nearly twice the rate in English parishes.[19] There is no indication of community objection to this freedom so long as marriage took place. No presentments for bridal pregnancy were made in any of the Maryland courts.[20]

The planter's wife was likely to be in her mid-twenties at marriage. An estimate of minimum age at marriage for servant women can be made from lists of indentured servants who left London over the years 1683–1684 and from age judgments in Maryland county court records. If we assume that the 112 female indentured servants going to Maryland and Virginia whose ages are given in the London lists served full four-year terms, then only 1.8 percent married before age twenty, but 68 percent after age twenty-four.[21] Similarly, if the 141 women whose ages were judged in Charles County between 1666 and 1705 served out their terms according to the custom of the county, none married before age twenty-two, and half were twenty-five or over.[22] When adjustments are made for the ages at which wives may have been purchased, the figures drop, but even so the majority of women waited until at least age twenty-four to marry.[23] Actual age at marriage in Maryland can be found for few seventeenth-century female immigrants, but observations for Charles and Somerset counties place the mean age at about twenty-five.[24]

Because of the age at which an immigrant woman married, the number of children she would bear her husband was small. She had lost up to ten years of her childbearing life[25]—the possibility of perhaps four or five children, given the usual rhythm of childbearing.[26] At the same time, high mortality would reduce both the number of children she would bear over the rest of her life and the number who would live. One partner to a marriage was likely to die within seven years, and the chances were only one in three that a marriage would last ten years.[27] In these circumstances, most women would not bear more than three or four children . . . to any one husband, plus a posthumous child were she the survivor. The best estimates suggest that nearly a quarter, perhaps more, of the children born alive died during their first year and that 40 to 55 percent would not live to see age twenty.[28] Consequently, one of her children would probably die in infancy, and another one or two would fail to reach adulthood. Wills left in St. Mary's County during the seventeenth century show the results. In 105 families over the years 1660 to 1680, only twelve parents left more than three children behind them, including those conceived but not yet born. The average number was 2.3, nearly always minors, some of whom might die before reaching adulthood.[29]

For the immigrant woman, then, one of the major facts of life was that although she might bear a child about every two years, nearly half would not reach maturity. The social implications of this fact are far-reaching. Because she married late in her childbearing years and because so many of her children would die young, the number who would reach marriageable age might not replace, or might only barely replace, her and her husband or husbands as child-producing members of society. Consequently, so long as immigrants were heavily predominant in the adult female population, Maryland could not grow much by natural increase.[30] It remained a land of newcomers.

This fact was fundamental to the character of seventeenth-century Maryland society, although its implications have yet to be fully explored. Settlers came from all parts of England and hence from differing traditions—in types of agriculture, forms of landholding and estate management, kinds of building construction, customary contributions to community needs, and family arrangements, including the role of women. The necessities of life in the Chesapeake required all immigrants to make adaptations. But until the native-born became predominant, a securely established Maryland tradition would not guide or restrict the newcomers. . . .

A hazard of marriage for seventeenth-century women everywhere was death in childbirth, but this hazard may have been greater than usual in the Chesapeake. Whereas in most societies women tend to outlive men, in this malaria-ridden area it is probable that men outlived women. Hazards of childbirth provide the likely reason that Chesapeake women died so young. Once a woman in the Chesapeake reached forty-five, she tended to outlive men who reached the same age. Darrett and Anita Rutman have found malaria a probable cause of an exceptionally high death rate among pregnant women, who are, it appears, peculiarly vulnerable to that disease.[31] . . .

However long they lived, immigrant women in Maryland tended to out-live their husbands—in Charles County, for example—by a ratio of two to one. This was possible, despite the fact that women were younger than men at death, because women were also younger than men at marriage. Some women were widowed with no living children, but most were left responsible for two or three. . . .[32]

This fact had drastic consequences, given the physical circumstances of life. People lived at a distance from one another, not even in villages, much less towns. The widow had left her kin 3,000 miles across an ocean, and her husband's family was also there. She would have to feed her children and make her own tobacco crop. Though neighbors might help, heavy labor would be required of her if she had no servants, until—what admittedly was usually not difficult—she acquired a new husband.

In this situation dying husbands were understandably anxious about the welfare of their families. Their wills reflected their feelings and tell some-thing of how they regarded their wives. In St. Mary's and Charles counties during the seventeenth century, little more than one-quarter of the men left their widows with no more than the dower the law required—one-third of his land for her life, plus outright ownership of one-third of his personal prop-erty (see Table I). If there were no children, a man almost always left his widow his whole estate. Otherwise there were a variety of arrangements (see Table II).

During the 1660s, when testators begin to appear in quantity, nearly a fifth of the men who had children left all to their wives, trusting them to see that the children received fair portions. . . . As the century progressed, hus-bands tended instead to give their wives all or a major part of the estate for her life, and to designate how it should be distributed after her death. Either

TABLE I *Bequests of Husbands to Wives, St. Mary's and Charles Counties, Maryland, 1640 to 1710*

	N	DOWER OR LESS	
		N	%
1640s	6	2	34
1650s	24	7	29
1660s	65	18	28
1670s	86	21	24
1680s	64	17	27
1690s	83	23	28
1700s	74	25	34
Totals	402	113	28

Source: Wills, I–XIV, Hall of Records, Annapolis, Md.

TABLE II Bequests of Husbands to Wives with Children, St. Mary's and Charles Counties, Maryland, 1640 to 1710

	N	ALL ESTATE		ALL OR DWELLING PLANTATION FOR LIFE		ALL OR DWELLING PLANTATION FOR WIDOWHOOD		ALL OR DWELLING PLANTATION FOR MINORITY OF CHILD		MORE THAN DOWER IN OTHER FORM		DOWER OR LESS OR UNKNOWN	
		N	%	N	%	N	%	N	%	N	%	N	%
1640s	3	1	33									2	67
1650s	16	1	6	2	13	1	6	1	6	4	25	7	44
1660s	45	8	18	8	18	2	4	3	7	9	20	15	33
1670s	61	4	7	21	34	2	3	3	5	13	21	18	30
1680s	52	5	10	19	37	2	4	2	4	11	21	13	25
1690s	69	1	1	31	45	7	10	2	3	10	14	18	26
1700s	62			20	32	6	10	2	3	14	23	20	32
Totals	308	20	6	101	33	20	6	13	4	61	20	93	30

Source: Wills, I-XIV.

way, the husband put great trust in his widow, considering that he knew she was bound to remarry. Only a handful of men left estates to their wives only for their term of widowhood or until the children came of age. When a man did not leave his wife a life estate, he often gave her land outright or more than her dower third of his movable property. Such bequests were at the expense of his children and showed his concern that his widow should have a maintenance which young children could not supply.

A husband usually made his wife his executor and thus responsible for paying his debts and preserving the estate. Only 11 percent deprived their wives of such powers.[33] In many instances, however, men also appointed overseers to assist their wives and to see that their children were not abused or their property embezzled. Danger lay in the fact that a second husband acquired control of all his wife's property, including her life estate in the property of his predecessor. . . . On the whole, the absence of [detailed] provisions for the protection of the children points to the husband's overriding concern for the welfare of his widow and to his confidence in her management, regardless of the certainty of her remarriage. Evidently, in the politics of family life women enjoyed great respect.[34] . . .

Maryland men trusted their widows, but this is not to say that many did not express great anxiety about the future of their children. They asked both wives and overseers to see that the children received "some learning." . . . Often present was the fear that orphaned children would be treated as servants and trained only to work in the fields.[35] With stepfathers in mind, many fathers provided that their sons should be independent before the usual age of majority, which for girls was sixteen but for men twenty-one. Sometimes fathers willed that their sons should inherit when they were as young as sixteen, though more often eighteen. The sons could then escape an incompatible stepfather, who could no longer exploit their labor or property. If a son was already close to age sixteen, the father might bind him to his mother until he reached majority or his mother died, whichever came first. If she lived, she could watch out for his welfare, and his labor could contribute to her support. If she died, he and his property would be free from a stepfather's control.[36]

What happened to widows and children if a man died without leaving a will? There was great need for some community institution that could protect children left fatherless or parentless in a society where they usually had no other kin. By the 1660s the probate court and county orphans' courts were supplying this need.[37] If a man left a widow, the probate court . . . usually appointed her or her new husband administrator of the estate with power to pay its creditors under court supervision. Probate procedures provided a large measure of protection. These required an inventory of the movable property and careful accounting of all disbursements, whether or not a man had left a will. . . .

Once the property of an intestate had been fully accounted and creditors paid, the county courts appointed a guardian who took charge of the property and gave bond to the children with sureties that he or she would not waste it. If the mother were living, she could be the guardian, or if she had re-married, her new husband would act. Through most of the century bond was waived in these circumstances, but from the 1690s security was required of all guardians, even of mothers. Thereafter the courts might actually take away an orphan's property from a widow or stepfather if she or he could not find sureties—that is, neighbors who judged the parent responsible and hence were willing to risk their own property as security. Children without any par-ents were assigned new families, who at all times found surety if there were property to manage. If the orphans inherited land, English common law al-lowed them to choose guardians for themselves at age fourteen—another es-cape hatch for children in conflict with stepparents. Orphans who had no property, or whose property was insufficient to provide an income that could maintain them, were expected to work for their guardians in return for their maintenance. Every year the county courts were expected to check on the wel-fare of orphans of intestate parents and remove them or their property from guardians who abused them or misused their estates. From 1681, Maryland law required that a special jury be impaneled once a year to report neighbor-hood knowledge of mistreatment of orphans and hear complaints. . . .

Remarriage was the usual and often the immediate solution for a woman who had lost her husband.[38] The shortage of women made any woman eligible to marry again, and the difficulties of raising a family while running a plantation must have made remarriage necessary for widows who had no son old enough to make tobacco. One indication of the high inci-dence of remarriage is the fact that there were only sixty women, almost all of them widows, among the 1,735 people who left probate inventories in four southern Maryland counties over the second half of the century.[39] Most other women must have died while married and therefore legally without property to put through probate.

One result of remarriage was the development of complex family struc-tures. Men found themselves responsible for stepchildren as well as their own offspring, and children acquired half-sisters and half-brothers. Sometimes a woman married a second husband who himself had been previously married, and both brought children of former spouses to the new marriage. They then produced children of their own. The possibilities for conflict over the up-bringing of children are evident, and crowded living conditions, found even in the households of the wealthy, must have added to family tensions. Luckily, the children of the family very often had the same mother. In Charles County, at least, widows took new husbands three times more often than wid-owers took new wives.[40] The role of the mother in managing the relationships of half-brothers and half-sisters or stepfathers and stepchildren must have been critical to family harmony.

Early death in this immigrant population thus had broad effects on Maryland society in the seventeenth century. It produced what we might call a pattern of serial polyandry, which enabled more men to marry and to father families than the sex ratios otherwise would have permitted. It produced thousands of orphaned children who had no kin to maintain them or preserve their property, and thus gave rise to an institution almost unknown in England, the orphans' court, which was charged with their protection. And early death, by creating families in which the mother was the unifying element, may have increased her authority within the household.

When the immigrant woman married her first husband, there was usually no property settlement involved, since she was unlikely to have any dowry. But her remarriage was another matter. At the very least, she owned or had a life interest in a third of her former husband's estate. She needed also to think of her children's interests. If she remarried, she would lose control of the property. Consequently, property settlements occasionally appear in the seventeenth-century court records between widows and their future husbands. Sometimes she and her intended signed an agreement whereby he relinquished his rights to the use of her children's portions. Sometimes he deeded to her property which she could dispose of at her pleasure.[41] . . .

The wife's dower rights in her husband's estate were a recognition of her role in contributing to his prosperity, whether by the property she had brought to the marriage or by the labor she performed in his household. A woman newly freed from servitude would not bring property, but the benefits of her labor would be great. A man not yet prosperous enough to own a servant might need his wife's help in the fields as well as in the house, especially if he were paying rent or still paying for land. Moreover, food preparation was so time-consuming that even if she worked only at household duties, she saved him time he needed for making tobacco and corn. The corn, for example, had to be pounded in the mortar or ground in a handmill before it could be used to make bread, for there were very few water mills in seventeenth-century Maryland. The wife probably raised vegetables in a kitchen garden; she also milked the cows and made butter and cheese, which might produce a salable surplus. She washed the clothes, and made them if she had the skill. When there were servants to do field work, the wife undoubtedly spent her time entirely in such household tasks. . . .

We have suggested that wives did field work; the suggestion is supported by occasional direct references in the court records. Mary Castleton, for example, told the judge of probate that "her husband late Deceased in his Life time had Little to sustaine himselfe and Children but what was produced out of ye ground by ye hard Labour of her the said Mary."[42] Household inventories provide indirect evidence. Before about 1680 those of poor men and even middling planters on Maryland's lower Western Shore—the bottom two-thirds of the married decedents—[43] show few signs of household industry, such as appear in equivalent English estates.[44] Sheep and woolcards, flax and hackles, and spinning wheels all were a rarity, and such things as candle molds were nonexistent. Women in these households must have been busy at other work. In households with bound labor the wife doubtless was fully occupied preparing food and washing clothes for family and hands. But the wife in a household too poor to afford bound labor—the bottom fifth of the married decedent group—might well tend tobacco when she could.[45] Eventually, the profits of her labor might enable the family to buy a servant, making greater profits possible. From such beginnings many families climbed the economic ladder in seventeenth-century Maryland.[46] . . .

Stagnation of the tobacco economy, beginning about 1680, produced changes that had some effect on women's economic role.[47] As shown by inventories of the lower Western Shore, home industry increased, especially at the upper ranges of the economic spectrum. In these households women were spinning yarn and knitting it into clothing.[48] The increase in such activity was far less in the households of the bottom fifth, where changes of a different kind may have increased the pressures to grow tobacco. Fewer men at this level could now purchase land, and a portion of their crop went for rent. At this level, more wives than before may have been helping to produce tobacco when they could. And by this time they were often helping as a matter of survival, not as a means of improving the family position.

So far we have considered primarily the experience of immigrant women. What of their daughters? How were their lives affected by the demographic stresses of Chesapeake society?

One of the most important points in which the experience of daughters differed from that of their mothers was the age at which they married. In this woman-short world, the mothers had married as soon as they were eligible, but they had not usually become eligible until they were mature women in their middle twenties. Their daughters were much younger at marriage. A vital register kept in Somerset County shows that some girls married at age twelve and that the mean age at marriage for those born before 1670 was sixteen and a half years. . . .

Not only did native girls marry early, but many of them were pregnant before the ceremony. Bridal pregnancy among native-born women was not as common as among immigrants. Nevertheless, in seventeenth-century Somerset County, 20 percent of native brides bore children within eight and one half months of marriage. This was a somewhat higher percentage than has been reported from seventeenth-century English parishes.[49]

These facts suggest considerable freedom for girls in selecting a husband. Almost any girl must have had more than one suitor, and evidently many had freedom to spend time with a suitor in a fashion that allowed her to become pregnant. We might suppose that such pregnancies were not incurred until after the couple had become betrothed, and that they were consequently an allowable part of courtship, were it not that girls whose fathers were living were usually not the culprits. In Somerset, at least, only 10 percent of the brides with fathers living were pregnant, in contrast to 30 percent of those who were orphans.[50] Since there was only about one year's difference between the mean ages at which orphan and non-orphan girls married, parental supervision rather than age seems to have been the main factor in the differing bridal pregnancy rates.[51]

Native girls married young and bore children young; hence they had more children than immigrant women. This fact ultimately changed the composition of the Maryland population. Native-born females began to have enough children to enable couples to replace themselves. These children, furthermore, were divided about evenly between males and females. By the mid-1680s, in all probability, the population thus began to grow through reproductive increase, and sexual imbalance began to decline. In 1704 the native-born preponderated in the Maryland assembly for the first time and by then were becoming predominant in the adult population as a whole.[52]

This appearance of a native population was bringing alterations in family life, especially for widows and orphaned minors. They were acquiring kin. St. Mary's and Charles counties wills demonstrate the change.[53] . . . Before 1680, when nearly all those who died and left families had been immigrants, three-quarters of the men and women who left widows and/or minor children made no mention in their wills of any other kin in Maryland. In the first decade of the eighteenth century, among native-born testators, nearly three-fifths mention other kin, and if we add information from sources other than wills—other probate records, land records, vital registers, and so on—at least 70 percent are found to have had such local connections. This development of local family ties must have been one of the most important events of early Maryland history.[54]

Historians have only recently begun to explore the consequences of the shift from an immigrant to a predominantly native population.[55] We would like to suggest some changes in the position of women that may have resulted from this transition. It is already known that as sexual imbalance disappeared, age at first marriage rose, but it remained lower than it had been for immigrants over the second half of the seventeenth century. At the same time, life expectancy improved, at least for men. The results were longer marriages and more children who reached maturity.[56] In St. Mary's County after 1700, dying men far more often than earlier left children of age to maintain their widows, and widows may have felt less inclination and had less opportunity to remarry.[57]

We may speculate on the social consequences of such changes. More fathers were still alive when their daughters married, and hence would have been able to exercise control over the selection of their sons-in-law. What in the seventeenth century may have been a period of comparative independence for women, both immigrant and native, may have given way to a return to more traditional European social controls over the creation of new families. If so, we might see the results in a decline in bridal pregnancy and perhaps a decline in bastardy.[58]

We may also find the wife losing ground in the household polity, although her economic importance probably remained unimpaired. Indeed, she must have been far more likely than a seventeenth-century immigrant woman to bring property to her marriage. But several changes may have caused women to play a smaller role than before in household decision making. Women became proportionately more numerous and may have lost bargaining power. Furthermore, as marriages lasted longer, the proportion of households full of stepchildren and half-brothers and half-sisters united primarily by the mother must have diminished. Finally, when husbands died, more widows would have had children old enough to maintain them and any minor brothers and sisters. There would be less need for women to play a controlling role, as well as less incentive for their husbands to grant it. . . .

If this change occurred, we should find symptoms to measure. There should be fewer gifts from husbands to wives of property put at the wife's disposal. Husbands should less frequently make bequests to wives that provided them with property beyond their dower. A wife might even be restricted to less than her dower, although the law allowed her to choose her dower instead of a bequest.[59] As the same time, children should be commanded to maintain their mothers.

St. Mary's County wills show some of the symptoms (see Table III). Bequests of dower or less grew by nearly two-fifths, from 30 to 41 percent. On the other hand, widowhood restrictions did not increase, nor did fathers often exhort children to help their mothers or give them living space. Still, as demographic conditions became more normal and traditional family networks appeared, St. Mary's County widows began to lose ground to their children. This phenomenon deserves further study. . . .

If the demography of Maryland produced the effects here described, such effects should also be evident elsewhere in the Chesapeake. The four characteristics of the seventeenth-century Maryland population—immigrant predominance, early death, late marriage, and sexual imbalance—are to be found everywhere in the region, at least at first. The timing of the disappearance of these peculiarities may have varied from place to place, depending on date of settlement or rapidity of development, but the effect of their existence upon the experience of women should be clear. Should research in other areas of the Chesapeake fail to find women enjoying the status they achieved on the lower Western Shore of Maryland, then our arguments would have to be revised.[60]

Work is also needed that will enable historians to compare conditions in Maryland with those in other colonies. Richard S. Dunn's study of the British West Indies also shows demographic disruption.[61] When the status of wives is studied, it should prove similar to that of Maryland women. In contrast were demographic conditions in New England, where immigrants came in family groups, major immigration had ceased by the mid-seventeenth century, sex ratios balanced early, and mortality was low.[62] Under these conditions, demographic disruption must have been both less severe and less prolonged. If New England women achieved status similar to that suggested for women in

TABLE III Bequests of Husbands to Wives with Children, St. Mary's County, Maryland, 1710–1777

Date	All Estate		All or Dwelling Plantation for Life		All or Dwelling Plantation for Widowhood[a]		More than Dower in Other Form		Dower or Less or Unknown[b]	
	N	N	%	N	%	N	%	N	%	N	%
1710–1719	39	1	3	12	32	2	5	10	26	14	37
1720–1729	65	4	6	23	35	0	0	15	23	23	35
1730–1739	58	2	3	17	29	5	9	9	16	25	43
1740–1749	73	1	1	20	27	6	8	10	14	36	49
1750–1759	78	2	3	26	33	11	14	8	10	31	39
1760–1769	92	2	2	35	38	10	11	5	5	40	43
1770–1777	66	1	3	17	26	10	15	12	18	26	39
Totals	471	13	3	150	32	44	9	69	15	195	41

[a]Includes instances of all or dwelling plantation for minority of child (N = 11).

[b]Includes instances of provisions for maintenance or houseroom (N = 5).

Source: Wills XIII–XLI.

Ed. Note: This table is a revision of the table printed in the original published article.

the Chesapeake, that fact will have to be explained. The dynamics might prove to have been different;[63] or a dynamic we have not identified, common to both areas, might turn out to have been the primary engine of change. And, if women in England shared the status—which we doubt—conditions in the New World may have had secondary importance. The Maryland data establish persuasive grounds for a hypothesis, but the evidence is not all in.

NOTES

1. Russell R. Menard, "Economy and Society in Early Colonial Maryland" (Ph.D. diss., University of Iowa, 1975), 153–212, and "Immigrants and Their Increase: The Process of Population Growth in Early Colonial Maryland," in Aubrey C. Land, Lois Green, and Edward C. Papenfuse, eds., *Law, Society and Politics in Early Maryland* (Baltimore, 1977), 88–110, hereafter cited as Menard, "Immigrants and Their Increase"; Lorena S. Walsh and Russell R. Menard, "Death in the Chesapeake: Two Life Tables for Men in Early Colonial Maryland," *Maryland Historical Magazine,* LXIX (1974), 211–227. In a sample of 806 headrights Menard found only two unmarried women who paid their own passage ("Economy and Society," 187).

2. Menard, "Immigrants and Their Increase," Fig. 1; William Hand Browne *et al.,* eds., *Archives of Maryland* (Baltimore, 1883–), XXV, 256, hereafter cited as *Maryland Archives.*

3. The lists of immigrants are found in John Camden Hotten, ed., *The Original Lists of Persons of Quality: Emigrants; Religious Exiles; Political Rebels; . . . and Others Who Went from Great Britain to the American Plantations, 1600–1700* (London, 1874); William Dodgson Bowman, ed., *Bristol and America: A Record of the First Settlers in the Colonies of North America, 1654–1683* (Baltimore, 1976 [orig. publ. London 1929]); C. D. P. Nicholson, comp., *Some Early Emigrants to America* (Balti-

more, 1965); Michael Ghirelli, ed., *A List of Emigrants to America, 1682–1692* (Baltimore, 1968); and Elizabeth French, ed., *List of Emigrants to America from Liverpool, 1697–1707* (Baltimore, 1962 [orig. publ. Boston, 1913]) Folger Shakespeare Library, MS, V.B. 16 (Washington, D.C.), consists of 66 additional indentures that were originally part of the London records.

4. Campbell, "Social Origins of Some Early Americans," in Smith, ed., *Seventeenth-Century America*, 74–77; Galenson, "'Middling People' or 'Common Sort'?" *WMQ* (forthcoming). When the ages recorded in the London list (Nicholson, comp., *Some Early Emigrants*) and on the Folger Library indentures for servants bound for Maryland and Virginia are combined, 84.5% of the men (N = 354) are found to have been aged 17 to 30, and 54.9% were 18 through 22. Of the women (N = 119), 81.4% were 18 through 25; 10% were older, 8.3% younger, and half (51.2%) immigrated between ages 20 and 22. Russell Menard has generously lent us his abstracts of the London list.

5. Menard, "Immigrants and Their Increase," Table I.

6. Menard, "Economy and Society," 336–356; Lois Green Carr and Russell R. Menard, "Servants and Freedmen in Early Colonial Maryland," in Thad W. Tate and David A. Ammerman, eds., *The Chesapeake in the Seventeenth Century* (Chapel Hill, N.C., 1979); E. A. Wrigley, "Family Limitation in Pre-Industrial England," *Economic History Review*, 2d Ser., XIX (1966), 82–109; Michael Drake, "An Elementary Exercise in Parish Register Demography," *ibid.*, XIV (1962), 427–445; J. D. Chambers, *Population, Economy, and Society in Pre-Industrial England* (London, 1972).

7. John Hammond, *Leah and Rachel, or, the Two Fruitfull Sisters Virginia and Maryland . . .* , and George Alsop, *A Character of the Province of Maryland . . .* , in Clayton Colman Hall, ed., *Narratives of Early Maryland 1633–1684*, Original Narratives of Early American History (New York, 1910), 281–308, 340–387; Russell R. Menard, P. M. G. Harris, and Lois Green Carr, "Opportunity and Inequality: The Distribution of Wealth on the Lower Western Shore of Maryland, 1638–1705, *Md. Hist. Mag.,* LXIX (1974), 169–184; Russell R. Menard, "From Servant to Freeholder: Status Mobility and Property Accumulation in Seventeenth-Century Maryland," *WMQ,* 3d Ser., XXX (1973), 37–64; Carr and Menard, "Servants and Freedmen," in Tate and Ammerman, eds., *Essays on the Chesapeake;* Walsh, "Servitude and Opportunity," 111–133.

8. Menard, "Economy and Society," Table VII–5.

9. Lorena S. Walsh, "Charles County, Maryland, 1658–1705; A Study in Chesapeake Political and Social Structure" (Ph.D. diss., Michigan State University, 1977), chap. 4.

10. Lorena S. Walsh and Russell R. Menard are preparing an article on the history of illegitimacy in Charles and Somerset counties, 1658–1776.

11. Abbot Emerson Smith, *Colonists in Bondage: White Servitude and Convict Labor in America, 1607–1776* (Chapel Hill, N.C., 1947), 271–273. Marriage was in effect a breach of contract.

12. Lois Green Carr, "County Government in Maryland, 1689–1709" (Ph.D. diss., Harvard University, 1968), 267–269, 363. The courts pursued bastardy offenses regardless of the social status of the culprits in order to ensure that the children would not become public charges. Free single women were not being overlooked.

13. This impression is based on Walsh's close reading of Charles County records, Carr's close reading of Prince George's County records, and less detailed examination by both of all other 17th-century Maryland court records.

14. Walsh, "Charles County, Maryland," chap. 4; Carr, "County Government in Maryland," chap. 4, n. 269. Carr summarizes the evidence from Charles, Prince George's, Baltimore, Talbot, and Somerset counties, 1689–1709, for comparing punishment of fathers and mothers of bastards. Leniency toward fathers varied from county to county and time to time. The length of time served for restitution also varied over place and time, increasing as the century progressed. See Charles County Court and Land Records, MS, L #1, ff. 276–277, Hall of Records, Annapolis, Md. Unless otherwise indicated, all manuscripts cited are at the Hall of Records.

15. Alsop, *Character of the Province,* in Hall, ed., *Narratives of Maryland,* 358.

16. Maryland Headright Sample, 1658–1681 (N = 625): 257.1 men per 100 women; Maryland Inventories, 1658–1679 (N = 584): 320.1 men per 100 women. Menard, "Immigrants and Their Increase," Table I.

17. A comparison of a Virginia Headright Sample, 1648–1666 (N = 4,272) with inventories from York and Lower Norfolk counties, 1637–1675 (N = 168) shows less, rather than more, imbalance in inventories as compared to headrights. This indicates fewer purchases of wives than we have suggested for the period after 1660. However, the inventory sample is small.

18. Sixty women left inventories. The status of five is unknown. The two who died single died in 1698. Menard, "Immigrants and Their Increase," Table I.

19. Menard, "Demography of Somerset County," Table XVII; Daniel Scott Smith and Michael S. Hindus, "Premarital Pregnancy in America, 1640–1971: An Overview," *Journal of Interdisciplinary History,* V (1975), 541. It was also two to three times the rate found in New England in the late 17th century.

20. In Maryland any proceedings against pregnant brides could have been brought only in the civil courts. No vestries were established until 1693, and their jurisdiction was confined to the admonishment of men and women suspected of fornication unproved by the conception of a child. Churchwardens were to inform the county court of bastardies. Carr, "County Government in Maryland," text, 148–149, 221–223.

21. The data are from Nicholson, comp., *Some Early Emigrants.*

22. Charles County Court and Land Records, MSS. C #1 through B #2.

23. Available ages at arrival are as follows:

Age	under 12	13	14	15	16	17	18	19	20	21	22	23	24	25	26	27	28	29	30
Indentured (1682–1687)			1	1	6	2	9	9	8	29	19	6	5	6	2	3	1	2	3
Unindentured (1666–1705)	8	5	12	4	7	18	16	13	34	9	11	2	1	1					

24. Walsh, "Charles County, Maryland," chap. 2; Menard, "Demography of Somerset County," Tables XI, XII.

25. The impact of later marriages is best demonstrated with age-specific marital fertility statistics. Susan L. Norton reports that women in colonial Ipswich, Massachusetts, bore an average of 7.5 children if they married between ages 15 and 19; 7.1 if they married between 20 and 24; and 4.5 if they married after 24. Norton, "Population Growth in Colonial America: A Study of Ipswich, Massachusetts," *Pop. Studies,* XXV (1971), 444. Cf. Wrigley, "Family Limitation in Pre-Industrial England," *Econ. Hist. Rev.,* 2d Ser., XIX (1966), 82–109.

26. In Charles County the mean interval between first and second and subsequent births was 30.8, and the median was 27.3 months. Walsh, "Charles County, Maryland," chap. 2. Menard has found that in Somerset County, Maryland, the median birth intervals for immigrant women between child 1 and child 2, child 2 and child 3, child 3 and child 4, and child 4 and child 5 were 26, 26, 30, 27 months, respectively ("Demography of Somerset County," Table XX).

27. Walsh, "Charles County, Maryland," chap. 2.

28. Walsh and Menard, "Death in the Chesapeake," *Md. Hist. Mag.,* LXIX (1974), 222.

29. Menard, using all Maryland wills, found a considerably lower number of children per family in a similar period: 1.83 in wills probated 1660–1665; 2.20 in wills probated 1680–1684 ("Economy and Society," 198). Family reconstitution not surprisingly produces slightly higher figures, since daughters are often underrecorded in wills but are recorded as frequently as sons in birth registers. In 17th-century Charles County the mean size of all reconstituted families was 2.75. For marriages contracted in the years 1658–1669 (N = 118), 1670–1679 (N = 79), and 1680–1689 (N = 95), family size was 3.15, 2.58, and 2.86, respectively. In Somerset County, family size for immigrant marriages formed between 1665 and 1695 (N = 41) was 3.9. Walsh, "Charles County, Maryland," chap. 2; Menard, "Demography of Somerset County," Table XXI.

30. For fuller exposition of the process see Menard, "Immigrants and Their Increase."

31. George W. Barclay, *Techniques of Population Analysis* (New York, 1958), p. 136n; Darrett B. and Anita H. Rutman, "'Now-Wives and Sons-in-Law': Parental Death in a Seventeenth-Century Virginia County," in Tate and Ammerman, eds., *Essays on the Chesapeake;* Rutman and Rutman, "Of Agues and Fevers," *WMQ,* 3d Ser., XXXIII (1976), 31–60. Cf. Peter H. Wood, *Black Majority: Negroes in Colonial South Carolina from 1670 through the Stono Rebellion* (New York, 1974), chap. 3.

32. Among 1735 decedents who left inventories on Maryland's lower Western Shore, 1658–1705, 72% died without children or with children not yet of age. Only 16% could be proved to have a child of age. "Social Stratification." See note 39 below.

33. From 1640 to 1710, 17% of the married men named no executor. In such cases, the probate court automatically gave executorship to the wife unless she requested someone else to act.

34. We divided wills according to whether decedents were immigrant, native born, or of unknown origins, and found no differences in patterns of bequests, choice of executors, or tendency to appoint overseers. No change occurred in 17th-century Maryland in these respects as a native-born population began to appear.

35. For example, *ibid.*, 172, 182.

36. Lorena S. Walsh, " 'Till Death Do Us Part': Marriage and Family in Charles County, Maryland, 1658–1705," in Tate and Ammerman, eds., *Essays on the Chesapeake.*

37. The following discussion of the orphans' court is based on Lois Green Carr, 'The Development of the Maryland Orphans' Court, 1654–1715," in Land, Carr, and Papenfuse, eds., *Law, Society, and Politics in Early Maryland,* 41–61.

38. In 17th-century Charles County two-thirds of surviving partners remarried within a year of their spouse's death. Walsh, "Charles County, Maryland," chap. 2.

39. Only 8% of tenant farmers who left inventories in four Maryland counties of the lower Western Shore owned labor, 1658–1705. St. Mary's City Commission Inventory Project, "Social Stratification in Maryland, 1658–1705" (National Science Foundation Grant GS-32272), hereafter cited as "Social Stratification." This is an analysis of 1,735 inventories recorded from 1658 to 1705 in St. Mary's, Calvert, Charles, and Prince George's counties, which together constitute most of the lower Western Shore of Maryland.

40. Walsh, " 'Till Death Do Us Part,' " in Tate and Ammerman, eds., *Essays on the Chesapeake.*

41. Walsh, " 'Till Death Do Us Part,' " in Tate and Ammerman, eds., *Essays on the Chesapeake.*

42. Testamentary Proceedings, X, 184–185. Cf. Charles County Court and Land Records, MS, I #1, ff. 9–10, 259.

43. Among married decedents before 1680 (N = 308), the bottom two-thirds (N = 212) were those worth less than £150. Among all decedents worth less than £150 (N = 451), only 12 (about 3%) had sheep or yarn-making equipment. "Social Stratification."

44. See Everitt, "Farm Labourers," in Thirsk, ed., *Agrarian History of England and Wales,* 422–426, and W. G. Hoskins, *Essays in Leicestershire History* (Liverpool, 1950), p. 134.

45. Among married decedents, the bottom fifth were approximately those worth less than £30. Before 1680 these were 17% of the married decedents. By the end of the period, from 1700 to 1705, they were 22%. Before 1680, 92% had no bound labor. From 1700 to 1705, 95% had none. Less than 1% of all estates in this wealth group had sheep or yarn-making equipment before 1681. "Social Stratification."

46. On opportunity to raise from the bottom to the middle see Menard, "From Servant to Freeholder," *WMQ,* 3d Ser., XXX (1973), 37–64; Walsh, "Servitude and Opportunity," 111–133, and Menard, Harris, and Carr, "Opportunity and Inequality," *Md. Hist. Mag.,* LXIX (1974), 169–184.

47. For 17th-century economic development see Menard, Harris, and Carr, "Opportunity and Inequality," *Md. Hist. Mag.,* LXIX (1974), 169–184.

48. Among estates worth £150 or more, signs of diversification in this form appeared in 22% before 1681 and in 67% after 1680. Over the years 1700–1705, the figure was 62%. Only 6% of estates worth less than £40 had such signs of diversification after 1680 or over the period 1700–1705. Knitting rather than weaving is assumed because looms were very rare. These figures are for all estates. "Social Stratification."

49. *Ibid.*, Table XVII; P. E. H. Hair, "Bridal Pregnancy in Rural England in Earlier Centuries," *Pop. Studies,* XX (1966), 237; Chambers, *Population, Economy, and Society in England,* 75; Smith and Hindus, "Premarital Pregnancy in America," *Jour. Interdisciplinary Hist.,* V (1975), 537–570.

50. Menard, "Demography of Somerset County," Table XVIII.

51. Adolescent subfecundity might also partly explain lower bridal pregnancy rates among very young brides.

52. Menard develops this argument in detail in "Immigrants and Their Increase." For the assembly see David W. Jordan, "Political Stability and the Emergence of a Native Elite in Maryland, 1660–1715," in Tate and Ammerman, eds., *Essays on the Chesapeake.* In Charles County, Maryland, by 1705 at least half of all resident landowners were native born. Walsh, "Charles County, Maryland," chaps. 1, 7.

53. The proportion of wills mentioning non-nuclear kin can, of course, prove only a proxy of the actual existence of these kin in Maryland. The reliability of such a measure may vary greatly from area to area and over time, depending on the character of the population and on local inheritance customs. To test the reliability of the will data, we compared them with data from reconstituted families in 17th-century Charles County. These reconstitution data draw on a much broader variety of sources and include many men who did not leave wills. Because of insufficient information for female lines, we could trace only the male lines. The procedure compared the names of all married men against a file of all known county residents, asking how many kin in the male line might have been present in the county at the time of the married man's death. The

proportions for immigrants were in most cases not markedly different from those found in wills. For native men, however, wills were somewhat less reliable indicators of the presence of such kin; when non-nuclear kin mentioned by testate natives were compared with kin found by reconstitution, 29% of the native testators had non-nuclear kin present in the county who were not mentioned in their wills.

54. Not surprisingly, wills of immigrants show no increase in family ties, but these wills mention adult children far more often than earlier. Before 1680, only 11% of immigrant testators in St. Mary's and Charles counties mention adult children in their wills; from 1700 to 1710, 37% left adult children to help the family. Two facts help account for this change. First, survivors of early immigration were dying in old age. Second, proportionately fewer young immigrants with families were dying, not because life expectancy had improved, but because there were proportionately fewer of them than earlier. A long stagnation in the tobacco economy that began about 1680 had diminished opportunities for freed servants to form households and families. Hence, among immigrants the proportion of young fathers at risk to die was smaller than in earlier years.

In the larger population of men who left inventories, 18.2% had adult children before 1681, but in the years 1700–1709, 50% had adult children. "Social Stratification."

55. Examples of some recent studies are Carole Shammas, "English-Born and Creole Elites in Turn-of-the-Century Virginia," in Tate and Ammerman, eds., *Essays on the Chesapeake;* Jordan, "Political Stability and the Emergence of a Native Elite in Maryland," *ibid;* Lois Green Carr, "The Foundations of Social Order: Local Government in Colonial Maryland," in Bruce C. Daniels, ed., *Town and Country: Essays on the Structure of Local Government in the American Colonies* (Middletown, Conn., forthcoming); Menard, "Economy and Society," 396–440.

56. Allan Kulikoff has found that in Prince George's County the white adult sex ratio dropped significantly before the age of marriage rose. Women born in the 1720s were the first to marry at a mean age above 20, while those born in the 1740s and marrying in the 1760s, after the sex ratio neared equality, married at a mean age of 22. Marriages lasted longer because the rise in the mean age at which men married—from 23 to 27 between 1700 and 1740—was more than offset by gains in life expectancy. Kulikoff, "Tobacco and Slaves: Population, Economy, and Society in Eighteenth-Century Prince George's County, Maryland" (Ph.D. diss., Brandeis University, 1976), chap. 3; Menard, "Immigrants and Their Increase."

57. Inventories and related biographical data have been analyzed by the St. Mary's City Commission under a grant from the National Endowment for the Humanities, "The Making of a Plantation Society in Maryland" (R 010585-74-267). From 1700 through 1776 the percentage of men known to have had children, and who had an adult child at death, ranged from a low of 32.8% in the years 1736–1738 to a high of 61.3% in the years 1707–1709. The figure was over 50% for 13 out of 23 year-groups of three to four years each.

58. On the other hand, these rates may show little change. The restraining effect of increased parental control may have been offset by a trend toward increased sexual activity that appears to have become general throughout Western Europe and the United States by the mid-19th century. Smith and Hindus, "Premarital Pregnancy in America," *Jour. Interdisciplinary Hist.,* V (1975), 537–570; Edward Shorter, "Female Emancipation, Birth Control, and Fertility in European History," *American Historical Review,* LXXVIII (1973), 605–640.

59. Acts 1699, chap. 41, *Maryland Archives,* XXII, 542.

60. James W. Deen, Jr., "Patterns of Testation: Four Tidewater Counties in Colonial Virginia," *American Journal of Legal History,* XVI (1972), 154–176, finds a life interest in property for the wife the predominant pattern before 1720. However, he includes an interest for widowhood in life interest and does not distinguish a dower interest from more than dower.

61. Richard S. Dunn, *Sugar and Slaves: The Rise of the Planter Class in the English West Indies, 1624–1713* (Chapel Hill, N.C., 1972), pp. 326–334. Dunn finds sex ratios surprisingly balanced, but he also finds very high mortality, short marriages, and many orphans.

62. For a short discussion of this comparison see Menard, "Immigrants and Their Increase."

63. James K. Somerville has used Salem, Massachusetts, wills from 1660 to 1770 to examine women's status and importance within the home ("The Salem [Mass.] Woman in the Home, 1660–1770," *Eighteenth-Century Life,* I ([1974], 11–14). See also Alexander Keyssar, "Widowhood in Eighteenth-Century Massachusetts: A Problem in the History of the Family," *Perspectives in American History,* VIII (1974), 83–119, which discusses provisions for 22 widows in 18th-century Woburn, Massachusetts. Both men find provisions for houseroom and care of the widow's property enjoined upon children proportionately far more often than we have found in St. Mary's

County, Maryland, where we found only five instances over 136 years. However, part of this difference may be a function of the differences in age at widowhood in the two regions. Neither Somerville nor Keyssar gives the percentage of widows who received a life interest in property, but their discussions imply a much higher proportion than we have found of women whose interest ended at remarriage or the majority of the oldest son.

Authors' Postscript

"The Planter's Wife" . . . began life in 1975 as the Bernard Steiner Lecture at the Maryland Historical Society.

The part of our essay that perhaps has attracted the most attention focuses on inheritance and the decisions husbands and fathers made in distributing family property. We must warn readers that there are difficulties in standardizing the provisions of wills that we did not foresee when we first wrote. After publication of "The Planter's Wife," we discovered that hidden discrepancies in interpreting wills had led to errors in Table III and required a modification of our findings for the eighteenth century. These changes have been incorporated into later reprintings of the essay, including this one.

4

The Beginnings of the Afro-American Family in Maryland

Allan Kulikoff

The scarcity of surviving documents written by African-American women in the colonial period forces historians to employ indirect means to explore their experience. Allan Kulikoff relies upon a quantitative analysis of the black population in colonial Virginia and Maryland to explore change over time. His analysis charts the emergence of an African-American family and community between 1650 and 1750. Two findings stand out: first, the mother–children group was central for the initial generation of African-born slaves. Second, over time an increasing share of slave parents lived together, but the small size of plantations and the frequent separation of family members meant that kinship and family bonds among slaves crossed plantation boundaries. Kulikoff presents evidence on the origins of patterns of slave family life in the nineteenth century, which are explored more fully in the article by Deborah G. White.

How did Afro-Americans organize their families in the Chesapeake colonies during the eighteenth century? Who lived in slave households? How many Afro-American fathers lived with their wives and children? What was the impact of arbitrary sale and transfer of slaves upon family life? How did an Afro-American's household and family relationships change through the life cycle?

This paper attempts to answer these questions.[1] While literary documents by or about slaves before 1800, such as runaway narratives, WPA freed-slave interviews, black autobiographies, or detailed travel accounts are very infrequently available to historians of colonial slave family life, they can gather age and family data from probate inventories, personal information from runaway advertisements, and depositions in court cases. These sources, together with several diaries and account books, kept by whites, provide a great deal of material about African and Afro-American family life in the Chesapeake region.

Almost all the blacks who lived in Maryland and Virginia before 1780 were slaves. Because their status precluded them from enjoying a legally secure family life, slave households often excluded important family members. Households, domestic groups, and families must therefore be clearly distin-

Excerpted from "The Beginnings of the Afro-American Family in Maryland," by Allan Kulikoff, Chapter 8 in *Law, Society, and Politics in Early Maryland*, Aubrey Land, Lois Green Carr, and Edward C. Papenfuse, eds. (Baltimore: The Johns Hopkins University Press, 1977).

"The Old Plantation," c. 1790. Colonial Williamsburg Foundation, Williamsburg, Va.

guished. A household, as used here, is a coresidence group that includes all who shared a "proximity of sleeping arrangements," or lived under the same roof. Domestic groups include kin and nonkin, living in the same or separate households, who share cooking, eating, childrearing, working, and other daily activities. Families are composed of people related by blood or marriage. Several distinctions are useful in defining the members of families. The immediate family includes husband and wife or parents and children. Near kin include the immediate family and all other kin, such as adult brothers and sisters or cousins who share the same house or domestic tasks with the immediate family. Other kinfolk who do not function as family members on a regular basis are considered to be distant kin.[2]

The process of family formation can perhaps best be understood as an adaptive process. My ideas about this process owe much to a provocative essay by Sidney Mintz and Richard Price on Afro-American culture. Blacks learned to modify their environment, learned from each other how to retain family ties under very adverse conditions, and structured their expectations about family activities around what they knew the master would permit. If white masters determined the outward bounds of family activities, it was Africans, and especially their descendants, who gave meaning to the relationships between parents and children, among siblings, and with more distant kinfolk. As a result, black family structure on the eve of the Revolution differed from both African and white family systems.[3]

Africans who were forced to come to the Chesapeake region in the late seventeenth and early eighteenth centuries struggled to create viable families and households, but often failed. They suffered a great loss when they were herded into slave ships. Their family and friends, who had given meaning to their lives and structured their place in society, were left behind and they found themselves among strangers. They could never recreate their families and certainly not devise a West African kinship system in the Chesapeake. The differences between African communities were too great. Some Africans lived in clans and lineages, others did not; some traced their descent from women but others traced descent from men; mothers, fathers, and other kin played somewhat different roles in each community; initiation ceremonies and puberty rites, forbidden marriages, marriage customs, and household structures all varied from place to place.[4]

Though African immigrants did not bring a unified West African culture with them to the Chesapeake colonies, they did share important beliefs about the nature of kinship. Africans could modify these beliefs in America to legitimate the families they eventually formed. They saw kinship as the principal way of ordering relationships between individuals. Each person in the tribe was related to most others in the community. The male was father, son, and uncle; the female was mother, daughter, and aunt to many others. Because their kinship system was so extensive, Africans included kinfolk outside the immediate family in their daily activities. For example, adult brothers or sisters of the father or mother played an important role in childrearing and domestic activities in many African societies.[5]

Secondly, but far less certainly, African immigrants may have adapted some practices associated with polygyny, a common African marital custom. A few men on the Eastern Shore of Maryland in the 1740s, and perhaps others scattered elsewhere, lived with several women. However, far too few African women (in relation to the number of men) immigrated to make polygynous marriages common. Nevertheless, the close psychological relationship between mothers and children, and the great social distance between a husband and his various wives and children found in African polygynous societies might have been repeated in the Chesapeake colonies. In any event, African slave mothers played a more important role than fathers in teaching children about Africa and about how to get along in the slave system. Both African custom, and the physical separation of immigrant men and women played a role in this development.[6]

Africans faced a demographic environment hostile to most forms of family life. If Africans were to start families, they had to find spouses, and that task was difficult. Most blacks lived on small farms of less than 11 slaves; and the small black population was spread thinly over a vast territory. Roads were rudimentary. Even where concentrations of larger plantations were located, African men did not automatically find wives. Sex ratios in southern Maryland rose from 125 to 130 (men per 100 women) in the mid-seventeenth century to about 150 in the 1710s and 1720s, and to around 180 in the 1730s. In Surry County, Virginia, the slave sex ratio was about 145 in the 1670s and 1680s, but over 200 in the 1690s and 1700s. . . . The larger the plantation, the higher the sex ratio tended to be.[7]

African men had competition for the available black women. By the 1690s, some black women were natives, and they may have preferred Afro-American men. White men were also competitors. Indeed, during the seventeenth and early eighteenth centuries, white adult sex ratios were as high (or higher) than black adult sex ratios. At any period whites possessed a monopoly of power and some of them probably took slave women as their common-law wives. African men competed for the remaining black women, and probably some died before they could find a wife. In 1739 African men planned an uprising in Prince George's County partly because they could not find wives.[8] . . .

Unlike most African men, African women commonly lived with their children. Some African women may have been so alienated that they refused to have children, but the rest bore and raised several offspring, protected by the master's reluctance to separate very young children from their mothers. Since the children were reared by their mothers, and eventually joined them in the tobacco fields, these households were domestic groups, although incomplete as families.[9]

A greater proportion of African women than African men lived with both spouses and children. These opportunities usually arose on large plantations. There was such a surplus of men on large plantations that African women who lived on them could choose husbands from several African or Afro-American men. The sex ratio on large plantations in Prince George's during the 1730s, a period of heavy immigration, was 249. This shortage of women prevented most recently arrived African men from finding a wife on the plantation. For them the opportunity to live with a wife and children was rare. More Africans probably lived with their immediate families in the 1740s; immigration declined, large planters bought more African women, and the sex ratio on big plantations fell to 142.[10]

Because African spouses were usually separated, African mothers reared their Afro-American children with little help from their husbands. Even when the father was present, the extended kin so important in the lives of African children was missing. Mothers probably taught them the broad values they brought from Africa and related the family's history in Africa and the Chesapeake. When the children began working in the fields, they learned from their mothers how to survive a day's work and how to get along with master and overseer.

Each group of Africans repeated the experiences of previous immigrants. Eventually, more and more Afro-American children matured and began families of their own. The first large generation of Afro-Americans in Maryland probably came of age in the 1690s; by the 1720s, when the second large generation had matured, the black population finally began increasing naturally.[11]

The changing composition of the black population combined with other changes to restructure Afro-American households and families. Alterations in the adult sex ratio, the size of plantations, and black population density provided black people with opportunities to enjoy a more satisfying family life. The way masters transferred slaves from place to place limited the size and composition of black households, but Afro-American family members separated by masters managed to establish complex kinship networks over many plantations. Afro-Americans used these opportunities to create a kind of family life that differed from African and Anglo-American practices.

Demographic changes led to more complex households and families. As the number of adult Africans in the population decreased, the sex ratio in Maryland declined to between 100 and 110 by the 1750s. This decline gave most men an opportunity to marry by about age 30. The number of slaves who lived on plantations with more than 20 blacks increased; the density of the black population in tidewater Maryland and Virginia rose; the proportion of blacks in the total population of Prince George's County, in nearby areas of Maryland, and throughout tidewater Virginia rose to half or more by the end of the century; and many new roads were built. The number of friends and kinfolk whom typical Afro-Americans saw every day or visited with regularity increased, while their contact with whites declined because large areas of the Chesapeake became nearly black counties.[12]

How frequently masters transferred their Afro-American slaves, and where they sent them, affected black household composition. Surviving documents do not allow a systematic analysis of this point, but several conclusions seem clear. First, planters kept women and their small children together but did not keep husbands and teenage children with their immediate family. Slaveowner after slaveowner bequeathed women and their "increase" to sons or daughters. However, children of slaveowners tended to live near their parents; thus, even when members of slave families were so separated, they remained in the same neighborhood.[13] Secondly, Afro-Americans who lived on small farms were transferred more frequently than those on large plantations. At their deaths small slaveowners typically willed a slave or two to their widows and to each child. They also frequently mortgaged or sold slaves to gain capital. If a slaveowner died with many unpaid debts, his slaves had to be sold.[14] Finally, relatively few blacks were forced to move long distances. Far more blacks were affected by migrations of slaves from the Chesapeake region to the new Southwest in the nineteenth century than by long-distance movement in the region before the Revolution.[15] These points should not be misunderstood. Most Afro-Americans who lived in Maryland or Virginia during the eighteenth century experienced separations from members of their immediate families sometime in their lives. Most, however, were able to visit these family members occasionally.

These changes led to a new social reality for most slaves born in the 1750s, 1760s, and 1770s. If unrelated people and their progeny stay in a limited geographic area for several generations, the descendants of the original settlers must develop kin ties with many other people who live nearby. Once the proportion of adult Africans declined, this process began. African women married and had children; the children matured and married. If most of them remained near their first homes, each was bound to have siblings, children, spouses, uncles, aunts, and cousins living in the neighborhood. How these various kinspeople were organized into households, families, and domestic groups depended not only upon the whims of masters but also upon the meaning placed on kinship by the slaves themselves.

The process of household and family formation and dissolution was begun by each immigrant woman who lived long enough to have children. The story of Ann Joice, a black woman who was born in Barbados, taken to England as a servant, and then falsely sold into slavery in Maryland in the 1670s, may have been similar to that of other immigrant women once she became a slave. The Darnall family of Prince George's owned Ann Joice. She had seven children with several white men in the 1670s and 1680s; all remained slaves the rest of their lives. Three of her children stayed on the Darnall home plantation until their deaths. One was sold as a child to a planter who lived a few miles away; another was eventually sold to William Digges, who lived about five miles from the Darnall farm. Both the spatial spread and the local concentration of kinfolk continued in the next generation. Peter Harbard, born between 1715 and 1720, was the son of Francis Harbard, who was Ann Joice's child. Peter grew up on the Darnall farm, but in 1737 he was sold to George Gordon, who lived across the road from Darnall. As a child, Peter lived with or very near his grandmother Ann Joice, his father, and several paternal uncles and aunts. He probably knew his seven cousins (father's sister's children), children of his aunt Susan Harbard, who lived on William Digges's plantation. Other kinfolk lived in Annapolis but were too far away to visit easily.[16]

As Afro-American slaves were born and died, and as masters sold or bequeathed their slaves, black households were formed and reformed, broken and created. Several detailed examples can illustrate this process. For example, Daphne, the daughter of Nan, was born about 1736 on a large plantation in Prince George's owned by Robert Tyler, Sr. Until she was two, she lived with her mother, two brothers, and two sisters. In 1738, Tyler died and left his slaves to his wife, children, and grandchildren. All lived on or near Tyler's farms. Three of Daphne's siblings were bequeathed to grand-daughter Ruth Tyler, who later married Mordecai Jacob, her grandfather's next-door neighbor. Daphne continued to live on the Tyler plantation. From 1736 to 1787, she had six different masters, but she still lived where she was born. Daphne lived with her mother until her mother died, and with her ten children until 1779. Children were eventually born to Daphne's daughters; these infants lived with their mothers and near their maternal grandmother. When Robert Tyler III, Robert senior's grandson and Daphne's fifth master, died in 1779, his will divided Daphne's children and grandchildren between his son and daughter. Daphne was thus separated from younger children, born between 1760 and 1772. They were given to Millicent Beanes, Robert III's daughter, who lived several miles away. Daphne continued to live on the same plantation as her four older children and several grandchildren. An intricate extended family of grandmother, sons, daughters, grandchildren, aunts, uncles, nieces, nephews, and cousins resided in several households on the Tyler plantation in 1778, and other, more remote kinfolk could be found on the neighboring Jacob farm.[17]

Family separations might be more frequent on smaller plantations. Rachael was born in the late 1730s and bore ten children between 1758 and 1784. As a child she lived on the plantation of Alexander Magruder, a large slaveowner in Prince George's; before 1746, Alexander gave her to his son Hezekiah, who lived on an adjoining plantation. Hezekiah never owned more than ten slaves, and when he died in 1769, he owned only two—including one willed to his wife by her brother. Between 1755 and 1757, he mortgaged nine slaves, including Rachael, to two merchants. In 1757, Samuel Roundall (who lived about five miles from the Magruders) seized Rachael and six other slaves mortgaged to him. This and subsequent transfers can be seen on Figure 1. In 1760 Roundall sold Rachael and her eldest daughter to Samuel Lovejoy,

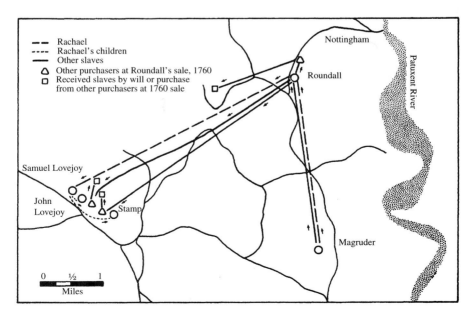

FIGURE 1 Sale and Later Transfer of Hezekiah Magruder's Slaves, 1755–1780.

who lived about nine miles from Roundall. At the same time, four other former Magruder slaves were sold: two to planters in Lovejoy's neighborhood, one to a Roundall neighbor, and one to a planter living at least fifteen miles away in Charles County. Rachael's separation from friends and family members continued. In 1761, her eldest child was sold at age three to George Stamp, a neighbor of Lovejoy. By the time Samuel Lovejoy died in 1762, she had two other children. She and her youngest child went to live with John Lovejoy, Samuel's nephew and near-neighbor, but her second child, about age two, stayed with Lovejoy's widow. Her third child was sold at age six, but Rachael and her next seven children lived with John Lovejoy until at least 1787.[18]

These three examples suggest how Afro-American households and families developed in the eighteenth century. Husbands and wives and parents and children were frequently separated by the master's transfers of family members. At the same time, as generation followed generation, households, or adjacent huts, became increasingly complex, and sometimes included grandparents, uncles, aunts, or cousins, as well as the immediate family. Since other kin lived on nearby or distant plantations, geographically concentrated (and dispersed) kinship networks that connected numbers of quarters emerged during the pre-Revolutionary era.

How typical were the experiences suggested by the examples? How were families organized into households and domestic groups on large and small quarters? Data from three large planters' inventories taken in 1759, 1773–74, and 1775, and from a Prince George's census of 1776 permit a test of the hypotheses concerning changes in household structure, differences between large and small units, and the spread of kinfolk across space. Table 1 details household structure on large quarters of over twenty and Table 2 shows the kinds of households on small farms. About half of all slaves probably lived on each plantation type.[19] This evidence provides a good test, because by the 1770s most Afro-Americans could trace a Chesapeake genealogy back to immigrant grandparents or great-grandparents.[20]

Kinfolk (immediate families and near kin) on large plantations were organized into three kinds of residence groups. Most of the slaves of some quarters were interrelated by blood or marriage. Domestic groups included kinfolk who lived on opposite sides of duplex slave huts and who shared a common yard and eating and cooking arrangements. Finally, most households included members of an immediate family.

The kinship structure of large plantations is illustrated by a household inventory taken in 1773–74 of 385 slaves owned by Charles Carroll of Carrollton on thirteen different quarters in Anne Arundel County. Because Carroll insisted that the inventory be "taken in Familys with their Ages," the document permits a detailed reconstruction of kinship networks.[21] Though the complexity and size of kinship groups on Carroll's quarters were probably

TABLE 1 *Afro-American Household Structures on Three Large Plantations in Prince George's and Anne Arundel Counties, Maryland, 1759–1775*

HOUSEHOLD TYPE	PERCENTAGE IN HOUSEHOLD TYPE				PERCENTAGE OF TOTAL IN HOUSEHOLD TYPES
	MALES 15 +	FEMALES 15 +	CHILDREN 0–9	CHILDREN 10–14	
Husband–wife– children	40	43	55	44	47
Mother–children	2	17	22	10	14
Mother–children– other kin	4	14	8	13	9
Siblings	7	4	6	12	7
Husband–wife– children–other kin	2	2	2	2	2
Father–children	5	0	3	5	3
Husband–wife	2	2	0	0	1
Three generation	1	2	2	3	2
Unknown or mixed	36	16	3	12	15
Total percentage	99	100	101	101	100
Number of people	142	129	178	77	526

Sources: PG Inventories, GS No. 1, f. 73 (1759; James Wardrop's, 32 slaves); and GS No. 2, ff. 334–36 (1775; Addison's 3 plantations, 109 slaves) and Charles Carroll Account Book, Maryland Historical Society (rest of slaves). The three-generation households include grandparents and grandchildren, but not the generation in between. The unknown or mixed category includes all those apparently living away from all kinfolk, but perhaps living near them. Some of the slaves in this category probably belong in the others, but the sources (especially the Addison and Wardrop documents) do not permit location of them.

greater than on other large plantations, the general pattern could easily have been repeated elsewhere.[22]

The ten men and three women who headed each list were probably leaders of their quarters. Five of the quarters were named for these individuals.[23] They tended to be old slaves who had been with the Carroll family for many years. While the mean age of all adults was 37 years, the mean age of the leaders was 49, and six of the thirteen were over 55.[24] The leader often lived with many kinfolk; he or she was closely related to about 36 to 38 percent of all the other slaves on the quarter. For example, Fanny, 69 years of age, was surrounded by at least 40 near kinfolk on the main plantation at Doohoregan, and Mayara James, 65 years of age, lived with 23 relatives on his quarter.[25]

The slave genealog[y] presented in Figure 2 provides a detailed example of the kinds of kinship networks that could develop on quarters after several generations of relative geographic stability. Because most slave quarters had between fifteen and thirty slaves, the network included just two or three

TABLE 2 *Afro-American Household Structures on Small Plantations (1–8 Slaves), Prince George's County, Maryland, 1776*

HOUSEHOLD TYPE	PERCENTAGE IN HOUSEHOLD TYPE				PERCENTAGE OF TOTAL IN HOUSEHOLD TYPES
	MALES 15 +	FEMALES 15 +	CHILDREN 0–9	CHILDREN 10–14	
Husband–wife–children	17	18	22	10	18
Mother–children	2	35	56	29	32
Father–children	2	*	4	1	2
Siblings	7	5	6	17	8
Mixed	72	42	12	43	41
Total percentage	100	100	100	100	101
Number of people	275	276	325	162	1038

Source: 1776 Census. The household types were assumed from black age structures on individual farms. Children and mothers were matched if a woman in the household could have been a mother to children in the same household (e.g., a woman 25 years old was assumed to be a mother of children aged 4, 2, and 1 years on the same plantation). Men and women were linked as husband and wife if a man and woman in the same household were close in age (e.g., a man of 35 linked with a woman of 25). Children and young adults (to c. 25) were assumed to be siblings if no parents were in the household, and the ages of the children were close. (Children aged 8, 10, 13 were linked as siblings when no adult in household could be their parent.) A man was assumed to be father to children who lived on the same farm if no other person who could be a parent was present (man aged 35 was father to children aged 12, 10, 8 when no woman was present in household to be wife). The mixed category included all others who could not be placed: these could include kinfolk like older siblings, or brothers or parents to women with children in the same household, or they could be unrelated. If more than one type was found on a farm, it was counted as two households despite the probability that the people lived in the same hut. The statistics must be treated as educated guesses. Since slave mothers and their children were usually kept together in slave sales and in wills of masters, it is fairly certain that all the children in the first two categories lived with their mothers. The other linkages must include many errors.

* = less than ½%.

households. The kin group shown in Figure 2 may have been typical. Thirteen of the seventeen slaves who lived at Annapolis Quarter in 1774 were descendants of Iron Works Lucy. Ten were children and grandchildren of Sall. One of Sall's sons-in-law and his brother also lived there. Peter and Charles, other descendants of Lucy, lived on the quarter but had families elsewhere.

Nearly half the slaves who resided on Riggs Quarter, Carroll's main plantation, were kinfolk (63/130). A network of this size could develop only on the home plantation of the largest Chesapeake planters.[26] Each of the members of the group was either a direct descendant or an affine (inlaw) of old Fanny. She was surrounded on her quarter by five children, nineteen grandchildren, nine great-grandchildren, four children-in-law, and three grandchildren's spouses. The network grew through the marriage of Fanny's children and grandchildren to children of other residents of the quarter. For

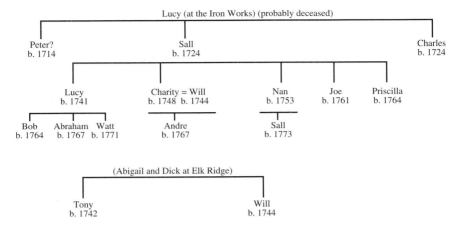

FIGURE 2 Kinship Ties Among Charles Carroll's Slaves at Annapolis Quarter, 1774.
Source: Charles Carroll Account Book, Maryland Historical Society.
Note: Will, son of Abigail and Dick and Charity's husband, appears twice. Peter may not be Lucy's son, but it seems probable. Mark (b. 1758) and Jem (b. 1754) apparently were not related to others on the quarter, but had relatives elsewhere on Carroll's plantation.

example, Cooper Joe, his wife, and thirteen children and grandchildren were closely related to Fanny's family. By the early 1750s Cooper Joe had married Nanny of Kate, and about 1761 Fanny's son Bob married Frances Mitchell of Kate. Joe and Nanny's children were first cousins of the children of Bob and Frances, and thereby more remotely connected to all the rest of Fanny's descendants. The alliance of the two families was cemented in 1772, when Dinah, the daughter of Kate of Fanny, married Joe, the son of Cooper Joe.[27]

The intraquarter kinship network was also a work group. Fanny's and Lucy's adult and teenage kinfolk worked together in the fields. Masters separated their slaves by sex, age, and strength, and determined what each would do, but blacks judged each other in part by the reciprocal kinship obligation that bound them together. Afro-Americans worked at their own pace and frequently thwarted their master's desires for increased productivity. Part of this conflict can be explained by the Afro-American's preindustrial work discipline, but part may have been due to the desires of kinfolk to help and protect each other from the master's lash, the humid climate, and the malarial environment.[28] . . .

When Afro-Americans came home each night from the fields, they broke into smaller domestic groups. Their habitat set the scene for social intercourse. On large plantations "a Negro quarter is a Number of Huts or Hovels, built at some distance from the Mansion House; where the Negroes reside with their wives and families and cultivate at vacant times the little spots allow'd them."[29] Four early-nineteenth-century slave houses still standing in Southern Maryland suggest that slave families living on the same quarter were very close. Each house included two rooms of about sixteen-by–sixteen feet, separated by a thin wall. In three of the homes, the two huts shared the same roof but had separate doorways. Two had separate fireplaces, the residents of one duplex shared a fireplace, and one quarter (which was over a kitchen) did not have a fireplace.[30] Neither family had much privacy, and communication between them must have been commonplace. No activity could occur on one side of the hut without those on the other knowing about it. And the two halves of the hut shared a common yard, where residents could talk, eat, or celebrate.

On the quarters the smallest local residence unit to contain kinfolk was the household. Household members were not isolated from other kinfolk; they worked with their relatives in the fields, associated with neighbors in the common yard, and cooked meals or slept near those who lived on the other side of their duplex. Nevertheless, kinfolk who lived in the same household were spatially closer when at home than any other group of kin. Who lived in typical households on slave quarters? How many husbands lived with their wives and children? How many children were separated from their parents? Did kin other than the immediate family live in many households?

Nearly half of all the Afro-Americans who lived on the three large plantations described in Table 1 resided in households that included both parents and at least some of their children. Over half of the young children on all three plantations lived with both parents, but a far higher proportion of adults and children 10 to 14 years of age lived in two-parent households on the Carroll quarters than on the three Addison farms and Wardrop's plantation in Prince George's. While 49 percent of the women, 51 percent of the men, and 52 percent of children between ages 10 and 14 on Carroll's farms lived in two-parent households, only 28 percent of the women, 24 percent of the men, and 30 percent of those 10 to 14 year olds could be found in two-parent homes on the other farms. Almost all the other children lived with one parent, usually the mother; but over a quarter of those 10 to 14 years of age lived with siblings or with apparently unrelated people.

The differences between Carroll and the other two large slaveowners is striking. Carroll, unlike all but a few other Chesapeake gentlemen, was able to provide his people with spouses from his own plantations and chose to keep adolescent children with their parents. Over six-tenths of the men (62 percent) and 28 percent of the women on Addison's and Wardrop's plantations lived with siblings, were unmarried, or lived away from spouses and children. On Carroll's quarters only 27 percent of the men and 12 percent of the women were similarly separated from spouses and children.

Many blacks on these three large farms lived with or near kin other than their parents or children. About 7 percent were in the household of a brother or sister, and over a tenth (13 percent) of parents and children shared their homes with another kinsperson. There were several types of these extended households: seven included parent(s), children, and sibling(s) of the mother; two included a grandmother living with her children and grandchildren; in one household grandparents took care of two young grandchildren; and in one hut, an adult brother and sister lived with her children and one grandchild.

Far less can be learned about families on small plantations. On these farms, the slave quarter could be in an outbuilding or in a small hut.[31] All the slaves, whether kin or not, lived together, cooked together, reared children together, and slept in the same hut. Table 2 very roughly suggests the differences in household composition of large plantations and small farms. Only 18 percent of the blacks on small units lived in two-parent households. About a third resided in mother–child households, and that included over half the young children and three-tenths of those 10 to 14 years of age. Nearly three-quarters of the men and two-fifths of the women—some unmarried—lived with neither spouse nor children. Over two-fifths of the youths 10 to 14 years of age lived away from parents and siblings. . . .

On large plantations, mothers could call upon a wide variety of kin to help them raise their children: husbands, siblings, cousins, and uncles or aunts might be living in nearby huts. Peter Harbard learned from his grandmother, father, and paternal uncles how his grandmother's indentures were burned by Henry Darnall and how she was forced into bondage. He "frequently heard his grandmother Ann Joice say that if she had her just right that she ought to be free and all her children. He hath also heard his Uncles David Jones, John Wood, Thomas Crane, and also his father Francis Harbard declare as much." Peter's desire for freedom, learned from his kinfolk, never left him. In 1748, he ran away twice toward Philadelphia and freedom. He was recaptured, but later purchased his freedom.[32] . . .

As Afro-American slaves moved from plantation to plantation through the life cycle, they left behind many friends and kinfolk, and established relationships with slaves on other plantations. And when young black men married off their quarter, they gained kinfolk on other plantations. Both of these patterns can be illustrated from the Carroll plantations. Sam and Sue, who lived on Sam's quarter at Doohoregan Manor, had seven children between 1729 and 1751. In 1774, six of them were spread over four different quarters at Doohoregan: one son lived with his father (his mother had died); a daughter lived with her family in a hut near her father's; a son and daughter lived at Frost's; one son headed Moses' quarter; and a son lived at Riggs. . . . Marriages increased the size and geographic spread of Fanny's relations. A third of the slaves (85/255) who lived away from Riggs Quarter (the main plantation) were kin to Fanny or her descendants. Two of Kate's children married into Fanny's family; Kate and one son lived at Frost's and another son lived at Jacob's. Cecilia, the daughter of Carpenter Harry and Sophia, married one of Fanny's grandchildren. Harry and Sophia lived with three of their children at Frost's, and two of their sons lived at Riggs, where they were learning to be wheelwrights with kinsperson Joe, son of Cooper Joe.[33]

Since husbands and wives, fathers and children, and friends and kinfolk were often physically separated, they had to devise ways of maintaining their close ties. At night and on Sundays and holidays, fathers and other kinfolk visited those family members who lived on other plantations. Fathers had regular visiting rights. Landon Carter's Guy, for instance, visited his wife (who lived on another quarter) every Monday evening.[34] Kinfolk, friends, and neighbors gathered in the yard around the slave cabins and talked, danced, sang, told stories, and drank rum through many an evening and special days on larger plantations.[35] These visits symbolized the solidarity of slave families and permitted kinfolk to renew their friendships, but did not allow nonresident fathers to participate in the daily rearing of their children.

The forced separation of Afro-American kinfolk by masters was not entirely destructive. Slave society was characterized by hundreds of interconnected and interlocking kinship and friendship networks that stretched from plantation to plantation and from county to county. A slave who wanted to run away would find kinfolk, friends of kinfolk, or kinfolk of friends along his route who willingly would harbor him for a while.[36] As Afro-American kinship and friendship networks grew ever larger, the proportion of runaways who were harbored for significant periods of time on slave quarters seemed to have increased in both Maryland and Virginia.[37]

There were three different reasons for slaves to use this underground. . . . In 1756, Kate, 30 years old, ran away from her master, who lived near Georgetown on the Potomac. She went to South River about thirty miles distant, where she had formerly lived. Friends concealed her there. Her master feared that since "she had been a great Rambler, and is well known in *Calvert* and *Anne Arundel* Counties, besides other parts of the Country," Kate would "indulge herself a little in visiting her old Acquaintances," but spend most of her time with her husband at West River.[38]

Indeed, 20 of 233 Maryland runaways (9 percent) left masters to join their spouses. Sue and her child Jem, 18 months old, went from Allen's Freshes to Port Tobacco, Charles County, a distance of about ten miles, "to go and see her husband." Sam, age 30, lived about thirty miles from his wife in Bryantown, Charles County, when he visited her in 1755. Will had to go over a hundred miles, from Charles to Frederick County, to visit his wife, because her master had taken her from Will's neighborhood to a distant quarter.[39]

This essay has pointed to the basic cultural and demographic cleavage between African and Afro-American families. African immigrants, like free and servant immigrants from Britain, remembered their native land but had to adjust to the new conditions of the Chesapeake. As free Africans they had lived among many kinfolk; in the Chesapeake, kin ties were established with difficulty. Because most immigrants were young adult males and because plantations were small, two-parent households were rare. Mothers by default became the major black influence upon Afro-American children.

After immigration from Africa slowed, the sex ratio declined, and plantation sizes increased. As generation followed generation, Afro-Americans in Maryland and Virginia created an extensive kinship system. More households, especially on large plantations, included two parents and their children. Although most households did not include kinfolk other than the immediate family, other relations lived in adjacent huts. Mothers and children worked in the tobacco fields with kinfolk, ate and celebrated with many relations, and invited kin who lived elsewhere to share in the festivities. Afro-Americans forcibly separated from relatives managed to maintain contact with them. And finally, slave resistance—whether expressed in the fields or by running away—was fostered and encouraged by kinfolk.

NOTES

1. Pioneering essays by Russell Menard, "The Maryland Slave Population, 1658–1730: A Demographic Profile of Blacks in Four Counties," *William and Mary Quarterly*, 3d ser. 32 (1975):29–54, and Peter Wood, *Black Majority: Negroes in Colonial South Carolina through the Stono Rebellion* (New York, 1974), ch. 5, suggest some characteristics of colonial black families. Much more is known about slave families in the nineteenth century. Herbert G. Gutman, *The Black Family in Slavery and Freedom, 1750–1925* (New York, 1976) is the standard reference. Other studies include Eugene D. Genovese, *Roll, Jordan, Roll: The World the Slaves Made* (New York, 1974), pp. 443–524; E. Franklin Frazier, "The Negro Slave Family," *Journal of Negro History* 15 (1930):198–266; John Blassingame, *The Slave Community: Plantation Life in the Ante-Bellum South* (New York, 1972), ch. 3; George P. Rawick, *From Sundown to Sunup: The Making of the Black Community* (New York, 1972), ch. 5.

2. There are no standard definitions of household, domestic group, and family. I have borrowed my definitions of household and domestic group from Donald R. Bender, "A Refinement of the Concept of Household: Families, Co-residence, and Domestic Functions," *American Anthropologist* 69 (1967):493–504, quote on p. 498. The use of "immediate family," "near kin," and "distant kin" were suggested to me by Herbert Gutman, and would be rejected by Bender.

3. Sidney W. Mintz and Richard Price, "The Study of Afro-American Culture History: Some Suggestions" (working paper presented to the Schouler Lecture Symposium, Creole Societies in the Americas and Africa, John Hopkins University, April 1973) cited with the permission of Mr. Mintz. This paper will be published in fall, 1976 by Ishi Publications, Philadelphia, as *An Anthropological Approach to the Afro-American Past: A Caribbean Perspective*, Occasional Papers in Social Change. A more systematic application of these hypotheses to the colonial Chesapeake will be found in Allan Kulikoff, "Tobacco and Slaves: Population, Economy, and Society in Eighteenth-Century Prince George's County, Maryland" (Ph.D. diss., Brandeis University, 1976), ch. 6.

4. It is difficult to be more precise because most data on African kinship systems comes from twentieth-century anthropological works. The following works suggest variations in African kinship patterns: A. R. Radcliffe-Brown, "Introduction" to *African Systems of Kinship and Marriage*, ed. Radcliffe-Brown and Daryll Ford (London, 1950), pp. 1–85; Meyer Fortes, "Kinship and Marriage among the Ashanti," ibid., pp. 252–84; Jack Goody, *Comparative Studies in Kinship* (Stanford, 1969), ch. 3; Robert Bain, *Bangwa Kinship and Marriage* (Cambridge, England, 1972); William J. Goode, *World Revolutions and Family Patterns* (New York, 1963), pp. 167–200.

5. Mintz and Price, "Afro-American Culture History," pp. 56–78 but esp. pp. 61–62; John S. Mbiti, *African Religions and Philosophy* (New York, 1969), pp. 104–9.

6. Goode, *World Revolutions*, pp. 167–68, 196; Mbiti, *African Religions*, pp. 142–45. Women in polygynous societies also nursed infants for three to four years and abstained from intercourse during part of that period. If this pattern was repeated in the Chesapeake, it was partially responsible for the low gross birth rate among blacks in seventeenth-century Maryland; see Kulikoff,

"Tobacco and Slaves," ch. 4; Menard, "Maryland Slave Population," p. 41; Mbiti, *African Religions*, p. 111. For polygyny on the Eastern Shore, see "Eighteenth-Century Maryland as Portrayed in the 'Itinerant Observations' of Edward Kimber," *Maryland Historical Magazine* 51 (1956):327.

7. For Maryland, see Kulikoff, "Tobacco and Slaves," ch. 4, table 4-3; Menard, "Maryland Slave Population," p. 32, for sex ratios; Kulikoff, "Tobaco and Slaves," ch. 6, for density. For Virginia, see Robert A. Wheeler, "Mobility of Laborers in Surry County, Virginia, 1674–1703 (paper presented at the Stony Brook, N.Y., Conference on Early Social History, June 1975), p. 6.

8. For the uprising of 1739 and some evidence concerning the competition of whites and Afro-American for African and Afro-American women, see Kulikoff, "Tobacco and Slaves," ch. 6.

9. White common-law husbands found open cohabitation with black women socially undesirable. When William Hardie of Prince George's accused Daniel Carroll of Upper Marlborough, a wealthy merchant of the same county, of buggery and of keeping mulattoes, since "he . . . could use them as he pleased," Carroll sued him for slander, finding both charges equally harmful; see Clinton Ashley Ellefson, "The County Courts and the Provincial Courts of Maryland, 1733–1764" (Ph.D. diss., University of Maryland, 1963), pp. 544–46.

10. PG Inventories, 1730–44.

11. Menard, "Maryland Slave Population," pp. 42–46; Kulikoff, "Tobacco and Slaves," ch. 4.

12. These points are fully developed in Kulikoff, "Tobacco and Slaves," ch. 6.

13. These statements are based upon PG Wills, 1730–69 and court cases discussed below.

14. PG Wills, 1730–69; mortgages in PG Land Records, libers T, Y, and PP, mss. Estate sales were sometimes advertised in the *Maryland Gazette*. Slaves could not be sold from an estate until all other moveable property had been used to pay debts. Elie Valette, *The Deputy Commissary's Guide within the Province of Maryland* (Annapolis, 1774), pp. 91, 134–35.

15. Eighteenth-century migrations of slaves are discussed in Kulikoff, "Tobacco and Slaves," ch. 4, and slave migrations in the nineteenth century are analyzed in Kulikoff, "Black Society and the Economics of Slavery," *Maryland Historical Magazine* 70 (1975):208–10.

16. Court of Appeals of the Western Shore, BW no. 10(1800–1801), ff. 456–83, but esp. ff. 459–60, mss.

17. Chancery Papers no. 5241 (1788) mss; PG Wills 1:280–5; PG Original Wills, box 7, folder 66, and box 13, folder 51, mss.; PG Inventories DD no. 1 ff. 22–24; DD no. 2, ff. 379–86; GS no. 1 ff. 246–48; and ST no. 1, ff. 96–100.

18. Chancery Records 16:298–304, ms.; PG Land Record PP (second part) 4; NN, f. 407; PG Original Wills, box 7, folder 3, and box 9, folder 52; PG Inventories DD no. 1, ff. 438–41, and GS no. 2, ff. 111–12.

19. About 40 percent of Prince George's slaves lived on large units from 1750 to 1779 (estimate based upon probate inventories), and 52 percent of the slaves in that county lived on big units in 1790 (federal census); see Kulikoff, "Tobacco and Slaves," table 6–1 for references.

20. Large in-migrations of Africans to the Chesapeake region occurred in the 1670s and 1690s (see Kulikoff, "Tobacco and Slaves," ch. 4, and references there). The great-grandmother of a man born in 1755 could have immigrated from Africa as a young woman in the 1690s.

21. "A List of Negroes on Dooheregan Manor taken in Familys with their Ages Decr 1 1773," and other lists of slaves at Popular Island, Annapolis Quarter, and Annapolis taken in February and July 1774, Carroll Account Book. There were ten quarters on the 10,500 acres of Doohoregan. I am greatly endebted to Edward Papenfuse for calling this list to my attention.

22. Only a handful of people in the Chesapeake colonies owned as many slaves as Carroll. He could therefore afford to keep most of his slave families together, an option not open even to the very large slaveowner with several children and 100 slaves. Nevertheless, two-thirds of Carroll's slaves lived on units with less than 40 people, and 57 percent of them on quarters with less than 30. Only the 130 slaves who lived at Riggs (the main plantation at Doohoregan) developed more extensive kinship networks on a single quarter than was possible for slaves who lived on other large Chesapeake quarters of 15 to 30 slaves.

23. See Menard, "Maryland Slave Population," pp. 35–36 for seventeenth-century examples of quarters named for slave residents.

24. There were 139 married adults (all ages) and single people 21 years and over in the group. While 46 percent of the leaders were over 55, only 11 percent (15/138) of all adults were over 55. The oldest member of a quarter kin group did not necessarily head the list. For example, Carpenter Harry, 46, headed Frost's Quarter even though his mother, Battle Creek Nanny, 78, was also living there.

25. The statistics are means: 36 percent of all slaves counted together, 38 percent with each quarter counted separately (sum of means). The number of people related to leaders on each quarter was as follows:

QUARTER	LEADER	AGE (YEARS)	NO. OF KIN TIES	NO. ON QUARTER (EXCLUDING LEADER)
Riggs	Fanny	69	40	129
Sukey's	Sukey	69	9	21
Moses'	Moses	41	7	18*
Jacob's	Jacob	34	2	21*
Mayara James	Mayara James	65	23	27
Folly	Nacy	45	7	19*
Sam's	Sam	57	6	21
Frost's	Carpenter Henry	46	8	36
Sten's	Judith†	21	7	22
Capt. Field's	Phil	34	3	7*
House Servants at Annapolis	Johnny	30	4	12
Annapolis	Peter	60	13	16
Popular Island	James	73	3	25*

Note: The first ten quarters listed were all on Doohoregan. Because affines were unknown (except for Riggs, where they were eliminated for the sake of comparison), the figures are minimums.

*Only known relations were immediate family.

†Daughter of Long Grace, 47, on that quarter, who had lost the use of her feet.

26. Only a maximum of 6 percent of all the slaves in Prince George's, Anne Arundel, Charles, and St. Mary's Counties, Md., in 1790, lived on units of more than 100. (The 6 percent is a maximum number because the census taker sometimes put slaves from several of the same master's quarters in the same entry.) *Heads of Families at the First Census of the United States Taken in the Year 1790; Maryland* (Washington, 1907), pp. 9–16, 47–55, 92–98, 104–9.
27. Joe married his mother's sister's husband's mother's grandchild.
28. See Kulikoff, "Tobacco and Slaves," ch. 7.
29. Kimber, "Itinerant Observations," p. 327. See Kulikoff, "Tobacco and Slaves," ch. 6, for a fuller description of slave quarters.
30. Three of the structures are in St. Mary's; the other once stood in Prince George's. I am indebted to Cary Carson, coordinator of research, St. Mary's City Commission, for sharing the data on St. Mary's with me, and to Margaret Cook (a local historian, who lives in Oxon Hill, Md.) for her descriptions and slides of the Prince George's hut. These ideas will be expanded elsewhere.
31. On a small plantation a slave quarter located in a kitchen is described in Provincial Court Judgments, EI no. 4, ff. 110–12, ms.
32. Court of Appeals of the Western Shore, BW no. 10 (1800–1801), ff. 459–60; *Maryland Gazette*, 2 Nov. 1748.
33. Carroll Account Book.
34. Greene, *Diary of London Carter*, pp. 329, 348, 648, 845, 1109–10; *Maryland Gazette*, 11 July 1771.
35. See references cited in Kulikoff, "Tobacco and Slaves," ch. 6, note 44.
36. My work on slavery owes much to the pioneering book of Gerald Mullin, *Flight and Rebellion: Slave Resistance in Eighteenth-Century Virginia* (New York, 1972), but my perspective on run-

aways differs from the ones he presents in chapters 3 and 4 of his book. Mullin has, I believe, missed the significance of kin networks in helping most runaways.

37. See table 8.5; Kulikoff, "Tobacco and Slaves," table 6–4; Mullin, *Flight and Rebellion*, p. 129, shows that the proportion of visitors (as defined in table 8.5) increased from 29% before 1775 to 38% of all runaways whose destinations can be determined from 1776 to 1800. The major problem with this data and Mullin's is the large number of unknowns (52% in Maryland and 40% in Virginia).

38. Ibid., 4 Oct. 1749; 11 Nov. 1756; for other extensive visiting networks, see ibid., 11 Aug. 1751; 12 March 1772; 30 Jan. and 22 May 1777.

39. Ibid., 9 March 1758, 6 Feb. 1755, and 12 Aug. 1773; table 8.7. John Woolman claimed that husbands and wives were often separated, *The Journal of John Woolman* (Corinth ed., New York, 1961), p. 59.

5

"To Use Her as His Wife": An Extraordinary Paternity Suit in the 1740s

Kathryn Kish Sklar

This account of a fornication and paternity case in the 1740s examines one aspect of the crumbling of premodern family structures. In a period before the advent of modern or "Victorian" family structures, young women frequently became pregnant before marriage and found themselves at the center of controversies about who and how they should wed. Kathryn Sklar examines the different ways that religious and secular authorities treated one such case.

Although we think of the family as a "private" institution, the public dimensions of family life have historically been just as important as the private.[1] Indeed, from Puritan times to the present, family life has offered historians a rich site to analyze the intersection of public and private life. Studies of family life have helped us understand large social and cultural paradigms in American history, such as those associated with seventeenth-century Puritans and nineteenth-century Victorians.[2] Yet the eighteenth-century shift between those "premodern" and "modern" paradigms remains relatively uninvestigated. This essay explores private and public themes associated with that shift. It examines an incidence of "fornication" that developed into a paternity case adjudicated in both civil and religious venues. The case shows us how changes in family life were being treated by public authorities, and it gives us insight into the social and cultural changes that were reshaping public and private life in the 1740s.

Our story unfolds at the midpoint between two well-studied models of domestic life. A rich literature about seventeenth-century family and community structures has shown us how propertied families were governed by patriarchal authority, relied on the economic productivity of wives and daughters, maintained high fertility rates, and formed new families in a process that was controlled by parents and based on economic considerations.[3] Similarly, ample writings about nineteenth-century middle-class family and community life have demonstrated how patriarchal authority was eroded, the economic

An earlier version of this article appeared in conference proceedings as "Culture Versus Economics: A Case of Fornication in Northampton, Massachusetts in the 1740's," *University of Michigan Papers in Women's Studies* (May 1978), 35–56. Copyright © 1978, 2001 by Kathryn Kish Sklar. Used by permission of the author.

productivity of wives and daughters reduced, fertility rates dramatically declined, and new families were formed in a process dominated by romantic love.[4] Each of these paradigms of family life was embedded in public contexts that monitored and supported their shape.

But what of the century between? How did the transition occur? How did private behavior and public authority mark the passage from one model of family life to the other? Fornication cases and paternity suits help us address those questions because they illuminate one of the most fundamental features of eighteenth-century family life: bridal pregnancy. Demographic studies have shown that the most visible sign of the transition from premodern to modern family structures was a remarkable rise in premarital pregnancy, which by 1790 meant that one in every three brides throughout the new American republic was pregnant at marriage.[5] This widespread but relatively understudied phenomenon left a paper trail in the form of civil proceedings that awarded child support to unwed mothers. This essay examines an extraordinary case in which religious authorities opposed the civil settlement, providing a window through which to view the changes that were shaping private and public behavior.

In the North American British colonies, premarital pregnancy rose from one in ten in 1710 to one in three in 1790. Demographic historians believe that this long-term rise signaled the disintegration of premodern family structures, particularly those governing the creation of new families. Another marker supporting that view was the end of marriage-by-birth-order as a means by which parents controlled the marriage market. Strict adherence to the rule that limited each child's access to marriage only after the marriage of their next eldest same-sex sibling meant that parents with young adult children had only one child of the same sex available for marriage at a time. This system had collapsed by 1790.[6]

Yet while premodern structures governing the creation of new families were crumbling between 1710 and 1790, modern structures had not yet emerged to take their place. After 1830 premarital pregnancy rates returned to their pre-1710 lows, reflecting the stability of the new "modern" or "Victorian" patterns of sexual behavior in which women exercised greater control over sexual access to their bodies and courting couples generally abstained from sex. New forms of courtship were governed by romantic love rather than parental control. Many Victorians denounced the sexual double standard that had characterized eighteenth-century sexual relations. And fertility rates declined precipitously in the 1840s and 1850s as couples began to limit the size of their families, creating long-term decline from high to low birth rates, called "the demographic transition."[7]

Women held a central place in the private and public dramas that occurred during the eighteenth-century transition from premodern to modern family forms. They made decisions that led to prebridal pregnancies; they took risks that their Victorian descendants avoided. How did they experience the consequences of those decisions and risks? What private and public responses did they make to the challenges they faced?

Demographic historians have concluded that the impact of rising bridal pregnancies on women was minimal because bastardy rates did not rise. Thus, although many more women were pregnant before marriage, by the time they gave birth they were married. In this view, community coercion "overcame the more serious consequences of pregnancy for women."[8] Yet that very coercion illuminates the problematic status of unmarried pregnant women in premodern societies. Communities enforced the norm of marriage to reduce the likelihood of the town's need to support fatherless children with public funds. Bastard births were rare because they were treated as serious transgressions of social norms. The social stigma attached to their plight reduced women's value on the marriage market, and delayed their ability to form independent households. Economically and culturally prohibited from creating their own households, single mothers had to find a place in other households, usually those in which they had been raised. Therefore, although many pregnant brides may have married their lovers and lived happily ever after, other potential outcomes rendered this remarkable rise in premarital pregnancy rates highly problematic for many young women.

Other forms of historical evidence point to women's vulnerability during this transition. Literary scholars have noted that the novel came into being in the eighteenth century largely as a way to tell stories of seduction and betrayal. From Samuel Richardson's *Pamela* of 1740 to Susanna Rowson's *Charlotte Temple* of 1791, the seduction novel captivated three generations of Anglo-American readers.[9] Similarly, recent research in New England court records has uncovered a gendered pattern of increasing male privilege when matters pertaining to sexual offenses, such as rape and fornication, were decriminalized around 1740. Rules that were once enforced by the community to provide child support in cases of children born outside of marriage gave way to civil suits by individual women who (with the fathers and male kin who supported them economically) had to assume the costs of such proceedings. In this new civil context, legal tactics of evasion and not-guilty pleas gave unscrupulous men a new advantage.[10]

How did women in yeoman families respond to these new circumstances? Could they find assistance in religious authorities who stepped in to represent the interests of the community? Did they face class as well as gender prejudice in the civil courts? This essay addresses these questions by focusing on an extraordinary paternity suit in Northampton, Massachusetts, in the 1740s. In many ways the suit was quite ordinary: a young woman sought child support after being abandoned by her faithless lover. Yet the suit had unusual dimensions that illuminate the cultural and institutional contexts in which it occurred. Because the conflict was heard by both religious and civil bodies, it discloses differences between the religious and civil discourses used in the case. And because each side of the conflict was championed by powerful men who invested the case with exceptional significance, it reveals the full range of resources that could be brought to bear on such cases.

At the center of the conflict was Martha Root, an unmarried young woman of a propertied yeoman family, who in 1747 at the age of twenty-seven gave birth to twins. On either side of the conflict powerful male leaders represented opposing religious and secular views of whether the babies' father should be required to marry her. At issue was the church's ability to hold men accountable for their sexual behavior, versus men's ability to evade marriage by paying damages in the secular courts.

For Martha Root the stakes were high, including whether she might marry her lover, Elisha Hawley, the twenty-one-year-old son of one of Northampton's most prestigious families, and whether she alone would bear the costs of their sexual union. The stakes were also high for the two male protagonists who argued the case. Pressing the church's case that Elisha Hawley should marry Martha Root was Jonathan Edwards (1703–1758), pastor of Northampton's First Congregational Church from 1729 to 1750, who in the 1740s was at the height of his career as one of the most powerful clergymen in colonial America.[11] Joseph Hawley (1723–1788), representing his younger brother in the civil courts, was just beginning a long and successful political career. In 1748 he was elected to the Northampton Board of Selectmen, three years later he began to represent the town in the Massachusetts assembly, and after 1760 he represented Hampshire County for 20 years in the General Court.[12]

Edwards and Hawley brought to this struggle over Martha Root the full strength of trends that were reshaping their culture and society. Edwards represented revitalized religious institutions, which, during the "Great Awakening" of the 1730s and 1740s, launched the revival emphasis within Protestant denominations that would by the 1830s transfer a great deal of power from the ministry to the laity.[13] Hawley represented the growth of vibrant local civil institutions that by the 1770s would seize political power in this corner of the British empire. Both men were masters of the era's chief tool of persuasion: oratory.[14] And in this test of wills both had deeply personal motivations to defeat the other. Edwards and Hawley articulated opposing sides of the family issues in Martha Root's case fully and forcefully, not only because they believed in the issues, but also because they each desperately needed to win.

Each man brought considerable oratorical power to the struggle. One of the most effective public speakers in colonial America, Edwards was well known for the emotional impact of his sermons. One listener described his delivery as "easy, natural, and very solemn."[15] The power of his sermons arose in part from his emphasis on human feelings and lived experience rather than theological abstractions, and from the erotic, feminized images with which he equated human love for God and marital love between wives and husbands.[16] Twenty years younger than Edwards, Joseph Hawley was beginning to construct a career that also relied on the spoken word. Hawley's style was decisively masculine. One observer later said of him: "Many men have spoken with more elegance and grace—I never heard one speak with more force."[17]

Each man also brought deeply personal issues of family identity to this struggle. They were cousins; both of their mothers were daughters of Esther Warham (1644–1736) and Solomon Stoddard (1643–1729). As Northampton's minister for fifty-seven years, Solomon Stoddard became one of the most powerful religious leaders in the Puritan colony of Massachusetts. Known for his "zeal and boldness in the cause of Truth and Holiness," for many years Stoddard preached the public lecture on the day following Harvard commencement, the only annual event attended by every minister in the colony. Stoddard used his position in Northampton's pulpit to reform church governance and church practice, for example, breaking with Puritan tradition by opening church membership to all who were over fourteen years old and of "non-scandalous behavior."[18] By 1748, when they took opposite sides in the Martha Root case, Jonathan Edwards and Joseph Hawley were locked in a personal conflict over Edwards's ability to exercise communal power on the patriarchal scale of their grandfather.

Premodern families were important not only as the sites of social organization and power, but also as the vessels that carried family lineage through time. Lines of descent mattered as much as wealth, and indeed were an important means by which wealth, prestige, and power were maintained. Esther and Solomon Stoddard had eleven children, six of whom were daughters. Their oldest surviving daughter, Esther, married clergyman Timothy Edwards and became the mother of Jonathan Edwards. Named for her mother, Esther became renowned for her piety and good works, raising Jonathan and his ten sisters in a household that valued female achievements, both spiritual and temporal.[19] Their youngest surviving daughter, Rebekah, married merchant-farmer Joseph Hawley, and became the mother of Joseph and Elisha Hawley. With the appointment of Jonathan Edwards to succeed Stoddard in the Northampton pulpit, the power and prestige of Solomon Stoddard began to flow through Esther Edwards's line of descent, and Rebekah Hawley's line faltered.

Rebekah was the only Stoddard daughter who did not marry a minister, and the only daughter who remained in the town of her birth after marriage. She became a widow in 1734 when her husband committed suicide by cutting his throat (Joseph was twelve and Elisha eight at the time). Described as a person of "strong prejudices and aristocratic tendencies," Rebekah contributed to her own and her sons' support by becoming "an expert dairy woman," making more butter and cheese "than any other person in town," and marketing her products throughout the region. Her privileged position in the community was marked by her seating allotment in church. Rather than sitting with the majority of the community's widows on the women's side of the aisle, she sat in a pew adjoining the minister's family with her brother John Stoddard, by far the wealthiest man in town until his death in 1748.[20]

Joseph's suicide occurred when he sank into a depression during his nephew's first revival success in his father-in-law's pulpit. Edwards attributed his uncle's suicide to the work of the devil and to bad Hawley blood, writing cooly in his *Narrative of Surprising Conversions*, published in 1736:

> In the later part of May, it began to be very sensible that the spirit of God was gradually drawing from us, and after this time Satan seemed to be more let loose, and raged in a dreadful manner. The first instance, wherein it appeared, was a person's putting an end to his own life, by cutting his throat. He was a gentleman of more than common understanding, of strict morals, religious in his behavior, and an useful, honorable person in the town; but was of a family that are exceeding prone to the disease of melancholy, and his mother was killed with it.[21]

This suicide quickened the lineage rivalry between Edwards and the fatherless Joseph. The open expression of the rivalry was facilitated in June 1748 by the death of the most important intermediary between them—their uncle, John Stoddard, the town's most powerful secular figure, who frequently represented the town in the state assembly and served as Justice of the Hampshire County Court. Joseph Hawley quickly claimed John Stoddard's mantle of political leadership, and in practically the same motion, turned to do battle with his cousin, Jonathan Edwards, on the question of whether Elisha Hawley should marry Martha Root.

*   *   *

Martha Root was the daughter of Hezekiah and Martha Root, born in 1720, the fourth of eight children, the second of four daughters. Although Hezekiah's estate was less than three-fifths the value listed for widow Rebekah Hawley and her two sons in 1739, Martha's father ranked in the wealthiest fourth of the town's population. An important sign of the family's standing was the marriage of Martha's older sister, Dorothy, at the age of 25 to Charles Phelps, a wealthy Justice of the Peace in Hadley.[22]

In 1747 Martha, at age of 27, was the family's oldest unmarried daughter. Five other siblings probably still lived at home, Simeon, age 30; Jemina, age 26; Joseph, age 19; Hannah, age 17; and Orlando, age 14. Jemina married in 1753, at age 31, and Martha herself married John Miller and left Northampton in 1754, at age 34.[23] Therefore, at the time of her "fornication" with Elisha, Martha was a primary candidate for marriage in a family whose social standing placed them among the solid citizenry of the town. She recovered from her relationship with Elisha and was ultimately able to form her own household, but for six years between 1748 and 1754 that outcome must have seemed far from certain, and her union with Miller might have had "last-chance" aspects that placed her at a disadvantage in her marital household.

Bastard births in propertied families were highly unusual in colonial America. The recorded incidence of illegitimacy in eighteenth-century New England has been estimated on an annual basis as occurring to approximately one in every 200 unmarried women of child-bearing age. While over a period of ten years this would include ten in every 200 (or five percent of the female population at risk), most of these women were much poorer than Martha Root, and came from economic groups in which male desertion was much more frequent than it was among propertied families.[24]

For reasons that remain unclear, Martha did not succeed in marrying someone else during the course of her pregnancy—a strategy that must have been frequently pursued in cases of abandonment. Thus Martha and Elisha's behavior raised the question: What if others followed their example? The urgency of that question was heightened by the fact that she came from the upper-middle ranks of the town's families. Martha, Elisha, and their illegitimate twins constituted a sharp anomaly in their community—an anomaly that could not be condoned as due to Elisha's class privilege alone. Economic differences between the Hawleys and Roots were not decisive enough to permit him to escape community scrutiny and censure. Like most well-off families in New England, the Hawleys were not wealthy enough to support idle sons. Although Elisha's family was considerably wealthier than Martha's, he, like her father and brothers, needed to work for a living. Lacking a college education, Elisha had, in 1746 at the age of 23, entered a business partnership with Joseph, his only sibling and older brother. They traded in hides, exporting from their region to Rhode Island "skins" that were byproducts of pickled meat, the region's other local export.[25] Nevertheless, the Hawleys had pretentions that reached beyond their means. Fueled by Rebekah's pride, they considered themselves the social superiors of yeoman families like the Roots, and they measured this difference in terms of lineage. Descended from Stoddards, they sought marriage partners whom they believed were similarly distinguished.

To understand how Elisha was able to marry into a more prestigious lineage after fathering a child with Martha, we must turn from census data to the written documents pertaining to the case. These show that the controversy had three basic elements:

1) a civil settlement in May 1748, wherein Martha Root received £155 from Elisha Hawley "in full satisfaction for and towards the Support and maintenance of a Bastard Child, now living";

2) a vote by the "brethern" of the First Church sometime before August 1748 to excommunicate Elisha for refusing to marry Martha Root; and

3) a vote by a Council of Ministers called in June 1749 "to hear a matter of Grievances between the Church and Hawley," and to consider "whether it appears [to] this Council to be the duty of Lt. Elisha Hawley to marry Martha Root with whom he has been guilty of fornication . . . and also rather because she lays a Child to him that is now living."[26]

None of these documents quoted Martha directly; her testimony in the case has not been preserved. Yet surviving documents show that she sided with her minister's advocacy on her behalf and pushed her claim against Elisha even though her actions incurred further risks to her reputation and hence to her future ability to marry.

We gain a glimpse of her relationship with Edwards in a letter he wrote to his wife, Sarah, on June 22, 1748, who was in Boston attending the deathbed of John Stoddard. Describing their household in her absence, Edwards wrote: "Your two eldest daughters went to Bed last night, both sick. . . . We got Hannah Root to help them yesterday in the afternoon, expect her again today."[27] This employment of Martha's eighteen-year-old younger sister in the Edwards home suggests that he knew the family well enough to entrust his own daughters to the care of one of their daughters.

Edwards had another reason for paternalistic concern about the welfare of Martha Root. His ministry was characterized by a special concern for young people, especially during his revival of 1735–1736, which brought many young souls to church membership.[28] Edwards had also encountered children in the Root family in less happy circumstances. Early in 1744 Simeon Root and Timothy Root, a twenty-six-year-old unmarried cousin, confessed to "contemptuous behavior toward the authority of this church" after they and about eight other young men were called before a special committee convened by Edwards to investigate reports that they were insulting young women on the street. Having acquired a midwife's book that described menstruation, the young men were running up to young women, calling them "nasty creatures," and saying, "when will the moon change, girls come I'll look on you and see whether there be a blue circle round your eyes."[29] This unseemly behavior on the part of adult unmarried children was accentuated when witnesses to the church committee said that Timothy Root swore that he would not "worship a wig," referring to one of the minister's signs of power, and that he did not "care a turd" or "a fart" for the authority of the committee.[30]

These rebellions by young adults were part of the cost the community was paying for its relatively late age at marriage. Postponed marriage was the main strategy by which premodern European societies reduced fertility in times of economic constraints, and land shortages in western Massachusetts were making it more difficult for young adults to set up their own households. Martha Root's liaison with Elisha Hawley was part of a larger pattern of misbehavior by young people of marriageable age who were not able to create their own households. They were becoming a population that was seriously imperiling constituted authority.

In this context, Elisha Hawley tried to limit his paternal obligations with a civil agreement in which he made a cash payment to Martha in exchange for her releasing him from future responsibility. Thanks to the fact that Elisha was packed off to a military career (commissioned lieutenant in March

1747 by his uncle, Colonel John Stoddard, and appointed commander of Fort Massachusetts), correspondence between Joseph and Elisha survives to inform us about both civil and religious proceedings in the case. Relative to the former, Joseph wrote Elisha in February 1748:

> As to yr affair that I was to manage I tried for an agreement before Court [but they] insisted on £150 down which I thought was too much Considering what risque there is of ye Ch[il]d[']s life, I therefore thought best to tarry awhile longer before I concluded ye affair, and till I could have some account of yr mind .... I hope before next session I Shall accomodate ye affair upon easier Terms than they seem at present to insist upon, if not I should think it best to abide by ye Order of the Court.[31]

From this letter we learn that one twin had apparently died and the other was not well. Without engaging in unseemly opposition to the court, Joseph was intent on obtaining the best bargain possible for the Hawley family.

Martha Root's receipt of £155 in May 1748 shows that one child lived, and that the Hawleys did not get off as cheaply as Joseph had hoped. Since we have no record of the court proceedings, we do not know what considerations were used to determine the sum of £155. The civil settlement referred only to child support in exchange for her promise "that I never will hereafter my self or by any other acting for or under me ask Sue for or demand anything for the future maintenance of the Child."[32]

That document, which was signed by Martha and two witnesses but not by Elisha, began:

> Know all men by these presents that I Martha Root of Northampton in the County of Hampshire in the Province of the Massachusetts Bay in New England Spinster have received of Elisha Hawley of Sd Northampton, Gent. the Sum of One Hundred and fifty-five pounds Old Tenr.

In the titles it appended to their names, calling him a "gentleman" and her a "spinster," this civil settlement articulated social distinctions of class and gender that privileged Elisha. Calling Elisha a "gentleman" imputed class privileges to him, while naming her a "spinster" highlighted her gendered identity as an unmarried woman.[33] He might just as well have been called the son of Rebekah Hawley and she the daughter of Hezekiah and Martha Root.

As a lump sum, Martha's paternity settlement of £155 was far greater than the weekly support of four to six shillings usually awarded by the Court of Common Pleas to prevent bastardy cases from relying on the town's poor relief. Given her family's economic resources, the sum came close to the amount she might be expected to receive as a dowry from her father. Averaged over ten years, however, the approximate length of time before a child could be apprenticed and earn his or her own support, Martha's award amounted to only six shillings a week. From one point of view, therefore, this settlement provided Martha with a dowry commensurate with her family's wealth. From another point of view, it did not provide her child with economic advantages commensurate with legitimate Hawley birth, it could not guarantee her a household of her own, and it placed primary responsibility for the child's future with her. The civil agreement represented the double sexual standard in its most official form.

The civil agreement did not mention damages to Martha's reputation, nor any responsibility Elisha bore to Martha herself. Her payment was only for child support:

> in full Satisfaction for and towards ye Support and maintenance of a Bastard Child born of my Body Now living, which child with Another Sometime Since deceased which was a Twin with ye first mentioned Child, I the Sd Martha Root Charged upon the Sd Elisha as their father.[34]

Were the class and gender inequalities represented in this civil agreement by "gentleman" and "spinster" large enough to justify the cultural and social anomaly that they and their child represented in the community? Apparently not, since the case was tried again in a religious venue. Martha, Elisha and Joseph were all church members and therefore subject to church discipline.[35]

The church, following Edwards's leadership, took up the issue and voted to excommunicate Elisha sometime in Fall 1748, soon after John Stoddard's death. We first hear of Elisha's excommunication in a letter to him from Joseph in December. Joseph's attitude prior to the excommunication shows that he did not expect such an outcome. In a letter to Elisha, he was not unduly alarmed. He felt that the church was taking a stronger stand than the occasion warranted, but he saw no vital threat to Hawley family interests. Those interests could be defended by the claim that Martha was not a virgin and that Elisha did not entice her. That letter began:

> I believe its best for you to Come down as soon as you can with any Convenience. I have thought a great deal of your affr am abundantly Clear in it yt no Church on earth Can by their Censures inforce a Match in Such Case, until ye two points absolute virginty and enticement on ye mans Side are fully proved.

Assuming that these points could not be proven, Joseph continued:

> I should have no regard at all to anything they pretend to do authoritatively in ye particular of Matrimony, nor would I attempt or labour to prove anything against her Since the burden of proof beyond all dispute lies wholly on either ye woman or the Church.

Joseph claimed that Martha and her family opposed the church's actions.

> [T]he woman declares against asking you, in ye form ye Church talk of as also her father and mother. So that if they proceed, they would impose more than

the Jewish Yoke which St. Peter declares Neither the Jews in his time nor their fathers were able to bear.

Joseph meant that the requirement of marriage by the church would be similar to the requirement of circumcision among the early Christians—imposing arcane articles of faith that were unnecessary to Christian belief. His advice struck an optimistic note, but ended obscurely with a reference to Elisha's private conscience.

> All therefore that I at present would do (let the Church take what Course they would) should be, to offer them proper Confessn and rest the Matter. As to Matrimy, I would Do what I knew was right in Conscience and before God, if there was anything [that I] knew of, that was particularly binding that Nobody else knew of.[36]

Joseph seems to be implying something like the following: whatever binding commitments you may have made are a matter for you and God alone. I don't want to hear about them and neither does anyone else. As long as you both shared in the enticement and/or she could not prove "absolute virginity," that was all that mattered.

What this letter did not count on was a minister who was willing to argue for matrimony even though the woman entered into the relationship willingly and was not a virgin at the time. Edwards later used those terms to defend Elisha's excommunication, and he may well have expressed those ideas in the instructions he gave to the brethren the day they voted against Elisha. Excommunication procedures, as defined in the Cambridge Platform, called for a vote by a majority of the "brethren" or male church members, and needed pastoral approval.[37] Elisha's ouster probably resembled that described in the church discipline of Simeon and Timothy Root in the midwifery book case, when, at the conclusion of Sunday worship, Edwards "desired the brethren of the church to stop, told them what evidence and information he had received, and put the question to them."[38]

A form of community ostracism designed to correct offensive behavior, excommunication was prevented by law from affecting a citizen's legal or political rights, and in Elisha's case his attendance at church was largely immaterial, since military duties took him away from Northampton anyway. While the church had no legal power to force couples to marry, excommunication nevertheless marked Elisha as a deviant and made it more difficult for the Hawleys to stare down community opinion and obtain what they deemed a more appropriate marriage for Elisha.

Sometime after December 1748, the Hawleys decided to try to overturn their congregation's decision and began processes that convened a Council of Ministers in June 1749. At that council Edwards argued against virginity and enticement as determining issues in the case. Joseph Hawley rose to the occasion by lying about Martha Root. Edwards's statement shows us that the religious council probed more deeply into the justice of the gender relations of the case than had the civil agreement of 1748. Hawley's later apology to Martha Root shows us that to win his case in this religious council, he felt compelled to lie about her.

The report of the Council, preserved in Hawley's papers, began by naming the five ministers from Hampshire County who convened "at the desire of the First Church of Northampton and Elisha Hawley to hear a matter of Grievances," and to determine:

> whether it appears . . . to be the Duty of Lt. Elisha Hawley to Marry Martha Root with whom he has been guilty of fornication . . . and also further because she lays a Child to him that is now living.[39]

Edwards's remarks on that occasion were almost certainly drawn from six pages of undated notes in his hand. In his remarks, Edwards innovatively and unexpectedly reinterpreted the relevant text in Deuteronomy 22:28–29:

> If a man find a damsel that is a virgin, which is not betrothed, and lay hold on her and lie with her, and they be found; then the man that lay with her shall give unto the damsel's father fifty shekels of silver, and she shall be his wife, because he has humbled her, he may not put her away all his days.[40]

Edwards argued against the double standard of sexual behavior implied in the passage, which expected virginity in women but not in men. He said that the Scriptural prescription applied to sexual relations not only between men and virginal women but between all unmarried women and men. "Tis evident by many Passages in the Prophets & other Parts of the Old Testament," he wrote, "that Fornication was a sin frequently committed in Israel," and that many unmarried women were not virgins. He also argued that a cash payment was inadequate compensation for the damage Elisha had done. "Reparation should be made by something that is equivalent in weight & value," he maintained, which "the nature of the injury demands." He emphatically reinterpreted the Old Testament text.

> The words can't be reasonably understood otherwise than thus. *Seeing he hath Humbled Her; and taken the Liberty to use her as his wife, and as tis proper none should use any woman but a wife; Therefore tis FIT & SUITABLE that she should indeed be his wife: seeing he has made so bold with her, & had Her once, tis fit He should have her alwaies, & not put her away all his days. 'Tis utterly unfit men should think to put away at their Pleasure, those whom They have seen Cause for their Pleasure, thus to unite themselves to.*[41]

With these words Edwards directly addressed the gendered injustice of the case. He insisted that this interpretation expressed "the moral nature of the Rule" and protected the welfare of the entire community. He was arguing, he said, not "meerly that Justice [be] done to the woman or the Repairing the outward injury done to Her. . . . For Gods law in this Case has not only Regard to any particular temporal Rights & Priviledges of the Parties Join'd, but to the . . . order decency & Health of Human society in general." Edwards thereby argued that the cultural and community aspects of the case were more important than its civil and private elements.

Another set of notes in Edwards's hand apparently outlined the terms that both parties agreed to follow in their council arguments. Those notes said that "Lieut Hawley was allowed to speak first" and "endeavor to prove 1. That she has been a Person of a grossly Lascivious Character before Lieut. Hawley's Acquaintance with Her & also Lascivious in her Conduct since this Acquaintance began. 2. That she rather enticed him to the Fact than He her." Although Edwards's notes did not provide for Joseph to assist his brother, Joseph also testified against Martha at the council meeting. Then Martha took her turn "to endeavour to prove 1. That He has enticed her 2. That He is of a Lascivious Character by his Behavior with other persons."[42]

If Edwards's notes were followed, they gave Martha two advantages. She was encouraged to make the point that Elisha entered into their relationship with a full knowledge of her previous sexual activity. "That if He proves any Facts of a Lascivious nature against her she be allowed opportunity if she pleases & thinks she is able to prove that He was acquainted with these Facts before his Fornication." And that Elisha was required to tell Edwards beforehand what allegations he planned to make about Martha. "That Lieut Hawleys particular allegations against Martha Root be brought in to the Pastor touching her Lascivious Character in writing a week before the publick hearing."[43]

Although we do not know what Martha said on this occasion, her minister provided her with the strongest possible opportunity to argue that Elisha should not be allowed to abandon her and their child simply because she was not a virgin at the time of their union or because she had enticed him. Whether Edwards's remarks or Martha's testimony seemed to sway the council, Joseph Hawley apparently thought the truth of the matter was not sufficient to sustain Hawley family interests, for, as later acknowledged, he testified falsely before the council about Martha.

Hawley's remarkable apology to Martha Root, written a year later in August 1750, had a self-justifying and defensive tone, suggesting it was written in response to outside pressure rather than as a voluntary act. His papers contain two copies, each with cautious editorial adjustments. Joseph's apology indicates the degree to which cultural values relating to gender and sexuality became the explicit focus of the Council's proceedings, depriving him of the class-based protection that he sought for his brother as a "gentleman" in the civil agreement. His apology began:

> When I was before the Ecclesiastical Council which sat at Northampton . . . to determine a dispute between the first Church of Sd Northampton and my

Brother respecting his Obligation to Marry you, In giving an Evidence to Sd
Council to prove yt you had been industrious in seeking my brothers Company
for some time before you charged him with being unlawfully familiar with you,
among other things I said yt within ye space of half a year . . . I had seen you in
our street (as I judged) forty several times, putting a Certain number for an uncertain, and yt I did not doubt, but that, at least it was so often. and further yt I
had seen you in almost all parts of our street, at ye Corners or where ye Paths
met particularly at ye Corner by the Bridge and Near the school house. Now so
far as this acct represented ye Matter beyond ye truth I not only so far wronged
ye truth but injured you.

He concluded on a public note:

I acted presumptuously. For which I am heartily sorry, and in observance of the
Divine rule James 5.16, I confess this to you, and do freely and humbly ask yr
pardon and forgiveness. and shall always be ready to Own what is above
written.[44]

Joseph's apology contradicted his earlier letter to Elisha in which he said "he
would not attempt or labour to prove anything against her, since the burden of
proof . . . lies wholly on either the woman or the Church." By the time Joseph
testified at the church council, the burden of proof seems to have shifted from
Martha and the church to Joseph and the Hawley family. Joseph's moral resources were equal to the occasion, and included both the willingness to provide false testimony to defend his family's interests and the ability to
acknowledge his falsehoods later without apparent damage to his career.

Unaware of the falsity of Joseph's statements about Martha, the Council
ruled in favor of Elisha, concluding: "we are far from determining that Lt.
Hawley is not bound in conscience to marry Martha Root [but] that it doesn't
appear to us . . . that it is his duty. We therefore determine it must be left to
the determination of his own conscience."[45] Although no church records survive from these years to tell whether or when Martha publicly confessed the
sin of fornication, Elisha apparently did so only after the council meeting,
since the council recommended that the First Church "receive Mr. Hawley
(upon his making a penitent confession of the Sin of fornication) to the
Christian charity and fellowship."[46]

This protracted struggle continued to affect the lives of its protagonists
after the 1749 council meeting. Most remarkably, in 1750 Jonathan Edwards
was dismissed from his pulpit. Scholars have not given the Martha Root case
the attention it deserves as a contributing cause of Edwards's firing, but his rivalry with Joseph Hawley was thoroughly enmeshed in the politics of his dis-
missal.[47] Another Council of Ministers convened in June 1750 to determine
whether the First Church should be allowed to dismiss Edwards as their pastor. There, Joseph Hawley was the congregation's chief spokesman against
Edwards. In another extraordinary confession, Hawley later admitted that he
made "groundless, and slanderous imputations on Mr. Edwards, expressed in

bitter language . . . which I could never have done if I had not had a wicked relish for perverse things: which conduct of mine I confess very sinful, and highly provoking to God; for which I am ashamed, confounded, and have nothing to answer."[48] For his part, Edwards believed that Hawley "Not only helped the People gain their End in dismissing me, but much encouraged and promoted the spirit with which it was done; your confident, magisterial, vehement manner had a natural and direct tendency to it."[49]

Six weeks after his "slanderous imputations" against Edwards, Hawley penned his apology to Martha Root. Perhaps his father's melancholy example prompted Joseph to be cautious with his own conscience and unload the burden of Martha Root while he was adjusting to the burden of Jonathan Edwards. That way he avoided his father's total solution. Martha Root left no record of what, if any, satisfaction she took in Joseph Hawley's apology to her. Perhaps Edwards directly or indirectly prompted the apology as his final act in the conflict. In any case, the document must have been widely known in and around Northampton, and probably repaired some of the damage that Martha's reputation incurred during this bruising battle, possibly contributing to her ability to marry in 1754.

In 1751 Elisha Hawley married Elizabeth Pomeroy, whose father ranked in the wealthiest tenth of the taxed population and was a deacon in the church.[50] In 1752 Joseph married Mercy Lyman, whose family, like the Pomeroys, were active opponents of Edwards. Neither marriage produced children. Elisha died in battle at Crown Point during the French and Indian War in 1755. Since Martha Root's illegitimate child left no trace in public records, it is impossible to know whether Rebekah Hawley's lineage survived genetically in spite of its legal termination with her childless sons. In 1753 Rebekah built an addition to her house with an expanded cheese room and buttery, as well as a separate apartment for herself now that Mercy lived in the Hawley home with Joseph.[51]

After his firing Edwards retired to frontier Stockbridge, where he wrote many of the theological works that later established him as a major figure in American Enlightenment thought. Named President of Princeton University in 1758, he died of smallpox shortly before taking office.[52] Joseph Hawley went on to become his colony's leading opponent of religious authority. His biographer later characterized his career as "a steady struggle against clerical infallibility and church interference in civil affairs."[53] As the Commonwealth's chief anticleric, Hawley vigorously opposed the continued support of religious institutions through taxation contained in Article III of the new Massachusetts Constitution. Advocating the Virginia solution of total religious disestablishment, Hawley "denied that the people had a right to require the towns to support and maintain public worship and protestant teachers of religion."[54] Believing that his conscience was for him and him alone to evaluate, he retired from public life in 1779 after refusing to take the oath of religious belief required for state senators under the new Constitution.

Explaining his position to fellow senators, he struck a personal note amid his generally principled stand, saying:

> I have been a professed Christian nearly 40 years and altho' I have been guilty of many things unworthy of that character whereof I am ashamed; yet I am not conscious that I have been guilty of anything wholly inconsistent with the truth of that profession.[55]

Yet for Hawley "the truth of that profession" could always be shaped to suit his personal needs.

Martha Root occupied a culturally anomalous position from which two charismatic male leaders were trying to remove her: Edwards in the name of "human society in general," to the culturally normative ranks of the married; Hawley in defense of his family's interests, to the ranks of the culturally and sexually deviant. Hawley's view prevailed and the final deliberating body gave a negative answer to the question of whether it was Elisha's duty to marry Martha. In this respect, the religious council validated the civil agreement with which the case began. Yet Jonathan Edwards's innovative defense of Martha Root's needs and Joseph Hawley's apology show that alternative views of gender justice could challenge the era's civil empowerment of male privilege.

The struggle between Edwards and Hawley symbolized the decline of premodern religious authority and communal forms of justice and the rise of modern secular power and its enshrinement of individual conscience. But as Edwards's career showed, Protestant Christianity was in the process of revitalizing itself. That process came to fruition during the "Second Great Awakening" (1798–1857), a cultural event that empowered women in many ways, most particularly by endorsing new modern forms of family life. By 1830 the wave of prebridal pregnancies that signaled the end of premodern family structures had itself ended, and Victorian values demonized male sexual privileges of the sort that Elisha Hawley displayed.

With the vast expansion of civil society in the 1830s, women began to form their own organizations independent of ministerial authority and thereby gained a powerful means of assaulting traditional gender inequalities. In 1848 the American Female Moral Reform Society and their crusade to assert a single standard of sexual morality for men and women successfully organized community opinion to oppose just the kind of male privilege that Elisha Hawley had exercised in 1748. That year, a petition drive obtained the passage in New York of an antiseduction law that made it a crime for men to impregnate women and abandon them. The law especially targeted upper-class men, who were no longer able to make a cash settlement with their victims.[56] After 1830 women parishioners did not need champions like Jonathan Edwards; in the new public culture that generated social movements independent of both church and state, they were able to take collective action to defend their own interests.

NOTES

I am grateful to David Hall of Harvard University and Patricia Tracy of Williams College for calling my attention to the documents analyzed in this essay, and to Ken Minkema of the Jonathan Edwards editorial project at Yale University for providing me with transcriptions of many pertinent documents in the case and guiding me through recent Edwards historiography. For helpful comments on earlier drafts, I thank Joyce Appleby, Victoria Brown, Richard Bushman, David Hall, Ken Minkema, Tiziana Rota, Daniel Scott Smith, and Patricia Tracy.

1. On this theme, see Nancy F. Cott, *Public Vows: A History of Marriage and the Nation* (Cambridge, Mass.: Harvard University Press, 2000).

2. See, for example, Edmund Morgan, *The Puritan Family: Religion and Domestic Relations in Seventeenth-Century New England* (New York: Harper & Row, 1966); and Kathryn Kish Sklar, *Catharine Beecher: A Study in American Domesticity* (New Haven, Conn.: Yale University Press, 1973).

3. See Philip J. Greven, *Four Generations: Population, Land, and Family in Colonial Andover, Massachusetts* (Ithaca, N.Y.: Cornell University Press, 1970); Nancy Folbre, "Patriarchy in Colonial New England," *Review of Radical Political Economics* 12 (1980): 4–13; Laurel Thatcher Ulrich, *Good Wives: Image and Reality in the Lives of Women in Northern New England, 1650–1750* (New York: Knopf, 1982); and Laurel Thatcher Ulrich, *A Midwife's Tale: The Life of Martha Ballard, Based on her Diary, 1785–1812* (New York: Knopf, 1990).

4. See Mary P. Ryan, *Cradle of the Middle Class: The Family in Oneida County, New York, 1790–1865* (New York: Cambridge University Press, 1981); and Lewis Perry, *Childhood, Marriage, and Reform: Henry Clarke Wright 1797–1870* (Chicago: University of Chicago Press, 1980).

5. Daniel Scott Smith and Michael S. Hindus, "Premarital Pregnancy in America, 1640–1971: An Overview and Interpretation," *Journal of Interdisciplinary History* 5 (Spring 1975): 537–70.

6. Daniel Scott Smith, "Population, Family and Society in Hingham, Massachusetts, 1635–1880" (Ph.D. diss., University of California, Berkeley, 1973), p. 247.

7. For Victorian sexual ideology, see Nancy F. Cott, "Passionlessness: An Interpretation of Victorian Sexual Ideology, 1790–1850," *Signs* 4 (1978–79): 219–36. For the sexual double standard, see Keith Thomas, "The Double Standard," *Journal of the History of Ideas* 20 (1959): 195–216. The demographic transition also included long-term declines in death rates. See Robert V. Wells, *Uncle Sam's Family: Issues in and Perspectives on American Demographic History* (Albany: State University of New York Press, 1985), pp. 5–8, 58, 104.

8. Smith and Hindus, "Premarital Pregnancy," 544. The authors support this conclusion by comparing the proportion of premarital pregnancies among couples in which the "bride's" father was of higher economic standing than the "groom's" father to the proportion among couples (like Elisha and Martha) in which the "bride's" father was of lower economic standing than the "groom's." They assumed that a smaller proportion of premarital pregnancies among the latter group might indicate the presence of concealed bastard births or of pregnancies not followed by marriage, but found that the proportion of premarital pregnancies was the same in both groups.

9. See, for example, Cathy N. Davidson, *Revolution and the Word: The Rise of the Novel in America* (New York: Oxford University Press, 1986).

10. Cornelia Hughes Dayton, *Women before the Bar: Gender, Law, and Society in Connecticut, 1639–1789* (Chapel Hill: University of North Carolina Press, 1995), pp. 157–230.

11. A good entry into the voluminous scholarly literature on Edwards is Patricia J. Tracy, *Jonathan Edwards, Pastor: Religion and Society in Eighteenth-Century Northampton* (New York: Hill and Wang, 1979). See also the eighteen-volume edition of *The Works of Jonathan Edwards* (New Haven, Conn.: Yale University Press, 1957–2000).

12. E. Francis Brown, *Joseph Hawley, Colonial Radical* (New York: Columbia University Press, 1931), p. 98.

13. For a useful collection of primary sources, see Richard L. Bushman, ed., *The Great Awakening: Documents on the Revival of Religion, 1740–1745* (Chapel Hill: University of North Carolina Press, 1969).

14. For the importance of oratory, see Sandra M. Gustafson, *Eloquence Is Power: Oratory and Performance in Early America* (Chapel Hill: University of North Carolina Press, 2000); and Jane Kamensky, *Governing the Tongue: The Politics of Speech in Early New England* (New York: Oxford University Press, 1997).

15. Samuel Hopkins, *The Life and Character of the Late Reverend, Learned and Pious Mr. Jonathan Edwards* (Boston, 1765), p. 52, quoted in Tracy, *Jonathan Edwards*, p. 83.

16. See Ruth H. Bloch, "Women, Love, and Virtue in the Thought of Edwards and Franklin," in Barbara B. Oberg and Harry S. Stout, eds., *Benjamin Franklin, Jonathan Edwards, and the Representation of American Culture* (New York: Oxford University Press, 1993), pp. 134–51; Amanda Porterfield, *Feminine Spirituality in America from Sarah Edwards to Martha Graham* (Philadelphia: Temple University Press, 1980), pp. 19–50; and Sandra M. Gustafson, "Jonathan Edwards and the Reconstruction of 'Feminine' Speech," *American Literary History* 6 (1994): 185–212.

17. Timothy Dwight, *Travels in New England and New York*, 4 Vols. (London, 1823), 1: 300, quoted in Brown, *Joseph Hawley*, p. 49.

18. Benjamin Colman, *The Faithful Ministers of Christ Mindful of their own Death. . . . upon the Death of the Learned and Venerable Solomon Stoddard* (Boston, 1729), quoted in Tracy, *Jonathan Edwards*, p. 19. See also Ralph J. Coffman, *Solomon Stoddard* (Boston: Twayne, 1978).

19. For Jonathan Edwards's childhood household, see Ola Elizabeth Winslow, *Jonathan Edwards, 1703–1758* (New York: Collier Books, 1961).

20. James Russell Trumbull, *History of Northampton, Massachusetts from its Settlement in 1654*, 2 Vols. (Northampton: Gazette Printing, 1902), 2: 79–82, quote 82.

21. Quoted in Brown, *Joseph Hawley*, p. 10.

22. Author's computations based on 1739 Northampton tax list. Northampton Town Papers, 5.71 Tax Assessors, Tax Valuation lists, 1739–1781, Microfilm, Forbes Library, Reel 146. Northampton Vital Records, Ms. Town Clerk's Office. Unpublished Vol. 3 of Northampton Genealogies 1640–1838, Forbes Library, Reel 21, Northampton.

23. Northampton Vital Records.

24. George E. Howard, *A History of Matrimonial Institution*, 2 Vols. (Chicago, 1904), 2: 193, counted illegitimacy cases from the court records of Middlesex County, Massachusetts, in 1764. Using his figures, Daniel Scott Smith estimated a rate between 4.6 and 5.6 illegitimate births per 1,000 unmarried women, aged 15–44. Smith, "A Survey of Illegitimacy and Premarital Pregnancy in American History" in Peter Laslett and Karla Oosterveen, eds., *Bastardy and Its Comparative History: Studies in the History of Illegitimacy and Marital Nonconformism in Britain, France, Germany, Sweden, North America, Jamaica, and Japan* (Cambridge, Mass.: Harvard University Press, 1980). See also Cissie Fairchilds, "Female Sexual Attitudes and the Rise of Illegitimacy: A Case Study," *Journal of Interdisciplinary History* 3 (1977–1978): 627–67; Peter Laslett, "The Bastardy Prone Sub-Society," in Laslett, *et al.*, eds., *Bastardy and its Comparative History* pp. 217–46; Laurel Ulrich, "Psalm-tunes, Periwigs, and Bastards: Ministerial Authority in Early Eighteenth Century Durham," *Historical New Hampshire* 36 (1981): 255–79; Cornelia Hughes Dayton, "Taking the Trade: Abortions and Gender Relations in an Eighteenth-Century New England Village," *William and Mary Quarterly*, 3rd Ser. 48 (1991): 19–49.

25. Joseph Hawley to Elisha Hawley, December 23, 1748, "Letters and Papers of Major Joseph Hawley" (henceforth LPJH), ms. 2 Vols., New York Public Library, 1: 12. (Available on microfilm, Forbes Library, Northampton.) See also Bruce C. Daniels, "Money-Value Definitions of Economic Classes in Colonial Connecticut, 1700–1776," *Histoire Sociale—Social History* 7 (1974): 346–52; and Mark Valeri, "The Economic Thought of Jonathan Edwards," *Church History* 60 (March 1991): 37–54.

26. LPJH, May 17, 1748, Vol. I, 7 (Civil Agreement); Joseph to Elisha, December 23, 1748; and LPJH, Vol. I, 8 (Report of Council of Ministers, June 29, 1749).

27. Jonathan Edwards to Sarah Pierpont Edwards, Northampton, June 22, 1748, in Harry S. Stout, General Editor, *The Works of Jonathan Edwards*, Vol. 16, George Claghorn, ed., *Jonathan Edwards: Letters and Personal Writings* (New Haven, Conn.: Yale University Press, 1998), p. 247.

28. Tracy, *Jonathan Edwards*, pp. 71–89.

29. Notes by JE, quoted in Tracy, *Jonathan Edwards*, p. 162. See also Thomas H. Johnson, "Jonathan Edwards and the 'Young Folks' Bible,'" *New England Quarterly* 5 (1932): 37–54; and Ava Chamberlain, "Bad Books and Bad Boys: The Transformation of Gender in 18th-Century Northampton," paper read at "Jonathan Edwards in Historical Memory" Conference, Coral Gables, Florida, March 2000. For Edwards's own fascination with the female body, see Ava Chamberlain, "The Immaculate Ovum: Jonathan Edwards and the Construction of the Female Body," *William and Mary Quarterly* 57 (2000): 289–322.

30. Hopkins, *Life and Character of . . . Edwards*, pp. 53–55, quoted in Tracy, *Jonathan Edwards*, p. 162.

31. Joseph Hawley to Elisha Hawley, February 16, 1748, LPJH, I, 6.

32. LPJH, May 17, 1748, Vol. I, 7.

33. The *Oxford English Dictionary* tells us that "spinster" had by 1650 changed from an occupational appendage for *some* women regardless of marital status, to a legal term embracing "all unmarried women from the viscount's daughter downward." It was not until the 19th century that "spinster" came primarily to mean an *older* woman who has never married or an "old maid."

34. LPJH, May 17, 1748, Vol. I, 7.

35. Church Records, First Church of Christ, Northampton, microfilm, Forbes Library, Northampton. For established church discipline and church–state relations, see David D. Hall, *The Faithful Shepherd: A History of the New England Ministry in the Seventeenth Century* (Chapel Hill: University of North Carolina Press, 1972), 133–36.

36. Joseph to Elisha, December 23, 1748.

37. The Cambridge Platform (Evans microfilm), Chapter X, p. 14, paragraph 11: "Power of judgement in matters of Censor . . . remaineth with the Brotherhood."

38. Sereno Edwards Dwight, *The Life of President Edwards* (New York: Carvill, 1830), p. 299.

39. LPJH, Vol. I, 8.

40. *The Bible,* King James Version, Deuteronomy 22:28–29.

41. Jonathan Edwards, Some Reasons briefly hinted at, why Those Rules Exod. 22. 16. & Deut 22. 28, 29. Relating to the Obligation of a man to marry a virgin that He had humbled, ought to be esteemed, as to the substance of them, as moral & of perpetual Obligation, with hints of Answers to Objections. "Some Reasons," Edwards Papers, Folder "No Date" #2, item 15, Andover Newton Theological School, Newton Center, Massachusetts. Emphasis in original.

42. [Memoranda on Hawley/Root Case], Edwards Papers, Folder "No Date" # 1, item 11, Andover Newton Theological School.

43. Memoranda on Hawley/Root Case

44. Joseph Hawley to Martha Root, August 8, 1750, LPJH, Vol. I, 9.

45. LPJH, Vol. I, 8.

46. LPJH, Vol. I, 8.

47. Other conflicts with his parishioners that contributed to Edwards's firing are discussed in Tracy, *Jonathan Edwards,* pp. 171–96; and David D. Hall, ed., *Jonathan Edwards: Ecclesiastical Writings* (New Haven, Conn.: Yale University Press, 1994), pp. 2–4, 17–18, 52, 55, 60, 77–79.

48. Joseph Hawley to Rev. David Hall of Sutton, Northampton, May 9, 1760, quoted in Dwight, *President Edwards,* pp. 423–24.

49. Jonathan Edwards to Joseph Hawley, Stockbridge, November 18, 1754, in Claghorn, *Letters and Personal Writings,* p. 650.

50. Author's computations based on Northampton Tax Valuation list, 1739.

51. Trumbull, *History of Northampton,* 1: 82.

52. See Tracy, *Jonathan Edwards,* pp. 180–84.

53. Brown, *Joseph Hawley,* p. 180.

54. See Mary C. Clune, "Joseph Hawley's Criticism of the Constitution of Massachusetts," *Smith College Studies in History* 3 (October 1917): 32–49. Quote from William G. McLoughlin, *New England Dissent, 1630–1833: The Baptists and the Separation of Church and State,* 2 Vols. (Cambridge, Mass: Harvard University Press, 1971), 1: 607–608.

55. Hawley to Massachusetts Senate, October 28, 1780, quoted in Brown, *Joseph Hawley,* p. 183.

56. Carroll Smith-Rosenberg, "Beauty, the Beast and the Militant Woman: A Case Study in Sex Roles and Social Stress in Jacksonian America," in this volume; Barbara Meil Hobson, *Uneasy Virtue, The Politics of Prostitution and the American Reform Tradition* (New York: Basic Books, 1987), pp. 66–70; and Daniel Wright, "What Was the Appeal of Moral Reform to Antebellum Northern Women?" in *Women and Social Movements in the U.S., 1820–1940,* at http://womhist.binghamton.edu.

6

"Daughters of Liberty": Religious Women in Revolutionary New England

Laurel Thatcher Ulrich

Religious practices in the late eighteenth-century English colonies prepared colonial women, in Laurel Thatcher Ulrich's view, to become active contributors to the American Revolution. Ulrich demonstrates the crucial role of ministers and religious culture in the emergence of spinning meetings in the decade before the outbreak of the Revolution. She illuminates the significance of the organized activity of women within their churches as a factor supporting the Revolutionary cause.

Women's historians working in the Revolutionary period have shown little interest in religion. This is a striking omission given the importance of religion not only in the larger history of American women but in the recent history of the American Revolution. Intellectual, political, social, and even military histories of the period emphasize religious themes, yet the major works in women's history have interpreted the Revolution almost exclusively in secular terms.

For New England this approach is particularly misleading. Mary Beth Norton's assertion that before the war "no one, male or female, wrote or thought about the possibility that women might affect the wider secular society through their individual or collective behavior" makes sense only if one excludes religious discourse.[1] For New England that is impossible to do. A providential view of history obliterated the distinction between secular and religious acts, making it possible for any believer, female or male, to affect the larger society. As Harry S. Stout has explained it, "Covenanted peoples like those of ancient Israel and New England were the hub around which sacred (that is, real) history revolved. Such people might be ignored or reviled by the world and figure insignificantly in the great empires of profane history, but viewed through the sacred lens of providential history they were seen as God's special instruments entrusted with the task of preparing the way for messianic deliverance."[2] . . .

Excerpted from "Daughters of Liberty": Religious Women in Revolutionary New England, by Laurel Thatcher Ulrich in *Women in the Age of the American Revolution*, Ronald Hoffman and Peter J. Albert, eds. (Charlottesville: Published for the United States Capitol Historical Society by the University Press of Virginia, 1989), pp. 211–15, 217–28, 243. Used by permission of the author and the publisher.

This essay will argue that a providential interpretation of history framed the contributions of New England women during the Revolutionary era, that the weekly sermons through which most people in the region interpreted political events included rather than excluded women, and that far from representing an ideological discontinuity in women's lives the Revolution enlarged and reaffirmed the terms of public participation that had prevailed during the intercolonial wars. It will proceed through the reinterpretation of two historical remnants from the period, the first a set of newspaper stories from the 1760s describing spinning meetings ostensibly organized by New England's "Daugh-

The *E S S E X* GAZETTE.

Containing the freſheſt Advices,   *both foreign and domeſtic.*

VOL. I.   NUMB. 44.

OMNE TULIT PUNCTUM,   QUI MISCUIT UTILE DULCI. Hoy.

From TUESDAY, *May* 23, to TUESDAY, *May* 30, 1769.

A gentleman of New-Port [R.I.] writes--- " . . . being at the Sign of the Pitt's Head in this Town, on Tuesday last, [I] was extremely pleased by having Admittance into the Company of Eleven of the Daughters of Liberty, Ladies of Character, and Lovers of British Freedom, and Industry; each being laudably employed . . . on . . . a Spinning Wheel. . . . I was still more pleased with the Ladies Company, (when by Inquiry) I had learnt more of their Love of Liberty, and strict Attachment to their Country's Welfare, and of their Determination of preserving in such laudable Exercise and good Oeconomy, as is a Credit to their fair Sex, and an Honour to America.

For I found that, as these Daughters of Liberty delight in each other's Company, they had agreed to make circular Visits to each of their Houses, and in order to excite Emulation in serving their Country, promoting Temperance and Industry, had determined to convert each Visit into a spinning Match, and to have no Entertainments but what is the Produce of their own Country; and to appear as much as possible clothed with our own Manufactures, and that more especially which is the Effects of their own Labour--The aforesaid Ladies spun between 6 o'Clock in the Morning, and 6 o'Clock in the Evening, 37 skeins and 15 Threads which, upon an Average make three Skeins five Knots and five Threads."

Contemporary Account, May 1769, of "Daughters of Liberty"

ters of Liberty," the second a woodcut of a female soldier published in 1779 on a broadside attributed to "a Daughter of Liberty, Living in Marblehead."[3]

At first glance both items fit well with prevailing secular interpretations. Most historians agree that the conflict with Britain politicized the household, giving ordinary domestic tasks a significance they had not had before, and that the war also pulled women beyond their traditional roles, inviting them to assume male duties, if not on the battlefield then at home on the farm. In this view the spinning meetings are a visible manifestation of a much larger politicization of private duties, the female soldier a flamboyant emblem of a widespread (though temporary) bending of gender roles. Thus, by 1775 a Connecticut farm girl could record in her diary "that she had carded all day, then spun ten knots of wool in the evening, '& felt Nationally into the bargain,'" while a New Hampshire woman, during her husband's second term in Congress, could begin writing of "our farming business" rather than "your farming business."[4]

This paper will attempt to uncover another layer of interpretation, arguing that the spinning meetings were as much artifacts of Congregationalism as of revolution. . . . This is not to argue that women's culture in early New England was merely an extension of Congregational theology. Beneath the . . . celebratory words of Congregational ministers lay a female world sustained by neighborliness, personal piety, and petty trade. The spinning bees were a visible but by no means comprehensive manifestation of that world. . . . Religious women helped to shape their own identities through support of Congregational churches. They used the language of war to question the male culture that it nourished, overcoming their own dependence to instruct and chasten their neighbors.

Most historians have assumed that the first of the pre-Revolutionary spinning meetings was the model for all the others. In Providence, on March 4, 1766, "eighteen daughters of liberty, young ladies of good reputation," met at the house of Dr. Ephraim Bowen to spin, to dine without the pleasure of tea, and to declare as a body that the Stamp Act was unconstitutional, that they would purchase no more British manufactures until it was repealed, and that they would spurn any suitor who refused to oppose it.[5] This was obviously a self-conscious political demonstration by young ladies related to whig leaders in Rhode Island—but it was atypical.

I have been able to document forty-six spinning meetings held between 1768 and 1770, thirty in 1769 alone. . . . Some of these were clearly spinning *matches,* that is, contests with a few women spinning a great deal of yarn, but most were also spinning *demonstrations,* public events attracting large numbers of spectators, as well as spinning *bees,* work parties to benefit a single household—usually that of the local minister. In fact, thirty-one of the forty-six meetings were held in ministers' houses. When we consider the number of participants listed in the various accounts, the religious setting becomes even more pronounced. Of the 1,644 women known to have attended spinning meetings in this two-year period, 1,539 (94 percent) gathered at a minister's house.

At one level this is simply further evidence of the political involvement of the New England clergy. Spinning meetings can now be added to election sermons in the political arsenal of the "black regiment." But such an explanation is too simple. Although patriotism was an important theme in many accounts, in only six of the forty-six meetings were spinners described as "Daughters of Liberty." "Young women" was the usual designation, though terms like "Daughters of Industry," "the fair sex," and even "noble-hearted Nymphs" were occasionally used.[6] Although reports from Roxbury and Chebacco alluded to political events, referring to "intolerable Burdens now Laid upon us" and to the necessity of recovering "our rights, properties and privileges," the article from Harpswell cautioned that "the Ladies are impressed with such a nice Sense of their Liberties derived from their Maker, as not to be very fond of the tyrannic Restraints or the scheming Partisans of any Party," closing with a sentiment that seemed to imply that if politicians would behave more like women, the problems could soon be solved: "That People can never be ruined who thrive by their Losses, and conquer by being conquered."[7]

Descriptions of refreshments show a similar range of commitment. A number of accounts followed the lead of the Providence demonstration by emphasizing the use of tea substitutes, though few communities were quite so devoted to American produce as Berwick, Maine, where the spinners, "as true Daughters of Liberty . . . made their Breakfast on Rye coffee, and their Dinner on that sort of Venison call'd Bear," the correspondent adding that "among the Provisions sent on the occasion was a Carrot, which after it was trim'd weighed two Pounds and a half."[8] The correspondent from Beverly, on the other hand, insisted that "the young Gentlewomen were not moved in the least by political Principles . . . yet they are cordial Lovers of Liberty, particularly of the Liberty of drinking Tea with their Bread and Butter, to which their Pastor consents."[9] The various plays on the word *liberty* suggest the complexity of the motives involved.

Yet these were obviously highly contrived and carefully orchestrated public events. The size and pageantry of most meetings contrasts with the more spontaneous (and sometimes raucous) character of the huskings, barn raisings, and quiltings that were traditional forms of collective work in the New England countryside. Spinning is not in fact a particularly appropriate candidate for a large work party. Consider the nature of the craft. Unlike barn raising, spinning was easily accomplished alone, nor was there a season for spinning as for husking. Also consider the shape and size of the implements involved. While a dozen women might comfortably fit around a quilt, few houses in the New England countryside could accommodate fifty-five women with thirty-four wheels, as did the minister's house in Brookfield in August 1769. The average number of participants in the spinning meetings was forty-seven, though there were ninety-two women in Ezra Stiles's house in Newport in the spring of 1770.[10]

The form of the meetings seems to have derived from a public demonstration held in Boston in August 1753. This event had nothing to do with the Revolution; in fact, its sponsors, the gentlemen of the United Society for Manufactures and Importation, were prerogative men. Their particular intention was to publicize the opening of a spinning factory; their broader intent was to encourage textile production as a form of poor relief, not only in Boston but in outlying towns. The day began with a sermon in the Old South Meeting House, followed by a spinning match in the afternoon with 300 spinners, some as young as seven years old, working together on the common. There was also a musical program and a parade.[11]

The spinning factory failed, as Gary B. Nash has shown us; poor women preferred to spin at home (or for other women) rather than in a workhouse.[12] Yet several key elements of the 1753 demonstration—the sermon, the musical accompaniment, the assembly of spinners on the green, and even, in simplified form, the procession—reappeared in the 1760s in the spinning bees held at ministers' houses. There were sermons at Gloucester, Chebacco, Linebrook, Newburyport, Braintree, and Rowley, spinning on the green at Dorchester and Brookfield, a procession at Braintree, and a program of anthems at Rowley. At Bridgewater the women walked in parade to the meeting house where they heard a discourse on Dorcas from Acts 9:36 followed by a song composed in their honor.[13]

The larger objectives of the 1753 event were as appropriate in New England in the 1760s as in the decade before. It is not accidental that most of the spinning meetings occurred in towns that had either outgrown their agricultural base or had never been farming communities at all. In fact, the depth of commitment to textile production implied in the newspaper accounts, the meticulous measuring of knots and skeins, the obvious presence not only of appropriate equipment but also of skilled spinners, suggests that by 1769 textile production had *already* become a female counterpart to the boatbuilding, shoemaking, and maritime crafts that were central to subsistence in these towns.[14] At one level, then, the spinning meetings simply ratified long-standing economic strategies. As in 1753, such meetings simultaneously promoted commonplace assumptions about the responsibility of a good society to cultivate industry among its populace and upheld biblical prescriptions for appropriate feminine behavior. Such a meshing of secular and religious values had a long history in England and America. The frontispiece of Thomas Firmin's seventeenth-century English tract "Some Proposals for the Imployment of the Poor," an early plea for a spinning factory, used the very biblical quotation that New England ministers enlarged upon in many spinning sermons.[15]

The spinning meetings fit well with other aspects of the religious culture of the mid-eighteenth century—the singing schools, for example, or the young men's and young women's meetings that became so important during the Great Awakening (the emphasis in the newspaper accounts on the youth of the spinners is striking). The meetings can also be seen as a form of what might be called "domesticated spirituality," a religious sensibility manifested in bed curtains with hymns embroidered around the valance or perky samplers giving cheerful renditions of the primal drama in Eden.[16] Spinning meetings bonded domesticity and piety, giving material form to women's religious commitments and at the same time sacralizing daily work.

Since participants contributed both fiber and labor, the meetings were also a visible manifestation of benevolence. This aspect of the meetings is well described in the diary of Ezra Stiles of Newport, who benefited from five spinning meetings between 1769 and 1775. On April 26, 1769, he wrote: "Spinning Match at my House, thirty-seven Wheels; the Women bro't their flax—& spun ninety-four fifteen-knotted skeins. . . . They made us a present of the whole. The Spinners were two Quakers, six Baptists, twenty-nine of my own Society. There were beside fourteen Reelers, &c. . . . We dined sixty persons. My p'ple sent in 4 lb Tea, 9 lb Coffee, Loaf Sugar, above 3 qrs. veal, 1 1/2 doz. Wine, Gammons, Flour, Bread, Rice, &c., &c., &c., to Amount of 150. Old Tenor, or about twenty Dollars: of which we spent about one-half. In the course of the day, the Spinners were visited by I judge six hundred Spectators."[17]

Obviously this was more than a denominational meeting. It was a contest, a public demonstration, a party—and for the members of Stiles's society an opportunity for generosity through contributions of food as well as flax. A minister may have inspired such an event, but he could hardly have organized it since he and his family were the recipients of the yarn. What we have here, I think, is an early form of women's religious or charitable activity, a precursor of the nineteenth-century missionary or educational societies that raised money or sewed shirts for traveling ministers or divinity students.

In some communities the spinning meetings were a creative response by women to the economic stress of their ministers. Women did not control taxes, but they did control their own labor and at least some portion of the raw materials with which they worked. The meetings may also have been a direct answer to particular need. The women who came to Stiles's house, including the Baptists and Quakers, were probably paying neighborly debts to Elizabeth Stiles, who was revered in her community for her medical skills as well as for her benevolence, and who was in declining health during this period.[18] Similar concerns were important in other towns. When the spinning bee was held in Chebacco, John Cleaveland was a new widower with seven children between the ages of six and twenty. The wives of Amos Adams of Roxbury and John Chipman of Beverly died in 1769; Samuel Eaton of Harpswell, whose fair followers presented him with wool for suit, was not yet married.[19]

Women in Congregational churches had an eminent but equivocal position; they predominated among the covenanted members who made up an inner elite in each congregation, but unlike Baptist or Quaker women they neither voted nor spoke in public. Because characteristic forms of participation were indirect, their activities are extraordinarily difficult to document. This is one reason why the spinning accounts are so interesting. Regardless of what they tell us about women's political consciousness, they confirm other evidence about the organizational activity of religious women in this period. Female "praying societies" existed in Boston and probably in other towns by the end of the seventeenth century, a period in which Cotton Mather first discussed the disproportion of women among communicants in local churches. By the pre-Revolutionary decades women made up 67 percent of new members in eastern Massachusetts churches.[20] In discussing this process of "feminization," historians have given too much attention to ministers and not enough to the efforts of devout women who, working around the edges of formal organization, managed to evangelize their sisters and sometimes influence their ministers as well.

The most visible of these leaders was Sarah Osborn of Newport who, in the 1760s, led a revival in her town without deviating from the outward form of the "private" association. By 1766, as Barbara E. Lacey has shown, there were one or more meetings at the Osborn house every evening of the week except Saturday: "a society of young men; a society of Baptist brethren; the female society; a society of Congregational brethren; the black society; groups of children; and number of Baptist women 'with whom we have a sweet harmony.'" Osborn claimed that the meetings were simple affairs, "Nothing more attempted than reading, singing, prayers perform'd by my Husband or any christian friend . . . and a plain familiar conversing about the things that belong to their everlasting peace," but when her church was bitterly divided over the selection of a pastor it was "the Sorority of her Meeting," according to Ezra Stiles, that determined the outcome.[21]

The activities of other praying women were quieter but no less earnest. In the 1760s Hannah Winslow of Boston was corresponding with Eleazar Wheelock on behalf of a "Religious Society of Women" interested in his Indian Charity School at Lebanon, Connecticut. Like Sarah Osborn, these women were involved in finding a pastor "after Gods own Heart" for their "Bereaved Church," and like Osborn they were interested in racial minorities. While she was praying with Newport blacks, they were helping support Wheelock's Indian school, from time to time sending "a few Articles . . . pact up in A Cask." Wheelock's papers contain letters from ordinary as well as eminent women, from Esther Wright of Lebanon, who offered three good sheep for the use of their school as well as from Lady Mary Pepperrell of Kittery, Maine, the wife of the hero of Louisbourg.[22]

The spinning meetings were a broader manifestation of that kind of spiritual energy and charitable intent. In the coastal towns of Essex County, Massachusetts, they followed within a couple of years a religious revival in which young women had taken a central part. According to John Cleaveland of Chebacco, the revival began at a "Conference Meeting" attended by "a

considerable Number of the Youth, chiefly Females." The first of the converts, a young woman, had been brought "under great Concern" through private conversations with her mother. In a seven- or eight-month period,
Cleaveland reported, ninety persons were added to his church, two-thirds of
them female. The revival spread to other towns as ministers exchanged pul-
pits and converts testified to the redeeming work. Samuel Chandler of
Gloucester, Jedidiah Jewett of Rowley, George Leslie of Linebrook, and
Jonathan Parsons of Newburyport, all of whom were later involved in spinning meetings, preached in Cleaveland's church.[23]

Mary Beth Norton has suggested that the spinning meetings were "ideological showcases; they were intended to convince American women that they
could render essential contributions to the struggle against Britain."[24] Certainly that is the way they were presented in the Boston papers. But if an
event like Pope's Day could mean different things to children, to radical
whigs, and to street leaders like Ebenezer MacIntosh, surely a spinning bee
might mean different things to the editor of the *Boston Evening Post,* to the
ministers who seem to have provided most of the newspaper stories, and to
the women who gathered to spin.

The range of meanings in these events is beautifully presented in the
words of a song performed in Bridgewater, at one of the more explicitly patriotic meetings. The poet, who was probably the Reverend Mr. Porter, began
with an obvious allusion to the woman of Proverbs whose price was above ru-
bies, then went on to the virtues of nonimportation:

> Foreign productions she rejects
> With nobleness of Mind,
> For Home commodities, to which
> She's prudently inclin'd.

He then returned to the immediate objective of the spinning match,
the support of the ministry, ending with more generated praise of feminine
charity:

> She works, she lends, she gives away
> The labors of her Hand.
> The priest, the poor, the people all,
> Do find in her the Friend.
> She cloaths herself and family,
> And all the Sons of need;
> Were all thus virtuous, soon we'd find
> Our Land from Slav'ry free'd.[25]

Look again at the last two lines of the song: "Were all thus virtuous,
soon we'd find/Our Land from Slav'ry free'd." For the ardent supporter of

the boycotts, those words probably meant, "If all the women of New England refused to purchase English products, Parliament would be forced to relent." But in religious terms, they conveyed a much more traditional message: "If more New Englanders would cultivate Christian virtues and uphold the churches and their neighbors, God would give us peace and prosperity in the land."

The importance of that dual message becomes more apparent when we compare accounts of the spinning demonstrations with accounts of concurrent activities of the Sons of Liberty. On August 14, 1769, Boston's Sons of Liberty celebrated the anniversary of the first Stamp Act demonstrations by meeting at the Liberty Tree in South Boston, where "fourteen Toasts were drunk; After which they proceeded in Carriages to Mr. Robinson's at the Sign of Liberty-Tree in Dorchester; where three large Piggs barbicued and a Variety of other Provision were prepared for dinner. . . . After dinner 45 patriotic Toasts were drank, and the Company spent the afternoon in social Mirth," returning to Boston about six, "the Cavalcade" passing "in Procession thro' the Main Street." Considering the riots that followed the original Stamp Act demonstrations, the author was probably wise to add, "The whole was conducted with the greatest Decency and good Order."[26]

That same month many papers carried a story of a spinning bee at Brookfield. The ladies assembled at their minister's house at 5 A.M., spinning until evening when they went out of the house into the front yard and continued to work until seven. "The young lady that excelled at the linen wheel, spun 70 knots," the minister reported, while "among the matrons there was one, who did the morning work of a large family, made her cheese, etc. and then rode more than two miles, and carried her own wheel, and sat down to spin at nine in the morning, and by seven in the evening spun 53 knots, and went home to milking."[27]

Ideological showcase indeed! While New England's Sons of Liberty indulged in rum, rhetoric, and roast pig, her Daughters worked from sunup to sundown to prove their commitment to "the cause of liberty and industry." While the contrasting accounts surely illustrate a differing standard of male and female behavior, they also suggest a potential conflict within the religious culture itself between the fear of tyranny and the dangers of anarchy. The jubilant toast drinking of the Sons of Liberty easily lent itself to parody, as in an *Essex Gazette* story that reported on the activities of certain "young gentlemen" of New Haven who in October 1769 drank 45 glasses, became 45 degrees extreme drunk by 45 after midnight, and then went to the college yard where they bawled in concert 45 times for 45 minutes.[28] The conclusion is inescapable that certain New England ministers eagerly embraced the Daughters of Liberty because they could not unequivocally defend her Sons. In publicizing the spinning bees, they promoted a form of political resistance built upon sacrifice, self-discipline, and personal piety rather than on street action, drinking, and flamboyant self-assertion.

During the Stamp Act crisis, Ezra Stiles was horrified when American Anglicans began accusing New England Congregationalists of fomenting riots. "I have uniformly persisted from the beginning to this Time in declaring for myself my own Resolution of not opposing this or any other Act of Parliament however grievous," he wrote Benjamin Franklin.[29] Amos Adams, another of the spinning ministers, rejoiced in the repeal of the Stamp Act, though he did not give the credit to political demonstrations but to God acting on the hearts of men. In the midst of the new crisis he urged patience, obedience, and moral reformation. "Perhaps by the suppression of extravagance, and the improvement of trades and manufactures; by the practice of frugality and industry, what was designed to bring us to a more absolute dependence may turn out, in its consequences, to be a blessing."[30]

Thus there is less contradiction than we might suppose between John Chipman's assertion that "the young women were not moved in the least by political principles" and John Cleaveland's claim that "women might recover to this country the full and free enjoyment of all our rights, properties and privileges (which is more than the men have been able to do): And so have the honour of building not only for their own, but the houses of many thousands, and, perhaps, prevent the ruin of the whole British Empire." Perhaps earlier studies had it backwards. The spinning bees were an attempt not so much to politicize the household as to feminize the body politic, to build public policy upon the example of New England's daughters.

. . . the evidence of the spinning bees documents the existence in coastal New England of organized religious and charitable activity by women in the years before the war . . . shows how women drew status and identity from religious values, subordinating the military and domestic struggle to the great war against Satan . . . [and] express[ing] an ongoing and unresolved tension between the ancient liberties (and disciplines) of Christian piety and the new liberties (and excesses) of revolution.

NOTES

1. Mary Beth Norton, *Liberty's Daughters: The Revolutionary Experience of American Women, 1750–1800* (Boston, 1980), p. 297. Norton's book includes a sympathetic discussion of Sarah Osborn, the Newport religious leader, but fails to connect her to her own period, suggesting that Osborn was an isolated figure who "helped to blaze the trail that generations of pious nineteenth-century American women were to follow" (pp. 126–32). Linda Kerber has examined similar material, but her interest is primarily secular rather than religious. Arguing that Revolutionary women operated in an ideological vacuum, she failed to note the *biblical* origins of the models for female patriotism used in the period and in early nineteenth-century defenses of female public activity (*Women of the Republic: Intellect and Ideology in Revolutionary America* [Chapel Hill, 1980], pp. 102–3, 112). Ruth H. Bloch's recent effort to trace the sources of republican womanhood in evangelical Protestantism, Scottish moral philosophy, and literary sentimentalism is better balanced yet confusing in its use of the New England sources ("The Gendered Meanings of Virtue in Revolutionary America," *Signs* 13 [1987]:37–58).

2. Harry S. Stout, *The New England Soul: Preaching and Religious Culture in Colonial New England* (New York, 1986), p. 7. For a good recent summary of the literature on religion and the

Revolution, see Melvin B. Endy, Jr., "Just War, Holy War, and Millennialism in Revolutionary America," *William and Mary Quarterly,* 3d ser. 42 (1985):3–25.

3. The woodcut appears in Alfred F. Young, ed., *The American Revolution: Explorations in the History of American Radicalism* (De Kalb, Ill., 1976), p. 383, Linda K. Kerber, *Women of the Republic: Intellect and Ideology in Revolutionary America* (Chapel Hill, 1980), p. 107, and on the cover of Linda Grant DePauw and Conover Hunt, *"Remember the Ladies": Women in America, 1750–1815* (New York, 1976). The full broadside is reproduced in DePauw and Hunt, *"Remember the Ladies,"* p. 94.

4. Norton, *Liberty's Daughters,* pp. 169, 219. Also see Kerber, *Women of the Republic,* pp. 39, 41, and, for a dissenting view, Joan Hoff-Wilson, "The Illusion of Change: Women and the American Revolution," in Young, ed., *American Revolution,* pp. 385–415.

5. *Providence Gazette,* Mar. 12, 1766. In 1758 Ephraim Bowen was on a committee to build a public market and in 1770 was one of the Providence leaders appointed to visit merchants who had allegedly violated the non-importation agreement (William R. Staples, *Annals of the Town of Providence* [Providence, 1843], pp. 201, 226).

6. Three of the six were in ministers' houses (Sept. 4, 1769, in Providence; Oct. 16, 1769, in Berwick; and Nov. 27, 1769, in Pomfret) and three in other private homes (May 1, 1769, in Newport and May 2, 1769, in Jamestown, in addition to the 1766 match in Providence). Four of these matches were in Rhode Island, one in Maine, and one in Connecticut.

7. *Boston Evening Post,* Oct. 10, 1768; *Essex Gazette,* June 6, 1769; *Boston Evening Post,* Nov. 6, 1769.

8. *New Hampshire Gazette,* Oct. 16, 1769.

9. *Boston Evening Post,* June 9, 1769.

10. *Providence Gazette,* Aug. 6, 1769; Franklin B. Dexter, ed., *The Literary Diary of Ezra Stiles,* 2 vols. (New York, 1901), 1:53 ("Afternoon seventy wheels going at the same Time for part of the time").

11. *Boston Gazette,* Aug. 14, 1753. Rolla Tryon, *Household Manufactures in the United States, 1640–1860* (1917; reprint ed., New York, 1966), p. 86, discusses this spinning bee. Tryon believes there was another held in Boston in 1721. My reading of his source (Samuel G. Drake, *History and Antiquities of Boston* [Boston, 1856], p. 561) suggests that he and Drake have both misattributed a description of the 1753 event to 1721.

12. Gary B. Nash, "The Failure of Female Factory Labor in Colonial Boston," *Labor History* 20 (1979):165–88. Nash maintains that "the public spinning exhibition and the attempt to induce lower-class women to spin by using upper-class daughters as examples . . . were taken straight from Richard Cox's description of his Irish linen experiment" (p. 179, n. 29; the reference is to *A Letter from Sir Richard Cox* [Boston, 1750]). I see less similarity in the exhibition itself, though I agree that the general strategy was the same. Spinning demonstrations were an old idea in textile-producing areas of England. See, for example, E. Lipson, *The History of the Woollen and Worsted Industries* (1921; reprint ed., London, 1965), pp. 62–63.

13. *Essex Gazette,* Nov. 22, 1763, June 6 and Aug. 15, 1769; *Boston Gazette,* May 9, 1768; *Boston Evening Post,* Oct. 30, July 3, June 12, Sept. 11, 1769; *Providence Gazette,* Aug. 6, 1769.

14. The nature of female participation in the prewar economy is unknown, though there are interesting leads in James A. Henretta, "The War for Independence and American Economic Development," in Ronald Hoffman, John J. McCusker, Russell R. Menard, and Peter J. Albert, eds., *The Economy of Early America: The Revolutionary Period, 1763–1790* (Charlottesville, 1988), and in Elaine F. Crane, "When More Means Less: Women and Work in Colonial American Seaports" (Paper presented at the Sixth Berkshire Conference on the History of Women, Smith College, June 1984). In Newport, Aaron Lopez was selling products made by local artisans, including women, as early as 1757. In the 1770s, according to Stanley F. Chyet, "his records showed some thirty Newporters, mostly women, producing cloth and garments for him from raw material which he furnished" (*Lopez of Newport: Colonial American Merchant Prince* [Detroit, 1970], p. 130). This question needs careful study, though current evidence suggests that most textile production remained outside the mercantile economy.

15. Thomas Firmin, *Some Proposals for the Imployment of the Poor, And for the Prevention of Idleness and the Consequence Thereof, Begging, In a Letter to a Friend* (London, 1681). This "Letter" is a precursor to the one by Cox (see n. 12, above), who also used Prov. 31 on his title page. Firmin urged Englishmen to learn the "Dutch trick" of letting poor children earn their own keep. Favorite texts for spinning bee sermons included, in addition to Prov. 31, Exod. 35:25 ("the women

that were wise hearted did spin"), Rom. 12:11 ("Not slothful in business; fervent in spirit; serving the Lord"), Acts 9:39 ("the coats and garments which Dorcas made"), Prov. 6:6–8 ("Go to the ant thou sluggard"), and Prov. 14:1 ("Every wise woman buildeth her house").

16. Ulrich, *Good Wives,* pp. 113–17.

17. Dexter, ed., *Diary of Stiles,* pp. 8–9.

18. Ibid., pp. 563–65.

19. Christopher M. Jedrey, *The World of John Cleaveland: Family and Community—Eighteenth-Century New England* (New York, 1979), p. 105; Clifford K. Shipton, *Biographical Sketches of Those Who Attended Harvard College in the Classes 1751–1755,* Sibley's Harvard Graduates, vol. 13 (Boston, 1965), pp. 178–86; *Essex Gazette,* July 11, 1769; George Augustus Wheeler and Henry Warren Wheeler, *History of Brunswick, Topsham, and Harpswell, Maine* (Somersworth, 1974), p. 736. Samuel Chandler's wife may have been mentally ill (Clifford K. Shipton, *Biographical Sketches of Those Who Attended Harvard College in Classes 1731–1735,* Sibley's Harvard Graduates, vol. 9 [Boston, 1956], p. 488).

20. On women's meetings, see Mary Maples Dunn, "Saints and Sisters: Congregational and Quaker Women in the Early Colonial Period," *American Quarterly* 30 (1978):582–601; Charles E. Hambrick-Stowe, *The Practice of Piety* (Chapel Hill, 1982), pp. 140–41; Cotton Mather, *Awakening Thoughts on the Sleep of Death* (Boston, 1712), p. vii, and idem, *Parentalia* (Boston, 1715), p. 32; Shiels, "Feminization of Congregationalism," p. 62. Records for three "spinning ministers," John Cleaveland, Jeremy Belknap, and Ezra Stiles, confirm the broader point. Jedrey, *World of Cleaveland,* p. 116; *Dover Historical Collections* 1 (1894):206–11; Dexter, ed., *Diary of Stiles,* pp. 28, 82. In Stiles's church, meetings of members were often held in Sisters' homes, but only males voted (Dexter, ed., *Diary of Stiles,* pp. 53, 58, 91, 145).

21. Norton, *Liberty's Daughters,* pp. 129–33, and Barbara E. Lacey, "The Bonds of Friendship: The Rev. Joseph Fish and Sarah Osborn, 1743–1779" (Paper presented at the fall meeting of the New England Historical Society, Roger Williams College, October 1983).

22. Papers of Eleazar Wheelock, microfilm, Dartmouth College Library, Hanover, N.H., 764306, 765557, 764517.2, 764661, 765330.

23. John Cleaveland, *A Short and Plain Narrative of the Late Work of God's Spirit* (Boston, 1767), pp. 4–16.

24. Norton, *Liberty's Daughters,* p. 168.

25. *Boston Evening Post,* Sept. 11, 1769.

26. *New Hampshire Gazette,* Aug. 25, 1769.

27. Ibid., Aug. 18, 1769.

28. *Essex Gazette,* Oct. 10–17, 1769.

29. Edmund S. Morgan, *The Gentle Puritan: A Life of Ezra Stiles, 1727–1795* (New Haven, 1962), pp. 231–33.

30. Amos Adams, *A Concise Historical View* (Boston, 1769), pp. 48–50. Christopher Jedrey sees political import in John Cleaveland's allusion to the Sons of Liberty during a conflict with another church in 1767. Even if the comment was intended as "praise" for the Sons of Liberty, it can hardly be construed as praise for the kind of excess Cleaveland elsewhere deplored. In 1774 he urged "repentance" as a means to victory in the conflict (see Jedrey, *World of Cleaveland,* p. 134).

7

Women and Rural Outwork in Nineteenth-Century New England

Thomas Dublin

Even before large numbers of farm women sought employment in New England's expanding cotton textile industry, many engaged in rural outwork during slack times on their family's farms. Weaving cloth and braiding straw and palm leaf hats provided credits at the local store that permitted women and their families to participate in the expanding consumer economy of the period. The work was traditional in the way that it was fully integrated into the family farm economy; but at the same time, by offering the possibility of individual wage labor, it facilitated the transition to factory employment for New England women.

Opportunities for wage work expanded steadily for rural women in New England in the first third of the nineteenth century. Yet there was something quite unconscious about this process; women continued to work at home as they shifted from production for family consumption to production for wider markets without realizing the full implications of the new activity. The handweaving of machine-spun cotton yarn into cloth and the braiding of split palm leaf into men's and children's hats became important economic activities for farm women in the years after 1810. Organized by local merchants, manufacturers, or middlemen, this work represented a significant departure from previous rural practice. No longer did farm families work up materials they produced on the farm; rather, they relied on outsiders who distributed or "put out" the yarn or split palm leaf into the countryside. Members of farm families performed the "outwork"—weaving cloth or braiding hats—and typically received credit toward store purchases for their labors.

The years after 1800 saw a significant proliferation of putting-out industries in New England. In their rural homes, young women integrated outwork into the fabric of their daily lives. Unmarried daughters in their teenage years attended district school about a third of the year, typically concentrated in the winter months.[1] In summer and fall they assisted their mothers in the cultivation of home gardens; throughout the year they tended poultry and cows and produced cheese and butter. When farm chores declined in the winter

"*The Idyll of the Palm Leaf Hat,*" *from* Frank Leslie's Illustrated Newspaper, *July 15, 1871.*
This romanticized view has one woman splitting palm leaf while a second braids the rim of a
hat on a wooden mold.

and early spring, they often turned their energies to weaving yarn from local spinning mills or braiding palm-leaf hats for the local storekeeper. In this manner, young women gained experience at waged work without ever leaving home, and they fit the demands of such work into the rhythms of their daily lives. If caring for younger siblings, cooking meals, preserving food, or nursing the sick took a great deal of time, daughters did little outwork. The flexibility of outwork appealed to members of rural families and eased concerns farmers might otherwise have felt working for others. The fact that the fathers or husbands of female outworkers typically were credited with the proceeds of their labors meant that outwork meshed well with the power dynamics of patriarchal farming families.

There was little overt opposition to women undertaking these new activities because they were well integrated on several levels into the operations of the family farm. Over time, however, women outworkers began to claim the proceeds of their labors, and the first signs of conflict between individual and familial interests became apparent. The spread of outwork into the New England countryside before 1850 shows some of the more general implications of wage labor for women across the nineteenth century. Rural outwork, in the end, proved something of a way station on the path from unwaged labor on the family farm to individual wage work in urban factories. In this manner, outwork simultaneously propped up the traditional family farm economy while preparing the way for the individual wage economy that would eventually displace it. . . .

Outwork grew dramatically in the course of the first half of the nineteenth century, although the production activities organized in this manner shifted over time. A brief boom of handloom weaving provided the first outwork employment. The practice first developed with the cutoff of English imports that accompanied the passage of the Embargo Act in December 1807.[2] Subsequently, the Non-Intercourse Act and war with Great Britain further stimulated American reliance on domestic textiles, giving a tremendous boost to New England's fledgling cotton-spinning industry.[3] The new firms expanded between 1808 and 1815 and developed their market by putting out cotton yarns to rural weavers in the surrounding countryside. Outwork weaving peaked around 1820, employing approximately twelve thousand weavers across New England.[4] With the adoption of the power loom and the consequent decline of outwork weaving after 1820, the rise of straw braiding and palm-leaf hat making more than made up for the loss of weaving employment. By 1837, hat production in Massachusetts had reached $1.9 million in value and employed more than 51,000 women and children.[5] The hats produced by New England outworkers found their way to the South and the Midwest, where slaves, farmers, and farm laborers wore them for inexpensive protection while working outdoors.[6] Although mechanization undermined outwork weaving by 1830, the Civil War, with its resulting interruption of interregional trade, spelled the end of the outwork manufacture of palm-leaf hats. Straw braiding, on the other hand, survived for several decades after the war, declining as outmigration reduced the rural labor supply and changing fashions reduced the demand for straw bonnets.

Shoes were another consumer good that occupied the energies of rural outworkers in New England in the antebellum decades. Beginning in the 1820s, manufacturers in Lynn and Haverhill, Massachusetts, routinely cut out the thin leather for shoe uppers and shipped the pieces by express team or railroad into the countryside, where farmers' wives and daughters stitched and bound them for three or four cents a pair.[7] As rural outwork increased, shoe manufacturers established central shops, bringing the cutting of the leather and the finishing and inspecting of shoes under their direction. Nonetheless, virtually all the binding and much of the shoemaking continued to be done in the countryside. Paul Faler has estimated that in 1855, 60 percent of Lynn shoes were made outside of the city by rural outworkers. The first cracks in this system came with the application of the sewing machine to the stitching of uppers in the 1850s. Then, with the adoption of the McKay stitcher during the Civil War years, New England shoemaking moved irreversibly from rural outwork to urban factory production.[8]

Even with the decline of rural shoebinding and shoemaking, outwork did not disappear. After the Civil War, it persisted in the New England countryside, where Boston garment manufacturers sent work to take advantage of the rural labor market. . . . Sewing for the urban market offered rural women the credits at the local store for purchases needed to supplement farm production that weaving cloth, braiding hats, and binding shoes had provided them before the Civil War. By 1870, this new trade linking Boston wholesale clothiers, country storekeepers, and members of farming families in New Hampshire and Maine was providing $2 million in wage payments annually to a workforce that probably consisted of 50,000 farm women.[9] . . . The domestic employment of New England farm women in geographically dispersed outwork networks persisted for more than sixty years.

Two features of rural outwork contrasted sharply with the defining aspects of factory production in the same period. First, production under the outwork system grew by extension over a growing geographical area rather than by the intensification of its demands on individual workers. Despite numerous efforts, textile manufacturers (and hat merchants and shoe and garment manufacturers after them) were largely unsuccessful at increasing the productivity of dispersed rural outworkers or at imposing uniform standards of quality. These difficulties resulted from the second defining characteristic of outwork in rural New England. Under the outwork system, merchants and manufacturers had remarkably little control over their workforce. Workers were members of rural property-owning families who engaged in outwork in slack periods when it suited their purposes. . . . The limited control that manufacturers exerted over outworkers necessitated a stupendous effort at distribution and introduced significant costs associated with the length of time intermediate goods were out in the hands of otherwise preoccupied workers. . . .

The geographical spread of weaving outwork is particularly striking. At first, textile firms often employed artisan weavers in rooms adjacent to their factories; over time, however, such weavers were too expensive or they could not keep up with factory output, and mill managers began giving out yarn to local residents to be woven.[10] . . . Outwork weaving also appeared in the vicinity of rural mills. For instance, in the town of Griswold, Connecticut, "the sound of the loom was heard increasingly, for the cotton spun in the village factory was woven in the homes of the people, and the price paid, from seven to ten cents per yard, wonderfully stimulated production." The picture in New Ipswich, New Hampshire, was similar: "Almost every farmhouse in the country was furnished with a loom, and most of the adult females were skilled weavers. Mr. Batchelder [the mill agent] made contracts with many of them . . . to weave cloth for him, and often had in his employ more than a hundred weavers, some of whom came six or eight miles, to receive the yarn and to return the woven cloth."[11] Rural and urban mills alike depended on outworkers from nearby farming families. Outwork weaving typically engaged a considerably larger number of workers than did the spinning mills themselves and thus broadened the impact of the early factories on the surrounding countryside.

As the growing production of yarn outstripped the ability of outworkers in the immediate vicinity of the mills to weave it into cloth, mill-owners began to look further afield. . . . [C]ompanies employed agents who loaded a wagon with yarn and drove regular routes through the countryside to supply yarn and pick up completed pieces of cloth. . . . Outwork middlemen typically acted as agents for the textile firms with which they contracted for yarn to put out. They were held responsible for the quality of the woven cloth they returned to the firm and were paid according to the quantity of weaving done under their direction. They, in turn, paid weavers a piece wage for each yard woven, the price varying with the complexity of the fabric. They also enforced a system of fines and deductions intended to ensure uniformity and quality in the woven cloth. . . .

Despite an array of threatened deductions, textile firms and outwork organizers remained unable to control outworkers. Many manufacturers needed the services of weavers, and farming families had other sources of support, so that they could not be effectively coerced to work at terms that did not suit them. Moreover, storekeepers needed their customers' business and thus could not or would not discipline outworkers as well as textile manufacturers desired.

The character of outwork emerges clearly in accounts kept by Silas Jillson, of Richmond, New Hampshire, between September 1822 and June 1829. In all, he recorded 2,041 separate transactions and credited account holders more than $12,000 for their output, about half of which was completed in

1823 and 1824.[12] Richmond residents did not become dependent on weaving earnings. Although Jillson put out yarn to be woven for almost seven years, few accounts remained open over the entire period. On average, individual account holders returned 5.4 pieces of cloth, totaling 579 yards in length, over a period of seventeen months, work for which they received $31.81. A typical weaver completed a piece of cloth of about 108 yards in length every three months.[13] . . . Even given the fact that outwork was concentrated in the winter and spring months, weaving likely occupied no more than three days a week during the busy season.[14]

Outwork weaving was widespread in Richmond in this period. At least 42 percent of families living in Richmond in 1830 had taken yarn from Jillson in the previous decade.[15] . . . Weaving output varied according to the sex and family status of account holders. Virtually all males who held accounts with Jillson were household heads; in contrast, only about a fourth of female account holders headed their own households. Unmarried daughters made up fully 60 percent of women with accounts, and their earnings from weaving were comparable with those of male household heads. Sons, in contrast, averaged only $9 for their weaving, compared with more than $31 for daughters. The data suggest that unmarried daughters did most of the outwork weaving, either within parental accounts or on their own.

A comparison of female household heads and married women with accounts in their own names is also instructive. Widows had the largest accounts of any group, averaging over $44 in weaving credits. Married women, by contrast, earned only $14 on average for weaving. Widows undoubtedly were credited for weaving done by other family members; married women probably were credited simply for weaving they completed interspersed with their other domestic duties. Unmarried daughters had earnings between those of wives and widows. Daughters had strong motivation to weave diligently, most likely contributing to their marriage portions.[16] Still, the overall picture that emerges from examining Jillson's weaving accounts is one of male household heads being credited with the majority of proceeds of outwork weaving performed by female family members. . . .

Just as Richmond and Fitzwilliam residents were returning their last pieces of handwoven cloth to Silas Jillson, however, a Fitzwilliam storekeeper, Dexter Whittemore, was inaugurating a new form of outwork, the braiding of children's and men's palm-leaf hats. Whittemore bought palm leaf from Boston wholesale merchants, who imported it from the Caribbean. He had it split locally and sold the split leaf (on credit) to his customers.[17] They, in turn, braided the hats, following directions he supplied, and sold them back to Whittemore for credits against their store purchases. Typically, customers brought back about fifteen hats at a time, picked up additional split palm leaf, and utilized their credit to buy store items. The frequency of hat transactions suggests that customers came in once every two months, which indicates that they were making perhaps two hats a week.

Palm-leaf hats were summer wear, and braiding hats was a seasonal activity, concentrated between October and April. . . . Hat making became a major element in Whittemore's business and continued to expand throughout the antebellum period. In 1830, Dexter Whittemore employed more than 250 individuals making 23,000 hats a year, and their earnings made up almost half of all credits in his store accounts.[19] This represented a dramatic increase in outwork, for between 1821 and 1824, handwoven cloth had totaled only about $270 a year, accounting for less than 10 percent of the credits of Whittemore's customers. In contrast, hat credits averaged about $5,000 per year in the early 1830s and more than $15,000 annually twenty years later.[20] By the early 1850s Whittemore employed more than 800 hat makers producing 80,000 hats annually. Outwork promoted a tremendous expansion in his store trade and made him one of the richest men in Fitzwilliam.[21] . . .

The composition of Whittemore account holders in 1830 speaks to the place of different groups in broader exchange. Among adults there were 145 accounts held in the names of male household heads compared with only 16 widows and 8 wives. These figures suggest that adult men had formal control of much of the exchange economy operating through the store. Moreover, the credit profiles of these accounts varied dramatically along gender lines. Male household heads averaged $12 in agricultural credits in their accounts, widows mustered only $7 of such credits, and wives had still fewer, with a trifling $1.25 in farm products on average. Finally, household heads had more access to cash and notes than did wives. More than 57 percent of the accounts for male household heads and 62 percent for widows had cash credits; none of the wives' accounts did. Similarly, no wives gave Whittemore notes to cover outstanding balances in their accounts, whereas 25 percent of widows and 38 percent of male household heads had such notes. The economic disabilities of married women are clearly evident.[22]

The place of hat credits in these accounts reflected the differing work roles and power relations of husbands, wives, and widows in the local farm economy. For husbands, who controlled a diverse family economy, hats accounted for only 41 percent of all credits; for widows, 47 percent; and for wives, more than 77 percent. The hat-making activity of married women in Fitzwilliam was generally subsumed within a family economy governed by their husbands. In the rare cases in which wives traded in their own names, they bought store goods from the limited proceeds of their own and their children's hat making. . . .

Among unmarried children with accounts in their own names, a different pattern emerged, with girls making more hats than did boys. In 1830, unmarried sons were 5.7 percent of individuals with accounts but only 3.1 percent of those with hat credits, and they were credited with only 1.4 percent of the hats made for Whittemore. Unmarried daughters, in contrast, made up at that date 17.8 percent of Whittemore account holders and 20.4 percent of those with hat credits. They were credited, moreover, for 21.7 percent of the hats sold to Whittemore. Daughters outnumbered sons by three to one among account holders, but their hat output exceeded that for sons by a factor of fifteen. These figures reveal that despite conventions by which most store accounts were kept in the names of males, hat making was primarily a female activity. . . .

A more fine-tuned analysis of family hat making lends further support to this finding. For all Fitzwilliam families in the 1830 ledger, the mean value of hats made in a year came to $18.62, but this figure varied according to the number of daughters between the ages of 10 and 19. Families with no daughters in this age group averaged about $12 of hat credits each year; families with one or two daughters averaged almost $25; and families with three or more teenage daughters averaged more than $33 in hat business. This concentration of hat making in families with teenage daughters became still greater over the next two decades. By 1850, Whittemore families with three or more teenage daughters were making four times as many hats annually as families with no teenage daughters.[23]

What factors had the greatest impact on the hat making of daughters for their own accounts? Two influences stand out: the age of the young woman and the sex of the household head. Age was a strong influence on daughters' hat making. Girls under nineteen averaged about $19 per year of hat credits, whereas by their late twenties, daughters were earning more than $27 a year through their efforts. The evidence is clear: the older the daughters, the greater the hat credits in their accounts. The greatest influence on hat making in daughters' accounts was the sex of the household head. In male-headed households—the predominant form—daughters marketed hats on their own account valued at a bit more than $20 annually. Daughters in female-headed households, by contrast, marketed hats worth more than $43 a year. If we control for age and the presence of parental accounts, daughters in female-headed households braided more than twice as many hats as those in male-headed households. This evidence reveals the importance of hat making as a source of income in some households. The death (or absence) of the male household head dramatically cut into the agricultural labor and wage income of a farming family. Members of the family responded by earning wages however they could. Sons found work as farm laborers or in woodenware shops; daughters braided palm-leaf hats. Their hat-making activity showed up in the high level of hat credits in their accounts at the Whittemore store. Daughters' wages played a significant role in the subsistence of female-headed farming families—much more so than in male-headed ones. . . .

Braiding palm-leaf hats never took on the same urgency in rural New England as straw plaiting did in parts of England, but it did provide a source of supplementary income well suited to the varying demands on farm women at different points in their lives. And although hat making was concentrated among single daughters in their teens and twenties, farm women made hats at all points in the life cycle—as daughters working for their families, as young women working on their own account, as newly married women in accounts under their husbands' names, and as widows, again in accounts under their own names.

A specific example illustrates the influence of life cycle transitions on women's hat making. Martha Alexander had an account with Whittemore from January 1831 until October 1834, the month of her marriage. She was 18 years of age when she opened an account in her own name, and in a forty-five–month period braided 341 hats. Her annual output of 91 hats was comparable with that of other unmarried daughters. In October 1834, Martha Alexander married Edward Allen, two years her senior, also of Fitzwilliam. He had not previously had a store account, but he opened one forthwith, his first transaction being the purchase of split palm leaf. Martha Alexander Allen kept right at her hat making, with 162 hats credited in the next two years. This output represented only a slight decline from the pace just before her marriage.

Martha Alexander's account in the two-year period before her marriage suggests that she was using hat credits to purchase items to bring into her marriage. Her purchases included teacups and saucers, a tea set, plates, platters, and butterboats, as well as yards of muslin, cord, calico, and shirting.

Men's store purchases commonly underwent a shift with their marriages. In the months before marriage, their purchases generally were not focused on items likely to be useful in their new homes. After their marriages, the purchases take on a more utilitarian bent. The month he married Rebecca Whittemore, Edmund Blodgett purchased a rocking chair and six dining chairs. In succeeding months his new bride brought to the store forty palm-leaf hats, the credits for which amounted to slightly more than the cost of the chairs.

Martha Alexander Allen and Rebecca Whittemore Blodgett were typical of other unmarried daughters who had accounts in their own names and married in the course of the 1830s. For twelve of sixteen such women noted in Whittemore's accounts, the exact dates of their marriages are known. On average these women opened accounts in their own names almost five years before their marriages. Thus they would have had ample time to build up credit or make purchases of goods to bring into their marriages. Moreover, twelve husbands subsequently had store accounts. Only five of the men had accounts before their marriages, three of whom had had previous hat credits. All twelve husbands, however, did have hat credits in their postmarriage accounts. The median output for these young wives amounted to 265 hats in the first five years of their marriages. Hat making was a skill well adapted to the family economy in Fitzwilliam. In terms of the store goods these young women brought into marriage and the store credit their hat making provided in the first years of their marriages, it is evident that outwork permitted women to make a significant contribution to their new families.[24] . . .

Contemporaries were aware of the place of outwork hat making in rural New England. Writing in 1878, Charles Carleton Coffin, the local historian of Boscawen, New Hampshire, recalled the concentration of hat making among poorer farming families of that community.

> The industry [of hat making] was not a universal one. The merchants paid cash only in part, making, of course, a large profit on the goods sold. Families in comfortable circumstances would not engage in an employment in which they would be at the mercy of the merchant, who, though he might be scrupulously honest, yet could fix his own profit and their measure of gain. It was a jug with only one handle, and that in the hands of the merchant. Notwithstanding this drawback, the industry gave employment to a large number of women and girls, who otherwise had little chance of earning money.[25]

This New Hampshirite had an understanding of the place of hat making in the rural economy that is confirmed by the Fitzwilliam evidence.

The impact of outwork on rural communities in New England in the first half of the nineteenth century was significant. Outwork income permitted rural families to supplement their agricultural earnings and to support themselves on steadily smaller holdings in the face of increasing competition from more productive midwestern farms. . . .

Outwork had a contradictory impact on the transition to wage labor for New England women in the nineteenth century. It offered women an alternative to factory employment, permitting them to live at home and continue to participate in the family farm economy while earning wages. Thus it allowed married women both to contribute to their families' purchasing power and to fulfill their domestic responsibilities. In this respect, outwork was an alternative to the emerging system of urban female wage labor.

On the other hand, outwork was an early form of wage labor; members of farming families provided labor for outwork organizers and in return were paid in yarn, cash, or store credit. They were dependent on their suppliers for raw materials—machine-spun yarn, split palm leaf, or leather uppers—and for the marketing of finished products. Outworkers were no longer independent producers of agricultural goods that might be consumed, traded with neighbors, or sold to a variety of purchasers. In this regard outwork did not offer women and their families the kind of independence offered in this period by dairying and butter making.[26]

Still, outwork shielded women workers (and their families) from a number of the consequences generally associated with wage labor. Their labor did not require them to leave their own homes. Moreover, their work remained entirely unsupervised. There was no disjuncture between home and workplace and no factory discipline dictating their every action while at work. These facts meant that women could work at a pace dictated by their own (or their families') needs and circumstances. The lack of any sort of industrial work discipline among dispersed outworkers was a source of distress to mill agents and shoe manufacturers, but it must have been a source of satisfaction to rural workers unwilling to accept the new discipline of factory production.

In this context, rural outwork must be viewed as transitional; it shared characteristics of earlier labor practices and at the same time opened the way for new ones. It was integrated within the rural family economy, and the income earned by farm women helped them sustain the family farm in this period. Yet, at the same time, outwork provided prospects for and imperceptibly merged into individual wage labor. As such it inconspicuously facilitated the entry of New England women into wage labor as the century progressed.

NOTES

1. Carl F. Kaestle and Maris A. Vinovskis, *Education and Social Change in Nineteenth-Century Massachusetts* (Cambridge; Cambridge University, Press, 1980), ch. 2, especially figs. 2.1, 2.3, 2.4, and 2.5. Recalculating means from data offered by Kaestle and Vinovskis suggests that in Massachusetts in 1840, children who attended school did so for about one hundred days annually.

2. For a good discussion of earlier attempts to employ skilled male handloom weavers in shops adjacent to power-spinning operations, see Gail Fowler Mohanty, "Experimentation in Textile Technology, 1788–1790, and Its Impact on Handloom Weaving and Weavers in Rhode Island," *Technology and Culture* 29 (1988): 1–31. On the shift to outwork and its subsequent decline, see Mohanty, "Putting Up with Putting-Out," *Journal of the Early Republic* 9 (1989): 191–216.

3. Caroline Ware, *Early New England Cotton Manufacture* (1931), ch. 3, and Peter J. Coleman, "Rhode Island Cotton Manufacturing," *Rhode Island History* 23 (1964): 65–80. Mohanty, "Putting Up with Putting-Out," pp. 193–94, takes issue with Coleman's assessment of Rhode Island manufacturers as particularly conservative in their adoption of the power loom, viewing outwork "as the most proper and profitable method of cloth production" at the time.

4. U.S. Department of the Treasury, *Letter from the Secretary of the Treasury . . . on the Subject of American Manufactures* (Washington: Roger C. Weightman, 1810), table D and p. 11; for 1820, see Robert Brooke Zevin, "The Growth of Textile Production after 1815," in Robert Fogel and Stanley Engerman, eds., *The Reinterpretation of American Economic History* (New York: Harper & Row, 1971), pp. 123–24.

5. Mass. Secretary of the Commonwealth, *Statistical Tables Exhibiting the Condition and Products of Certain Branches of Industry in Massachusetts for the Year Ending April 1, 1837* (Boston: Dutton and Wentworth, 1838), p. 181. The employment figures are derived from my study of the palm-leaf hat making network organized by Dexter Whittemore of Fitzwilliam, N.H., discussed below. There I found that the most committed outworkers, single women working on their own account, produced on average one hundred hats a year. Applying that figure to overall Massachusetts output data yielded the employment estimate noted here. By using a mean output figure derived from the most productive workers in one network, I likely understate the total number of outworkers who braided hats at some point in the year. For other states, see Conn. Secretary of State, *Statistics of the Condition and Products of Certain Branches of Industry in Connecticut, for the Year Ending October 1, 1845* (Hartford: J. L. Boswell, 1846), p. 217, and R.I. Secretary of State, *Report upon the Census of Rhode Island, 1865* (Providence: Providence Press, 1867), p. 92. For treatment of one palm hat network in Massachusetts, see Christopher Clark, *The Roots of Rural Capitalism: Western Massachusetts, 1780–1860* (Ithaca, N.Y.: Cornell University Press, 1990), pp. 181–90.

6. One Alabama planter's account book, for instance, reveals the purchase of "12 palm leaf hats—for women" in 1843. These were probably slave women. Henry Watson, Jr., Account Book, 1841–1844, Manuscript Department, William R. Perkins Library, Duke University, Durham, N.C., entry of June 6, 1843. For a similar record of a Noxubee County, Mississippi, storekeeper, see A. H. Jones Invoice Book, 1848–1849, Manuscript Department, William R. Perkins Library, Duke University, Durham, N.C., entry for February 21, 1848. I thank Anne F. Scott for these two references. For invoices of the palm hat purchases of a St. Genevieve, Mis-

souri, storekeeper, see the Francis C. Rozier collection, 1841–1857, Historical Society of Pennsylvania, Philadelphia.

7. Mary H. Blewett, "Women Shoeworkers and Domestic Ideology: Rural Outwork in Early Nineteenth-Century Essex County," *New England Quarterly*, 60 (1987): 403–28.

8. Paul G. Faler, *Mechanics and Manufacturers in the Early Industrial Revolution: Lynn, Massachusetts, 1780–1869* (Albany: State University of New York Press, 1981), p. 223; and Mary H. Blewett, *Men, Women, and Work: Class, Gender, and Protest in the New England Shoe Industry, 1780–1910* (Urbana: University of Illinois Press, 1988), pp. 142–53.

9. Mass. Bureau of Statistics of Labor, *Annual Report*, 1870–71, pp. 201–2.

10. Mohanty, "Experimentation in Textile Technology."

11. Daniel L. Phillips, *Griswold—A History: Being a History of the Town of Griswold, Connecticut from the Early Times to the Entrance of the Country into the World War in 1917* (New Haven, Conn.: Tuttle, Morehouse & Taylor, 1929), p. 107; and William R. Bagnail, *The Textile Industries of the United States*, vol. 1 (Cambridge, Mass.: Riverside Press, 1893), pp. 476–77. For further references to dispersed outwork weaving, see Federal Manuscript Census of Manufactures, 1820, N.H. returns, microfilm, BL, pp. 83–92, and Sarah Anne Emery, *Reminiscences of a Newburyport Nonagenarian* (Newburyport, Mass.: William H. Huse, 1879), pp. 72–73.

12. The most common outwork products were denims, plaids, checks, and stripes, fabrics that required four harnesses or multiple shuttles and that power looms could not handle in this period.

13. The shift in language here is purposeful. It is impossible to be certain of the output of individual weavers from an account held in the name of a male household head because several family members could have been contributing to the output credited to the account. The output figure noted in this final sentence reflects cloth credited to unmarried daughters with accounts in their own name—the group of account holders most likely to be exchanging with Jillson the product of their own labor.

14. November and December accounted for just over 26 percent of all webs given out; in contrast, in July–October, Jillson gave out less than 21 percent of his webs. Unfortunately, Jillson did not record the dates that woven cloth was returned, so we do not know precisely when the work was completed. Jillson's weavers do not appear to be unrepresentative of outworkers generally. See Jonathan Prude, *Coming of Industrial Order* (1983), pp. 76–77; Fowler, "Rhode Island Handloom Weavers," pp. 145–47, 168–71; and Coleman, "Rhode Island Cotton Manufacturing," p. 74.

15. This figure is based on the linkage of Jillson account holders with households enumerated in the 1830 federal manuscript census for Richmond, Cheshire County, N.H.

16. For an autobiographical account of one young Connecticut woman who did outwork weaving to provide for her trousseau, see *Bessie; or, Reminiscences of a Daughter of a New England Clergyman; Simple Facts, Simply Told by a Grandmother* (New Haven, Conn.: J. H. Benham, 1861), chap. 18.

17. Outworkers "bought" the split leaf and "sold" their hats to Whittemore, but they were not really independent producers of palm-leaf hats. Prices for leaf and braided hats reflected a competitive market in which storekeepers competed for rural customers. For convenience, it is likely that outworkers purchased leaf where they sold their hats and bought other store goods; it did not make sense to buy leaf at one store and trade hats at another given the distances involved.

18. Volumes 87 and 88, Dexter Whittemore & Son Collection, Harvard Business School, provide solid evidence of this seasonality as they include Whittemore's accounts with hat processors in neighboring Worcester County and with the urban wholesalers with whom he dealt.

19. Whittemore was not unique in his adoption of hat making; in fact, neighboring Worcester County, Massachusetts, was the center for palm-leaf hat making. By 1832, residents of that county were braiding 1.5 million hats annually. See Louis McLane, "Report of the Secretary of the Treasury, 1832," *Documents Relative to the Manufactures of the United States*, vol. 1 (Washington: Duff Green, 1833), pp. 474–577.

20. Dexter Whittemore & Son Collection, vols. 3, 4, 87, 88.

21. New Hampshire, vol. 2, p. 192, R. G. Dun & Co. Collection, Harvard Business School. For discussion of an even larger palm-leaf hat operation in Amherst, Massachusetts, see Clark, *Roots of Rural Capitalism*, pp. 182–84.

22. For the broader legal ramifications of these disabilities and women's efforts to provide legislative remedies, see Norma Basch, *In the Eyes of the Law: Women, Marriage, and Property in Nineteenth-Century New York* (Ithaca, N.Y.: Cornell University Press, 1982).

23. The differences evident here between families' production of hats in 1830 and 1850 are significant in statistical terms. For the 1830 breakdown, $F = 7.05$, with a significance of .009; for 1850, $F = 20.29$, with a significance of .0001.

24. There is a striking similarity here to the pattern described for English outwork knitting regions in David Levine, *Family Formation in an Age of Nascent Capitalism* (New York: Academic Press, 1977), pp. 51, 61–62.

25. Charles Carleton Coffin, *The History of Boscawen and Webster from 1733 to 1878* (Concord, N.H.: Republican Press Association, 1878), p. 641.

26. Joan M. Jensen, *Loosening the Bonds: Mid-Atlantic Farm Women, 1750–1850* (New Haven, Conn.: Yale University Press, 1986). On the changing character of farm women's roles in butter making in the second half of the nineteenth century, see Nancy Grey Osterud, *Bonds of Community: The Lives of Farm Women in Nineteenth-Century New York* (Ithaca, N.Y.: Cornell University Press, 1991).

8

The Sexual Division of Labor and the Artisan Tradition in Early Industrial Capitalism: The Case of New England Shoemaking, 1780–1860

Mary H. Blewett

The history of the transformation of shoemaking in the course of the nineteenth century was a well-explored topic, but it had been viewed almost entirely in terms of the changing work patterns and attitudes of skilled male shoemakers until Mary Blewett began examining the historical record. A much richer, and more nuanced, picture emerges when we take gender into consideration. Blewett demonstrates the way a gendered division of labor between shoemaking and shoebinding in the domestic system carried over into the factory beginning in the 1850s. She also explores the divided interests of women factory workers and homeworkers during the Lynn shoe strike of February 1860. Her work demonstrates the limitations of examining relations of power within the industrial revolution without keeping gender (as well as class) at the forefront of the analysis.

Labor historians who in the 1970s investigated the connections between nineteenth-century culture and class experience came to regard the preindustrial male artisan and his work culture as the source of working-class consciousness. As Bryan Palmer put it in an article in 1976: "The artisan, not the debased proletariat, fathered the labour movement. . . . The working class was born, not in the factory, but in the [artisan] workshop."[1] This metaphorical claim to hegemony in class formation as well as human procreation is symbolic of the invisibility of women in this conception of the working class: their invisibility as workers and as a gender.

The artisan's workshop was indeed a male world, and much of the new labor history assumes that the experience of female members of artisan families who were drawn into preindustrial production was indistinguishable from male experience. Labor historians regard the artisan workshop as the center of preindustrial political and cultural life and the source of the ideology and consciousness of the American working class. Such an assumption underestimates

Reprinted from Mary H. Blewett, "The Sexual Division of Labor and the Artisan Tradition in Early Industrial Capitalism: The Case of New England Shoemaking, 1780–1860," in "*To Toil the Livelong Day,*" edited by Carol Groneman and Mary Beth Norton. Copyright © 1987 by Cornell University. Used by permission of the publisher, Cornell University Press.

Meeting of striking women shoeworkers, Lynn, Mass., February, 1860. Lynn Museum.

the importance of changes in the sexual division of labor within a craft of skilled male artisans, such as the New England shoemakers in the late eighteenth century. These artisans came to view women shoe workers as persons in separate and immutable gender categories that defined both their work and their relationship to the family and to artisan life. The artisan tradition fostered the sexual division of labor and perpetuated the preindustrial patterns of work and life that shaped the family wage system of the nineteenth century. Gender categories made it difficult for male artisans to regard women as fellow workers, include them in the ideology and politics based on their work culture, or see in the experience of working women what awaited all workers under industrialization. The failure of male artisans to perceive or accommodate the interests of the women involved in shoe production weakened their ability to resist the reorganization of work by early industrial capitalism.[2]

Women in eighteenth-century New England shoemaking families were recruited to new work as a result of a shift in the control of profits when markets expanded after 1780 and production increased. Before this expansion, women had contributed as "helpmeets" to the family economy in ways tied to their domestic duties: by boarding apprentices and journeymen and by spinning flax into shoe thread. A cutoff of British imports during the American Revolution stimulated efforts to secure tariff protection and create new domestic markets. Merchants began to supply capital in the form of raw materials (tanned leather) to workers in artisan shops and marketed the finished shoes in towns and cities along the Atlantic seaboard. Since merchant control over raw materials and access to markets meant merchant control of profits, artisan masters borrowed money if they could to purchase their own leather. Those shoemakers who owned no leather divided up the work among the men in their shops and augmented their own income by recruiting (unpaid) female members of their families to sew shoe uppers. Robert Gilman, traveling through Essex County in 1797, observed the early involvement of women in shoemaking work: "In our way to Salem we passed through a number of pretty little villages one of which, Lynn, is scarcely inhabited by any but shoemakers. . . . The women work also and we scarcely passed a house where the trade was not carried on."[3]

The male head of the shoemaking family assigned and controlled work on shoes in both the home and the shop. The merchant capitalists welcomed the new potential for production, but they paid no wages directly to women workers and did not supervise them. Direction of work remained in the hands of male artisans. Women simply added this new chore to their traditional household labor. The recruitment of women to shoe production was a carefully controlled assignment of work designed to fit women's role in family life and maintain gender relationships in the family, while preserving the artisan system as a training ground for the craft and part of the process of male gender formation. Apprentices continued to learn their craft as shoemakers and find their place in the gender hierarchy of the shoe shop by performing services and running errands for the master and journeymen. Women in shoemaking families were recruited to do only a small part of the work—the sewing of the upper part of the shoe—and not to learn the craft itself. They were barred from apprenticeships and group work and isolated from the center of artisan life: the shoe shop.[4]

The new work assigned to women in shoemaking families took on social connotations appropriate to female gender. "Shoebinding," a new word for this sexual division of labor, became a category of women's work in the early nineteenth century. The activity, combined with domestic chores and child care, took place in the kitchen. The shoemaker did not straddle a shoemaker's bench. She used a new tool, the shoe clamp, which rested on the floor and accommodated her long skirt and apron while providing a flexible wooden holder for leather pieces. The binder held the clamp tightly between her knees, freeing her hands to use her awl and needle. The use of women expanded production, met the needs of both capitalist and artisan, and threatened no change in the traditional patterns of gender and craft formation. The sexual division of labor guaranteed the subordination of women by separating the work of shoebinding from additional knowledge of the craft and by maintaining separate workplaces for men and women. These patterns survived the transformation of shoe production into the factory system at midcentury and constituted a fundamental social dimension of industrial work.

As shoebinders worked in their kitchens, the demands of the artisan shop intruded upon and shaped their time. The binding of uppers by shoemakers' wives and daughters was essential to the timing and pace of the work of shoemakers. Women's work in the home combined both task labor (their domestic duties) and timed labor: the erratic but compelling need to keep all the men in the shoe shop supplied with sewn shoe uppers. One historian of shoework in nineteenth-century Lynn described the process:

> Then there would be a little delay, perhaps, until a shoe was bound, with which to start off the new lot. But generally, before the "jour" got his "stock" seasoned, one or two "uppers" were ready, and enough were usually bound ahead to keep all hands at work. And so, now and then, the order would be heard—"Come John, go and see if your mother has got a shoe bound: I'm all ready to last it."[5]

Shoebinders remained, however, socially and physically isolated from the group life of the shop. The collective nature of men's work in the artisan shop supported a militant tradition of resistance to the reorganization of production in early industrialization, but this tradition did not mirror the experience of women workers.

Binders in shoemaking families earned no wages before 1810 but simply contributed their labor to the family economy. However, the capacity of women to bind uppers for the shoe shop while also performing all kinds of domestic tasks had its limits. The domestic setting of shoebinding contradicted the increasing demands by merchant capitalists for production, but the recruitment of additional women outside the shoemaking family required some kind of a payment for their labor. After 1810, shoebinding, while still performed by hand in the home, gradually shifted to part-time outwork paid in goods (often in the new factory-made cotton textiles) and later in wages. Women's work on shoes came to be increasingly dissociated from the family labor system and done more and more by female workers outside of shoemaking families. As a result, the merchant capitalist or shoe boss assumed responsibility for hiring female workers, including those in shoemaking families, and directed their work from a central shop; his authority replaced that of shoemaking husbands and fathers.[6]

The shift in the coordination of the work process out of the hands of shoemakers and into the hands of the shoe boss represented a decline in the ability of male artisans to control their work. As shoebinding moved onto the wage labor market, its character as women's work without craft status kept wages low. These wages became part of the family wage, earnings pooled in the family's interests by its members. In New England shoemaking, the male artisan contributed the primary source of family income; it was supplemented by the much lower wages of shoebinders.

By the 1830s, shoebinders in Massachusetts outnumbered female operatives in cotton textile factories. Women shoe workers still combined sewing uppers with household tasks, a situation that continued to limit their productivity and to characterize their work as part time, intermittent, and poorly paid. In order to expand production, shoe bosses built networks of rural female outworkers in eastern Massachusetts and southern New Hampshire. This recruitment of rural New England women undercut the strikes against low wages that occurred among shoebinders in the early 1830s in the shoe towns of Essex County. The objective conditions of shoebinding—performed in isolation from group work and combined with domestic tasks—discouraged collective activity.[7]

Artisan shoemakers in Essex County burst into labor activity in the 1840s, organizing with other workers into workingmen's associations. They sought to include women in their activities but offered no way in which shoebinders as workers could associate themselves ideologically or strategically with the artisan protest societies. Rebellious shoemakers saw women as persons whose lives were defined primarily by family and morality. In 1844 the editor of *The Awl*, the newspaper of the Lynn Cordwainers' Society, cast women's support of labor protest in moral terms: "Thank heaven our movement is not a political one. If it were, it would not be warmed into life by the bright sunshine of woman's smiles, nor enriched by the priceless dower of her pure affections. But as it is strictly a moral enterprise, it opens to her willing heart a wide field of usefulness."[8] Oblivious of the implications of the domestic setting of shoebinding and offering no solutions for the problems that isolated outworkers faced in dealing with shoe bosses, artisan shoemakers received little support from shoebinders in the 1840s.

The expansion of markets in the developing West and the South created new demands for increased production in the early 1850s. The adaptation of the Singer sewing machine in 1852 to stitch light leather solved many of the problems of low productivity and coordination of production which characterized shoebinding as outwork. Capitalists had already centralized cutting and finishing operations in central shops, to which they added sewing machines run first by hand cranks or foot treadles and then by steam power in 1858. Because the Singer Company marketed its machines exclusively to garment manufacturers rather than immediately developing the market for home sewing machines, the initial unfamiliarity of Essex County women with the sewing machine in the early 1850s provoked some organized resistance by shoebinders, who feared that machine operations would destroy their work:

In 1853 . . . the first stitching machine was brought into [Haverhill]. A Mr. Pike was the first operator and so many people came from far and near to see how the great curiosity worked, that the firm was obliged to keep the factory doors locked. The women were fully excited as the men, and some of them shook their fists in Mr. Goodrich's face telling him that he was destroying their means of livelihood.[9]

Manufacturers, especially in Lynn, responded by training young women as stitchers on machines in central shops and leasing machines to women who chose to work at home. A new female factory work force was recruited from local families, but by 1860 sizable numbers of native-born, young, single New England women, once the source of industrial workers for the textile factories of the Merrimack Valley, were seeking employment in the shoe shops of eastern Massachusetts. As machine operators in steam-powered factories, they came under the direct control of their employers and the time discipline of industrial work. However, factory work offered women new opportunities for full-time employment, higher wages (three times those of homeworkers) and group work, an experience that contrasted sharply with their situation as outworkers.

The mechanization of women's work and the productivity of factory stitchers changed the composition of the work force throughout the shoe industry. One factory girl working full time at her machine replaced eleven shoebinders. As a result, the number of women employed in shoe work decreased quickly in the 1850s. But higher productivity by women workers in factories stimulated the demand for additional male workers; by contemporary estimates, one sewing machine operator could supply enough work for twenty shoemakers. The new male recruits had little craft knowledge or artisan experience; they were rural migrants, Irish and German immigrants, and country shoemakers who resided in the villages and towns of eastern Massachusetts and southern New Hampshire. As a result, the sex ratio of men and women in the Lynn shoe industry sharply reversed in the 1850s from 63 percent females and 37 percent males in 1850 to 40 percent females and 60 percent males in 1860. Wages for female factory operatives rose by 41 percent between 1852 and 1860, but wages fell for female homeworkers, unable to keep up with the productivity of centralized sewing machine operations. (Men's wages increased by only 10 percent and were severely cut during the depression of 1857.)[10] The mechanization of women's work intensified the hard conditions of all outworkers.

Intense competition among shoe manufacturers, the recruitment of large numbers of male outworkers, and the collapse of market demand for shoes in 1857 brought a crisis to the shoe industry of New England and precipitated in 1860 the largest demonstration of labor protest by American workers before the Civil War. The manufacturers blamed low wages on the laws of supply and demand, while male shoeworkers reasserted the moral and political values of the artisan tradition. The ideological emphasis on the brotherhood of the craft inherent in artisan culture prevented divisions between the new male recruits and more experienced shoemakers. The target of the strikers was the emerging factory system and the threat of mechanization and centralization to the preindustrial family wage system based on out-work. The new female factory workers seemed an alien group, while those who remained outside factory walls reaffirmed family, craft, and community values.

Significant divisions surfaced among shoe workers over the objectives of the 1860 strike in Lynn, the principal shoe town of Essex County.[11] Factory girls, realizing the power of their strategic location as machine operators in centralized production, sought increases in wages for all women workers. Their productivity on steam-powered machinery was the key to shutting down the largest manufacturers in Lynn and preventing them from sending machine-sewn uppers and leather stock by express teams to country shoe-makers. This tactic powerfully aided the cause of the shoemakers' regional strike. Identifying themselves with female homeworkers, the factory girls pro-posed a coalition to raise wages for both categories of women's work: home-work and factory work. Many of the factory girls lived as boarders in the households of Lynn families but had relatively little connection with the com-munity or its artisan culture. Their leader, twenty-one-year-old Clara H. Brown of Medford, Massachusetts, boarded with another factory stitcher in the household of a Lynn shoemaker. However, living with a young shoemaker and his wife and infant son did not deter Clara Brown from speaking for the interests of the factory girls, and it may have inspired her vision of an alliance of women working at home and in the factory.

The factory girls insisted that their proposed coalition represented the interests of *all* women workers in Lynn. They were in effect proposing an al-ternative to the family wage as the objective of the strike. An alliance based on gender would protect working women wherever the location of their work or whatever their marital status, and would offer homeworkers a vital and powerful link with female workers in the new factories. For example, the wage demands voted by the women strikers in 1860 included prices for home-work high enough to offset the customary costs to homeworkers of furnishing their own thread and lining material, a practice that cut earnings. In return, the factory girls could anticipate that when they married, they too could do shoe work at home for decent wages. They also tried to organize machine stitchers in the shoe factories of other towns. For these new industrial work-ers, it was just as important to increase women's wages as it was to increase men's wages during the strike. Their support of female homeworkers offered a bridge between preindustrial patterns of work for women and the factory system. Three times during the early meetings held by home and factory workers, the majority of striking women voted for the gender alliance.

Some female homeworkers, however, identified their interests with the men of the Lynn strike committee, who sought to protect the preindustrial family wage system and decentralized work. Shoemakers, who controlled the strike committees in each New England town, sought—as they had in the 1840s—to organize women's support for the strike on the basis of female moral stature and loyalty to family interests. In addition, the men's strike committee in Lynn insisted that wage increases for men were primary. Male workers opposed efforts to raise wages for women, fearing that an increase in the wages of female factory workers might promote a centralization of all stitching operations and thereby entirely eliminate women's work in the home and its supplemental earnings. For striking shoemakers and their allies among the female homeworkers, the best protection for the family wage lay in obtaining higher wages for men's work while defending homework for women. Implicit in their defense of the family wage was the subordinated role of women's contribution to family income.

The shoemakers of Lynn and their female allies seized control of the women's strike meetings and ended the emerging coalition of women shoeworkers. They ignored the votes at the women's strike meetings, substituted a wage proposal written by homeworkers, and circulated this altered wage list in Lynn for the signatures of strikers. The factory girls confronted the betrayal of their leadership at a tumultuous meeting on March 2, 1860. Above the uproar, Clara Brown angrily demanded to know who had dared to change the women's strike objectives. During the long debate, disgruntled homeworkers characterized the factory operatives as "smart girls," motivated by selfish individualism and the desire for lavish dress, an urge "to switch a long-tailed skirt."[12] In vain, Clara Brown tried to rally the supporters of the women's alliance. She emphasized the power of the machine operatives, who as industrial workers could obtain higher wages for all women workers: "For God's sake, don't act like a pack of fools. We've got the bosses where we can do as we please with 'em. If we won't work our machines, and the out-of-town girls won't take the work, what can the bosses do?"[13] The issue had become a test of loyalty: to the family wage or to the possibility of an alliance among female workers. Swayed by pressure from the leaders and supporters of the men's strike committee and their arguments for the family wage, the majority of women strikers at the March 2 meeting reversed themselves, voted against the factory girls, and agreed to march with the male strikers in a giant procession through the streets of Lynn on March 7. One of the banners carried by the striking women indicated their acceptance of moral and family values as primary to their role in labor protest: "Weak in physical strength but strong in moral courage, we dare to battle for the right, shoulder to shoulder with our fathers, husbands and brothers."[14]

The well-known sketches of women's participation in the Lynn strike of 1860 which appeared in *Frank Leslie's Illustrated Newspaper* depict the triumph of the artisan cause and the family wage but obscure the conflict among the women shoeworkers. The factory girls dropped out of the strike, which went on another two months but ended without a resolution of the wage issue.

The Lynn shoe workers in 1860 had failed to see the strategic potential for labor protest of female factory workers, ignored and opposed their articulated interests, and refused to recognize the implications for women of the mechanization and centralization of their work. The artisans of Lynn and their female allies fought in the 1860 strike to defend the traditions and ideology of preindustrial culture and decentralized production for men and women. This strategy cut off the new female factory work force from contributing to labor protest. The failure of the alliance among women shoe workers meant a continuation of the family wage system in which women workers were subordinated to male wage earners and divided from each other by marital status and the location of their work. The perceptions that shoemakers had developed of work and gender in the early nineteenth century made it difficult for them to regard women as fellow workers outside of family relationships, to include them as equals in the ideology and politics built on artisan life, or to represent the interests of female factory workers. The experiences of these women workers in centralized production symbolized what awaited all workers as capitalism in the New England shoe industry moved toward the factory system.

While male artisans defended their craft and its traditions between 1780 and 1860, women workers experienced the cutting edge of change in the reorganization of production: a sexual division of labor that denied women craft status; the separation of women's work from the family labor system; the loss of control over the coordination of work by artisans; the development of the family wage system; the isolation and vulnerability of the individual shoebinder in the outwork system; and the mechanization and centralization of work. The submersion of women's work experience within artisan culture in the new labor history has obscured the penetration of home life and household production by early industrial capitalism and has sustained the illusion of the home as a refuge from the marketplace. Artisan culture prevented men from perceiving the circumstances and accommodating the interests of women as workers, and thus weakened their ability to challenge the reorganization of production in early industrialization. The patriarchal ideology of artisan culture and the sex structuring of labor in the New England shoe industry worked together to prevent women workers from contributing to the most vital tradition of collective protest among the workers of early nineteenth-century New England.

NOTES

1. Bryan D. Palmer, "Most Uncommon Common Men: Craft and Culture in Historical Perspective," *Labour/Le Travailleur* 1 (1976): 14. For overviews of the artisan tradition in American labor history, see Sean Wilentz, "Artisan Origins of the American Working Class," *International Labor and Working Class History* 19 (1981): 1–22; and Jim Green, "Culture, Politics and Workers' Response to Industrialization in the US," *Radical America* 16 (1982): 101–28.
2. For an overall discussion of the political and ideological implications of the sexual division of labor in shoe production, see Mary H. Blewett, "Work, Gender and the Artisan Tradition in New England Shoemaking, 1780–1860," *Journal of Social History* 17 (1983): 221–48.
3. George F. Dow, ed., *Two Centuries of Travel in Essex County* (Topsfield, Mass., 1921), 182; Alan Dawley, *Class and Community* (1976), 16–25.

4. For similar patterns, see Natalie Zemon Davis, "Women in the Crafts in Sixteenth–Century Lyon," *Feminist Studies* 8 (1982): 47–80.

5. David Newhall Johnson, *Sketches of Lynn; or, The Changes of Fifty Years* (Lynn, Mass., 1880), 331.

6. Among the account books that illustrate the shift of shoebinders' work out of the family labor system are those at the Lynn Historical Society: Jonathan Boyce (1793–1813), John Burrell (1819–20), Unidentified Manufacturer's Stockbook (1830–31), and Untitled Ledger, Lynn (1790–1820), and those at the Old Sturbridge Village Archives: Samuel Bacheller Papers (1795–1845), vol. 2; James Coburn, Boxford (1804–21); Robert Brown, West Newburyport (1813–28); and Caleb Eames, Wilmington (1819–25). Alan Dawley regarded the head of the household as the coordinator of production in both kitchen and shop and offered no comment on the implications of the sexual division of labor (*Class and Community*, 16–20).

7. In 1837, 15,366 women worked as shoebinders, while 14,759 worked in cotton textile factories (Massachusetts, Secretary of the Commonwealth, *Statistical Information Relating to Certain Branches of Industry in Massachusetts for the Year Ending 1837* [Boston, 1837]).

8. "Woman," *Awl*, 21 December 1844. Women shoe workers had already claimed a moral *and* political role for women in labor protest in the early 1830s. By 1845, 18,678 women in Massachusetts were working as shoebinders, compared with 14,407 in cotton textile factories; in 1855, 32,826 women worked on shoes and 22,850 in textile factories. Shoe work was part-time work performed in the home; textile work was full-time work in factories (Massachusetts, Secretary of the Commonwealth, *Statistics of the Condition and Production of Certain Branches of Industry in Massachusetts* [Boston, 1845, 1855]).

9. Philip C. Swett, "History of Shoemaking in Haverhill, Massachusetts," manuscript, Haverhill Public Library, 16–17.

10. Sex ratios and wage increases are based on the schedules for Lynn in the federal census of manufacture for 1850 and 1860 and on the statistics of industry for Massachusetts in 1855. Also see *Lynn Weekly Reporter*, 31 March, 16 and 21 April 1860; *Salem Observer*, 3 March 1860; *Marblehead Ledger*, 29 February 1860; *Tri-Weekly Publisher* (Haverhill), 3 and 10 March 1860; *New York Herald*, 22 March 1860; *Boston Journal*, 28 February 1860. Helen L. Sumner noted the high productivity of the machine operators in relation to the shoemakers after the introduction of the sewing machine (*History of Women in Industry in the United States* [Washington, D.C., 1910], 172).

11. The regional shoe strike in 1860 has had attention from labor historians, but the role of women in the strike has had little systematic analysis. The most detailed account is in Philip S. Foner, *Women and the American Labor Movement: From Colonial Times to the Eve of World War I* (New York, 1979), 90–97. Foner emphasized the heroic and exemplary aspects of the strike, especially the women's militancy and the unity between working-class men and women, but he dismisses the dissension over strike objectives as "some discussion." Overreliance by other historians on the labor press in Lynn, especially the pro-strike *Bay State*, resulted in their missing the debate over women's roles in the strike as workers and as family members (Dawley, *Class and Community*, 79–90; Paul Faler, *Mechanics and Manufacturers* (1981), chap. 11; Norman Ware, *The Industrial Worker, 1840–1860* [Chicago, 1964], 47; John B. Andrews and W. D. P. Bliss, *History of Women in Trade Unions* [Washington, D.C., 1911], 108). The evidence in the Boston and New York newspapers whose editors sent reporters to Lynn to cover the events as eyewitnesses reveals the conflict during the four women's meetings. See the accounts from 28 February to 6 March 1860, in *Boston Herald, New York Times, New York Herald, Boston Post, Boston Journal*, and *Boston Advertiser*.

12. *New York Times*, 6 March 1860.

13. *New York Times*, 6 March 1860. For a detailed analysis of the strike, see chap. 5 in Mary H. Blewett, *Men, Women, and Work: A Study of Class, Gender, and Protest in the Nineteenth-Century New England Shoe Industry* (Urbana, Ill., 1988).

14. *Bay State* (Lynn), 8 March 1860. Marxist feminists have debated whether the family wage served the interests of patriarchy or served the ability of working-class families to resist exploitation by employers. See Heidi Hartmann, "The Unhappy Marriage of Marxism and Feminism: Towards a More Progressive Union," *Capital and Class* 8 (1979): 1–43; and Jane Humphries, "Class Struggle and the Persistence of the Working-Class Family," *Cambridge Journal of Economics* 1 (1979): 241–58. The two models appear to have operated in conflict during the Lynn strike in 1860.

9

The Domestic Balance of Power: Relations Between Mistress and Maid in Nineteenth-Century New England

Carol Lasser

Much has been written about domestic service in Europe and the United States, but only in recent years have servants themselves received much attention. Carol Lasser places power relations between mistress and maid at the center of her study. She argues that what was viewed as "decline" by employers was simply evidence of an improving bargaining position for servants. Lasser documents the ways in which Yankee and Irish servants used their newfound bargaining power to secure improvements in the terms of their employment. Increasingly, mistresses had to accommodate to a free labor system in which servants staunchly defended what freedom they did possess. The nature of domestic service and discrimination in the broader labor market limited options for Irish servants at mid-century, but they did exercise a measure of agency, as Lasser emphasizes.

After a long period of neglect, the history of domestic service, particularly in its American context, has begun to receive the scholarly attention it deserves. Careful study of the development of service and servants has begun to reveal the intriguing and complex nature of relations between mistress and maid, relations that cross class but not gender boundaries, and connect women to each other as employer and employee in the private arena of the upper- and middle-class home, not the traditional public realm of exchange. Although much remains to be explored, a decade of research has made clear that the status of servants, and, with this, relations within American households, changed significantly in the first half of the 19th century. Especially in urbanizing areas, native born "help"—those farmers' daughters who traded youthful energy for training in housewifery (and perhaps a little extra cash)—were replaced by immigrant domestics; paralleling this shift, the service relation lost its reciprocal character and came to resemble more closely wage relations of the typical external workplace.[1]

Following the lead of 19th-century observers who lived through the change, historians have generally interpreted this shift as a "decline" in service; but the concept of "decline" explains only part of the story. Influenced

Excerpted from "Domestic Balance of Power: Relations Between Mistress and Maid in Nineteenth-Century New England," by Carol Lasser in *Labor History* 28 (1987): 5–22.

Domestic servants posing for photographer. Smithsonian Institution/Office of Imaging, Printing, and Photographic Services.

by the relative abundance of sources reflecting the employers' point of view, scholars have too readily accepted at face value the nostalgic lamentations of mistresses longing for a lost age. For the diaries and letters of employers and the household manuals and advice books to which they turned can also reveal what the changes in the service relation meant "from the bottom up." A growing body of works in women's and labor history has demonstrated the ability of human beings working in oppressive and often despised conditions to create for themselves ways to maintain their dignity, and to exercise some power over their lives. Drawing upon this scholarship, the historian of domestic service should ask whether the loss of the personal, almost feudalistic tie between mistress and maid was an unmitigated and equal loss for both parties to the relationship.[2]

Once the question is posed from the servants' perspective, the traditional elite sources yield new insights. The lamentations of declension suggest employers' protests against their relative loss of power, and in particular, loss of their nonmonetary influence in an increasingly competitive market in labor. Seen in this way, it is clear that the curtailment of what has been called "benevolent maternalism" paralleled the growth of a new set of more impersonal, market mediated labor relations, constituting for servants a kind of "bourgeois freedom" which they slowly learned to use to develop leverage and to bargain more openly, thus asserting a new kind of control over their conditions of employment. While domestic work remained a physically demanding and often demeaning employment, 19th century servants found ways to exercise some power in the houses in which they worked, and with this, to establish for themselves a limited but significant sense of their own autonomy and agency.[3]

Drawing largely on materials from southern New England, especially Boston, an area in the forefront of economic and social change in the 19th century, this essay suggests how some servants used the leverage of the market to free themselves from some of the most grating restraints of the personal bonds with their employers. First, it examines the potential female labor force and the limited market for women's wage labor in the opening years of the 19th century; then, it analyzes the attraction of service for immigrant women arriving in large numbers in the 1840s in the midst of the transition. Finally, it explores the rhetoric of mistresses' complaints, finding in it evidence of employers' growing awareness of the pressures the labor market placed upon them. What employers experienced as threats to their domestic comfort and maternal authority, servants understood as avenues for at least limited autonomy in an oppressive relationship.

*   *   *

Throughout the 19th century, the wage-earning options available to women were quite limited and domestic service remained the single most important source of women's paid employment. Yet amid this continuity, the larger meaning of wage work, as well as the character of the female labor force, changed substantially. In New England, young, native-born women working within the context of a rural family economy often spent time as "help" in the household of a neighbor. Such employment did not represent long-term commitment to, nor a serious dependence upon, wage work. Rather, the earning strategy was temporary, since even if women were expected to generate cash the choice was not so much between service and other forms of paid employment as it was between working for others and engaging in some sort of commodity production for market—dairy or poultry work, raising butter or eggs for sale, weaving, spinning, or making palm leaf hats.[4]

During the first few decades of the 19th century, increasingly marginalized farms were hard pressed to sustain a household economy based on commodity production, even with the regular contribution of women's labor. Wage-earning employment off the farm gained significance for both men and women. As family orientations shifted from the lineal to the conjugal unit, the out migration of marriageable young men increased, and the need for individual wage-earning strategies for young women intensified. Some joined Lucy Larcom in New England's first textile factories; others explored the region's cities, particularly Boston.[5]

The expanding urban economy did offer work for women, but the range of choices remained narrow, particularly for the unskilled. Sewing, an occupation which required no special training for women who had from childhood been taught the use of the needle, was, as a result, characterized by "low wages, underemployment, and overwork." Despite its position as the second most common employment for women, it held little attraction for those who sought to support themselves. Even married women who took in some sewing to supplement their husbands' earnings complained bitterly about the exploitive pay structure. But alternatives were few; even in Boston, only a handful of women found employment in such light manufacturing as paper, tobacco, and trusses. Moreover, at mid-century, none of these occupations was particularly well-paying.[6] Thus women migrating from the New England countryside regularly turned to domestic service.

In this situation, the typical young, native-born woman who took a place in an urban household in ante-bellum New England was probably not motivated by hopes of the protection and maternal benevolence of her employer. Nor was she likely to desire an apprenticeship in housewifery. Rather, the simple cash nexus was, increasingly, the likely inducement; she wanted money and the autonomy money could buy.[7]

Young women with such aims did not make the most docile of servants, and reactions to them were mixed. As Hezekiah Niles reported in his *Weekly Register:*

Europeans . . . have a universal complaint to make about the "impertinence of servants," . . . These girls will not call the lady of the house *mistress* or drop a *curtsey* when honored with a command; and if they do not like the usage they receive, will be off in an instant. . . . They think that the employer is quite as much indebted to them as they are to the employer. . . .

But American mistresses accustomed to the peculiarities of "help" were less surprised by such behavior. Catharine Sedgwick found the paradox of the "republican independent dependent" salutary, for, she believed, it produced "the very best servant . . . for capability and virtue of a self-regulating and self-respecting agent." The independence of domestics, she noted with satisfaction, was indicative of the relative freedom enjoyed even by young women to contract their time for the best available wages, whether in service or in other employments. For them, work was a means to an end. As Sedgwick noted, such women "used their power; they had something better before them than domestic subordination and household service."[8]

By the 1830s and 1840s, the ability of native-born women to use the market for domestic service to their own advantage was strengthened by several additional factors. First, the economy of rural New England which had forced young women beyond the boundaries of the household economy began to stabilize as birth rates fell and out migration rose. Thus, it was less imperative for large numbers of young women to leave their parental homes; indeed, there were relatively fewer women to leave, and hence fewer native-born women seeking work as servants in the city. Second, women could choose from a growing number of alternative employments in the region, including school teaching, shoe work, and greater opportunities in the textile factories. Third, those who did migrate to cities in search of employment in service found a rapidly rising urban population, and with it, a fast growing market for domestic servants. Between 1820 and 1850, for example, Boston's population more than tripled; and, as wealth and inequality rose in tandem, a larger number of families undoubtedly sought servants to enable them to participate in the "cult of domesticity," which mandated higher standards of comfort, cleanliness and gentility. . . . Taken together, all these factors suggest that an increasing demand for servants among a growing urban population, combined with a relatively stable, or perhaps even declining, supply of native-born women, meant the market in domestic labor favored the laborer.[9]

Employers' diaries and letters of the 1830s complained constantly about their difficulty in finding and keeping servants. Desperate employers expressed their feelings as a sense of their own victimization by those who were supposed to serve them. When young Lucy Pierce married the Transcendentalist minister Frederic Henry Hedge, her mother in outlying Brookline searched the countryside as well as Boston itself for appropriate household help to send to her frantic daughter in Cambridge. Louisa Lee Waterhouse complained to her husband that in the past, she had been able to hire several able servants, but, in the late 1830s, could secure now only one and "I can't depend on her and had rather bear and forbear a while than change." Most telling, perhaps, was the letter Mehitable Mary Dawes Goddard wrote to her sister in 1830 expressing her gratitude for a downturn in the local economy, noting that it meant a momentary advantage for the mistress: "wages are lower, & of course there is a corresponding improvement in the behavior of this class of people—I do not wish them to suffer for suffering's sake, but I do fear nothing but absolute want will compel them to do their duty. . . ." Yet she admitted the change could be only temporary, for "the instant the pressure is over, they will be as topping as ever."[10]

The vast international migrations beginning in the late 1840s should have marked a turning point in the labor market balance by bringing to New England cities a large unskilled female labor force eager to take employment as domestic servants; and, in an economy based on simple supply and de-mand, mistresses should then have gained the upper hand. Certainly, there were more women available; Irish women were particularly attracted to ser-vice for the advantages it offered to them. Many had come to America alone and needed housing as well as employment; moreover, live-in service meant that most of a woman's earnings could be sent back to Ireland to support family members left behind, or perhaps finance their migration. In addition, service promised year-round employment, avoiding the periodic or seasonal layoffs that accompanied work in many industries, especially the needle trades. For all these reasons, immigrant Irish women found in domestic ser-vice an excellent opportunity. Yet the sheer availability of new laborers did not end the employers' perceptions of an ongoing crisis in service.[11]

For a time, prejudice seems to have played a role in imposing an artifi-cial limit on what mistresses defined as the supply of appropriate workers thus exacerbating for some old school mistresses their sense of exasperation. While it maintained great strength, discrimination hindered the ability of willing immigrant workers to make the best of their situation. Yet slowly, even the most prestigious families accepted their dependence on Irish servants. Mary Gardner Lowell, brought up in one prominent New England family and married into another, noted in her 1849 diary that she had, for the first time, hired Irish women, to work as cook and chambermaid in her country home in Waltham for the summer. Louisa Crowninshield Bacon, a descendant of one of the great merchant families of Salem, noted that before 1850, the do-mestics in her house were "always American," but thereafter, "when no more American servants could be found, like everyone else we had Irish. In fact, they were the only ones available." . . . Yet the eventual acceptance of servants from so distinctly different a cultural background marked an important tran-sition in the evolution of New England service toward a simple cash nexus.[12]

Once they entered the homes of the Yankee middle and upper classes, Irish domestics proved no more docile nor settled than their Yankee prede-cessors. Moreover, the immigrant servants soon found that they too could shop for the best situation. They learned to bargain—sometimes with their feet—for the highest wages, the most conducive working conditions, and the best locations. From the servants' point of view, the loss of the reciprocity of "benevolent maternalism" was balanced by two key acquisitions; first, they now had access to places for which they never would have been hired as "help"; and second, they could use their growing knowledge of the labor market for immediate, personal gain.

It was not that servants had never before bargained for higher wages and better conditions. . . . But employers and didactic writers were especially distressed by the attempts of Irish domestics to assert their own needs and to bargain for their own ends. Reacting with alarm, they charged that these recent immigrants were not yet ready to understand and enjoy the privileges of a republic, including the contractualism of its market system. As Catharine Beecher complained in 1869:

> . . . the Irish and German servants . . . became more or less infected with the spirit of democracy. They came to this country with vague notions of freedom and equality . . . they repudiated many of those habits of respect and courtesy which belonged to their former condition, and asserted their own will and way in the round unvarnished phrase which they supposed to be their right as republican citizens. Life became a sort of domestic wrangle and struggle between the employers, who secretly confessed their weakness, but endeavored openly to assume the air and bearing of authority, and the employed, who knew their power and insisted on their privileges.

Yet Beecher recognized that the clock could not be turned back toward the older notions of domestic apprenticeship. Thus, to counteract what she saw as the excessive power enjoyed by servants, Beecher pointedly advised employers to take their best advantage of the freedom of contract:

> The more strictly and perfectly the business matters of the first engagement of domestics are conducted, the more likelihood there is of mutual quiet and satisfaction in the relation. . . . It is much better to regulate such affairs by cool contract in the outset than by warm altercations and protracted domestic battles.

So the struggle of servants to establish their economic rights, buying and selling their own labor power, clearly threatened Beecher and the women for whom she wrote. And Beecher's answer for employers rested on the abandonment of the notions of reciprocity and responsibility which, she asserted, immigrants were incapable of understanding. She sought for mistresses to recover not only some vague emotional satisfaction, but, more importantly, real power in the household relationship as well.[13]

Yet even when mistresses tried to reconcile themselves to the exigencies of the new relations, they charged that the transition of servants to the ethics of a marketplace economy was at best incomplete. Commentators and employers complained that domestics were annoyingly casual about the niceties of contracts, the touchstone of free labor engagements. Under the pen name "Gail Hamilton," New England author Mary Abigail Dodge charged that servants "lack a moral sense, a mental perception, or whatever the faculty is which makes one capable of contracting an engagement." Employers recounted with annoyance the myriad of incidents in which domestics verbally committed never arrived or left abruptly without giving the expected and customary notice. Few employers, however, understood the inconsistencies of their position, demanding feudal loyalty on the one hand, and free market contractualism on the other. One observer who placed this problem in its particular 19th century American context was E. L. Godkin, editor of the progressive periodical *The Nation.* As he noted, the behavior of household employees was simply an accurate assessment of their labor market position: "The only real restraint on laborers of any class among us nowadays, is the difficulty of finding another place." He admitted that it appeared a servant's "sense of the obligations of contracts is feeble," yet he reminded his readers:

> her spirit about contracts is really that of the entire community in which she lives. . . . Native mechanics and seamstresses are just as perfidious as Bridget, but incur less obloquy, because their faithlessness causes less annoyance. . . . What makes [her] so fond of change is that she lives in a singularly restless society, in which everybody is engaged in a continual struggle to "better himself"— her master, in nine cases out of ten, setting her an example of dislike to steady industry and slow gains.[14]

In short, the servant was learning from the surrounding society how to perform as a well-informed actor on the expanding urban labor market.

A rare piece of advice literature aimed directly at the immigrant domestic, not her mistress, dignified the servant's attempts to make the best of the market, urging even further that it was, at times, a duty. The "Nun of Kenmare," writing *Advice to Irish Girls in America,* counseled her readers not to change their places for transient reasons, but noted that "there is no harm in changing a place to better oneself. . . . If you have a father and mother or other relatives depending on you, whom you ought to support, or if you are engaged to be married, and want to lay by something for your future home, then you would be quite right" to leave when offered higher wages. "The Nun" expected and even encouraged servants to exercise their bargaining powers as free persons and free laborers.[15]

But critics proved reluctant to acknowledge fully the right of servants to use to their own advantage a market they had not created; and in their resistance, employers and their advisors often obscured the relationship of the domestic to her own labor power. Such mystification is apparent in the attacks of advice books on housekeepers who offered high wages to lure good servants away from the homes of friends and acquaintances. Eunice Beecher, the wife of Henry Ward Beecher and sister-in-law of Catharine Beecher, devoted an entire chapter in her 1875 work, *Motherly Talks with Young Housekeepers,* to the evil of "stealing" servants. According to her analysis,

> We object to no one's obtaining the full value for his [*sic*] work, but claim that there should be no meddling, no underhand work to buy servants or laborers

from another, by private offer of larger wages. Advertising is open to all, and brings the needed help.

Beecher seemed reluctant to recognize that it was the employees themselves and not their employers who were selling their labor, and, moreover, that "full value" might be a larger amount than prevailing wage rates. Her conclusion that enticing servants to leave their positions represented an *employer's* violation of the golden rule overlooked the other parties in the relation to whom justice was also due. Another domestic handbook charged that offers of enticing raises were "a kind of larceny [that] should be punished." Yet what was theft from the employer's point of view was power to the employee.[16]

The intelligence office, or employment agency, incontrovertible proof of the growing market orientation of relations between housewife and hireling, became a favorite target for critics of the transformation of service; as "Gail Hamilton" commented acerbically, it "was the last place in the world to look for intelligence." Maternalistic mistresses blamed these employment agencies for undermining older notions of a reciprocal, benevolent relationship by turning the delicate matter of matching mistress and maid into a profit-oriented business. At intervals throughout the 19th century, wealthy women worked through orphan asylums, female moral reform societies and charitable agencies to provide institutional alternatives to these crassly commercial enterprises.[17]

By the second half of the 19th century, mistresses had no choice but to accept the commercial intelligence office as a necessary evil. Employers' diaries and letters chronicle the seemingly endless numbers of agencies on which they called in their search for servants, and record as well employers' resentment at being at the mercy of the market. In 1870, for example, Elizabeth Ellery Dana lamented that the cook her mother had just engaged decided not to come since she heard that the family work was too hard. "Lily" Dana then visited four intelligence offices in the morning, and her mother called upon a fifth. Less than two months later, the sudden flight of another new servant sent Dana to six intelligence offices one morning, and an additional four (not counting a charitable society) three days later. As Dana made clear, she took little pleasure in her task, but found no alternative. She resented, but could not resist, trading in the market for labor power.[18]

Dana well knew the relationship that had been lost between mistress and servant. As part of an old Boston Brahmin family, she had long observed the closeness between her imperious aunt Charlotte Dana, and Maria, her aunt's steadfast privileged domestic who enjoyed almost familial standing. Aunt Charlotte defended the prerogatives of her servant against the encroachments of less established newcomers; Maria's sleeping accommodations rivaled those of Dana's sisters, and the care taken of her health was comparable to that taken of family members, not other servants. In return,

Aunt Charlotte was richly rewarded with the devotion and endurance of faithful Maria who remained with her hot-tempered mistress despite arbitrary and pre-emptive commands and general unpredictability. Indeed, the symbiosis of this mistress and maid contrasted sharply with the crassly materialistic ties which often failed to secure the service of other wage-labor employees in the various Dana households. Domestics hired at commercial agencies tested the limits of family patience and proved the buoyancy of the market. For Lily Dana, the result of the passing of benevolent maternalism was her frequent and frustrating visits to Boston intelligence offices to replenish the supply of household help.[19]

But the eloquent testimony to the transformation of employers' experiences in hiring servants left in the diaries and letters of the Dana family, and similar households, should not, however, blind historians to the other side of the story. If the Danas—and even Aunt Charlotte's Maria—mourned the growing distance between employer and employee, the passing of sponsored mobility, and the end of surrogate familial relationships, few 19th century domestics shared their longing for household harmony reconstructed on an earlier model. By the middle of the 19th century, domestics were increasingly different from their employers, in class and culture. For these servants, their work was primarily a way to earn cash and independence. They did not seek ersatz mothers or benevolent guardians.

These new servants were *not* loyal, docile employees; they *did* leave what employers viewed as essentially suitable situations to suit their own convenience, and they *did* often evaluate their satisfaction according to narrowly materialistic standards. From their perspective, benevolent maternalism represented anachronistic inequality in the marketplace. Kindness and reciprocity often cloaked the locus of power in the caretaker relationship; benevolent mistresses defined the care to be taken, imposing it upon the object of benevolence. In the name of charity and uplift, mistresses had waged unconscious and unintentional wars of "cultural imperialism" upon their maids, struggling to win the hearts and minds of their employees, assuming that both sides could establish a unity of interests. Early in the century, when class and culture of mistress and maid had been more similar, genuine collaboration was more likely; and sympathy and tradition served to soften the lines of power on either side. But the growing impersonality of urban market relations shifted the context in which employer and employee met and negotiated, and employers felt victimized. Unwilling to recognize the existence of a growing conflict of interests between the two sides in the marketplace, employers charged servants with at best ingratitude, at worst treason, to the family state.[20]

But servants declared independence from arbitrary rule and sought to exercise their limited but significant "freedom"—the power to sell their labor to the highest bidder. There were, of course, limits to this freedom. Domestics needed work, so their ability to exercise choice was never unlimited. And servants' separation from their employers could be only at best incomplete while domestics still lived in. . . . And, in addition, hard work and deplorable situations often characterized both the employment itself and the conditions which drove women to seek it. Nonetheless, mid-19th century domestics were beginning to learn to use the market relations on which service was increasingly based to their own advantage.

Domestics learned to bargain, but it is important to remember that the transformation of service was not wholly a revolution from the bottom up. Perhaps more than they realized, mistresses themselves were at least in part responsible for the deteriorating viability of benevolent materialism. The growth of cities, foreign immigration, and increasingly complex exchange relations in broader society are all important, but one suspects another factor as well.

Beginning in the 1840s, the authors of household manuals, cookbooks, and didactic literature noted the declension of housekeepers from the "noble matronage" who had helped their men secure the freedom of the land during the American revolution. In scathing indictments, they charged that academic and ornamental education had expanded at the cost of practical housekeeping instruction; mid-century middle- and upper-class girls, they asserted, lacked the experience that would have allowed them to teach their domestics what their surrogate daughters should know. In the years after the Civil War, advisors modified their expectations of young homemakers by suggesting that the ability to perform housework was not as important as the capacity to manage effectively; but many expressed their doubts that mistresses could operate even at this level.

Thus, neither benevolent mistresses nor competent managers, middle-class women trained to be merely decorative lacked practical skills and then lost their ability to exert competent authority. Enclosed within Victorian domesticity, these "ladies" confronted a sophisticated labor market of which they could make little sense despite dizzying dashes from domestic enclosure into the maze of intelligence offices in their efforts to hire other women to perform work that they could neither undertake, nor describe, nor direct.

The isolation of the mistress in her own "separate sphere" from the market further enlarged the growing chasm between employer and employee and contributed to their different interpretations of the shifting relations of service. As domestics learned to bring market pressures to bear—pressures their employers perceived as lack of faithfulness, unfair wage inflation, and instability—mistresses expressed resentment at the "power" of those who were supposed to be their servants. By the late 19th century, within the domestic service relation, "bourgeois woman" confined by patriarchal domesticity confronted "economic woman" forced to assert her bourgeois rights in the marketplace. "Economic woman" often suffered at the invisible hands of the market and, as a woman employed by a woman, found herself as the dependent of a dependent; but she nonetheless acted as an agent transforming the relationship of women to society, both within and outside the home. Mistresses might wistfully look back to an earlier age, but for servants, the decline of the surrogate familial relations of benevolent maternalism was not an unmitigated loss. The market offered, although it did not always provide, the opportunity for a new kind of economic independence, if not self-sufficiency. Servants learned to exercise new "power" while their mistresses perceived their own enslavement by the market.

NOTES

1. The most important recent works on domestic service are: David M. Katzman, *Seven Days A Week: Women and Domestic Service in Industrializing America* (New York, 1978); and Faye E. Dudden, *Serving Women: Household Service in Nineteenth-Century America* (Middletown, 1983).
    Daniel E. Sutherland, *Americans and Their Servants: Domestic Service in the United States from 1800 to 1920* (Baton Rouge, 1981) disagrees with the idea of a major transformation in service. Hasia R. Diner, *Erin's Daughter in America: Irish Immigrant Women in the Nineteenth Century* (Baltimore, 1983) gave a particularly good account of Irish servants.
2. Among the best known 19th century authors who articulated notions of "decline" were Catharine Beecher, *Letters to Persons Who Are Engaged in Domestic Service* (New York, 1842); Lydia Maria Child, *History of the Condition of Women* (Boston, 1835); Sarah Josepha Hale, *Sketches of American Character* (Boston, 1831); [Elizabeth Stuart Phelps,] *The Sunny Side; Or, the Country Minister's Wife.* Writing in the tradition of "progressive history," Lucy Maynard Salmon in *Domestic Service* (New York, 1897) evaluated the 19th century trend as one of decline.
3. The term "bourgeois freedom" is used here in the sense that Karl Marx suggested it in "Manifesto of the Communist Party," *The Marx-Engels Reader*, Robert C. Tucker, ed. (New York, 1972), 348. Thomas Dublin argues that New England women in the 1830s and 1840s viewed their wages as their own, and saw them as a part of their "independence." See Thomas Dublin, "Introduction," *Farm to Factory: Women's Letters, 1830–1860* (New York, 1981), 23–25; and *Women at Work: The Transformation of Work and Community in Lowell, Massachusetts, 1826–1860* (New York, 1979), especially chapt. 3.
4. Michael Merrill, "Cash is Good to Eat: Self-Sufficiency and Exchange in the Rural Economy of the United States," *Radical History Review* 4(Fall 1976), 42–71 describes the flexibility of the early market economy; Dudden, *Serving Women*, 12–19 places domestic service in the context of the rural economy.
5. On the shift from the lineal to the conjugal family, see James A. Henretta, "Families and Farms: *Mentalité* in Pre-Industrial America," *William and Mary Quarterly* 3d ser., 35 (1978), 3–32.
6. The quotation characterizing sewing is from Christine Stansell, "The Origins of the Sweatshop: Women and Early Industrialization in New York City," in *Working-Class America: Essays on Labor, Community, and American Society*, Michael H. Frisch and Daniel J. Walkowitz, eds. (Urbana, IL, 1983), 78. For one view of the female labor market in Boston and the relationship of work to migration patterns, see Carol Lasser, "'The World's Dread Laugh': Singlehood and Service in Nineteenth-Century Boston," in *The New England Working Class and the New Labor History*, Donald H. Bell and Herbert C. Gutman, eds. (Urbana, IL, 1987).
    Wage rates for Boston women in industrial work in approximately 1830 ranged from 33 to 75 cents per day, out of which women had to pay for food, clothing and shelter; wage rates for servants were approximately $1.00 to 2.00 per week, and domestic servants received food and shelter, and often clothing as well.
7. Dublin, *Farm to Factory*, includes writings by Mary Paul, 97–99, and Mary Edwards, 83, both of whom undertook work as domestic servants for short periods of time. See also "Clarissa Packard" [Caroline Gilman], *Recollections of a Housekeeper* (New York, 1986), 32.
    Two well-known New England authors reiterated this theme later in the century. See Louisa May Alcott, *Work: A Story of Experience* (1873; reprint New York, 1977). Alcott herself worked in service for a short period of time when her parents' finances were especially bad; see Dudden, *Serving Women*, 87–89. Also Charlotte Perkins Gilman's heroine Diantha Bell in *What Diantha Did* quite explicitly sees service as a means to independence—in this case towards learning the skills she will need to open her own cleaning company. For an excerpt from the novel

which makes clear the role of service in Diantha's quest for earning power, see "What Diantha Did," 123–140, *The Charlotte Perkins Gilman Reader,* Ann J. Lane, ed. (New York, 1980).

Prevailing wage rates, described above, note 6, provided women who worked in service with a very modest, but nonetheless significant, amount of disposable cash.

8. *Niles Weekly Register,* 9 (Dec. 2, 1815), 238–239; Catharine Sedgwick, *Home* (Boston, 1839), 72; Catharine Sedgwick, *A New England Tale* (1852), 10–11; Mary E. Dewey, ed., *Life and Letters of Catharine M. Sedgwick* (New York, 1871), "Recollections of Childhood," 22.

9. J. Potter . . . concluded that the overall American birth rate declined between 1800 and 1860, particularly in New England: see "The Growth of Population in America, 1700–1860," in D. V. C. Glass and D. Eversley, *Population in History: Essays in Historical Demography* (Chicago, 1965), 672–673. More recently, Maris Vinovskis, *Fertility in Massachusetts from the Revolution to the Civil War* (New York, 1981), provides an analysis of declining birth rates including regional varia-tions within the state; he concludes that, although urban fertility declined faster than rural fertil-ity, the decline in rural fertility was, nonetheless, significant and a major factor in the overall decline of Massachusetts fertility in the years before 1860. See especially 100–101.

On the new occupations available for women workers, see Richard M. Bernard and Maris A. Vinovskis, "The Female School Teacher in Ante-Bellum Massachusetts," *Journal of Social History* 10 (1977), 332–345, which analyzes the expansion in opportunities for school teaching; shoe-making is described by Alan Dawley, *Class and Community: The Industrial Revolution in Lynn* (Cam-bridge, MA, 1976); the expansion in the textile industry is detailed by Caroline Ware, *The New England Cotton Manufacture: A Study in Industrial Beginnings* (New York, 1931); and the expansion of Lowell in particular is chronicled in Thomas Dublin, *Women at Work.*

10. Lucy Tappan Pierce to Lucy Pierce Hedge, undated letter attributed to 1830–1832 pe-riod, Box 2, Folder 16, Poor Family Papers, Schlesinger Library; Louisa Lee Waterhouse, Journal entry, undated [1841], Waterhouse Papers, Massachusetts Historical Society; Mehitable Mary Dawes Goddard to Lucretia Dawes, Boston, Feb. 21, 1830, May-Goddard papers, Schlesinger Li-brary.

11. Dudden, *Serving Women,* 60–61; see also, for example, Oscar Handlin, *Boston's Immigrants: A Study in Acculturation,* rev. ed. (New York, 1971), 61–62; and Diner, *Erin's Daughters,* 93–94.

12. Mary Gardner Lowell, Diary Volume 81 (1849) May 5, 1849, Francis Cabot Lowell II Pa-pers, Massachusetts Historical Society, Louisa Crowninshield Bacon, *Reminiscences* (Salem, 1922), 34–37.

13. Beecher and Stowe, *American Women's Home,* 320–321, 324.

14. "Gail Hamilton" [Mary Abigail Dodge,] *Woman's Worth and Worthlessness: The Complement to "A New Atmosphere"* (New York, 1872), 95–96. Edward Godkin, "Manners and Morals of the Kitchen," 63–64. *Reflections and Comments, 1867–1895* (New York, 1895); the piece originally ap-peared in the *Nation,* 16 (Jan 2, 1873), 6–7.

15. Sister Mary Francis Clare, *Advice to Irish Girls in America by the Nun of Kenmare* (New York, 1872), 28.

16. Eunice Beecher ("Mrs. Henry Ward Beecher"), *Motherly Talks with Young Housekeepers* (New York, 1875), 112–116; Mrs. Oakley, *From Attic to Cellar: A Book for Young Housekeepers* (New York, 1879), 26.

17. Dodge, *Woman's Worth,* 79; for one case study of orphan placement, see Carol Lasser, "'A Pleasingly Oppressive Burden': The Transformation of Domestic Service in Salem, 1800–1840," *Essex Institute Historical Collections,* 116 (1980), 156–175. Other Boston charitable agencies inter-ested in placement included the Society for the Mutual Benefit of Female Domestics and Their Employers, the New England Female Moral Reform Association, and the Boston Society for the Prevention of Pauperism.

18. Elizabeth Ellery Dana, Diary for 1870, entries for Mar. 19, May 20, and May 23, Dana Family Papers, Schlesinger Library.

19. Elizabeth Ellery Dana, Diary for 1868, entries for Oct. 9, Nov. 5, for example. The whole family commented on Aunt Charlotte's temper, and Lily Dana noted her readiness for a walk-out of household servants if her aunt assumed the task of overseeing the home.

20. I am indebted to Diana Grossman Kahn for her astute observations on maternal benevo-lence and cultural imperialism, or, as she has also called it, internal "colonization." Too much of the current literature on "maternal thinking" and caretaking lacks this critical perspective. See especially Sarah Ruddick, "Maternal Thinking," *Feminist Studies,* 6(1980), 842–67.

10

Women, Work, and Protest in the Early Lowell Mills: "The Oppressing Hand of Avarice Would Enslave Us"

Thomas Dublin

The emergence of factory employment between 1820 and 1850 had contradictory results. On the one hand, this new employment offered young, single women wages far in excess of anything else they could earn in teaching, sewing, or domestic service. On the other hand, it led to the first sustained collective labor protests by women workers.

Thomas Dublin attempts to explain this contradiction by exploring the nature of the female experience in the first cotton textile mills of Lowell, Massachusetts. He finds that work-sharing in the mills and shared mill housing contributed to the growth of a close-knit community among mill workers, and that the sense of community coupled with republican egalitarian traditions lead women to be sensitive to declining wages and working conditions. Women workers responded collectively to wage cuts, speedups, and stretchouts, and challenged the power of mill employers. While the protests rarely succeeded, they reveal well the clash of values that accompanied the industrial revolution.

In the years before 1850 the textile mills of Lowell, Massachusetts, were a celebrated economic and cultural attraction. Foreign visitors invariably included them on their American tours. Interest was prompted by the massive scale of these mills, the astonishing productivity of the power-driven machinery, and the fact that women comprised most of the work force.

Lowell was, in fact, an impressive accomplishment. In 1820, there had been no city at all—only a dozen family farms along the Merrimack River in East Chelmsford. In 1821, however, a group of Boston capitalists purchased land and water rights along the river and a nearby canal, and began to build a major textile manufacturing center. Opening two years later, the first factory employed Yankee women recruited from the nearby countryside. By 1840, ten textile corporations with thirty-two mills valued at more than ten million dollars lined the banks of the river and nearby canals.[1] Adjacent to the mills were rows of company boarding houses and tenements which accommodated most of the eight thousand factory operatives.

Adapted from "Women, Work, and Protest in the Early Lowell Mills: 'The Oppressing Hand of Avarice Would Enslave Us,'" by Thomas Dublin in *Labor History* 16 (1975): 99–116.

Women weavers, c. 1860. American Textile History Museum. Lowell, Mass.

As Lowell expanded and became the nation's largest textile manufacturing center, the experiences of women operatives changed as well. The increasing number of firms in Lowell and in the other mill towns brought the pressure of competition. Overproduction became a problem and the prices of finished cloth decreased. The high profits of the early years declined and so, too, did conditions for the mill operatives. Wages were reduced and the pace of work within the mills was stepped up. Women operatives did not accept these changes without protest. In 1834 and 1836 they went on strike to protest wage cuts, and between 1843 and 1848 they mounted petition campaigns aimed at reducing the hours of labor in the mills.

These labor protests in early Lowell contribute to our understanding of the response of workers to the growth of industrial capitalism in the first half of the nineteenth century. They indicate the importance of values and attitudes dating back to an earlier period and also the transformation of these values in a new setting.

The preconditions for the labor unrest in Lowell before 1850 may be found in the study of the daily worklife of its operatives. In their everyday, relatively conflict-free lives, mill women created the mutual bonds which made possible united action in times of crisis. The existence of a tight-knit community among them was the most important element in determining the collective, as opposed to individual, nature of this response.

The mutual dependence among women in early Lowell was rooted in the structure of mill work itself. Newcomers to the mills were particularly dependent on their fellow operatives, but even experienced hands relied on one another for considerable support.

New operatives generally found their first experiences difficult, even harrowing, though they may have already done much handspinning and weaving in their own homes. The initiation of one of them is described in fiction in the *Lowell Offering:*

> The next morning she went into the Mill; and at first the sight of so many bands, and wheels, and springs in constant motion, was very frightful. She felt afraid to touch the loom, and she was almost sure she could never learn to weave . . . the shuttle flew out, and made a new bump on her head; and the first time she tried to spring the lathe, she broke out a quarter of the treads.[2]

While other accounts present a somewhat less difficult picture, most indicate that women only became proficient and felt satisfaction in their work after several months in the mills.[3]

The textile corporations made provisions to ease the adjustment of new operatives. Newcomers were not immediately expected to fit into the mill's regular work routine. They were at first assigned work as sparehands and were paid a daily wage independent of the quantity of work they turned out. As a sparehand, the newcomer worked with an experienced hand who instructed her in the intricacies of the job. The sparehand spelled her partner for short stretches of time and occasionally took the place of an absentee. After the passage of some weeks or months, when she could handle the normal complement of machinery—two looms for weavers during the 1830s—and when a regular operative departed, leaving an opening, the sparehand moved into a regular job.

Through this system of job training, the textile corporations contributed to the development of community among female operatives. During the most difficult period in an operative's career, the first months in the mill, she relied upon other women workers for training and support. And for every sparehand whose adjustment to mill work was aided in this process, there was an experienced operative whose work was also affected. Women were relating to one another during the work process and not simply tending their machinery. Given the high rate of turnover in the mill workforce, a large proportion of women operatives worked in pairs. At the Hamilton Company in July 1836, for example, more than a fifth of all females were sparehands.[4] Consequently, over 40 percent of the females employed there in this month worked with one another. Nor was this interaction surreptitious, carried out only when the overseer looked elsewhere; rather, it was formally organized and sanctioned by the textile corporations themselves.

In addition to the integration of sparehands, informal sharing of work often went on among regular operatives. A woman would occasionally take off a half or full day from work either to enjoy a brief vacation or to recover from illness, and fellow operatives would each take an extra loom or side of spindles so that she might continue to earn wages during her absence.[5] Women were generally paid on a piece rate basis, their wages being determined by the total output of the machinery they tended during the payroll period. With friends helping out during her absence, making sure that her looms kept running, an operative could earn almost a full wage even though she was not physically present. Such informal work-sharing was another way in which mutual dependence developed among women operatives during their working hours.

Living conditions also contributed to the development of community among female operatives. Most women working in the Lowell mills of these years were housed in company boarding houses. In July 1836, for example, more than 73 percent of females employed by the Hamilton Company resided in company housing adjacent to the mills.[6] Almost three-fourths of them, therefore, lived and worked with each other. Furthermore, the work schedule was such that women had little opportunity to interact with those not living in company dwellings. They worked, in these years, an average of 73 hours a week. Their work day ended at 7:00 or 7:30 P.M., and in the hours between supper and the 10:00 curfew imposed by management on residents of company boarding houses there was little time to spend with friends living "off the corporation."

Women in the boarding houses lived in close quarters. A typical boarding house accommodated twenty-five young women, generally crowded four to eight in a bedroom.[7] There was little possibility of privacy within the dwelling, and pressure to conform to group standards was very strong. The community of operatives which developed in the mills carried over into life at home as well.

The boarding house became a central institution in the lives of Lowell's female operatives in those years, but it was particularly important in the initial integration of newcomers into urban industrial life. Upon first leaving her rural home for work in Lowell, a women entered a setting very different from anything she had previously known. One operative, writing in the *Offering*, described the feelings of a fictional character: ". . . the first entrance into a factory boarding house seemed something dreadful. The room looked strange and comfortless, and the women cold and heartless; and when she sat down to the supper table, where among more than twenty girls, all but one were strangers, she could not eat a mouthful."[8] In the boarding house, the newcomer took the first steps in the process which transformed her from an "outsider" into an accepted member of the community of women operatives.

Recruitment of newcomers into the mills and their initial hiring was mediated through the boarding house system. Women generally did not travel to Lowell for the first time entirely on their own. They usually came because they knew someone—an older sister, cousin, or friend—who had already worked in Lowell.[9] The scene described above was a lonely one—but the newcomer did know at least one boarder among the twenty seated around the supper table. The Hamilton Company Register Books indicate that numerous pairs of operatives, having the same surnames and coming from the same town in northern New England, lived in the same boarding houses.[10] Given the personal nature of recruitment in this period, therefore, newcomers usually had the company and support of a friend or relative in their first adjustment to Lowell.

Upon entering the boarding house, the newcomer came under pressure to conform with the standards of the community of operatives. Stories in the *Offering* indicate that newcomers at first stood out from the group in terms of their speech and dress. Over time they dropped the peculiar "twang" in their speech which so amused experienced hands. Similarly, they purchased clothing more in keeping with urban than rural styles. It was an unusual and strongwilled individual who could work and live among her fellow operatives and not conform, at least outwardly, to the customs and values of this larger community.[11]

Given the all-pervasiveness of this community, one would expect it to exert strong pressures on those who did not conform to group standards. Such appears to have been the case. The community influenced newcomers to adopt its patterns of speech and dress. In addition, it enforced an unwritten code of moral conduct. Henry Miles, a minister in Lowell, described the

way in which the community pressured those who deviated from accepted
moral conduct:

> A girl, suspected of immoralities, or serious improprieties, at once loses caste.
> Her fellow boarders will at once leave the house, if the keeper does not dismiss
> the offender. In self-protection, therefore, the patron is obliged to put the of-
> fender away. Nor will her former companions walk with her, or work with her;
> till at length, finding herself everywhere talked about, and pointed at, and
> shunned, she is obliged to relieve her fellow-operatives of a presence which they
> feel brings disgrace.[12]

One should not conclude, however, that women always enforced a
moral code agreeable to Lowell's clergy, or to the mill agents and overseers
for that matter. After all, the kind of peer pressure imposed on Hannah
could be brought to bear on women in 1834 and 1836 who, on their own,
would not have protested wage cuts. It was much harder to go to work when
one's roommates were marching about town, attending rallies, or circulating
strike petitions. Similarly, the ten-hour petitions of the 1840s were certainly
aided by the fact of a tight-knit community of operatives living in a dense
neighborhood of boarding houses. To the extent that women could not have
completely private lives in the boarding houses, they probably had to conform to group norms, whether these involved speech, clothing, relations with
men, or attitudes toward the ten-hour day. Group pressure to conform, so important to the community of women in early Lowell, played a significant role
in the collective response of women to changing conditions in the mills.

In addition to the structure of work and housing in Lowell, a third factor, the homogeneity of the mill workforce, contributed to the development
of community among female operatives. In this period, the mill work-force
was homogeneous in terms of sex, nativity, and age. Payroll and other records
of the Hamilton Company reveal that more than 85 percent of those employed in July, 1836, were women and that over 96 percent were native-
born.[13] Furthermore, over 80 percent of the female workforce were between
the ages of 15 and 30; and only 10 percent were under 14 or over 40.[14]

Workforce homogeneity takes on particular significance in the context
of work structure and the nature of worker housing. Together these factors
meant that women operatives had little daily interaction with men. Men and
women did not perform the same work in the mills, and generally did not
even labor in the same rooms. Men worked in the initial picking and card-
ing processes, in the repair shop, and on the watchforce and filled all super-
visory positions in the mills. Women held all sparehand and regular
operative jobs in drawing, speeding, spinning, weaving and dressing. A typical room in the mill employed eighty women tending machinery, with two
men overseeing the work and two boys assisting them. Women had little contact with men other than their supervisors in the course of the working day.
After work, women returned to their boarding houses, where once again

there were few men. Women, then, worked and lived in a predominantly female setting.

Ethnically the workforce was also homogeneous. Immigrants formed
only 3.4 percent of those employed at Hamilton in July, 1836. In addition,
they comprised only 3 percent of residents in Hamilton Company housing.[15]
The community of women operatives was composed of women of New England stock drawn from the hill-country farms surrounding Lowell. Consequently, when experienced hands made fun of the speech and dress of
newcomers, it was understood that they, too, had been "rusty" or "rustic"
upon first coming to Lowell. This common background was another element
shared by women workers in early Lowell.

The work structure, the workers' housing, and workforce homogeneity
contributed to the growth of community among Lowell's women operatives.
To understand the larger implications of community, it is necessary to examine the labor protests of this period. For in these struggles, the new values
and attitudes which developed in the community of women operatives are
most visible.

In February 1834, 800 of Lowell's women operatives "turned-out"—
went on strike—to protest a proposed reduction in their wages. They
marched to numerous mills in an effort to induce others to join them, and, at
an outdoor rally, they petitioned others to "discontinue their labors until
terms of reconciliation are made." Their petition concluded:

> Resolved, That we will not go back into the mills to work unless our wages are
> continued . . . as they have been.
> Resolved, That none of us will go back, unless they receive us all as one.
> Resolved, That if any have not money enough to carry them home, they shall be
> supplied.[16]

The strike proved to be brief and failed to reverse the proposed wage reductions. Turning-out on a Friday, the striking women received their back wages
on Saturday, and by the middle of the next week had returned to work or left
town. Within a week of the turn-out, the mills were running near capacity.[17]

This first strike in Lowell is important not because it failed or succeeded, but simply because it took place. In an era in which women had to
overcome opposition simply to work in the mills, it is remarkable that they
would further overstep the accepted middle-class bounds of female propriety
by participating in a public protest. The agents of the textile mills certainly
considered the turn-out unfeminine. William Austin, agent of the Lawrence
Company, described the operatives' procession as an "amizonian [sic] dis-
play." He wrote further, in a letter to his company treasurer in Boston: "This
afternoon we have paid off several of these Amazons & presume that they will
leave town on Monday."[18] The turn-out was particularly offensive to the
agents because of the relationship they thought they had with their opera-

tives. Mill agents assumed an attitude of benevolent paternalism toward their female operatives, and found it particularly disturbing that the women paid such little heed to their advice. The strikers were not merely unfeminine, they were ungrateful as well.

Such attitudes notwithstanding, women chose to turn-out. They did so for two principal reasons. First, the wage cuts undermined their sense of dignity and social equality, which was an important element in their Yankee heritage. Second, these wage cuts were seen as an attack on their economic independence.

A prime motive for the strike was outrage at the social implications of the wage cuts. In a statement of principles which circulated among operatives, women expressed well the sense of themselves which prompted their protests:

UNION IS POWER

Our present object is to have union and exertion, and we remain in possession of our unquestionable rights. We circulate this paper wishing to obtain the names of all who imbibe the spirit of our Patriotic Ancestors, who preferred privation to bondage, and parted with all that renders life desirable—and even life itself—to procure independence for their children. The oppressing hand of avarice would enslave us, and to gain their object, they gravely tell us of the pressure of the time, this we are already sensible of, and deplore it. If any are in want of assistance, the Ladies will be compassionate and assist them; but we prefer to have the disposing of our charities in our own hands; and as we are free, we would remain in possession of what kind Providence has bestowed upon us; and remain daughters of freemen still.[19]

At several points in the proclamation the women drew on their Yankee heritage. Connecting their turn-out with the efforts of their "Patriotic Ancestors" to secure independence from England, they interpreted the wage cuts as an effort to "enslave" them—to deprive them of their independent status as "daughters of freemen."

Though very general and rhetorical, the statement of these women does suggest their sense of their own worth and dignity. Elsewhere, they expressed the conviction that they were the social equals of the overseers, indeed of the mill owners themselves.[20] The wage cuts, however, struck at this assertion of social equality. These reductions made it clear that the operatives were subordinate to their employers, rather than equal partners in a contract binding on both parties. By turning-out, the women emphatically denied that they were subordinates; but by returning to work the next week, they demonstrated that in economic terms they were no match for their corporate superiors.

In point of fact, these Yankee operatives were subordinate in early Lowell's social and economic order, but they never consciously accepted this status. Their refusal to do so became evident whenever the mill owners attempted to exercise the power they possessed. This fundamental contradiction between the objective status of operatives and their consciousness of it was at the root of the 1834 turn-out and of subsequent labor protests in Lowell before 1850. The corporations could build mills, create thousands of jobs, and recruit women to fill them. Nevertheless, they bought only the workers' labor power, and then only for as long as these workers chose to stay. Women could always return to their rural homes, and they had a sense of their own worth and dignity, factors limiting the actions of management.

Women operatives viewed the wage cuts as a threat to their economic independence. This independence had two related dimensions. First, the women were self-supporting while they worked in the mills and, consequently, were independent of their families back home. Second, they were able to save out of their monthly earnings and could then leave the mills for the old homestead whenever they so desired. In effect, they were not totally dependent upon mill work. Their independence was based largely on the high level of wages in the mills. They could support themselves and still save enough to return home periodically. The wage cuts threatened to deny them this outlet, substituting instead the prospect of total dependence on mill work. Small wonder, then, there was alarm that "the oppressing hand of avarice would enslave us." To be forced, out of economic necessity, to lifelong labor in the mills would have indeed seemed like slavery.[21] The Yankee operatives spoke directly to the fear of a dependency based on impoverishment when offering to assist any women workers who "have not money enough to carry them home." Wage reductions, however, offered only the *prospect* of a future dependence on mill employment. By striking, the women asserted their actual economic independence of the mills and their determination to remain "daughters of freemen still."

While the women's traditional conception of themselves as independent daughters of freemen played a major role in the turn-out, this factor acting alone would not necessarily have triggered the 1834 strike. It would have led women as individuals to quit work and return to their rural homes. But the turn-out was a collective protest. When the wage reductions were announced, women began to hold meetings in the mills during meal breaks in order to assess tactical possibilities. Their turn-out began at one mill when the agent discharged a woman who had presided at such a meeting. Their procession through the streets passed by other mills, expressing a conscious effort to enlist as much support as possible for their cause. At a mass meeting, the women drew up a resolution which insisted that none be discharged for their participation in the turn-out. This strike, then, was a collective response to the proposed wage cuts. The existence of a tight-knit community among women turned individual opposition to the wage cuts into a collective protest.

In October 1836, women again went on strike. This second turn-out was similar to the first in several respects. Its immediate cause was also a wage reduction; marches and a large outdoor rally were organized; again, like the earlier protest, the basic goal was not achieved: the corporations refused to restore wages and operatives either left Lowell or returned to work at the new rates.

Despite these surface similarities between the turn-outs, there were some real differences. One involved scale: over 1500 operatives turned out in 1836, compared to only 800 earlier.[22] Moreover, the second strike lasted much longer than the first. In 1834 operatives stayed out for only a few days; in 1836, the mills ran far below capacity for several months. Two weeks after the second turn-out began, a mill agent reported that only a fifth of the strikers had returned to work: "The rest manifest *good 'spunk'* as they call it."[23] Several days later he described the impact of the continuing strike on operations in his mills: "We must be feeble for months to come as probably not less than 250 of our former scanty supply of help have left town."[24] These lines read in sharp contrast to the optimistic reports of agents following the turn-out in February 1834.

Differences between the two turn-outs were not limited to scale and duration. Women displayed a much higher degree of organization in 1836 than earlier. To coordinate strike activities, they formed a Factory Girls' Association whose membership reached 2500 at its height.[25] The new organization among women was reflected in the tactics employed. Strikers, according to one mill agent, were able to halt production to a greater extent than numbers alone could explain; and, he complained that although some operatives were willing to work, "it has been impossible to give employment to many who remained." He attributed this difficulty to the strikers' tactics: "This was in many instances no doubt the result of calculation and contrivance. After the original turn-out they [the operatives] would assail a particular room—as for instance, all the warpers, or all the warp spinners, or all the speeder and stretcher girls, and this would close the mill as effectually as if all the girls in the mill had left."[26] Now giving more thought than they had in 1834 to the specific tactics of the turn-out, the women made a deliberate effort to shut down the mills in order to win their demands. They attempted to persuade less committed operatives, concentrating on those in crucial departments within the mill. Such tactics anticipated those of skilled mulespinners and loomfixers who went out on strike in the 1880s and 1890s.

In their organization of a Factory Girls' Association and in their efforts to shut down the mills, the female operatives revealed that they had been changed by their industrial experience. Increasingly, they acted not simply as "daughters of freemen" offended by the impositions of the textile corporations, but also as industrial workers intent on improving their position within the mills.

There was a decline in protest among women in the Lowell mills following these early strike defeats. During the 1837–1843 depression, textile corporations twice reduced wages without evoking a collective response from operatives. Because of the frequency of production cutbacks and layoffs in these years, workers probably accepted the mill agents' contention that they had to reduce wages or close entirely. But with the return of prosperity and the expansion of production in the mid-1840s, there were renewed labor protests among women.

In contrast to the protests of the previous decade, the struggles now were primarily political. Women did not turn out in the 1840s; rather, they mounted annual petition campaigns calling on the state legislature to limit the hours of labor within the mills. These campaigns reached their height in 1845 and 1846, when 2,000 and 5,000 operatives respectively signed petitions. Unable to curb the wage cuts or the speed-up and stretch-out imposed by mill owners, operatives sought to mitigate the consequences of these changes by reducing the length of the working day. Having been defeated earlier in economic struggles, they now sought to achieve their new goal through political action. The Ten Hour Movement, seen in these terms, was a logical outgrowth of the unsuccessful turn-outs of the previous decade. Like the earlier struggles, the Ten Hour Movement was an assertion of the dignity of operatives and an attempt to maintain that dignity under the changing conditions of industrial capitalism.

The growth of relatively permanent labor organizations and institutions among women was a distinguishing feature of the 1840s. The Lowell Female Labor Reform Association was organized in 1845 by women operatives. It became Lowell's leading labor organization over the next three years, organizing the city's female operatives and helping to set up branches in other mill towns. The Association was affiliated with the New England Workingmen's Association and sent delegates to its meetings. It acted in concert with similar male groups and yet maintained its own autonomy. Women elected their own officers, held their own meetings, testified before a state legislative committee, and published a series of "Factory Tracts" which exposed conditions within the mills and argued for the ten-hour day.[27]

An important educational and organizing tool of the Lowell Female Labor Reform Association was the *Voice of Industry*, a labor weekly published in Lowell between 1845 and 1848 by the New England Workingmen's Association. Female operatives were involved in every aspect of its publication and used the *Voice* to further the Ten Hour Movement among women. Their Association owned the press on which the *Voice* was printed. Sarah Bagley, the Association president, was a member of the three-person publishing committee of the *Voice* and for a time served as editor. Other women were employed by the paper as travelling editors. They wrote articles about the Ten Hour Movement in other mill towns, raised money for the *Voice* and increased its circulation by selling subscriptions to the paper in their travels about New England, and used the *Voice* to appeal directly to their fellow operatives. They edited a separate "Female Department," which published letters and articles by and about women in the mills.

Another aspect of the Ten Hour Movement which distinguished it from the earlier labor struggles in Lowell was that it involved both men and women. At the same time that women in Lowell formed the Female Labor Reform Association, a male mechanics' and laborers' association was also organized. Both groups worked to secure the passage of legislation setting ten hours as the length of the working day. Both groups circulated petitions to this end, and when the legislative committee came to Lowell to hear testimony, both men and women testified in favor of the ten-hour day.

The two groups, then, worked together, and each made an important contribution to the movement in Lowell. Women had the numbers, comprising as they did over 80 percent of the mill workforce. Men, on the other hand, had the votes, and since the Ten Hour Movement was a political struggle, they played a crucial part. After the State committee reported unfavorably on the ten-hour petitions, the Female Labor Reform Association denounced the committee chairman, a state representative from Lowell, as a corporation "tool," and successfully worked for his defeat at the polls. Women took a more prominent part in the Ten Hour Movement in Lowell than did men, but they obviously remained dependent on male voters and legislators for the ultimate success of their movement.

Although co-ordinating their efforts with those of working men, women operatives organized independently within the Ten Hour Movement. For instance, in 1845 two important petitions were sent from Lowell to the state legislature. Almost 90 percent of the signers of one petition were females, and more than two-thirds of the signers of the second were males.[28] Clearly the separation of men and women in their daily lives was reflected in the Ten Hour petitions of these years.

The way in which the Ten Hour Movement was carried from Lowell to other mill towns also illustrated the independent organizing of women within the larger movement. For example, at a spirited meeting in Manchester, New Hampshire, in December, 1845—one presided over by Lowell operatives—more than a thousand workers, two-thirds of them women, passed resolutions calling for the ten-hour day. Later, those in attendance divided along male-female lines, each group meeting separately to set up parallel organizations. Sixty women joined the Manchester Female Labor Reform Association that evening, and by the following summer it claimed over three hundred members. Female operatives met in company boarding houses to involve new women in the movement. In their first year of organizing, Manchester workers obtained more than 4,000 signatures on ten-hour petitions.[29] While men and women were both active in the movement, they worked through separate institutional structures from the outset.

The women's Ten Hour Movement, like the earlier turn-outs, was based in part on the participants' sense of their own worth and dignity as daughters of freemen. At the same time, however, it indicated the growth of a new consciousness. It reflected a mounting feeling of community among women operatives and a realization that their interests and those of their employers were not identical, that they had to rely on themselves and not on corporate benevolence to achieve a reduction in the hours of labor. One woman, in an open letter to a state legislator, expressed this rejection of middle-class paternalism: "Bad as is the condition of so many women, it would be much worse if they had nothing but your boasted protection to rely upon; but they have at last learnt the lesson which a bitter experience teaches, that not to those who style themselves their 'natural protectors' are they to look for the needful help, but to the strong and resolute of their own sex."[30] Such an attitude, underlying the self-organizing of women in the ten-hour petition campaigns, was clearly the product of the industrial experience in Lowell.

Both the early turn-outs and the Ten Hour Movement were dependent upon the existence of a close-knit community of women operatives. Such a community was based on the work structure, the nature of worker housing, and workforce homogeneity. Women were drawn together by the initial job training of newcomers, by the informal work-sharing among experienced hands, by living in company boarding houses, and by sharing religious, educational, and social activities in their leisure hours. Working and living in a new and alien setting, they came to rely upon one another for friendship and support.

This evolving community as well as the common cultural traditions which Yankee women carried into Lowell were major elements that governed their response to changing mill conditions. The pre-industrial tradition of independence and self-respect made them particularly sensitive to management labor policies. The sense of community enabled them to transform their individual opposition to wage cuts and to the increasing pace of work into public protest. In these labor struggles women operatives expressed a new consciousness of their rights both as workers and as women. Such a consciousness, like the community of women itself, was one product of Lowell's industrial revolution.

The experiences of Lowell women before 1850 present a fascinating picture of the contradictory impact of industrial capitalism. Repeated labor protests reveal that female operatives felt the demands of mill employment to be oppressive. At the same time, however, the mills provided women with work outside the home and family, thereby offering them an unprecedented independence. That they came to challenge employer paternalism was a direct consequence of the increasing opportunities offered them in these years. The Lowell mills both exploited and liberated women in ways unknown to the pre-industrial political economy.

NOTES

1. *Statistics of Lowell Manufacturers,* January 1, 1840. Broadside available in the Manuscripts Division, Baker Library, Harvard Business School.
2. *Lowell Offering* I, p. 169.
3. *Ibid.* IV, p. 145–148, 169–172, 237–240, 257–259.
4. These statistics are drawn from the author's dissertation, "Women at Work: The Transformation of Work and Community in Lowell, Mass., 1826–1860" (Columbia Univ. 1975).

5. Harriet Hanson Robinson, *Loom and Spindle, Or Life Among the Early Mill Girls* (New York, 1898), p. 91.

6. Dublin, "Women at Work," Chapter 4.

7. Dublin, "Women at Work," Chapter 5. Statistics based on analysis of federal manuscript census listings of Hamilton boarding houses in 1830 and 1840.

8. *Lowell Offering* I, p. 169.

9. *Ibid.* II, pp. 145–155; I, pp. 2–7, 74–78.

10. *Hamilton Manufacturing Company Records*, vol. 283, *passim*. This volume, along with all the other company records cited in this article, is located in the Manuscript Division of Baker Library, Harvard Business School.

11. *Ibid.* I, p. 5; IV, p. 148.

12. Henry A. Miles, *Lowell As It Was and As It Is* (Lowell, 1845), pp. 144–145.

13. These statistics are based on the linkage of payroll and register books of the Hamilton Company as were the data on residence presented above. See Chapter 4 and Appendices of Dublin, "Women at Work."

14. These data are based on an analysis of the age distribution of females residing in Hamilton Company boarding houses as recorded in the federal manuscript censuses of 1830 and 1840. See Dublin, "Women at Work," Chapter 4.

15. Federal Manuscript Census of Lowell, 1830.

16. Boston *Evening Transcript*, February 18, 1834.

17. *Lawrence Manufacturing Company Records*, Correspondence, Vol. MAB-1, March 4 and March 9, 1834.

18. *Ibid.*, February 15, 1834.

19. Boston *Evening Transcript*, February 18, 1834.

20. Robinson, *Loom and Spindle*, p. 72; *Lowell Offering*, February 1841, p. 45. For an interesting account of conflict between an operative and an overseer, see Robinson, p. 57.

21. The wage cuts, in still another way, might have been seen as threatening to "enslave." Such decreases would be enacted by reductions in the piece rates paid women. If women were to maintain their overall earnings, given the wage cuts, they would have to speed up their work or accept additional machinery, both of which would result in making them work harder for the same pay. Opposition to the speed-up and the stretch-out were strong during the Ten Hour Movement in the 1840s, and although I have found no direct evidence, such feeling may have played a part in the turn-outs of the 1830s as well.

22. Robinson, *Loom and Spindle*, p. 83; Boston *Evening Transcript*, October 4 and 6, 1836.

23. *Tremont-Suffolk Mills Records*, unbound letters, Vol. FN-1, October 14, 1836.

24. *Ibid.*, October 18, 1836.

25. Hannah Josephson, *The Golden Threads: New England's Mill Girls and Magnates* (New York, 1949), p. 238.

26. *Tremont-Suffolk Mills Records*, Unbound Letters, Vol. FN-1, October 10, 1836.

27. Massachusetts *House Document* No. 50, 1845. Quoted in John R. Commons et al., *A Documentary History of American Industrial Society* (Cleveland, 1910), Vol. 3, pp. 133–151.

28. Based on author's examination of Ten Hour Petitions at Massachusetts State Archives, 1845, 1587/8 and 1587/9.

29. *Voice of Industry*, December 5 and 19, 1845, July 24, 1846, October 30, 1846, December 4, 1846, January 8, 1847.

30. *Voice of Industry*, March 13, 1846.

11

Female Slaves: Sex Roles and Status in the Antebellum Plantation South

Deborah G. White

Viewing the often contested subject of slave family life from the perspective of slave women, Deborah G. White analyzes women's centrality to slave family life and the importance of their economic contributions. Since the slave world was sex stratified, women's experience was separate from that of men. White explores the consequences of "matrifocality" for women, showing how women's family life and working lives generated female networks of mutual support. Not simply victims of an oppressive and exploitative labor system, slave women constructed their own culture, which nurtured and rewarded its members according to its own set of values.

In his 1939 study of the black family in America, sociologist E. Franklin Frazier theorized that in slave family and marriage relations, women played the dominant role. Specifically, Frazier wrote that "the Negro woman as wife or mother was the mistress of her cabin, and, save for the interference of master and overseer, her wishes in regard to mating and family matters were paramount." He also insisted that slavery had schooled the black woman in self-reliance and self-sufficiency and that "neither economic necessity nor tradition had instilled in her the spirit of subordination to masculine authority." The Frazier thesis received support from other social scientists, including historians Kenneth Stampp and Stanley Elkins, both of whom held that slave men had been emasculated and stripped of their paternity rights by slave masters who left control of slave households to slave women. In his infamous 1965 national report, Daniel Patrick Moynihan lent further confirmation to the Frazier thesis when he alleged that the fundamental problem with the modern black family was the "often reversed roles of husband and wife," and then traced the origin of the "problem" back to slavery.[1]

Partly in response to the criticism spawned by the Moynihan Report, historians reanalyzed antebellum source material, and the matriarchy thesis was debunked. For better or worse, said historians Robert Fogel and Stanley Engerman, the "dominant" role in slave society was played by men. Men were

Excerpted from Deborah G. White, "Female Slaves: Sex Roles and Status in the Antebellum Plantation South," *Journal of Family History* 8 (1983): 248–59, copyright © 1983. Reprinted by permission of Sage Publications, Inc.

Slave family of several generations, J. J. Smith Plantation, Beaufort, S.C. 1862. CORBIS and Library of Congress.

dominant, they said, because men occupied all managerial and artisan slots, and because masters recognized the male head of the family group. From historian John Blassingame we learn that by building furnishings and providing extra food for their families, men found indirect ways of gaining status. If a garden plot was to be cultivated, the husband "led" his wife in the family undertaking. After a very thoughtful appraisal of male slave activities, historian Eugene Genovese concluded that "slaves from their own experience had come to value a two-parent, male-centered household, no matter how much difficulty they had in realizing the ideal." Further tipping the scales toward patriarchal slave households, historian Herbert Gutman argued that the belief that matrifocal households prevailed among slaves was a misconception. He demonstrated that children were more likely to be named after their fathers than mothers, and that during the Civil War slave men acted like fathers and husbands by fighting for their freedom and by protecting their wives and children when they were threatened by Union troops or angry slaveholders.[2]

With the reinterpretation of male roles came a revision of female roles. Once considered dominant, slave women were now characterized as subordinated and sometimes submissive. Fogel and Engerman found proof of their subordinated status in the fact that they were excluded from working in plow gangs and did all of the household chores. Genovese maintained that slave women's "attitude toward housework, especially cooking, and toward their own femininity," belied the conventional wisdom according to which women unwittingly helped ruin their men by asserting themselves in the home, protecting their children, and assuming other normally masculine responsibilities. Gutman found one Sea Island slave community where the black church imposed a submissive role upon married slave women.[3]

In current interpretations of the contemporary black family the woman's role has not been "feminized" as much as it has been "deemphasized." The stress in studies like those done by Carol Stack and Theodore Kennedy, is not on roles per se but on the black family's ability to survive in flexible kinship networks that are viable bulwarks against discrimination and racism. These interpretations also make the point that black kinship patterns are not based exclusively on consanguineous relationships but are also determined by social contacts that sometimes have their basis in economic support.[4]

Clearly then, the pendulum has swung away from the idea that women ruled slave households, and that their dominance during the slave era formed the foundation of the modern day matriarchal black family. But how far should that pendulum swing? This paper suggests that we should tread the road that leads to the patriarchal slave household and the contemporary amorphous black family with great caution. It suggests that, at least in relation to the slave family, too much emphasis has been placed on what men could not do rather than on what women could do and did. What follows is not a comprehensive study of female slavery, but an attempt to reassess Frazier's claim that slave women were self-reliant and self-sufficient through an examination of some of their activities, specifically their work, their control of particular resources, their contribution to their households and their ability to cooperate with each other on a daily basis. Further, this paper will examine some of the implications of these activities, and their probable impact on the slave woman's status in slave society and the black family.

At the outset a few points must be made about the subject matter and the source material used to research it. Obviously, a study that concentrates solely on females runs the risk of overstating women's roles and their importance in society. One must therefore keep in mind that this is only one aspect, although a very critical one, of slave family and community life. In addition, what follows is a synthesis of the probable sex role of the average slave woman on plantations with at least twenty slaves. In the process of constructing this synthesis I have taken into account such variables as plantation size, crop, region of the South, and the personal idiosyncrasies of slave masters. Finally, in drawing conclusions about the sex role and status of slave women, I have detailed their activities and analyzed them in terms of what anthropologists know about women who do similar things in analogous settings. I took this approach for two reasons. First, information about female slaves cannot be garnered from sources left by slave women because they left few narratives, diaries or letters. The dearth of source material makes it impossible to draw conclusions about the slave woman's feelings. Second, even given the ex-slave interviews, a rich source material for this subject, it is almost impossible to draw conclusions about female slave status from an analysis of their individual personalities. Comments such as that made by the slave woman, Fannie, to her husband Bob "I don't want no sorry nigger around me," perhaps says something about Fannie, but not about all slave women.[5] Similarly, for every mother who grieved over the sale of her children there was probably a father whose heart was also broken. Here, only the activities of the slave woman will be examined in an effort to discern her status in black society.

Turning first to the work done by slave women, it appears that they did a variety of heavy and dirty labor, work which was also done by men. In 1853, Frederick Olmsted saw South Carolina slaves of both sexes carting manure on their heads to the cotton field where they spread it with their hands between the ridges in which cotton was planted. In Fayetteville, North Carolina, he noticed that women not only hoed and shovelled but they also cut down trees and drew wood. The use of women as lumberjacks occurred quite frequently, especially in the lower South and Southwest, areas which retained a frontier quality during the antebellum era. Solomon Northup, a kidnapped slave, knew women who wielded the ax so perfectly that the largest oak or sycamore fell before their well-directed blows. An Arkansas ex-slave remembered that her mother used to carry logs. On southwestern plantations women did all kinds of work. In the region of the Bayou Boeuf women were expected to "plough, drag, drive team, clear wild lands, work on the highway," and do any other type of work required of them. In short, full female hands frequently did the same kind of work as male hands.[6]

It is difficult, however, to say how often they did the same kind of field work, and it would be mistake to say that there was no differentiation of field labor on Southern farms and plantations. The most common form of differentiation was that women hoed while men plowed. Yet, the exceptions to the rule were so numerous as to make a mockery of it. Many men hoed on a regular basis. Similarly, if a field had to be plowed and there were not enough male hands to do it, then it was not unusual for an overseer to command a strong woman to plow. This could happen on a plantation of twenty slaves or a farm of five.

It is likely, however, that women were more often called to do the heavy labor usually assigned to men after their childbearing years. Pregnant women, and sometimes women breastfeeding infants, were usually given less physically demanding work.[7] If, as recent studies indicate, slave women began childbearing when about twenty years of age and had children at approximately two and a half year intervals, at least until age thirty-five, slave women probably spent a considerable amount of time doing tasks which men did not do.[8] Pregnant and nursing women were classified as half-hands or three-quarter hands and such workers did only some of the work that was also done by full hands. For instance, it was not unusual for them to pick cotton or even hoe, work done on a regular basis by both sexes. But frequently, they were assigned to "light work" like raking stubble or pulling weeds, which was often given to children and the elderly.

Slave women might have preferred to be exempt from such labor, but they might also have gained some intangibles from doing the same work as men. Anthropologists have demonstrated that in societies where men and women are engaged in the production of the same kinds of goods and where widespread private property is not a factor, participation in production gives women freedom and independence. Since neither slave men nor women had access to, or control over, the products of their labor, parity in the field may have encouraged equalitarianism in the slave quarters. In Southern Togo, for instance, where women work alongside their husbands in the field because men do not alone produce goods which are highly valued, democracy prevails in relationships between men and women.[9]

But bondswomen did do a lot of traditional "female work" and one has to wonder whether this work, as well as the work done as a "half-hand" tallied on the side of female subordination. In the case of the female slave, domestic work was not always confined to the home, and often "woman's work" required skills that were highly valued and even coveted because of the place it could purchase in the higher social echelons of the slave world. For example, cooking was definitely "female work" but it was also a skilled occupation. Good cooks were highly respected by both blacks and whites, and their occupation was raised in status because the masses of slave women did not cook on a regular basis. Since field work occupied the time of most women, meals were often served communally. Female slaves therefore were, for the most part, relieved of this traditional chore, and the occupation of "cook" became specialized.

Sewing too was often raised above the level of inferior "woman's work." All females at one time or another had to spin and weave. Occasionally each woman was given cloth and told to make her family's clothes, but this was unusual and more likely to happen on small farms than on plantations. During slack seasons women probably did more sewing than during planting and harvesting seasons, and pregnant women were often put to work spinning, weaving and sewing. Nevertheless, sewing could be raised to the level of a skilled art, especially if a woman sewed well enough to make the white family's clothes. Such women were sometimes hired out and allowed to keep a portion of the profit they brought their master and mistress.[10]

Other occupations which were solidly anchored in the female domain, and which increased a woman's prestige, were midwifery and doctoring. The length of time and extent of training it took to become a midwife is indicated by the testimony of Clara Walker, a former slave interviewed in Arkansas, who remembered that she trained for five years under a doctor who became so lazy after she had mastered the job that he would sit down and let her do all the work. After her "apprenticeship" ended she delivered babies for both slave and free, black and white.[11] Other midwives learned the trade from a female relative, often their mother, and they in turn passed the skill on to another female relative.

A midwife's duty often extended beyond delivering babies, and they sometimes became known as "doctor women." In this capacity they cared for men, women, and children. Old women, some with a history of midwifery and some without, also gained respect as "doctor women." . . . Old women had innumerable cures, especially for children's diseases, and since plantation "nurseries" were usually under their supervision, they had ample opportunity to practice their art. In sum, a good portion of the slave's medical care, particularly that of women and children, was supervised by slave women.

Of course, not all women were hired-out seamstresses, cooks, or midwives; a good deal of "female work" was laborious and mundane. An important aspect of this work, as well as of the field work done by women, was that it was frequently done in female groups. As previously noted, women often hoed while men plowed. In addition, when women sewed they usually did so with other women. . . . Such gatherings were attended only by women and many former slaves had vivid recollections of them. The "quiltin's and spinnin' frolics dat de women folks had" were the most outstanding remembrances of Hattie Anne Nettles, an Alabama ex-slave. Women also gathered, independent of male slaves, on Saturday afternoons to do washing. Said one ex-slave, "they all had a regular picnic of it as they would work and spread the clothes on the bushes and low branches of the tree to dry. They would get to spend the day together."[12]

In addition, when pregnant women did field work they sometimes did it together. On large plantations the group they worked in was sometimes known as the "trash gang." This gang, made up of pregnant women, women with nursing infants, children and old slaves, was primarily a female work gang. Since it was the group that young girls worked with when just being initiated into the work world of the plantation, one must assume that it served some kind of socialization function. Most likely, many lessons about life were learned by twelve-year-old girls from this group of women who were either pregnant or breastfeeding, or who were grandmothers many times over.

It has been noted that women frequently depended on slave midwives to bring children into the world; their dependence on other slave women did not end with childbirth but continued through the early life of their children. Sometimes women with infants took their children to the fields with them. Some worked with their children wrapped to their backs, others laid them under a tree. Frequently, however, an elderly woman watched slave children during the day while their mothers worked in the field. Sometimes the cook supervised young children at the master's house.[13] Mothers who were absent from their children most of the day, indeed most of the week, depended on surrogate mothers to assist them in child socialization. . . .

Looking at the work done by female slaves in the antebellum South, therefore, we find that sex role differentiation in field labor was not absolute but that there was differentiation in other kinds of work. Domestic chores were usually done exclusively by women, and certain "professional" occupations were reserved for females. It would be a mistake to infer from this differentiation that it was the basis of male dominance. A less culturally biased conclusion would be that women's roles were different or complementary. For example, in her overview of African societies, Denise Paulme notes that in almost all African societies, women do most of the domestic chores, yet they lead lives that are quite independent of men. Indeed, according to Paulme, in Africa, "a wife's contribution to the needs of the household is direct and indispensable, and her husband is just as much in need of her as she of him." Other anthropologists have suggested that we should not evaluate women's roles in terms of men's roles because in a given society, women may not perceive the world in the same way that men do.[14] In other words, men and women may share a common culture but on different terms, and when this is the case, questions of dominance and subservience are irrelevant. The degree to which male and female ideologies are different is often suggested by the degree to which men and women are independently able to rank and order themselves and cooperate with members of their sex in the performance of their duties. In societies where women are not isolated from one another and placed under a man's authority, where women cooperate in the performance of household tasks, where women form groups or associations, women's roles are usually complementary to those of men, and the female world exists independently of the male world. Because women control what goes on in their world, they rank and order themselves vis à vis other women, not men, and they are able to influence decisions made by their society because they exert pressure as a group. Ethnographic studies of the Igbo women of Eastern Nigeria, the Ga women of Central Accra in Ghana, and the Patani of Southern Nigeria confirm these generalizations.[15] Elements of female slave society—the chores done in and by groups, the intrasex cooperation and dependency in the areas of child care and medical care, the existence of high echelon female slave occupations—may be an indication, not that slave women were inferior to slave men, but that the roles were complementary and that the female slave world allowed women the opportunity to rank and order themselves and obtain a sense of self which was quite apart from the men of their race and even the men of the master class.

That bondswomen were able to rank and order themselves is further suggested by evidence indicating that in the community of the slave quarters certain women were looked to for leadership. Leadership was based on either one or a combination of factors, including occupation, association with the master class, age, or number of children. It was manifested in all aspects of female slave life. For instance, Louis Hughes, an escaped slave, noted that each plantation had a "forewoman who . . . had charge of the female slaves and also the boys and girls from twelve to sixteen years of age, and all the old people that were feeble." Bennett H. Barrow repeatedly lamented the fact that Big Lucy, one of his oldest slaves, had more control over his female slaves then he did: "Anica, Center, Cook Jane, the better you treat them the worse they are. Big Lucy, the Leader, corrupts every young negro in her power." When Elizabeth Botume went to the Sea Islands after the Civil War, she had as a house servant a young woman named Amy who performed her tasks slowly and sullenly until Aunt Mary arrived from Beaufort. In Aunt Mary's presence the obstreperous Amy was "quiet, orderly, helpful and painstaking."[16]

Another important feature of female life, bearing on the ability of women to rank and order themselves independently of men, was the control women exercised over each other by quarreling. In all kinds of sources there are indications that women were given to fighting and irritating each other. From Jesse Belflowers, the overseer of the Allston rice plantation in South Carolina, Adele Petigru Allston learned that "mostly mongst the Woman," there was "goodeal of quarling and disputing and telling lies." Harriet Ware, a northern missionary, writing from the Sea Islands in 1863 blamed the turmoil she found in black community life on the "tongues of the women."[17] The evidence of excessive quarreling among women hints at the existence of a gossip network among female slaves. Anthropologists have found gossip to be a principal strategy used by women to control other women as well as men.[18] Significantly, the female gossip network, the means by which community members are praised, shamed, and coerced, is usually found in societies where women are highly dependent on each other and where women work in groups or form female associations.[19]

In summary, when the activities of female slaves are compared to those of women in other societies a clearer picture of the female slave sex role emerges. It seems that slave women were schooled in self-reliance and self-sufficiency but the "self" was more likely the female slave collective than the individual slave woman. On the other hand, if the female world was highly stratified and if women cooperated with each other to a great extent, odds are that the same can be said of men, in which case neither sex can be said to have been dominant or subordinate.

There are other aspects of the female slave's life that suggest that her world was independent of the male slave's and that slave women were rather self-reliant. It has long been recognized that slave women did not derive traditional benefits from the marriage relationship, that there was no property to share and essential needs like food, clothing, and shelter were not provided by slave men. Since in almost all societies where men consistently control women, that control is based on male ownership and distribution of property and/or control of certain culturally valued subsistence goods, these realities of slave life had to contribute to female slave self-sufficiency and independence from slave men. The practice of "marrying abroad," having a spouse on a different plantation, could only have reinforced this tendency, for as ethnographers have found, when men live apart from women, they cannot control them. We have yet to learn what kind of obligations brothers, uncles, and male cousins fulfilled for their female kin, but it is improbable that wives were controlled by husbands whom they saw only once or twice a week. Indeed, "abroad marriages" may have intensified female intradependency.[20]

The fact that marriage did not yield traditional benefits for women, and that "abroad marriages" existed, does not mean that women did not depend on slave men for foodstuffs beyond the weekly rations, but since additional food was not guaranteed, it probably meant that women along with men had to take initiatives in supplementing slave diets. So much has been made of the activities of slave men in this sphere that the role of slave women has been overlooked.[21] Female house slaves, in particular, were especially able to supplement their family's diet. Mary Chesnut's maid, Molly, made no secret of the fact that she fed her offspring and other slave children in the Confederate politician's house. "Dey gets a little of all dat's going," she once told Chesnut. Frederick Douglass remembered that his grandmother was not only a good nurse but a "capitol hand at catching fish and making the nets she caught them in." Eliza Overton, an ex-slave, remembered how her mother stole, slaughtered, and cooked one of her master's hogs. Another ex-slave was not too bashful to admit that her mother "could hunt good ez any man." Women, as well as men, were sometimes given the opportunity to earn money. Women often sold baskets they had woven, but they also earned money by burning charcoal for blacksmiths and cutting cordwood. Thus, procuring extra provisions for the family was sometimes a male and sometimes a female responsibility, one that probably fostered a self-reliant and independent spirit.[22]

The high degree of female cooperation, the ability of slave women to rank and order themselves, the independence women derived from the absence of property considerations in the conjugal relationship, "abroad marriages," and the female slave's ability to provide supplementary foodstuffs are factors which should not be ignored in considerations of the character of the slave family. In fact, they conform to the criteria most anthropologists list for that most misunderstood concept—matrifocality. Matrifocality is a term used to convey the fact that women *in their role as mothers* are the focus of familial relationships. It does not mean that fathers are absent; indeed two-parent households can be matrifocal. Nor does it stress a power relationship where women rule men. When *mothers* become the focal point of family activity, they are just more central than are fathers to a family's continuity and survival as a unit. While there is no set model for matrifocality, Smith has noted that in societies as diverse as Java, Jamaica, and the Igbo of eastern Nigeria, societies recognized as matrifocal, certain elements are constant. Among these elements are female solidarity, particularly in regard to their cooperation within the domestic sphere. Another factor is the economic activity of women which enables them to support their children independent of fathers *if they desire to do so or are forced to do so.* The most important factor is the supremacy of the mother-child bond over all other relationships.[23]

Female solidarity and the "economic" contribution of bondswomen in the form of medical care, foodstuffs, and money has already been discussed; what can be said of the mother-child bond? We know from previous works on slavery that certain slaveholder practices encouraged the primacy of the mother-child relationship. These included the tendency to sell mothers and small children as family units, and to accord special treatment to pregnant and nursing women and women who were exceptionally prolific. We also know that a husband and wife secured themselves somewhat from sale and separation when they had children. Perhaps what has not been emphasized enough is the fact that it was the wife's childbearing and her ability to keep a child alive that were the crucial factors in the security achieved in this way. As such, the insurance against sale which husbands and wives received once women had borne and nurtured children heads the list of female contributions to slave households.[24]

In addition to slaveowner encouragement of close mother-child bonds there are indications that slave women themselves considered this their most important relationship. Much has been made of the fact that slave women were not ostracized by slave society when they had children out of "wedlock." Historians have usually explained this aspect of slave life in the context of slave sexual norms which allowed a good deal of freedom to young unmarried slave women. However, the slave attitude concerning "illegitimacy" might also reveal the importance that women, and slave society as a whole, placed on the mother role and the mother-child dyad. For instance, in the Alabama community studied by Charles S. Johnson in the 1930s, most black women felt no guilt and suffered no loss of status when they bore children out of wedlock. This was also a community in which, according to Johnson, the role of the mother was "of much greater importance than in the more familiar American family group." Similarly, in his 1956 study of the black family in British Guyana, Smith found the mother-child bond to be the strongest in the whole matrix of social relationships, and it was manifested in lack of condemnation of women who bore children out of legal marriage. If slave women were not ostracized for having children without husbands, it could mean that the mother-child relationship took precedence over the husband-wife relationship.[25]

The mystique which shrouded conception and childbirth is perhaps another indication of the high value slave women placed on motherhood and childbirth. Many female slaves claimed that they were kept ignorant of the details of conception and childbirth. For instance, a female slave interviewed in Nashville noted that at age twelve or thirteen, she and an older girl went around to parsley beds and hollow logs looking for newborn babies. "They didn't tell you a thing," she said. Another ex-slave testified that her mother told her that doctors brought babies, and another Virginia ex-slave remembered that "people was very particular in them days. They wouldn't let children know anything."[26] This alleged naiveté can perhaps be understood if examined in the context of motherhood as a *rite de passage*. . . . That conception and childbirth were cloaked in mystery in antebellum slave society is perhaps an indication of the sacredness of motherhood. When considered in tandem with the slave attitude toward "illegitimacy," the mother-child relationship emerges as the most important familial relationship in the slave family.

Finally, any consideration of the slave's attitude about motherhood and expectations which the slave community had of childbearing women must consider the slave's African heritage. In many West African tribes the mother-child relationship is and has always been the most important of all human relationships. To cite one of the many possible examples, while studying the role of women in Ibo society, Sylvia Leith-Ross asked an Ibo woman how many of ten husbands would love their wives and how many of ten sons would love their mothers. The answer she received demonstrated the precedence which the mother-child tie took: "Three husbands would love their wives but seven sons would love their mothers."[27]

When E. Franklin Frazier wrote that slave women were self-reliant and that they were strangers to male slave authority he evoked an image of an overbearing, even brawny woman. In all probability visions of Sapphire danced in our heads as we learned from Frazier that the female slave played the dominant role in courtship, marriage and family relationships, and later from Elkins that male slaves were reduced to childlike dependency on the slave master.[28] Both the Frazier and Elkins theses have been overturned by historians who have found that male slaves were more than just visitors to their wives' cabins, and women something other than unwitting allies in the degradation of their men. Sambo and Sapphire may continue to find refuge in American folklore but they will never again be legitimized by social scientists.

However, beyond the image evoked by Frazier is the stark reality that slave women did not play the traditional female role as it was defined in nineteenth-century America, and regardless of how hard we try to cast her in subordinate or submissive role in relation to slave men, we will have difficult reconciling that role with the plantation realities. When we consider the work done by women in groups, the existence of upper echelon female slave jobs, the interdependence of women in child care and medical care; if we presume that the quarreling or "fighting and disputing" among slave women is evidence of a gossip network and that certain women were elevated by their peers to positions of respect, then what we are confronted with are slave women who were able, within the limits set by slaveowners, to rank and order their female world, women who identified and cooperated more with other slave women than with slave men. There is nothing abnormal about this. It is a feature of many societies around the world, especially where strict sex role differentiation is the rule.

Added to these elements of female interdependence and cooperation were the realities of chattel slavery that decreased the bondsman's leverage over the bondswoman, made female self-reliance a necessity, and encouraged the retention of the African tradition which made the mother-child bond more sacred than the husband-wife bond. To say that this amounted to a matrifocal family is not to say a bad word. It is not to say that it precluded male-female cooperation, or mutual respect, or traditional romance and courtship. It does, however, help to explain how African-American men and women survived chattel slavery.

NOTES

1. E. Franklin Frazier, *The Negro Family in the United States* (Chicago: University of Chicago Press, 1939), 125; Kenneth Stampp, *The Peculiar Institution: Slavery in the Ante-Bellum South* (New York: Vintage, 1956), 344, Stanley M. Elkins, *Slavery: A Problem in American Institutional and Intellectual Life*, 2nd ed. (Chicago: University of Chicago Press, 1959), 130; Daniel Patrick Moynihan, *The Negro Family: The Case for National Action* (Washington, D.C.: Government Printing Office, 1965), 31.

2. Robert William Fogel and Stanley Engerman, *Time on the Cross: The Economics of American Negro Slavery* (Boston: Little, Brown, 1974), 141; John W. Blassingame, *The Slave Community: Plantation Life in the Antebellum South* (New York: Oxford University Press, 1972), 92; Eugene Genovese, *Roll, Jordan, Roll: The World the Slaves Made* (New York: Vintage, 1974), 491–92; Herbert Gutman, *The Black Family in Slavery and Freedom, 1750–1925* (New York: Pantheon, 1976), 188–91, 369–86.

3. Fogel and Engerman, *Time on the Cross*, 141–42, 500; Gutman, *The Black Family*, 72.

4. Carol Stack, *All Our Kin: Strategies for Survival in a Black Community* (New York: Harper and Row, 1974); Theodore R. Kennedy, *You Gotta Deal with It: Black Family Relations in a Southern Community* (New York: Oxford University Press, 1980).

5. Ophelia S. Egypt, J. Masuoka and Charles S. Johnson, eds., *Unwritten History of Slavery: Autobiographical Accounts of Negro Ex-slaves* (Nashville: Fisk University Press, 1945), 184.

6. Frederick L. Olmsted, *The Cotton Kingdom*, edited by David Freeman Hawke (New York: Bobbs-Merrill, 1971), 67, 81; Gilbert Osofsky, ed., *Puttin' on Ole Massa* (New York: Harper and Row, 1969), 308–09, 313; George Rawick, ed., *The American Slave: A Composite Autobiography,* 19 vols. (Westport, Connecticut: Greenwood Press, 1972), vol. 10, pt. 5:54.

7. See Rawick, *The American Slave*, vol. 4, pt. 3:160; vol. 10, pt 7:255; Louis Hughes, *Thirty Years a Slave* (Milwaukee: South Side Printing, 1897), 22; Frederick L. Olmsted, *A Journey in the Seaboard Slave States* (New York: Dix and Edwards, 1856), 430; Southern Historical Collection [SHC], *Plantation Instructions* (undated); Olmsted, *The Cotton Kingdom*, 78; Frances Anne Kemble, *Journal of a Residence on a Georgian Plantation*, edited by John A. Scott (New York: Alfred A. Knopf, 1961), 87, 179; Benjamin Drew, *The Refugee: A North Side View of Slavery* (Boston: Addison Wesley, 1969), 128; Edwin Adams Davis, *Plantation Life in the Florida Parishes of Louisiana, 1836–1846 as Reflected in the Diary of Bennet H. Barrow* (New York: Columbia University Press, 1943), 127.

8. Richard Dunn, "The Tale of Two Plantations: Slave Life at Mesopotamia in Jamaica and Mount Airy in Virginia, 1799–1828," *William and Mary Quarterly,* 34 (1977): 58; Gutman, *The Black Family,* 50, 74, 124, 171; James Trussell and Richard Steckel, "Age of Slaves at Menarche and Their First Birth," *Journal of Interdisciplinary History,* 8 (1978): 504.

9. Leith Mullings, "Women and Economic Change in Africa," in Nancy J. Hafkin and Edna G. Bay, eds., *Women in Africa: Studies in Social and Economic Change* (Stanford: Stanford University Press, 1976), 243–244; Karen Sacks, "Engels Revisited: Women, the Organization of Production,

and Private Property," in Michelle Rosaldo and Louise Lamphere, eds., *Women, Culture and Society* (Stanford: Stanford University Press, 1974), 213–222; Guy Rocher, R. Clignet, and F. N. N'sougan Agblemagon, "Three Preliminary Studies: Canada, Ivory Coast, Togo," *International Social Science Journal,* 14 (1962): 151–52.

10. Rawick, *The American Slave,* vol. 17, 158; vol. 2, pt. 2:114; SHC, *White Hill Plantation Books (1817–1860),* 13.

11. Rawick, *The American Slave,* vol. 10, pt. 5:21. For other examples of midwives, see Rawick, vol. 6:256; vol. 16:90–91; vol. 10, pt. 5:125.

12. Rawick, vol. 6:297, 360; vol. 7:315.

13. Olmsted, *A Journey,* 423; Ulrich B. Phillips, *Plantation and Frontier Documents 1649–1863,* vol. 1 (Cleveland: Arthur H. Clarke, 1909), 127.

14. Denise Paulme, ed., *Women of Tropical Africa* (Berkeley: University of California Press, 1963), 4; Susan Carol Rogers, "Woman's Place: A Critical Review of Anthropological Theory," *Comparative Studies in Society and History* 20 (1978): 152–62.

15. Nancy Tanner, "Matrifocality in Indonesia and Africa and Among Black Americans," in Rosaldo and Lamphere, eds., *Woman, Culture and Society,* 146–50; Claire Robertson, "Ga Women and Socioeconomic Change in Accra, Ghana," in Hafkin and Bay, *Women in Africa,* 115–32; Nancy B. Leis, "Women in Groups: Ijaw Women's Association," in Rosaldo and Lamphere, eds., *Women, Culture and Society,* 221–42.

16. Hughes, *Thirty Years a Slave,* 22; Davis, *Plantation Life,* 191; Elizabeth Hyde Botume, *First Days Amongst the Contrabands* (Boston: Lee and Shepard, 1893), 132.

17. J. E. Easterby, ed., *The South Carolina Rice Plantations as Revealed in the Papers of Robert W. Allston* (Chicago: University of Chicago Press, 1945), 291; Elizabeth Ware Pearson, ed., *Letters from Port Royal Written at the Time of the Civil War* (Boston: W. B. Clarke, 1906), 210.

18. Michelle Rosaldo, "Woman, Culture and Society: A Theoretical Overview," in Rosaldo and Lamphere, eds., *Woman, Culture and Society,* 10–11; Stack, "Engels Revisited," 109–15; Margery Wolf, "Chinese Women: Old Skill in a New Context," in Rosaldo and Lamphere, eds., *Woman, Culture and Society,* 162.

19. Gossip is one of many means by which women influence political decisions and interpersonal relationships. See Rosaldo, "Woman, Culture and Society," 10–11; Wolf, "Chinese Women," 162; and Stack, *All Our Kin,* 109–15.

20. Blassingame, *The Slave Community,* 77–103; John A. Noon, *Law and Government of the Grand River Iroquois* (New York: Viking, 1949), 30–31; Rosaldo, *Woman, Culture and Society,* 36, 39.

21. Blassingame, *The Slave Community,* 92; Genovese, *Roll, Jordan, Roll,* 486.

22. Mary Boykin Chesnut, *A Diary from Dixie,* edited by Ben Ames Williams (New York: D. Appleton and Company, 1905), 348; Frederick Douglass, *My Bondage and My Freedom* (New York: Arno Press, 1968 [originally published in 1855]), 35; Rawick, *The American Slave,* vol. 11:53, 267; vol. 7:23; Olmsted, *A Journey,* 26.

23. Nancie Gonzalez, "Toward a Definition of Matrifocality," in Norman E. Whitten, Jr. and John F. Szwed, eds., *Afro-American Anthropology: Contemporary Perspectives* (New York: The Free Press, 1970), 231–43; Raymond T. Smith, *The Negro Family in British Guiana: Family Structure and Social Status in the Villages* (London: Routledge and Kegan Paul, 1956), 257–60; Raymond T. Smith, "The Matrifocal Family," in Jack Goody, ed., *The Character of Kinship* (London: Cambridge University Press, 1973), 125, 139–42; Tanner, "Matrifocality in Indonesia and Africa,": 129–56.

24. John Spencer Bassett, *The Southern Plantation Overseer, As Revealed in His Letters* (Northampton, Mass.: Southworth Press, 1925), 31, 139, 141; Kemble, *Journal of a Residence,* 95, 127, 179; Phillips, *Plantation and Frontier Documents,* 1: 102, 312; Gutman, *The Black Family,* 76.

25. Genovese, *Roll, Jordan, Roll,* 465–66; Gutman, *The Black Family,* 74, 117–18; Charles S. Johnson, *Shadow of the Plantation* (Chicago: University of Chicago Press, 1934), 29, 66–70; Smith, *The Negro Family in British Guiana,* 109, 158, 250–51.

26. Egypt *et al., Unwritten History of Slavery,* 10; Rawick, *The American Slave,* vol. 16:15.

27. Egypt *et al., Unwritten History of Slavery,* 8; Rawick, *The American Slave,* vol. 16:25, vol. 7:3–24, vol. 2:51–52. See also Paulme, *Women of Tropical Africa,* 14; Tanner, "Matrifocality in Indonesia and Africa," 147; Mayer Fortes, "Kinship and Marriage Among the Ashanti," in A. R. Radcliffe-Brown and Daryll Forde, eds., *African Systems of Kinship and Marriage* (London: Routledge and Kegan Paul, 1939), 127.

28. Frazier, *The Negro Family,* 125; Elkins, *Slavery,* 130.

12

Women's Rights Emerges within the Antislavery Movement: Angelina and Sarah Grimké in 1837

Kathryn Kish Sklar

Women's rights emerged as a social force in American life in very specific circumstances in 1837. Kathryn Sklar examines the religious motivations and the antislavery impulse that combined to achieve this breakthrough. She draws on the lives and writings of Angelina and Sarah Grimké to show how their 1837 speaking tour against slavery required them to defend the rights of women to participate fully in the moral debates of their time. Their efforts laid a sturdy foundation on which Elizabeth Cady Stanton and Lucretia Mott built when they organized the historic women's rights convention held in Seneca Falls, New York, in July 1848.

In the summer of 1837, two sisters from South Carolina, Angelina and Sarah Grimké, age 32 and 45, respectively, began a speaking tour of New England that permanently altered American perceptions of the rights of women. What began as a tour to promote the abolition of slavery ended by introducing the new concept of women's rights into American public life. Between May and September, the Grimkés ignited a debate about the equality of the sexes that first enveloped the abolitionist movement and then extended into the lives of women who were active in other reforms, precipitating large changes in consciousness in a relatively short period of time.

The emergence of an autonomous women's rights movement from the struggle against slavery was not inevitable. Although women were also active in British antislavery circles, for example, their activism did not generate an equivalent women's rights movement in England. In the United States a movement arose out of the confluence of many causes in the 1830s, some rooted in the economic, social, and political significance of slavery in American society, some in the transformations occurring in American religious culture, and some arising from the growing power of white, middle-class women in American political culture. The movement began, however, with the unique position the Grimké sisters held, as exiles from South Carolina, within the campaign to end slavery.

Adapted from the introduction to Kathryn Kish Sklar, *Women's Rights Emerges within the Antislavery Movement: A Short History with Documents, 1830–1870* (Boston: Bedford Books, St. Martin's Press, 2000).

Angelina and Sarah Grimké rose rapidly to occupy a powerful position in the antislavery movement between 1835 and 1837 because they were the daughters of an elite southern slaveholding family who left the South and became lecturers for the American Anti-Slavery Society. Their compelling descriptions of the horrors of slavery attracted audiences that otherwise might have remained indifferent to the topic, especially since a wide range of economic livelihoods in the North were closely intertwined with the system of racial slavery in the South. For example, the politically powerful class of northern merchants profited substantially by selling southern cotton to English manufacturers. And even New England textile workers depended on southern cotton for their earnings.[1]

Before 1830 the Grimké sisters seemed an unlikely pair to launch a revolution. Born to a prominent slave-owning family of Huguenot (French Protestant) descent in Charleston, South Carolina, Sarah was the sixth and

Cover vignette from Lydia Maria Child, Authentic Anecdotes of American Slavery *(1838). Columbia University.*

Angelina the last of fourteen children. Their father was chief justice of the state's highest court; their mother's brother served as governor of North Carolina. The family's wealth derived from a distant plantation that they never visited, which was run by a hired overseer. Their substantial house in Charleston required the labor of many slaves, most of whom had relatives on the plantation.[2]

The seeds for the sisters' later abhorrence of slavery were sown by their privileged position within its embrace, when, during their childhood, they sympathized with the sufferings of slave children. For example, Angelina once witnessed the anguish of a young slave boy who had been so "dreadfully whipped that he could hardly walk." His "heartbroken countenance" moved her as much as his bloodied back.[3] Sarah and Angelina's mother, Mary Grimké, supervised her household with callous disregard for the well-being of the slaves who served her. Bondspeople slept on the floor without bed or bedding, ate from tin plates without a table, and had no lights in their quarters. Seamstresses were required to work after dark in winter by staircase lamps, so dim that they had to stand to see their work. "Mother," Angelina wrote in her diary in 1828, "rules slaves and children with a rod of fear."[4] After their father died in 1819, slave punishments became even more severe.

One important subtext of the cruelty within slave-owning households was, of course, the fact that slaves were held in bondage against their will. Charleston's 20,000 whites in 1820 were far outnumbered by the city's 60,000 slaves, a ratio that bred fears of slave revolts as well as brutal reprisals against potential uprisings. In Charleston in the summer of 1822, a free black carpenter, Denmark Vesey, secretly organized an extensive slave revolt that was discovered before it erupted. Vesey and thirty-six other black men were hanged.[5]

Yet like most southern critics of slavery, Angelina and Sarah Grimké would almost certainly have accepted their circumstances as beyond their ability to change had they not embarked on a search for a more meaningful religious faith than the comfortable Episcopalianism of their mother. Each in her own way came to reject slavery by first rejecting the religious alternatives available in Charleston and migrating to join the Quaker community in Philadelphia. There, each came to accept the Quaker view of slavery as sinful.[6]

Sarah, thirteen years older than Angelina, went first. Touched by the powerful forces of "the Second Great Awakening"—which transformed American Protestantism between 1800 and 1860 with the evangelical "good news" that individuals could will their own conversion from sin and achieve salvation—she had experienced religious conversion in Charleston under the guidance of a visiting Presbyterian minister in 1813. He preached that her soul would never be saved while she enjoyed fashionable Charleston society—dances, teas, house parties, and other frivolities.[7] In 1819, when Sarah traveled with her ailing father to consult Quaker physicians in Philadelphia and he died at a seaside resort they had recommended, she was befriended by

Quakers. After his death she lingered two months under their calming influence, absorbing their spirituality, their belief in the unmediated relationship between God and the individual conscience, their plain style of dress, few servants, orderly habits, and their condemnation of slavery as ungodly.[8] Two years later she returned to Philadelphia and soon thereafter converted to Orthodox Quakerism.

In 1827, Sarah used religious arguments to convince Angelina to join her in Philadelphia. That year Sarah spent the winter in Charleston, reviving the close relationship she had forged with Angelina since the time of her younger sister's birth. Sarah had served as Angelina's godmother at the time of her baptism, and in many ways became a more meaningful parent than their mother. Angelina's letters to Sarah in Philadelphia addressed her as "dearest Mother" and Sarah's called her "my precious child."[9] In 1827, at the age of 22, Angelina led a vibrant social life, the center of which was her young Presbyterian minister. She led a "colored Sunday school," participated in religious societies, did charity work among the poor, and attended a "female prayer meeting" where Baptists, Methodists, Congregationalists, and Presbyterians met monthly to discuss their responsibilities as women. At home, Angelina had organized daily prayer meetings that were attended by her mother and sisters, the family slaves, and slaves from other households.[10]

A struggle for Angelina's soul ensued, with her "beloved" Presbyterian minister on one side and Sarah's Quakerism on the other. At issue was the question of whether Quakers or Presbyterians offered the more reliable route to religious salvation. Sarah won, but only after an intense battle. The older sister's victory was sealed when Angelina cut up her Walter Scott novels and stuffed a cushion with the laces, veils, and trimmings that had adorned her clothing. In July 1828, three months after Sarah returned to Philadelphia, Angelina joined her there.

Years of uncertain focus followed. Because the sisters' escape from Charleston had religious rather than antislavery motives, and because they joined the conservative Quaker community that had taken Sarah in when their father died, they had no contact with the antislavery movement that began to disrupt Philadelphia in 1831.[11] Their Quaker community valued silence and prohibited mingling with outsiders. Participation in "popular" causes—that is, those that were not exclusively Quaker—was strongly discouraged.[12] In 1827 a schism had split American Quakers into two groups. One, called "Hicksite" (after their leader Elias Hicks, a Long Island farmer), continued the traditional Quaker belief in the power of individual conscience over all other sources of authority, sacred or secular. The others called themselves "Orthodox" but actually were innovators who were adopting a creed that took precedence over individual conscience. For example, they began to require members to profess a belief in the divinity of Jesus. In the great social issues of the day, including slavery, Hicksite Quakers tended to promote radical reform and Orthodox Quakers shunned controversy.

Angelina and Sarah's friends were affiliated with the Arch Street Meeting House, seat of Orthodox Quaker conservatism. "We mingle almost entirely with a Society which appears to know but little of what is going on outside of its own immediate precincts," Angelina wrote in 1829. By 1836, she put it more strongly, "My spirit is oppressed and heavy laden, and shut up in prison."[13] Cut off from the city around her, Angelina Grimké withdrew into a five-year moratorium between late 1829 and early 1835, during which she never spoke in Quaker meetings. Having left the South but not really integrating herself into Northern culture, Angelina emerged from this moratorium as a person without regional loyalties who could challenge race and gender norms of both the North and the South.[14]

The sisters' inheritance from their father made it unnecessary for them to work for a living, and they lived comfortably in the home of a Quaker woman who had befriended Sarah in 1819. Both sisters became Quaker ministers. Quakers did not support a paid ministry; instead their ministers were itinerants for whom the "inner light" of their calling sufficed to qualify them as clergy. Unlike other Protestants, Quakers sanctioned women ministers, though they expected women to minister primarily to the needs of their own sex. Separate women's meetings gave the Grimkés and other Quaker women the opportunity to gain speaking and leadership skills. Quaker religious meetings consisted of silence broken only by those (women as well as men) who were inspired, however briefly, to share their thoughts.[15]

Sarah took both her religious quest and her ministerial calling quite seriously. Although her speaking style was halting and tentative, she spoke regularly in Sunday meetings and traveled to visit and speak to other Quaker groups, especially groups of women. Angelina, by contrast, never spoke in public. Searching for other avenues of usefulness, she explored the possibility of becoming a teacher, and visited Catharine Beecher's renowned female seminary in Hartford, Connecticut. Beecher, the daughter of prominent evangelical Congregational minister Lyman Beecher, was promoting the feminization of the teaching profession as an opportunity for women to become self-supporting.[16] But Angelina's Quaker mentors disapproved because such a move would take her out of the community. Permitted by the congregation to return to Charleston to care for her mother in 1829, Angelina spent nine anguished months viewing slavery for the first time through eyes that judged it a sin. Returning to Philadelphia, Angelina found no outlet for her growing conviction that something should be done to stop slavery in the South.

Meanwhile, Hicksite Quakers in Philadelphia were taking the lead in a radical new movement to end slavery. In 1831, Lucretia Mott, a Hicksite Quaker minister and the leading abolitionist in Philadelphia, befriended William Lloyd Garrison, an antislavery journalist who that year founded *The Liberator*, the nation's first newspaper to call for immediate and unconditional emancipation. Mott helped Garrison develop a more effective speaking and writing style. In 1833, she participated in the founding of Garrison's militant

new organization, the American Anti-Slavery Society (AASS) and that year
she also helped create one of the largest new Garrisonian women's organizations, the Philadelphia Female Anti-Slavery Society.[17]

The founding of the AASS in 1833 marked a turning point in American
history because it fostered the growth of a social movement advocating the
immediate, unconditional abolition of slavery and the racial equality that im-
mediatism implied. Heretofore white northern and southern antislavery
opinion had been dominated by gradualists in the American Colonization Society, who viewed blacks as inferior, had no immediate plans for emancipation, imagined emancipation would occur only after slave owners were
compensated for the loss of their slave "property," and expected freed slaves
eventually to settle in Africa. Colonization did not threaten the economic, political, and social status quo; Garrison's uncompromising call for immediate
abolition did. By emphasizing the equality of blacks and whites, by attacking
the racial basis of slavery, and by denouncing race prejudice in the North, the
Garrisonian movement from Boston to Cincinnati was attacked by mobs that
included "gentlemen of property and standing" when it first appeared in the
1830s.[18]

The power of Garrison's vision flowed from his contact with free blacks,
who never accepted colonization as a strategy for ending slavery, from the
radicalism of Hicksite Quakers, and from religious ideas about human per-
fectibility generated by the Second Great Awakening. A tiny minority in the
1830s, Garrisonians argued that slavery was a sin because it deprived human
beings of the freedom they needed to choose their own salvation. Because all
humans were moral beings, created free by God to determine their own salvation, no person could rightfully deprive others of the ability to make their
own moral choices. To do so was a sinful abomination. The remedy? Immediate and unconditional abolition. In Garrison's movement the slave became a
child of God, created equal in the eyes of God, and the abolition of slavery
became the means by which the new nation could achieve a higher and purer
form of God-given liberty.[19]

Garrisonians denounced the trend in northern states that had recently
disfranchised free blacks—by 1840 over 90 percent of northern free blacks
lived in states that denied them the right to vote.[20] In his 1832 book, *Thoughts
on African Colonization,* Garrison scornfully asked those who believed that
blacks and whites could never live together harmoniously: "are we pagans,
are we savages, are we devils?" Quoting the Scripture, he declared: "In Christ
Jesus, all are one: there is neither Jew nor Greek, there is neither bond nor
free, there is neither male nor female."[21] This passage supported Garrison's
commitment to racial equality; it also endorsed a related principle of sexual
equality, which in 1837 the Grimké sisters would turn into a battle cry.

Large numbers of women responded to Garrison's new movement even
before the Grimkés joined their ranks in 1835.[22] Three white women, three
black men, and sixty white men were present at the founding of the AASS, a

meeting that was not publicly announced because its organizers feared the mobs that had plagued Garrison's public appearances ever since he called for the unconditional abolition of slavery. Although women could join the AASS and its local branches, women also formed separate female organizations, like the Philadelphia Female Anti-Slavery Society, which included white and black women among its founders. Such public action was new for women. In the 1820s, women had begun to create maternal societies where they discussed the new meaning of motherhood in their culture, but before 1835, these groups usually met under religious auspices with ministerial leadership. Lucretia Mott, though a gifted speaker, did not feel capable of chairing the founding meeting of the Philadelphia Female Anti-Slavery Society. Yet she did not follow the common path and ask a white minister to preside; women who attended that meeting were led by "James McCrummel, a colored man."[23]

Although black women joined the Philadelphia and other female anti-slavery societies, they also formed their own groups. Indeed in Salem, Massachusetts, in 1832, when black women formed the Female Anti-Slavery Society of Salem, they created the nation's first women's antislavery group. Before Garrison began to reach African Americans through *The Liberator*, many free blacks were politicized by David Walker's *Appeal to the Colored Citizens of the World*, an 1829 pamphlet that predicted and urged armed rebellion in the South. An African-American merchant in Boston, Walker was a member of the Massachusetts General Colored Association, formed in 1826 to combat racial prejudice in the North and slavery in the South.

Most black women's organizations stressed racial betterment as well as the abolition of slavery. For example, the Afric-American Female Intelligence Society of America, founded in Boston in 1831, opposed slavery, but its constitution emphasized "the welfare of our friends."[24] While many white as well as black women abolitionists spoke out against racial prejudice, black women dedicated themselves to the improvement of African-American communities— a project that distinguished them from most though not all white abolitionist women. In the 1830s this emphasis within black women's organizations meant that racial justice became a higher priority for them than the advancement of women's rights. Although black women were prominent in the abolitionist movement, their voices were not generally heard on the question of women's rights until the 1850s.[25]

Angelina Grimké was jarred out of her moratorium and joined Garrisonian abolitionism in 1835, when she learned of the AASS's efforts to carry its militant new message into the South. Despite the disapproval of her Orthodox Quaker community, she attended a Garrisonian meeting in Philadelphia in March 1835, met with the Philadelphia Female Anti-Slavery Society, and began to read *The Liberator*, where she found thrilling accounts of the heroism and martyrdom of abolitionists threatened by angry mobs.

In the summer of 1835, in a step that unofficially severed her ties with her Quaker community, Angelina publicly joined the vilified abolitionist movement. She did so just after Garrisonians carried their message to Charleston. The AASS had launched a "postal campaign" that sent vast amounts of abolitionist literature through the mails that summer, 175,000 pieces through the New York City post office in July alone.[26] Mobs reacted by destroying these "inflammatory appeals" and attacking abolitionist meetings. In Charleston a mob broke into the post office, seized the AASS literature, and burned it beneath a hanged effigy of Garrison. With the bonfires in Charleston on her mind, in August Angelina sent a letter to Garrison that emphasized her profoundly personal commitment, saying, "it is my deep, solemn, deliberate conviction, that *this is a cause worth dying for.*"[27] At the age of thirty, Angelina Grimké had found her voice.

When Angelina joined Garrison, Mott, and others in 1835 in the vanguard of her generation's concern for her nation's future as a land of freedom, three Americans who later played major parts in the national drama over slavery were relatively oblivious to its importance. Abraham Lincoln, twenty-six years old, was a freshman state legislator and law student in New Salem, Illinois. Jefferson Davis, twenty-six years old and later president of the Confederate States of America, had just moved with his bride and eleven slaves to begin a cotton plantation on rich Mississippi delta land. Harriet Beecher Stowe, twenty-four years old and future author of *Uncle Tom's Cabin* in 1852, was teaching school in Cincinnati. When Lincoln, Davis, and Stowe later became large public figures, they joined a discourse that had been shaped by the Grimké sisters and other Garrisonians.

At first, Sarah strongly disapproved of her sister's actions, writing in her diary, "The suffering which my precious sister has brought upon herself by her connection with the antislavery cause, which has been a sorrow of heart to me, is another proof how dangerous it is to slight the clear convictions of truth." Truth, for Sarah, lay in the Quaker admonition to be still and avoid conflict. Angelina wrote her, "I feel as though my character had sustained a deep injury in the opinion of those I love and value most—how justly, they will best know at a future day."[28]

Independently of her sister, Angelina moved ahead. She took refuge with a sympathetic friend in Shrewsbury, New Jersey, and spent the winter of 1836 writing *Appeal to the Christian Women of the South*. Writing as a southerner and a woman, she created a place for herself within the new Garrisonian movement. Promptly published and widely distributed by the AASS, her *Appeal* urged southern women to follow the example of northern women and mobilize against slavery. Rather than limiting their influence to their own domestic circle, Angelina argued, women should speak out and take public action. "Where *woman's* heart is bleeding," she insisted, "Shall woman's heart be hushed?" If championing the cause of the slave required them to break local laws, she called on her readers, in one of the nation's first expressions of civil disobedience, to follow higher laws.[29]

The exiled South Carolinian especially urged her readers to petition the national government to end slavery. The recent abolition of slavery in the British West Indies, she argued, was due to women's petitions. Sixty female antislavery societies in the North had already followed the British women's example, and she urged southern women to do the same. Petitions enlarged the public space that women occupied, and brought them into direct contact with their national government. At a time when the national government was a distant and somewhat ephemeral concept in the lives of most Americans, antislavery petitions made it a concrete reality. Women's antislavery petitions affirmed the potential power of the national government to redress grievances and restore "rights unjustly wrestled from the innocent and defenseless."[30]

Disfranchised individuals, like women and slaves, had petitioned the national government, particularly the U.S. House of Representatives, since the 1790s, drawing on the First Amendment to the Constitution, which guaranteed the right of "the people . . . to petition the government for a redress of grievances." What was new in the 1830s was the group petition with many signatures. Catharine Beecher organized the first national petition drive by women in the summer of 1829, opposing President Andrew Jackson's forced removal of Cherokee people from land they had historically occupied in Georgia.[31] In 1834, when the AASS organized petitions to end slavery in the District of Columbia, the Society printed a petition form especially designed for women.

The new Garrisonian women's antislavery societies dedicated themselves to gathering signatures, walking door to door, and driving wagons or carriages through their communities. Historians estimate that women contributed 70 percent of the signatures on antislavery petitions.[32] They collected three times as many signatures as those previously obtained by paid male AASS agents. By 1836 the petition campaign so disrupted the proceedings of the U.S. House of Representatives that a "gag rule" was passed to prevent congressmen from reading or otherwise presenting the petitions on the floor of the House. Passed with each Congress between 1836 and 1844, gag rules expanded support for the antislavery cause by linking it to free speech.[33]

Joining this insurgent movement in 1835, Angelina Grimké immediately attracted the attention of the AASS, which sent piles of her *Appeal* to Charleston. There, postmasters publicly burned the pamphlets. The city's mayor told Mrs. Grimké that her daughter would be arrested if she tried to enter the city.[34] Even before Angelina submitted her *Appeal* to the American Anti-Slavery Society, Elizur Wright, secretary of the society, invited her to come to New York and under the sponsorship of the AASS, meet with women in their homes and speak with them about slavery.

Sarah, meanwhile, was rebuked in the Arch Street Meeting House in a way that led her to leave Philadelphia. Although her speaking skills remained unimpressive, and her southern accent reminded her listeners that she remained an outsider in this elite Quaker community, Sarah often spoke in meetings. In July 1835, a presiding elder, probably expressing a consensus reached with other local leaders, rose and cut her off, saying: "I hope the Friend will now be satisfied." Silenced, Sarah sat down. His breach of Quaker discipline was clearly meant to silence her permanently in the meeting. For nine years she had struggled to develop ministerial speaking gifts, keenly aware of the cold indifference with which the elders viewed her efforts. That day she decided "that my dear Saviour designs to bring me out of this place." On learning the news, Angelina rejoiced, "I will break your bonds and set you free."[35] Within a few weeks Angelina had convinced Sarah of the righteousness of her Garrisonian views, and Sarah acknowledged her younger sister's leadership in setting their future course.

Renouncing the respectable comforts of northern as well as southern society, the sisters traveled to New York City in the autumn of 1836. There, for most of the month of November 1836, they joined a training workshop of about thirty men who were serving as the paid agents of the AASS. There they forged new identities as antislavery agitators. "We sit," Angelina wrote to a friend, "from 9 to 1, 3 to 5, and 7 to 9, and never feel weary at all," discussing biblical arguments against slavery and answering questions like "What is Slavery?"[36]

Although they declined to accept pay from the AASS, the sisters launched their new identity as the first women agents of the AASS on December 16, 1836, when they spoke in a Baptist meeting room, no home being large enough to hold the three hundred women who wanted to hear them. To speak in public they had to be willing to break the custom that prohibited respectable women from addressing large public gatherings, and oppose the Scriptural authority of Paul's admonition to the early Christians, "Let your women keep silence in the churches; for it is not permitted unto them to speak." Antislavery women had heretofore spoken to small groups of women, mostly neighbors, in their homes or churches. Angelina temporarily lost her nerve and feared it would be "unnatural" for her to proceed. Charismatic Theodore Weld, one of the leaders of their training group, whom Angelina would later marry, revived the sisters' courage by disparaging social norms that "bound up the energies of woman," and by reminding them of the high importance of their message.[37]

Public speaking was a form of performance in nineteenth-century culture that was strongly associated with the explicitly masculine virtues of virility, forcefulness, and endurance. Much of the vitality of the new nation's public life emanated from styles of oratory that began to emerge in the 1830s, first in the pulpit, then in politics. These new styles were part of the process by which the authority of the clergy and of traditional landed elites was being replaced in public life by the power of more popular groups, especially the broad middle class that ranged from artisans to professionals. The rise in public oratory placed great demands on both speaker and audience. Speakers were expected to engage their audiences' emotions in ways that entertained as well as enlightened, and they were not expected to be brief. Theirs was a culture in which "the word" carried great weight.[38]

Beyond the meetings of all-female societies, respectable women were permitted to enter this arena only as consumers, not as the producers of eloquence. The chief exceptions to this rule were itinerant women preachers, whose prophetic or visionary preaching was inspired by the new currents of expression within the Second Great Awakening. Yet the authority that these women claimed was spiritual, not social. One historian has called them "biblical feminists" because they asserted the spiritual but not the social equality of women. Women might have mystical powers but this did not translate into authority in society. Except among Quakers, female preachers were not ordained and worked outside the institutional religious authority of the clergy.[39] In 1836 and 1837, Angelina and Sarah Grimké would assert women's right to speak not only because women were the spiritual equals of men, but also because they were the moral and social equals of men. By so doing, they opened new channels to public life for women who were not visionaries or prophets.

Opponents tried to discredit women's public speaking by tainting it with the radicalism of Frances Wright, a British free thinker identified with the French Revolution, who spoke widely in the United States in the 1820s.[40] Even the term used to describe a mixed audience of men and women— promiscuous—conveyed the era's distrust of women moving freely in public space. Partly because public speaking was so central to the construction of contemporary civil society, the prohibition against respectable women's public speaking was a key ingredient in the practices that denied respectable women—that is, elite, white, middle-class, and artisan-class women—access to and equality within the new contours of public life. By speaking in public, the Grimké sisters precipitated a women's movement that rebelled against this exclusion. By breaking the prohibition against women's public speaking, they generated criticisms that denied their right to speak, which in turn prompted them to defend that right. This spiraling dynamic occurred because thousands of people wanted to hear the sisters speak more than they wanted to enforce customary strictures.[41]

Angelina's confidence in her public performances grew in the meetings that followed her first speaking date. Addressing a new audience each week, in January 1836, she wrote her Philadelphia friend, Jane Smith, "I love the work." By February she described her animated speaking style as yielding to "impulses of feeling." By then she was also beginning to defend women's "rights & duties" to speak and act on the topic of slavery.

The rapid growth of women's antislavery associations, and the stir that the Grimkés were making in their ranks, led to an unprecedented event in May 1837—a national convention of antislavery women. Organized by Angelina Grimké and other women abolitionist leaders, including Maria Weston Chapman of the Boston Female Anti-Slavery Society and Lucretia Mott and others in the Philadelphia Female Anti-Slavery Society, the convention was scheduled in conjunction with the annual meeting of the American Anti-Slavery Society. Planning for the meeting, Angelina urged Sarah Douglass, a black friend from Philadelphia, to attend it despite the prejudice she could expect to encounter there—from women abolitionists as well as the public at large. Accompanied by her mother, Sarah Douglass did attend. The three-day event attracted about two hundred women from nine states. About one in ten was African American.

The women's antislavery convention marked a new stage in the emergence of women's rights within the abolitionist movement. There Angelina presented her *Appeal to the Women of the Nominally Free States,* a lengthy pamphlet that defiantly defended women's right to speak and act. "The denial of our duty to act, is a bold denial of our right to act; and if we have no right to act, then may *we* well be termed 'the white slaves of the North'—for, like our brethren in bonds, we must seal our lips in silence and despair."[42]

At the convention, delegates adopted resolutions that urged women to circulate petitions that decried the indifference of American churches to the sin of slavery, that censured northerners who married southern slave holders, and that called for white women to associate with African-American women "as though the color of the skin was of no more consequence than that of the hair, or the eyes." Just as radically, the convention approved a resolution supporting women's rights. It declared that "certain rights and duties are common to all moral beings," and that it was the duty of woman "to do all that she can by her voice, and her pen, and her purse, and the influence of her example, to overthrow the horrible system of American slavery." Although most of the convention's resolutions were adopted without extensive discussion, this one "called forth an animated and interesting debate." Twelve delegates opposed the resolution so strongly that they had their names recorded in the minutes "as disapproving."[43]

Following the inaugural meeting of the Anti-Slavery Convention of American Women, the Grimkés launched their historic speaking tour of Massachusetts in the summer of 1837. Beginning in Boston, they felt that they pleaded "not the cause of the slave only" but "the cause of woman as a responsible moral being." In parlor meetings where they strategized with their supporters, men as well as women thought it was time their "fetters were broken." Many believed "that women could not perform their duties as moral beings, under the existing state of public sentiment." And very many thought "that a new order of things is very desirable in this respect." Angelina was stunned by this turn of events. "What an untrodden path we have entered upon," she wrote Jane Smith. "Sometimes I feel almost bewildered, amazed, confounded & wonder by what strange concatenation of events I came to be where I am and what I am."[44]

Reinforced by this support, Angelina declared before 300 members of the Female Moral Reform Society in Boston that they should see women's rights as a personal issue—"that this reform was to begin in ourselves." Women were "polluted" by the attitudes toward them, she said. For example, they felt "restraint and embarrassment" in the society of men. And the "solemn and sacred subject of marriage" was discussed in unseemly ways. Emphasizing the subjective, personal impact of gender inequalities, Angelina told her audience, "My heart is pained, my womanhood is insulted, my moral being is outraged continually."[45]

The sisters found support for this critique of male dominance when they left Boston to lecture in the surrounding countryside. Maria Weston Chapman, an elite leader of the Boston Female Anti-Slavery Society, sent a letter "to Female Anti-Slavery Societies throughout New England" supporting the Grimkés' discussion of "the condition of woman; her duties and her consequent rights." Disdaining those "who were grinding in the narrow mill of a corrupt publick opinion on this point," Chapman urged antislavery women to show the sisters "hospitality of the heart."[46]

In contrast to most British churchmen, who led public opinion in supporting abolition in the 1830s when Parliament ended slavery in the British West Indies, most American clergymen in the North did not support immediate abolition before the Civil War.[47] Thus most church doors were closed against them and ministers who invited the sisters to speak in their churches were exceptions to the rule.

People came to hear the sisters because they were curious about the phenomenon they now represented: southern women presenting in public their first-hand view of the horrors of slavery and defending their right to speak in public about those horrors. Their reception varied. "Great apathy" sometimes reigned in small outlying towns, but before large audiences in Boston and Lynn, Angelina found it "very easy to speak because there was great openness to hear." Men became an increasing part of their audiences. In Lynn on the evening of June 21, they addressed 500 women; a month later in that manufacturing town, they spoke to 1,500 men as well as women.[48] Seven months after their first speaking engagement they had successfully broken the customs against women speaking in public and against women speaking to mixed audiences.

The Grimkés maintained a grueling pace between June and November. Speaking every other day, sometimes twice a day, often for two hours at a time, they reached thousands. In June Angelina spoke seventeen times in ten towns, with over 8,000 attending. In July she gave nineteen lectures in fourteen towns, reaching nearly 12,000. In August, even though Angelina was ill for half the month, she gave eleven lectures in nine towns, with 6,000 present. In September, she spoke seventeen times in sixteen towns, with over 7,000 persons attending. In October she spoke fifteen times in fifteen towns, with 12,000 in her audiences. During these five months she lectured seventy-nine times to audiences totaling over 40,000 people.[49]

It does not seem that Sarah spoke independently of Angelina. Angelina was the one people came to hear. Her extraordinary oratory offered audiences the 1830s equivalent of an award-winning movie about slavery. "Never before or since have I seen an audience so held and so moved by any public speaker, man or woman," said a Massachusetts minister in whose pulpit she lectured.[50] Wendell Phillips, prominent Boston abolitionist, said that she "swept the cords of the human heart with a power that has never been surpassed, and rarely equalled." Phillips was impressed by "her serene indifference to the judgment of those about her. Self-poised, she seemed morally sufficient to herself." He thought her power derived from "the profound religious experience of one who had broken out of the charmed circle, and whose intense earnestness melted all opposition." Audiences felt that "she was opening some secret record of her own experience"; their "painful silence and breathless interest told the deep effect and lasting impression her words were making."[51]

Angelina's impact on her audiences issued partly from her mastery of an oratorical style that emphasized her feelings. Equally important, however, was her ability to use familiar language in new ways. She spoke in the religious discourse of her time, shaping it to fit her purposes. "Cast out the spirit of slavery from your own hearts," she said. "The great men of this country" and the "church" have become "worldly-wise, and therefore God in his wisdom, employs them not to carry on his plans of reformation and salvation." Instead, he has chosen "the weak to overcome the mighty." This use of familiar metaphors to convey new ideas had deep roots in Judeo-Christian traditions. Angelina stood in a long line of prophets who used that tradition to bring new concepts into their cultures. She equated herself to Isaiah and the Massachusetts clergy to old-testament Jewish priests. Like them, she was denounced by established religious authorities, who saw her as a defiant challenge to their leadership.[52]

Yet despite Angelina's greater oratorical gifts, the sisters' success was achieved jointly; neither could have done alone what they were able to accomplish together. Traveling among strangers, some of whom were friendly, some hostile, they could rely on one another as trusted family members and as dedicated colleagues with whom they shared the speaking platform. Neither had to bear all the burdens of their grueling schedule. Sarah was becoming a capable speaker on women's rights, and Angelina relied on her to elaborate that aspect of their message. "Sister Sarah does preach up woman's rights most nobly and fearlessly," Angelina wrote in July.[53]

One measure of the sisters' success was the exponential growth in membership of the American Anti-Slavery Society immediately after their speaking tour. Each meeting harvested new "subscribers" to the AASS. In 1837, the AASS claimed 1,000 auxiliaries and 100,000 members. A year later, their membership had more than doubled to 250,000, and the number of affiliated antislavery societies had increased by one third.[54]

A large number of these new members were women. Many women responded enthusiastically to the Grimkés' "breach in the wall of public opinion." Angelina wrote Jane Smith, "we find that many of our New England sisters are ready to receive these strange doctrines, feeling as they do, that our whole sex needs an emancipation from the thraldom of public opinion." In villages as well as cities, "the whole land seem[ed] roused to discussion on the *province of woman*."[55] While the sisters from South Carolina led the way, others willingly followed. Disciples attracted to their side—like Abby Kelley, a Quaker teacher in Lynn, Massachusetts—now embraced women's rights as well as Garrisonian abolition.

In June the Grimkés' campaign created a constituency for women's rights; in July their opponents emerged. Men within the Garrisonian movement, many of whom supported women's rights in the abstract, feared the issue would damage abolitionism by diffusing the movement's energies, and by linking antislavery with an even less popular idea. Sarah responded to this criticism in a letter to Amos Phelps, a Congregational minister who was an agent of the AASS. There was no going back on her right to speak to mixed assemblies, she said: "To close the doors *now* against our brethren wd. be a violation of our fundamental principle that man & woman are created equal, & have the same duties & the same responsibilities as moral beings. If, therefore, it is right for thee, my dear brother, to lecture to promiscuous assemblies, it is right for us to do the same."[56]

The sharpest criticism of the sisters came from a Pastoral Letter issued by the General Association of Massachusetts [Congregational] Churches, which in July condemned "those who encourage females to bear an obtrusive and ostentatious part in measures of reform, and countenance any of that sex who so far forget themselves as to itinerate in the character of public lecturers and teachers." The letter especially condemned the naming of "things which ought not to be named," as they delicately referred to the sisters' testimonials about the sexual exploitation of slave women. Indirectly the letter forbade clergymen to permit the sisters to speak in their churches.[57]

Clerical opposition to the Grimkés was fueled in part by ministers' desires to contain the power of the female laity in their own congregations. Historically excluded from leadership positions, except among Quakers, in the late 1830s women began to express views on a wide range of issues in their communities, including temperance and moral reform as well as abolition.[58] The growing power of women in the political culture of their communities on these and other issues threatened to undercut ministers' moral leadership. Reverend Albert Folsom of Hingham, Massachusetts, spoke for many clergymen when he sought to discredit women's participation in public life as "inappropriate and unlawful."[59] By August, Angelina felt that "a storm was gathering all around against our womanhood," and feared that even more ministers would close church doors against them.[60]

Increasingly the defense of women's rights came to occupy the sisters' attention. They had not sought this controversy, Angelina emphasized. "We are placed very unexpectedly in a very trying situation, in the forefront of an entirely new contest—a contest for the rights of woman as a moral, intelligent & responsible being."[61] In the summer of 1837, Sarah began to publish a series of essays in defense of women's rights. Theodore Weld, the most charismatic of their male colleagues in the AASS, urged them both to cease such publications and stay focused on slavery. As "*southerners*," he argued, they could "do more at convincing the North than twenty northern females," an advantage that they lost by pursuing "*another* subject."[62] Standing her ground, Angelina explained to Weld why she and Sarah felt they now had to defend women's rights in their speaking and writing. "If we surrender the right to speak to the public this year, we must surrender the right to petition next year & the right to write the year after &c.," she wrote. "What *then* can *woman* do for the slave, when she herself is under the feet of man and shamed into *silence?*"[63]

The annual reports of many women's antislavery societies endorsed the Grimkés' fight for women's rights. At an October 1837 meeting, the Ladies Anti-Slavery Society in Providence, Rhode Island, resolved "that we act as moral agents"; and "that our rights are sacred and immutable, and founded on the liberty of the gospel, that great emancipation act for women." A majority of the nation's largest and most powerful women's abolitionist group, the Philadelphia Female Anti-Slavery Society, also voted their approval.[64]

In October 1837, the sisters settled into the home of friends in Brookline, Massachusetts. Both wrote essays in the form of letters that were later published as books, Sarah's as *Letters on the Equality of the Sexes and the Condition of Woman* (1838); Angelina's as *Letters to Catherine E. Beecher* (1838).[65] Their writings became the standard for women's rights thinking until a decade later, when the Seneca Falls Women's Rights Convention sparked another outpouring of commentary. Glowing with a white-hot radiance, Angelina and Sarah left an enduring legacy for women's rights advocates.

The sisters' writings on women's rights relied primarily on religious arguments. Yet because they buttressed these arguments with enlightenment notions about human equality and natural rights contained in the Declaration of Independence, their vision of female equality extended further than the "biblical feminism" of itinerant female preachers. In these "letters" they explored the implications of the ideas they had developed during their speaking tour. Insisting that all rights were grounded in "moral nature," they explored the personal aspects of moral identity and of rights. And they analyzed the social and political meaning of women's rights from a multitude of perspectives inside and outside the antislavery movement.

Angelina even argued that women should have equal rights in the secular social and political world. When she supported woman's "right to be consulted in all the laws and regulation by which she is to be governed, whether in Church or State," she was making a very large claim indeed. In a passage with closing words that must have thrilled some readers and shocked others, she further insisted "that woman has just as much right to sit in solemn counsel in Conventions, Conferences, Associations, and General Assemblies, as man—just as much right to sit upon the throne of England, or in the Presidential chair of the United States, as man." Sarah offered a new interpretation of the biblical admonition "wives, submit yourselves unto your own husbands." For nineteenth-century women, this biblical admonition often meant submitting to unwanted sexual intercourse, and, since intercourse often led to pregnancy, to unwanted pregnancy. The passage, Sarah wrote, merely recommended a Christian spirit of humility, not a literal rule of husbands over wives.[66] Aware of the radical implications of their arguments, Angelina wrote Sarah Douglass in February 1838, "We Abolition Women are turning the world upside down."[67]

That month, Theodore Weld declared his love and proposed marriage to Angelina Grimké. To gain her consent he wrote only one letter. There, he said that her 1835 letter to Garrison "formed an era in my feelings and a crisis in my history that drew my spirit toward yours." Reminded of her state of mind in 1835 when she wrote Garrison "under tremendous pressure of feelings bursting up with volcanic violence from the bottom of my soul . . . the first long breath of *liberty* which my imprisoned spirit dared to respire whilst it pined in hopeless bondage, panting after freedom to *think aloud*," she agreed to marry Weld.[68] She loved him as "a kindred mind, a congenial soul" with whom she "longed to hold communion."[69] They set the wedding for May. The "volcanic violence" of Angelina Grimké's commitment to Garrisonian abolitionism helped her break customary limits on women's participation in public life. By thinking aloud—fearlessly—she and her sister brought new words and new concepts into public life and created the basis for new relationships in marriage.

Perhaps reflecting the burdens of her pathbreaking three years, Angelina retired from public life after her marriage to Theodore Weld, and Sarah joined the couple in their rural New Jersey retreat. Theodore had lost his voice after one particularly exhausting lecture tour in 1836, and never fully recovered it. Although he continued to play a part in the antislavery movement, Theodore supported his growing family by becoming a teacher.

By autumn of 1837, a new era had taken shape in gender relations and gender ideology in the United States. Although limited geographically to New England and contained within a small social movement to end slavery, the ideas launched by Angelina and Sarah Grimké steadily gained authority through the 1840s, contributing substantially to the first women's rights convention at Seneca Falls, New York, in 1848, and that convention's historic "Declaration of Sentiments."[70] A series of women's rights conventions met during the 1850s, and, after an interregnum during the Civil War in the

1860s, led in 1869 to the founding of national and local woman suffrage organizations, and in 1920 to the adoption of woman suffrage in the Nineteenth Amendment to the U.S. Constitution.[71] The conversion of Angelina and Sarah Grimké to Garrisonian abolitionism and their 1837 speaking tour played a pivotal role in the emergence of this greatest of social movements in American history.

NOTES

1. John Ashworth, *Slavery, Capitalism, and Politics in the Antebellum Republic,* vol. 1, *Commerce and Compromise, 1820–1850* (New York: Cambridge University Press, 1995), p. 365.
2. Brief biographies of Angelina and Sarah Grimké (hereafter AG and SG) and most other women mentioned in this essay can be found in Edward James, *et al.,* eds., *Notable American Women: A Biographical Dictionary* (Cambridge: Harvard University Press, 1971).
3. "Testimony of Angelina Grimké Weld," in Theodore D. Weld, ed., *American Slavery As It Is: Testimony of a Thousand Witnesses* (New York: American Anti-Slavery Society, 1839), pp. 54–55.
4. Large portions from AG's diary have been printed in Catherine H. Birney, *The Grimké Sisters: Sarah and Angelina Grimké: The First American Women Advocates of Abolition and Women's Rights* (Philadelphia: Lee and Shepard, 1885), pp. 55–93. The treatment of slaves in the Grimké household can be inferred from passages in "Testimony of Angelina Grimké Weld," and "Narrative and Testimony of Sarah M. Grimké," in *American Slavery As It Is,* pp. 52–57 and 22–24.
5. See John Lofton, *Denmark Vesey's Revolt: The Slave Plot that Lit a Fuse to Fort Sumter* (Kent, Ohio: Kent State University Press, 1983); and Edward A. Pearson, ed., *Designs Against Charleston: The Trial Record of the Denmark Vesey Slave Conspiracy of 1822* (Chapel Hill: University of North Carolina Press, 1999). The total slave population in the United States at this time was about two million.
6. This interpretation of the Grimké sisters draws on my research in primary materials. It builds on but is not the same as interpretations found in Birney, *The Grimké Sisters;* Larry Ceplair, ed., *The Public Years of Sarah and Angelina Grimké: Selected Writings, 1835–1839* (New York: Columbia University Press, 1989); Gerda Lerner, *The Grimké Sisters of South Carolina: Pioneers for Women's Rights and Abolitionism* (New York: Oxford University Press, 1967); Gerda Lerner, *The Feminist Thought of Sarah Grimké* (New York: Oxford University Press, 1998); and Katherine DePre Lumpkin, *The Emancipation of Angelina Grimké* (Chapel Hill: University of North Carolina Press, 1974).
7. For the feminist potential in the Second Great Awakening, see Nancy A. Hardesty, *Your Daughters Shall Prophesy: Revivalism and Feminism in the Age of Finney* (Brooklyn: Carlson, 1991). See also Nathan O. Hatch, *The Democratization of American Christianity* (New Haven: Yale University Press, 1989).
8. Quakers led the way in the abolition of slavery in the North. In 1758, the Philadelphia Yearly Meeting of the Society of Friends voted to exclude anyone who bought or sold slaves; in 1776, it excluded anyone who owned slaves. Between 1780 and 1800, most Northern states enacted statutes that abolished slavery, though this was usually accomplished gradually, as was the case in the Pennsylvania "Act for the Gradual Abolition of Slavery" of 1780, which immediately emancipated all children born after the passage of the act, but freed adults more gradually. See "Abolition Statutes," in Robert H. Bremner, et al., eds., *Children and Youth in America: A Documentary History,* Vol. I: 1600–1865 (Cambridge: Harvard University Press, 1970), pp. 324–26. In 1830, Negro slavery was still not totally abolished in the North; about 3,500 persons remained in bondage, mostly in New Jersey. See Leon F. Litwack, *North of Slavery: The Negro in the Free States, 1970–1860* (Chicago: University of Chicago Press, 1961), pp. 12–14.
9. Lumpkin, *The Emancipation of Angelina Grimké,* p. 20.
10. AG to Elizabeth Bascom, 23 July 1828; and AG to [her sister] Mrs. Anna Frost, 17 March 1828, both in Weld-Grimké Collection, William L. Clements Library, University of Michigan, Ann Arbor; Lerner, *The Grimké Sisters,* p. 54.
11. Although AG later claimed that antislavery motivations impelled her departure from South Carolina, the historical evidence supports a more gradual evolution of her antislavery views.

12. See Thomas D. Hamm, *The Transformation of American Quakerism: Orthodox Friends, 1800–1907* (Bloomington: Indiana University Press, 1988).

13. AG to Thomas Grimké [1829]; and AG to SG [1836], quoted in Birney, *The Grimké Sisters,* pp. 91, 137.

14. For another example of a young person who emerged from a moratorium to change his society, see Erik Erikson, *Young Man Luther* (New York: W. W. Norton, 1958).

15. For the endorsement of women's spiritual leadership within Quakerism, see Janis Calvo, "Quaker Women Ministers in Nineteenth Century America," *Quaker History* 63, no. 2 (1974): 75–93; and Margaret Hope Bacon, *Mothers of Feminism: The Story of Quaker Women in America* (New York: Harper, 1986).

16. See Kathryn Kish Sklar, *Catharine Beecher: A Study in American Domesticity* (New Haven: Yale University Press, 1973).

17. For Garrison and *The Liberator,* see William E. Cain, ed., *William Lloyd Garrison and the Fight Against Slavery: Selections from the Liberator* (Boston: Bedford Books, 1995). For Mott, see Margaret Hope Bacon, *Valiant Friend: The Life of Lucretia Mott* (New York: Walker, 1980); and Dana Greene, ed., *Lucretia Mott: Her Complete Speeches and Sermons* (New York: Mellen, 1980).

18. Paul Goodman, *Of One Blood: Abolitionism and the Origins of Racial Equality,* (Berkeley: University of California Press, 1998); and Leonard L. Richards, *"Gentlemen of Property and Standing": Anti-Abolition Mobs in Jacksonian America* (New York: Oxford University Press, 1970).

19. Robert H. Abzug, *Cosmos Crumbling: American Reform and the Religious Imagination* (New York: Oxford University Press, 1994), pp. 129–62; and Caroline L. Shanks, "The Biblication Anti-Slavery Argument of the Decade, 1830–1840," *Journal of Negro History* XVI (April 1931).

20. Litwack, *North of Slavery,* p. 75.

21. William Lloyd Garrison, *Thoughts on African Colonization* (Boston, 1832), reprinted in George M. Fredrickson, ed., *William Lloyd Garrison* (Englewood Cliffs, N.J.: Prentice Hall, 1968), pp. 29–37; quote, p. 33.

22. For the growth of women's antislavery organizations in the 1830s, see Julie Roy Jeffrey, *The Great Silent Army of Abolitionism: Ordinary Women in the Antislavery Movement* (Chapel Hill: University of North Carolina Press, 1998), pp. 53–95.

23. Anna Davis Hallowell, *James and Lucretia Mott, Life and Letters* (Boston: Houghton Mifflin, 1884), p. 121, reprinted in Kathryn Kish Sklar, ed., *Women's Rights Emerges within the Antislavery Movement, 1830–1870: A Brief History with Documents* (Boston: Bedford/St. Martin's Press, 2000), p. 78.

24. *The Liberator,* Jan. 7, 1832, reprinted in Sklar, *Women's Rights Emerges,* p. 79.

25. See Shirley J. Yee, *Black Women Abolitionists: A Study in Activism, 1828-1860* (Knoxville: University of Tennessee Press, 1992), pp. 136–54.

26. Bertram Wyatt-Brown, "The Abolitionists' Postal Campaign of 1835," *Journal of Negro History* 50 (October 1963), 227–38.

27. AG to William Lloyd Garrison, August 30, 1835, printed in *The Liberator,* September 19, 1835, and reprinted in Ceplair, *The Public Years,* pp. 24–27, quote, p. 26. For AG's state of mind, see AG to SG, Sept. 27, 1835, quoted in Birney, *The Grimké Sisters,* p. 127.

28. Diary of SG, Sept. 25, 1835, and AG to SG, Sept. 27, 1835, both quoted in Birney, *The Grimké Sisters,* pp. 128–29.

29. For the visual images associated with this appeal to women, see Jean Fagan Yellin, *Women and Sisters: The Antislavery Feminists in American Culture* (New Haven: Yale University Press, 1989).

30. AASS petition form for women reprinted in Sklar, *Women's Rights Emerges,* p. 85.

31. Mary Hershberger, "Mobilizing Women, Anticipating Abolition: The Struggle against Indian Removal in the 1830s," *Journal of American History* 86 (1999); 15–40.

32. Gerda Lerner, "The Political Activities of Antislavery Women," in Lerner, *The Majority Finds Its Past: Placing Women in History* (New York: Oxford University Press, 1979), and Deborah Bingham Van Broekhoven, "'Let Your Names Be Enrolled': Method and Ideology in Women's Antislavery Petitioning," in Jean Fagan Yellin and John C. Van Horne, eds., *The Abolitionist Sisterhood: Women's Political Culture in Antebellum America* (Ithaca: Cornell University Press, 1994).

33. William W. Freehling, *The Road to Disunion, Vol. I, Secessionists at Bay, 1776–1854* (New York: Oxford University Press, 1990), pp. 308–36, 345–52.

34. AG to SG, [Shrewsbury, summer 1836], quoted in Birney, *The Grimké Sisters,* p. 141. See also Stanley Harrold, *The Abolitionists and the South, 1831–1861* (Lexington: University Press of Kentucky, 1995).

35. Diary of Sarah Grimké, August 3, 1836; and AG to SG, n.d., both quoted in Birney, *The Grimké Sisters*, pp. 144–45.

36. AG to Jane Smith, Nov. 11, 1836, and AG to Jane Smith [November, 1836], both quoted in Birney, *The Grimké Sisters*, p. 159.

37. AG to Jane Smith, Dec. 17, 1836, reprinted in Sklar, *Women's Rights Emerges*, p. 89.

38. While literacy was universal in the North, the spoken word still had the authority that came in part from its identification with religious authority, as in "In the beginning was the Word, and the Word was with God, and the Word was God" (John 1:1).

39. Catherine Anne Brekus, *Strangers and Pilgrims: Female Preaching in America, 1740–1845* (Chapel Hill: University of North Carolina Press, 1998).

40. See A. J. G. Perkins and Theresa Wolfson, *Frances Wright, Free Enquirer: The Study of a Temperament* (New York: Harper & Bros., 1939).

41. For more on the Grimkés' oratory, see Stephen Howard Browne, *Angelina Grimké: Rhetoric, Identity, and the Radical Imagination* (East Lansing: Michigan State University, 1999); Lillian O'Connor, *Pioneer Women Orators: Rhetoric in the Ante-Bellum Reform Movement* (New York: Vantage Press, 1952); and Karlyn Kohrs Campbell, *Man Cannot Speak for Her: Volume I: A Critical Study of Early Feminist Rhetoric* (New York: Praeger, 1989). For an exploration of women's presence in public life, see Mary P. Ryan, *Women in Public: Between Banners and Ballots, 1825–1880* (Baltimore: Johns Hopkins University Press, 1990).

42. Angelina Grimké, *Appeal to the Women of the Nominally Free States* (New York: Dorr, 1837), reprinted in Sklar, *Women's Rights Emerges*, pp. 100–103.

43. The full proceedings of the convention have been published as *Turning the World Upside Down: The Anti-Slavery Convention of American Women, held in New York City, May 9–12, 1837* (New York: Feminist Press, 1987).

44. AG to Jane Smith, Boston, May 29, 1837, reprinted in Sklar, *Women's Rights Emerges*, pp. 110–12.

45. AG to Smith, May 29, 1837.

46. Maria Chapman, "To Female Anti-Slavery Societies throughout New England," Boston, June 7, 1837, reprinted in Sklar, *Women's Rights Emerges*, pp. 112–14. On Chapman and the Boston society, see Debra Gold Hansen, *Strained Sisterhood: Gender and Class in the Boston Female Anti-Slavery Society* (Amherst: University of Massachussetts, 1993); and Blanche Glassman Hersh, *The Slavery of Sex: Feminist-Abolitionists in America* (Urbana: University of Illinois Press, 1978).

47. See John R. McKivigan, *The War against Proslavery Religion: Abolitionism and the Northern Churches, 1830–1865* (Ithaca: Cornell University Press, 1984).

48. AG to Jane Smith, May 29, 1837; and AG to Jane Smith, Groton, Mass., Aug. 10, 1837, reprinted in Sklar, *Women's Rights Emerges*, pp. 122–24.

49. Lumkin, *The Emancipation of Angelina Grimké*, p. 128.

50. Birney, *The Grimké Sisters*, p. 190.

51. [Theodore D. Weld], *In Memory of Angelina Grimké Weld* (Boston: George Ellis, 1880).

52. For an example of AG's speaking style, see Sklar, *Women's Rights Emerges*, pp. 153–56, the only one of her lectures to be recorded by shorthand.

53. AG to Jane Smith, New Rowley, Mass., July 15, 1837, reprinted in Sklar, *Women's Rights Emerges*, p. 117.

54. Gilbert Hobbs Barnes, *The Antislavery Impulse, 1830–1844* (New York: Appleton-Century, 1933; reprint Smith, 1957), pp. 134–35; and Louis Filler, *The Crusade Against Slavery, 1830–1860* (New York: Harper, 1960), p. 67.

55. AG to Jane Smith, July 15, 1837.

56. Sarah and Angelina Grimké to Amos Phelps, Groton, Mass., August 3, 1837, reprinted in Sklar, *Women's Rights Emerges*, pp. 118–19.

57. "Pastoral Letter: The General Association of Massachusetts to Churches under Their Care," July 1837, reprinted in Sklar, *Women's Rights Emerges*, pp. 119–21.

58. For the temperance movement, see Ruth M. Alexander, " 'We Are Engaged As a Band of Sisters': Class and Domesticity in the Washingtonian Temperance Movement, 1840–1850," *Journal of American History* 75 (1988): 763–85. For moral reform, see Carroll Smith-Rosenberg, "Beauty, the Beast, and the Militant Woman: A Case Study in Sex Roles and Social Stress in Jacksonian America," in this volume, and Daniel Wright, "What Was the Appeal of Moral Reform to Antebellum Northern Women?" on *Women and Social Movements in the United States, 1830–1930*, a website at http://womhist.binghamton.edu.

59. "Lecture by Albert Folsom, Pastor, Universalist Church, Hingham, Mass., August 27, 1837," reprinted in Sklar, *Women's Rights Emerges*, pp. 121–22.

60. AG to Jane Smith, Groton, Mass., August 10, 1837, reprinted in Sklar, *Women's Rights Emerges*, pp. 122–24.

61. AG to Theodore Weld, Groton, Mass., August 12, 1837, reprinted in Sklar, *Women's Rights Emerges*, pp. 124–27.

62. Theodore Weld to Sarah and Angelina Grimké, Hartford, Conn., May 22, 1837, in Gilbert H. Barnes and Dwight L. Dumond, *Letters of Theodore Dwight Weld, Angelina Grimké Weld and Sarah Grimké, 1822–1844*, 2 vols. (New York: Appleton-Century Crofts, 1934; reprinted Gloucester, Mass.: Smith, 1965), I, 389.

63. AG to Theodore Dwight Weld and John Greenleaf Whittier, Brookline, Mass., August 20, 1837, reprinted in Sklar, *Women's Rights Emerges*, pp.130–34.

64. "Resolutions Adopted by the Providence, Rhode Island, Ladies' Anti-Slavery Society, October 21, 1837," and "Philadelphia Female Anti-Slavery Society Annual Report, 1837," reprinted in Sklar, *Women's Rights Emerges*, pp. 134–41.

65. Sarah M. Grimké, *Letters on the Equality of the Sexes, and the Condition of Woman, Addressed to Mary S. Parker, President of the Boston Female Anti-Slavery Society* (Boston: Knapp, 1838); and Angelina E. Grimké, *Letters to Catherine E. Beecher, in Reply to An Essay on Slavery and Abolitionism, Addressed to A. E. Grimké. Revised by the Author.* (Boston: Isaac Knapp, 1838), portions reprinted in Sklar, *Women's Rights Emerges*, pp. 142–52.

66. Reprinted in Sklar, *Women's Rights Emerges*, pp. 145, 152.

67. AG to Sarah Douglass, Brookline [Mass.] Feb. 25 [1838], in Barnes and Dumond, *Weld-Grimké Letters*, I, p. 574.

68. Theodore Weld to AG, New York, Feb. 8, 1838, and AG to Theodore Weld, Brookline [Mass.] February 11, [1838], in Barnes and Dumond, *Weld-Grimké Letters*, II, pp. 533–34, 536–37.

69. Theodore Weld to AG, New York, Feb. 8, 1838, and AG to Theodore Weld, Brookline [Mass.] February 11, [1838], in Barnes and Dumond, *Weld-Grimké Letters*, I, pp. 533–34, and 536–37.

70. "Report of the Woman's Rights Convention, Seneca Falls, N.Y., July 19–20, 1848," reprinted in Sklar, *Women's Rights Emerges*, pp. 172–79.

71. For more on the emergence of the woman's suffrage movement, see Sklar, *Women's Rights Emerges*, pp. 179–204.

13

Beauty, the Beast, and the Militant Woman: A Case Study in Sex Roles and Social Stress in Jacksonian America

Carroll Smith-Rosenberg

Transforming changes in American family life and in the organization of American religious institutions created unprecedented opportunities for women to undertake collective action in the 1830s. Changes in family life eroded patriarchal values by giving mothers rather than fathers primary responsibility for child rearing. The "disestablishment" of churches removed taxation as a form of support, forcing ministers to rely on the voluntary contributions of their congregations, most of whom were women. The female laity gained enormously in power from both of these developments. Analyzing the largest example of women's collective action before the Civil War, Carroll Smith-Rosenberg shows how women's mobilization was rooted in their distinctive cultural experience as women.

On a spring evening in May 1834, a small group of women met at the revivalistic Third Presbyterian Church in New York City to found the New York Female Moral Reform Society. The Society's goals were ambitious indeed; it hoped to convert New York's prostitutes to evangelical Protestantism and close forever the city's numerous brothels. This bold attack on prostitution was only one part of the Society's program. These self-assertive women hoped as well to confront that larger and more fundamental abuse, the double standard, and the male sexual license it condoned. Too many men, the Society defiantly asserted in its statement of goals, were aggressive destroyers of female innocence and happiness. No man was above suspicion. Women's only safety lay in a militant effort to reform American sexual mores—and, as we shall see, to reform sexual mores meant in practice to control man's sexual values and autonomy. The rhetoric of the Society's spokesmen consistently betrayed an unmistakable and deeply felt resentment toward a male-dominated society.[1]

Few if any members of the Society were reformed prostitutes or the victims of rape or seduction. Most came from middle-class native American

Excerpted from Caroll Smith-Rosenberg, "Beauty, the Beast and the Militant Woman," *American Quarterly* 23 (1971). 562–84. © The American Studies Association. Reprinted by permission of the Johns Hopkins University Press.

backgrounds and lived quietly respectable lives as pious wives and mothers. What needs explaining is the emotional logic which underlay the Society's militant and controversial program of sexual reform. . . .

I would like to suggest that [some 19th-century] women channeled frustration, anger and a compensatory sense of superior righteousness into the reform movements of the first half of the 19th century; and in the controversial moral reform crusade such motivations seem particularly apparent. While unassailable within the absolute categories of a pervasive evangelical worldview, the Female Moral Reform Society's crusade against illicit sexuality permitted an expression of anti-male sentiments. And the Society's "final solution"—the right to control the mores of men—provided a logical emotional redress for those feelings of passivity which we have suggested. It should not be surprising that between 1830 and 1860 a significant number of militant women joined a crusade to establish their right to define—and limit—man's sexual behavior.

Yet adultery and prostitution were unaccustomed objects of reform even in the enthusiastic and millennial America of the 1830s. The mere discussion of these taboo subjects shocked most Americans; to undertake such a crusade implied no ordinary degree of commitment. The founders of the Female Moral Reform Society, however, were able to find both legitimization for the expression of grievance normally unspoken and an impulse to activism in the moral categories of evangelical piety. Both pious activism and sex-role anxieties shaped the early years of the Female Moral Reform Society. This conjunction of motives was hardly accidental.

The lady founders of the Moral Reform Society and their new organization represented an extreme wing of that movement within American Protestantism known as the Second Great Awakening. These women were intensely pious Christians, convinced that an era of millennial perfection awaited human effort. In this fervent generation, such deeply felt millennial possibilities made social action a moral imperative. Like many of the abolitionists, Jacksonian crusaders against sexual transgression were dedicated activists, compelled to attack sin wherever it existed and in whatever form it assumed—even the unmentionable sin of illicit sexuality.

New Yorkers' first awareness of the moral reform crusade came in the spring of 1832 when the New York Magdalen Society (an organization which sought to reform prostitutes) issued its first annual report. Written by John McDowall, their missionary and agent, the report stated unhesitatingly that 10,000 prostitutes lived and worked in New York City. Not only sailors and other transients, but men from the city's most respected families, were regular brothel patrons. Lewdness and impurity tainted all sectors of New York society. True Christians, the report concluded, must wage a thoroughgoing crusade against violators of the Seventh Commandment.[2]

The report shocked and irritated respectable New Yorkers—not only by its tone of righteous indignation and implied criticism of the city's old and established families. The report, it seemed clear to many New Yorkers, was obscene, its author a mere seeker after notoriety.[3] Hostility quickly spread from McDowall to the Society itself; its members were verbally abused and threatened with ostracism. The Society disbanded.

A few of the women, however, would not retreat. Working quietly, they began to found church-affiliated female moral reform societies. Within a year, they had created a number of such groups, connected for the most part with the city's more evangelical congregations. These pious women hoped to reform prostitutes, but more immediately to warn other God-fearing Christians of the pervasiveness of sexual sin and the need to oppose it. Prostitution was after all only one of many offenses against the Seventh Commandment; adultery, lewd thoughts and language, and bawdy literature were equally sinful in the eyes of God. These women at the same time continued unofficially to support their former missionary, John McDowall, using his newly established moral reform newspaper to advance their cause not only in the city, but throughout New York State.[4]

After more than a year of such discreet crusading, the women active in the moral reform cause felt sufficiently numerous and confident to organize a second city-wide moral reform society, and renew their efforts to reform the city's prostitutes. On the evening of May 12, 1834, they met at the Third Presbyterian Church to found the New York Female Moral Reform Society.[5]

Nearly four years of opposition and controversy had hardened the women's ardor into a militant determination. They proposed through their organization to extirpate sexual license and the double standard from American society. A forthright list of resolves announced their organization:

> Resolved, That immediate and vigorous efforts should be made to create a public sentiment in respect to this sin; and also in respect to the duty of parents, church members and ministers on the subject, which shall be in stricter accordance with . . . the word of God. . . .
>
> Resolved, That the licentious man is no less guilty than his victim, and ought, therefore, to be excluded from all virtuous female society.
>
> Resolved, That it is the imperious duty of ladies everywhere, and of every religious denomination, to co-operate in the great work of moral reform.[6]

A sense of urgency and spiritual absolutism marked this organizational meeting, and indeed all of the Society's official statements for years to come. . . .

The motivating zeal which allowed the rejection of age-old proprieties and defied the criticism of pulpit and press was no casual and fashionable enthusiasm. Only an extraordinary set of legitimating values could have justified such commitment. And this was indeed the case. The women moral reformers acted in the conscious conviction that God imperiously commanded their work. As they explained soon after organizing their society: "As Christians we must view it in the light of God's word—we must enter into His feelings on the subject—engage in its overthrow just in the manner he would have us. . . . We must look away from all worldly opinions or influences, for they are perverted and wrong; and individually act only as in the presence of God."[7] Though the Society's pious activism had deep roots in the evangelicalism of the Second Great Awakening, the immediate impetus for the founding of the Moral Reform Society came from the revivals Charles G. Finney conducted in New York City between the summer of 1829 and the spring of 1834.[8]

Charles Finney, reformer, revivalist and perfectionist theologian from western New York State, remains a pivotal figure in the history of American Protestantism. The four years Finney spent in New York had a profound influence on the city's churches and reform movements. . . . Inspired by Finney's sermons, thousands of New Yorkers turned to missionary work; they distributed Bibles and tracts to the irreligious, established Sunday schools and sent ministers to the frontier.[9] A smaller, more zealous number espoused abolition as well, determined, like Garrison, never to be silent and to be heard. An even smaller number of the most zealous and determined turned—as we have seen—to moral reform. . . .[10]

The Society began its renewed drive against prostitution in the fall of 1834 when the executive committee appointed John McDowall their missionary to New York's prostitutes and hired two young men to assist him.[11] The Society's three missionaries visited the female wards of the almshouse, the city hospital and jails, leading prayer meetings, distributing Bibles and tracts. A greater proportion of their time, however, was spent in a more controversial manner, systematically visiting—or, to be more accurate, descending upon—brothels, praying with and exhorting both the inmates and their patrons. The missionaries were especially fond of arriving early Sunday morning—catching women and customers as they awoke on the traditionally sacred day. The missionaries would announce their arrival by a vigorous reading of Bible passages, followed by prayer and hymns. At other times they would station themselves across the street from known brothels to observe and note the identity of customers. They soon found their simple presence had an important deterring effect, many men, with doggedly innocent expressions, pausing momentarily and then hastily walking past. Closed coaches, they also reported, were observed to circle suspiciously for upwards of an hour until, the missionary remaining, they drove away.[12]

The Female Moral Reform Society did not depend completely on paid missionaries for the success of such pious harassment. The Society's executive committee, accompanied by like-thinking male volunteers, regularly visited the city's hapless brothels. . . . The members went primarily to pray and to exert moral influence. They were not unaware, however, of the financially disruptive effect that frequent visits of large groups of praying Christians would have.[13] The executive committee also aided the concerned parents (usually rural) of runaway daughters who, they feared, might have drifted to the city and been forced into prostitution. Members visited brothels asking for information about such girls; one pious volunteer even pretended to be delivering laundry in order to gain admittance to a brothel suspected of hiding such a runaway.[14]

In conjunction with their visiting, the Moral Reform Society opened a House of Reception, a would-be refuge for prostitutes seeking to reform. The Society's managers and missionaries felt that if the prostitute could be convinced of her sin, and then offered both a place of retreat and an economic alternative to prostitution, reform would surely follow. Thus they envisioned their home as a "house of industry" where the errant ones would be taught new trades and prepared for useful jobs—while being instructed in morality and religion. When the managers felt their repentant charges prepared to return to society, they attempted to find them jobs with Christian families—and, so far as possible, away from the city's temptations.[15]

Despite their efforts, however, few prostitutes reformed; fewer still appeared, to their benefactresses, to have experienced the saving grace of conversion. Indeed, the number of inmates at the Society's House of Reception was always small. In March 1835, for instance, the executive committee reported only fourteen women at the House. A year later, total admissions had reached but thirty—only four of whom were considered saved.[16] The final debacle came that summer when the regular manager of the House left the city because of poor health. In this absence, the executive committee reported unhappily, the inmates seized control, and discipline and morality deteriorated precipitously. The managers reassembled in the fall to find their home in chaos. Bitterly discouraged, they dismissed the few remaining unruly inmates and closed the building.[17]

The moral rehabilitation of New York's streetwalkers was but one aspect of the Society's attack upon immorality. The founders of the Female Moral Reform Society saw as their principal objective the creation of a woman's crusade to combat sexual license generally and the double standard particularly. American women would no longer willingly tolerate that traditional—and role-defining—masculine ethos which allotted respect to the hearty drinker and the sexual athlete. This age-old code of masculinity was as obviously related to man's social preeminence as it was contrary to society's explicitly avowed norms of purity and domesticity. The subterranean mores of the American male must be confronted, exposed and rooted out.

The principal weapon of the Society in this crusade was its weekly, *The Advocate of Moral Reform.* In the fall of 1834, when the Society hired John McDowall as its agent, it voted as well to purchase his journal and transform it into a national women's paper with an exclusively female staff. Within three years, the *Advocate* grew into one of the nation's most widely read evangelical papers, boasting 16,500 subscribers. By the late 1830s the Society's managers pointed to this publication as their most important activity.[18]

Two themes dominated virtually every issue of the *Advocate* from its founding in January 1835, until the early 1850s. The first was an angry and emphatic insistence upon the lascivious and predatory nature of the American male. Men were the initiators in virtually every case of adultery or fornication—and the source, therefore, of that widespread immorality which endangered America's spiritual life and delayed the promised millennium. A second major theme in the *Advocate's* editorials and letters was a call for the creation of a national union of women. Through their collective action such a united group of women might ultimately control the behavior of adult males and of the members' own children, particularly their sons.

The founders and supporters of the Female Moral Reform Society entertained several primary assumptions concerning the nature of human sexuality. Perhaps most central was the conviction that women felt little sexual desire; they were in almost every instance induced to violate the Seventh Commandment by lascivious men who craftily manipulated not their sensuality, but rather the female's trusting and affectionate nature. A woman acted out of romantic love, not carnal desire; she was innocent and defenseless, gentle and passive. . . .[19]

The male lecher, on the other hand, was a creature controlled by base sexual drives which he neither could nor would control. He was, the *Advocate's* editors bitterly complained, powerful and decisive; unwilling (possibly unable) to curb his own willfulness, he callously used it to coerce the more passive and submissive female. This was an age of rhetorical expansiveness, and the *Advocate's* editors and correspondents felt little constraint in their delineation of the dominant and aggressive male. "Reckless," "bold," "mad," "drenched in sin" were terms used commonly to describe erring males; they "robbed," "ruined" and "rioted." But one term above all others seemed most fit to describe the lecher—"The Destroyer."[20]

A deep sense of anger and frustration characterized the *Advocate's* discussion of such all-conquering males, a theme reiterated again and again in the letters sent to the paper by rural sympathizers. Women saw themselves with few defenses against the determined male; his will was far stronger than that of woman. Such letters often expressed a bitterness which seems directed not only against the specific seducer, but toward all American men. One representative rural subscriber complained, for example: "Honorable men; they would not plunder, . . . an imputation on their honour might cost a man his life's blood. And yet they are so passingly mean, so utterly contemptible, as basely and treacherously to contrive . . . the destruction of happiness, peace, morality, and all that is endearing in social life; they plunge into degradation, misery, and ruin, those whom they profess to love. O let them not be trusted. Their 'tender mercies are cruel.' "[21]

The double standard seemed thus particularly unjust; it came to symbolize and embody for the Society and its rural sympathizers the callous indifference—indeed at times almost sadistic pleasure—a male-dominated society took in the misfortune of a passive and defenseless woman. The respectable harshly denied her their friendship; even parents might reject her. Often only the brothel offered food and shelter. But what of her seducer? Conventional wisdom found it easy to condone his greater sin: men will be men and right-thinking women must not inquire into such questionable matters.[22]

But it was just such matters, the Society contended, to which women must address themselves. They must enforce God's commandments despite hostility and censure. "Public opinion must be operated upon," the executive committee decided in the winter of 1835, "by endeavoring to bring the virtuous to treat the guilty of both sexes alike, and exercise toward them the same feeling." "Why should a female be trodden under foot," the executive committee's minutes questioned plaintively, "and spurned from society and driven from a parent's roof, if she but fall into sin—while common consent allows the male to habituate himself to this vice, and treats him as not guilty."[23] . . .

Women must unite in a holy crusade against such sinners. The Society called upon pious women throughout the country to shun all social contact with men suspected of improper behavior—even if that behavior consisted only of reading improper books or singing indelicate songs. Church-going women of every village and town must organize local campaigns to outlaw such men from society and hold them up to public judgment.[24] "Admit him not to your house," the executive committee urged, "hold no converse with him, warn others of him, permit not your friends to have fellowship with him, mark him as an evildoer, stamp him as a villain and exclaim, 'Behold the Seducer.'" The power of ostracism could become an effective weapon in the defense of morality.[25]

A key tactic in this campaign of public exposure was the Society's willingness to publish the names of men suspected of sexual immorality. The *Advocate's* editors announced in their first issue that they intended to pursue this policy, first begun by John McDowall in his *Journal*.[26] "We think it proper," they stated defiantly, "even to expose names, for the same reason that the names of thieves and robbers are published, that the public may know them and govern themselves accordingly. We mean to let the licentious know, that if they are not ashamed of their debasing vice, we will not be ashamed to expose them. . . . It is a justice which we owe each other."[27] Their readers responded enthusiastically to this invitation. Letters from rural subscribers poured into the *Advocate,* recounting specific instances of seduction in their towns and warning readers to avoid the men described. The editors dutifully set them in type and printed them.[28]

Within New York City itself the executive committee of the Society actively investigated charges of seduction and immorality. A particular target of their watchfulness was the city's employment agencies—or information offices as they were then called; these were frequently fronts for the white-slave trade. The *Advocate* printed the names and addresses of suspicious agencies, warning women seeking employment to avoid them at all costs.[29] Prostitutes whom the Society's missionaries visited in brothels, in prison or in the city hospital were urged to report the names of men who had first seduced them and also of their later customers; they could then be published in the *Advo-cate*.[30] The executive committee undertook as well a lobbying campaign in Al-bany to secure the passage of a statute making seduction a crime for the male participant.[31] While awaiting the passage of this measure, the executive com-mittee encouraged and aided victims of seduction (or where appropriate their parents or employers) to sue their seducers on the grounds of loss of services.[32]

The Society's general program of exposure and ostracism, lobbying, and education depended for effectiveness upon the creation of a national as-sociation of militant and pious women. In the fall of 1834, but a few months after they had organized their Society, its New York officers began to create such a woman's organization. At first they worked through the *Advocate* and the small network of sympathizers John McDowall's efforts had created. By the spring of 1835, however, they were able to hire a minister to travel through western New York State "in behalf of Moral Reform causes."[33] The following year the committee sent two female missionaries, the editor of the Society's newspaper and a paid female agent, on a thousand-mile tour of the New England states. . . . The ladies rallied their sisters to the moral reform cause and helped organize some forty-one new auxiliaries. Each suc-ceeding summer saw similar trips by paid agents and managers of the Society throughout New York State and New England.[34] By 1839, the New York Fe-male Moral Reform Society boasted some 445 female auxiliaries, principally in greater New England.[35] So successful were these efforts that within a few years the bulk of the Society's membership and financial support came from its auxiliaries. In February 1838, the executive committee voted to invite rep-resentatives of these auxiliaries to attend the Society's annual meeting. The following year the New York Society voted at its annual convention to reorga-nize as a national society—the American Female Moral Reform Society; the New York group would be simply one of its many constituent societies.[36]

This rural support was an indispensable part of the moral reform move-ment. The local auxiliaries held regular meetings in churches, persuaded hesitant ministers to preach on the Seventh Commandment, and urged Sunday school teachers to confront this embarrassing but vital question. They raised money for the executive committee's ambitious projects, convinced at least some men to form male moral reform societies, and did their utmost to os-tracize suspected lechers. When the American Female Moral Reform Society decided to mount a campaign to induce the New York State legislature to pass a law making seduction a criminal offense, . . . hundreds of rural auxiliaries wrote regularly to their legislators, circulated petitions and joined their New York City sisters in Albany to lobby for the bill (which was finally passed in 1848).[37]

In some ways, indeed, the New York Female Moral Reform Society could be considered a militant woman's organization. Although it was not overtly part of the woman's rights movement, it did concern itself with a num-ber of feminist issues, especially those relating to woman's economic role. Society, the *Advocate's* editors argued, had unjustly confined women to domestic tasks. There were many jobs in society that women could and should be trained to fill. They could perform any light indoor work as well as men. In such positions—as clerks and artisans—they would receive decent wages and consequent self-respect.[38] And this economic emphasis was no arbitrary or inappropriate one, the Society contended. Thousands of women simply had to work; widows, orphaned young women, wives and mothers whose husbands could not work because of illness or intemperance had to support themselves and their children. Unfortunately, they had now to exercise these responsibilities on the pathetically inadequate salaries they received as domestics, washerwomen or seamstresses—crowded, underpaid and physically unpleasant occupations.[39] By the end of the 1840s, the Society had adopted the cause of the working woman and made it one of their principal concerns—in the 1850s even urging women to join unions and, when mechanization came to the garment industry, helping underpaid seamstresses rent sewing machines at low rates.[40]

The Society sought consciously, moreover, to demonstrate woman's ability to perform successfully in fields traditionally reserved for men. Quite early in their history they adopted the policy of hiring only women employees. From the first, of course, only women had been officers and managers of the Society. And after a few years, these officers began to hire women in preference to men as agents and to urge other charitable societies and government agencies to do likewise. . . . In February 1835, for instance, the executive committee hired a woman agent to solicit subscriptions to the *Advocate.* That summer they hired another woman to travel through New England and New York State organizing auxiliaries and giving speeches to women on moral reform. In October of 1836, the executive officers appointed two women as editors of their journal—undoubtedly among the first of their sex in this country to hold such positions.[41] In 1841, the executive committee decided to replace their male financial agent with a woman bookkeeper. By 1843 women even set type and did the folding for the Society's journal. All these jobs, the ladies proudly, indeed aggressively stressed, were appropriate tasks for women.[42]

The broad feminist implications of such statements and actions must have been apparent to the officers of the New York Society. And indeed the Society's executive committee maintained discreet but active ties with the broader woman's rights movement of the 1830s, 40s and 50s; at one point at least, they flirted with official endorsement of a bold woman's rights position. Evidence of this flirtation can be seen in the minutes of the executive committee and occasionally came to light in articles and editorials appearing in the *Advocate.* As early as the mid-1830s, for instance, the executive committee began to correspond with a number of women who were then or were later to become active in the woman's rights movement. Lucretia Mott, abolitionist and pioneer feminist, was a founder and secretary of the Philadelphia Female Moral Reform Society; as such she was in frequent communication with the New York executive committee.[43] Emma Willard, a militant advocate of women's education and founder of the Troy Female Seminary, was another of the executive committee's regular correspondents. Significantly, when Elizabeth Blackwell, the first woman doctor in either the United States or Great Britain, received her medical degree, Emma Willard wrote to the New York executive committee asking its members to use their influence to find her a job.[44] The Society did more than that. The *Advocate* featured a story dramatizing Dr. Blackwell's struggles. The door was now open for other women, the editors urged; medicine was a peculiarly appropriate profession for sensitive and sympathetic womankind. The Society offered to help interested women in securing admission to medical school.[45]

. . . Much of the Society's rhetorical onslaught upon the male's lack of sexual accountability served as a screen for a more general—and less socially acceptable—resentment of masculine social preeminence. Occasionally, however, the *Advocate* expressed such resentment overtly. An editorial in 1838, for example, revealed a deeply felt antagonism toward the power asserted by husbands over their wives and children. "A portion of the inhabitants of this favored land," the Society admonished, "are groaning under a despotism, which seems to be modeled precisely after that of the Autocrat of Russia. . . . We allude to the tyranny exercised in the HOME department, where lordly man, 'clothed with a little brief authority,' rules his trembling subjects with a rod of iron, conscious of entire impunity, and exalting in his fancied superiority." The Society's editorialist continued, perhaps even more bitterly: "Instead of regarding his wife as a help-mate for him, an equal sharer in his joys and sorrows, he looks upon her as a useful article of furniture, which is valuable only for the benefit derived from it, but which may be thrown aside at pleasure."[46] Such behavior, the editorial carefully emphasized, was not only commonplace, experienced by many of the Society's own members—even the wives of "Christians" and of ministers—but was accepted and even justified by society; was it not sanctioned by the Bible?

At about the same time, indeed, the editors of the *Advocate* went so far as to print an attack upon "masculine" translations and interpretations of the Bible, and especially of Paul's epistles. This appeared in a lengthy article written by Sarah Grimké, a "notorious" feminist and abolitionist.[47]

"Men have endeavored to entice, or to drive women from almost every sphere of moral action." Miss Grimké charged: "'Go home and spin' is the . . . advice of the domestic tyrant. . . . The first duty, I believe, which devolves on our sex now is to think for themselves. . . . Until we take our stand side by side with our brother; until we read all the precepts of the Bible as addressed to woman as well as to man, and lose . . . the consciousness of sex, we shall never fulfill the end of our existence."[48] . . .

Sarah Grimké's overt criticism of women's traditional role, containing as it did an attack upon the Protestant ministry and orthodox interpretations of the Bible, went far beyond the consensus of the *Advocate's* rural subscribers. The following issue contained several letters sharply critical of her and of the managers, for printing her editorial.[49] And indeed the *Advocate* never again published the work of an overt feminist. Their membership, the officers concluded, would not tolerate explicit attacks upon traditional family structure and orthodox Christianity. Anti-male resentment and anger had to be expressed covertly. It was perhaps too threatening or—realistically—too dangerous for respectable matrons in relatively close-knit semi-rural communities in New York, New England, Ohio or Wisconsin so openly to question the traditional relations of the sexes and demand a new and ominously forceful role for women.

The compromise the membership and the officers of the Society seemed to find most comfortable was one that kept the American woman within the home—but which greatly expanded her powers as pious wife and mother. In rejecting Sarah Grimké's feminist manifesto, the Society's members implicitly agreed to accept the role traditionally assigned woman: the self-sacrificing, supportive, determinedly chaste wife and mother who limited her "sphere" to domesticity and religion. But in these areas her power should be paramount. The mother, not the father, should have final control of the home and family—especially of the religious and moral education of her children. If the world of economics and public affairs was his, the home must be hers.[50]

And even outside the home, woman's peculiar moral endowment and responsibilities justified her in playing an increasingly expansive role, one which might well ultimately impair aspects of man's traditional autonomy. When man transgressed God's commandments, through licentiousness, religious apathy, the defense of slavery, or the sin of intemperance—woman had both the right and duty of leaving the confines of the home and working to purify the male world.

The membership of the New York Female Moral Reform Society chose not to openly espouse the women's rights movement. Yet many interesting emotional parallels remain to link the moral reform crusade and the suffrage movement of Elizabeth Cady Stanton, the Grimké sisters, and Susan B. Anthony. In its own way, indeed, the war for purification of sexual mores was far more fundamental in its implications for woman's traditional role than the demand for woman's education—or even the vote.

NOTES

1. "Minutes of the Meeting of the Ladies' Society for the Observance of the Seventh Commandment held in Chatham Street Chapel, May 12, 1834," and "Constitution of the New York Female Moral Reform Society," both in ledger book entitled "Constitution and Minutes of the

New York Female Moral Reform Society, May, 1834 to July 1839," deposited in the archives of the American Female Guardian Society (hereinafter referred to as A.F.G.S.), Woodycrest Avenue, Bronx, New York. For a more detailed institutional history of the Society see Carroll Smith Rosenberg, *Religion and the Rise of the American City* (Ithaca, N.Y.: Cornell Univ. Press, 1971), chaps. 4 and 7.

2. John R. McDowall, *Magdalen Report*, rpr. *McDowall's Journal*, 2 (May 1834); 33–38. For the history of the New York Magdalen Society see *First Annual Report of the Executive Committee of the New York Magdalen Society, Instituted January 1, 1830.* See as well Rosenberg, *Religion*, chap. 4

3. Flora L. Northrup, *The Record of a Century* (New York: American Female Guardian Soc., 1934), pp. 13–14; cf. *McDowall's Defence*, 1, No. 1 (July 1836), 3; *The Trial of the Reverend John Robert McDowall by the Third Presbytery of New York in February, March, and April, 1836* (New York, 1836). [Thomas Hastings Sr.], *Missionary Labors through a Series of Years among Fallen Women by the New York Magdalen Society* (New York: N.Y. Magdalen Soc., 1870), p. 15.

4. Northrup, *Record of a Century*, pp. 14–15; only two volumes of *McDowall's Journal* were published, covering the period Jan. 1833 to Dec. 1834. Between the demise of the New York Magdalen Society and the organization of the New York Female Moral Reform Society (hereinafter, N.Y.F.M.R.S.), McDowall was connected, as agent, with a third society, the New York Female Benevolent Society, which he had helped found in February of 1833. For a more detailed account see Carroll S. Rosenberg, "Evangelicalism and the New City," Ph.D. Diss. Columbia University, 1968, chap. 5.

5. *McDowall's Journal*, 2 (Jan. 1834), 6–7.

6. "Minutes of the Meeting of the Ladies' Society for the Observance of the Seventh Commandment . . . May 12, 1834," and "Preamble," "Constitution of the New York Female Moral Reform Society."

7. *Advocate of Moral Reform* (hereinafter, *Advocate*) 1 (Jan.–Feb. 1835), 6. The *Advocate* was the Society's official journal.

8. Close ties connected the N.Y.F.M.R.S. with the Finney wing of American Protestantism. Finney's wife was the Society's first president. The Society's second president, Mrs. William Green, was the wife of one of Finney's closest supporters. The Society's clerical support in New York City came from Finney's disciples. Their chief financial advisers and initial sponsors were Arthur and Lewis Tappan, New York merchants who were also Charles Finney's chief financial supporters.

9. Rosenberg, *Religion*, chaps. 2 and 3.

10. These reforms were by no means mutually exclusive. Indeed there was a logical and emotional interrelation between evangelical Protestantism and its missionary aspects and such formally secular reforms as peace, abolition and temperance.

11. *Advocate*, 1 (Jan.–Feb. 1835), 4; Northrup, *Record*, p. 19.

12. *Advocate*, 1 (Mar. 1835), 11–12; 1 (Nov. 1835), 86; N.Y.F.M.R.S., "Executive Committee Minutes, June 6, 1835 and April 30, 1836." These pious visitors received their most polite receptions at the more expensive houses, while the girls and customers of lower-class, slum brothels met them almost uniformly with curses and threats.

13. *Advocate*, 1 (Jan.–Feb. 1835), 7.

14. For a description of one such incident see *Advocate*, 4 (Jan. 15, 1838), 15.

15. *Advocate*, 1 (Sept. 1, 1835), 72; Northrup, *Record*, p. 19.

16. *Advocate*, 1 (Mar. 1835), 11; N.Y.F.M.R.S., "Executive Committee Minutes, Apr. 5, 1836, May 30, 1835."

17. N.Y.F.M.R.S., "Executive Committee Minutes, Oct. 4, 1836."

18. N.Y.F.M.R.S., "Executive Committee Minutes, June 6 and June 25, 1835, June (n.d.), 1836"; N.Y.F.M.R.S., *The Guardian or Fourth Annual Report of the New York Female Moral Reform Society presented May 9, 1838*, pp. 4–6.

19. "Budding," "lovely," "fresh," "joyous," "unsuspecting lamb," were frequent terms used to describe innocent women before their seduction. The *Advocate* contained innumerable letters and editorials on this theme. See, for example, *Advocate*, 4 (Jan. 1, 1838), 1; *Advocate*, 10 (Mar. 1, 1844), 34; *Advocate and Guardian* (the Society changed the name of its journal in 1847), 16 (Jan. 1, 1850), 3.

20. "Murderer of Virtue" was another favorite and pithy phrase. For a sample of such references see: *Advocate*, 4 (Feb. 1, 1838), 17, *Advocate*, 10 (Jan. 1, 1844), 19–20; *Advocate*, 10 (Jan. 15, 1844), 29; *Advocate*, 10 (Mar. 1, 1844), 33.

21. *Advocate,* 1 (Jan.–Feb. 1835), 3, *Advocate,* 1 (Apr. 1835), 19; *Advocate and Guardian,* 16 (Jan. 1, 1850), 3, *McDowall's Journal,* 2 (Apr. 1834), 26–27.

22. Many subscribers wrote to the *Advocate* complaining of the injustice of the double standard. See, for example: *Advocate,* 1 (Apr. 1835), 22; *Advocate,* 1 (Dec. 1835), 91; *Advocate and Guardian,* 16 (Jan. 1, 1850), 5.

23. *Advocate,* 1 (Jan.–Feb. 1835), 6–7.

24. This was one of the more important functions of the auxiliaries, and their members uniformly pledged themselves to ostracize all offending males. For an example of such pledges see *Advocate,* 4 (Jan. 15, 1838), 16.

25. *Advocate and Guardian,* 16 (Jan. 1, 1850), 3.

26. McDowall urged his rural subscribers to report any instances of seduction. He dutifully printed all the details, referring to the accused man by initials, but otherwise giving the names of towns, counties and dates. Male response was on occasion bitter.

27. *Advocate,* 1 (Jan.–Feb. 1835), 2.

28. Throughout the 1830s virtually every issue of the *Advocate* contained such letters. The *Advocate* continued to publish them throughout the 1840s.

29. For detailed discussions of particular employment agencies and the decision to print their names see: N.Y.F.M.R.S., "Executive Committee Minutes, Feb. 12, 1845, July 8, 1846."

30. N.Y.F.M.R.S., "Executive Committee Minutes, Mar. 1, 1838, Mar. 15, 1838"; *Advocate,* 4 (Jan. 15, 1838), 15.

31. The Society appears to have begun its lobbying crusade in 1838. N.Y.F.M.R.S., "Executive Committee Minutes, Oct. 24, 1838, Jan. 4, 1842, Feb. 18, 1842, Apr. 25, 1844, Jan. 8, 1845"; American Female Moral Reform Society (the Society adopted this name in 1839), *Tenth Annual Report for . . . 1844,* pp. 9–11; American Female Moral Reform Soc., *Fourteenth Annual Report for . . . 1848.*

32. The N.Y.F.M.R.S.'s "Executive Committee Minutes" for the years 1837, 1838, 1843 and 1844 especially are filled with instances of the committee instituting suits against seducers for damages in the case of loss of services.

33. N.Y.F.M.R.S., "Executive Committee Minutes, June 25, 1835."

34. N.Y.F.M.R.S., "Executive Committee Minutes, Oct. 4, 1836, and May 22, 1837, and Sept. 11, 1839." Indeed, as early as 1833 a substantial portion of John McDowall's support seemed to come from rural areas. See, for example, *McDowall's Journal,* 1 (Aug. 1833), 59–62.

35. N.Y.F.M.R.S., "Executive Committee Minutes, Oct. 4, 1838"; Northrup, *Record,* p. 22.

36. N.Y.F.M.R.S., "Executive Committee Minutes, May 10, 1839"; N.Y.F.M.R.S., "Quarterly Meeting, July, 1839." Power within the new national organization was divided so that the president and the board of managers were members of the N.Y.F.M.R.S., while the vice presidents were chosen from the rural auxiliaries. The annual meeting was held in New York City, the quarterly meetings in one of the towns of Greater New England.

37. Virtually every issue of the *Advocate* is filled with letters and reports from the auxiliaries discussing their many activities.

38. *Advocate and Guardian,* 16 (Jan. 15, 1850), 9.

39. *Advocate,* 1 (May 1835), 38; N.Y.F.M.R.S., *Guardian,* pp. 5–6. The Society initially became concerned with the problems of the city's poor and working women as a result of efforts to attack some of the economic causes of prostitution. The Society feared that the low wages paid seamstresses, domestics or washerwomen (New York's three traditional female occupations) might force otherwise moral women in turn to prostitution. The Society was, for example, among the earliest critics of the low wages and bad working conditions of New York's garment industry.

40. Significantly, the Society's editors and officers placed the responsibility for the low wages paid seamstresses and other female workers on ruthless and exploitative men. Much the same tone of anti-male hostility is evident in their economic exposés as in their sexual exposés.

41. N.Y.F.M.R.S., "Executive Committee Minutes, Feb. 20, 1835, Oct. 4 and Oct. 5, 1836"; N.Y.F.M.R.S., *Fifth Annual Report,* p. 5.

42. A.F.G.S., *Eleventh Annual Report,* pp. 5–6. For details for replacing male employees with women and the bitterness of the male reactions, see N.Y.F.M.R.S., "Executive Committee Minutes," *passim* for early 1843.

43. N.Y.F.M.R.S., "Executive Committee Minutes, Aug. 3, 1837."

44. N.Y.F.M.R.S., "Executive Committee Minutes, June 2, 1847, Mar. 28, 1849." The *Advocate* regularly reviewed her books, and indeed made a point of reviewing books by women authors.

45. *Advocate and Guardian,* 16 (Jan. 15, 1850), 10.
46. *Advocate,* 4 (Feb. 15, 1838), 28.
47. See Lerner, *The Grimké Sisters.*
48. *Advocate,* 4 (Jan. 1, 1838), 3–5.
49. See, for example, *Advocate,* 4 (Apr. 1, 1838), 55; 4 (July 16, 1838), 108.
50. For examples of the glorification of the maternal role see *Advocate,* 10 (Mar. 15, 1844), 47 and *Advocate and Guardian,* 16 (Jan. 15, 1850), 13–14.

14

Catharine Beecher Promotes Women's Entrance into the Teaching Profession

Kathryn Kish Sklar

Both the Grimké sisters and Catharine Beecher encouraged women to assume new public responsibilities within the larger male-dominated projects with which they affiliated in the Second Great Awakening—the Grimkés within Garrisonian abolitionism and Beecher within the westward expansion of New England evangelical Congregationalism. In this essay Kathryn Sklar explores Catharine Beecher's campaign to feminize the teaching profession in the United States. The vast expansion of the white population across the North American continent created an immense demand for a new supply of teachers that could not be met by men alone. Access to the teaching profession between 1840 and 1880 provided important employment opportunities for women and created a strong demand for the expansion of women's higher education. By 1880 one out of every three students enrolled in institutions of higher learning in the United States was a woman.

In an atmosphere congenial to her from both past acquaintance and future strategy, Catharine Beecher began to outline an ambitious new educational program in the summer of 1843. She was staying in New York City with Mrs. Cortlandt Van Rensselaer, and if she had been wandering all summer in search of the best means of launching her new career, Catharine could not have picked a better means than the Van Rensselaer family. Cortlandt Van Rensselaer was a descendant of old Dutch aristocracy and still held considerable wealth and social prestige. Though he was an ordained Presbyterian minister, his talents were not wasted by the church on a congregation but were instead used for fund-raising. At the time of Catharine's visit he was leading a campaign to raise one hundred thousand dollars for Princeton Theological Seminary. In 1846 he became president of the Presbyterian board of education and devoted his energies to raising funds to endow parochial schools and colleges. Catharine gained access to his skills and influence through her close friendship with Van Rensselaer's wife, her former Hartford seminary pupil, Catharine Cogswell. She stayed at the Van Rensselaers' home for a week and succeeded in gaining their support for her plan to create a national organization for the training and placement of women

Adapted from Kathryn Kish Sklar, *Catharine Beecher: A Study in Domesticity*, chapter 12. Copyright © 1973 Yale University Press. Used by permission of the publisher and the author.

teachers. Catharine's last act of the summer was to accept fifty dollars from the Van Rensselaers as the first contribution toward the funding of the proposed organization.

During the mid-1840s Catharine Beecher successfully promoted the inclusion of women in the male-dominated teaching profession. She sought out people who were either themselves wealthy or could open doors to the wealth of other evangelical individuals and groups. She toured constantly in both East and West, raising funds, seeking sites for schools and seminaries, and recruiting teachers to occupy them. Her 1843 *Treatise on Domestic Economy* made her nationally known, and her frequent speaking tours kept her immediately in the public view. By the end of the 1840s she was one of the most widely known women in America.[1]

Over the course of the decade, as she met with greater and greater success in promoting the primacy of women in American education, Catharine's public and private lives converged. Finally she had found a role commensurate with her personal needs and desires, and much of her achievement during this decade may have arisen from that congruence. As she traveled about the country advocating a special role for her sex, she became the living embodiment of that role. This new consistency in Catharine's life lent conviction to her activities and greatly enhanced her powers of persuasion.

Catharine Beecher returned to Cincinnati in the fall of 1843 and spent the winter striving to create a national organization to promote "the cause of popular education, and as intimately connected with it, the elevation of my sex by the opening of a profession for them as educators of the young." All that winter and spring she corresponded with prominent individuals in the East and West, soliciting their endorsement of such an organization.[2]

By the winter of 1845, her efforts bore fruit in a successful speaking tour during which she visited almost every major city in the East, delivering a standard speech and organizing local groups of church women to collect and forward funds and proselytize her views.[3]

*   *   *

Beecher's addresses were subsequently published in three volumes by Harpers: *The Duty of American Women to Their Country* in 1845, and in 1846 *The Evils Suffered by American Women and American Children: The Causes and the Remedy* and *An Address to the Protestant Clergy of the United States.*[4]

These addresses clarified the ideas she had evolved over the course of the last two decades. Now however like a practiced evangelist she played expertly upon the feelings and fears of her audience and ultimately brought them to commit themselves to her vision of a nation redeemed by women. The full meaning of Beecher's exhortation was not revealed until halfway through her addresses. First she gained her audiences' sympathy for the sufferings of masses of American children under cruel teachers and in degenerate environments. She quoted from several reports to state legislatures that described "the comfortless and dilapidated buildings, the unhung doors, broken sashes, absent panes, stilted benches, gaping walls, yawning roofs, and muddy moldering floors," of contemporary schools and "the self-styled teachers, who lash and dogmatize in these miserable tenements of humanity." Many teachers were "low, vulgar, obscene, intemperate," according to one report to the New York State legislature, "and utterly incompetent to teach anything good."[5]

To remedy this situation Beecher then proposed a national benevolent movement, similar to the temperance movement or the missionary boards, to raise money for teachers and schoolrooms. Yet her plan went even beyond the contemporary benevolent models. Her chief goal was to "elevate and dignify" her sex, and this goal was inextricably bound to her vision of a more consolidated society. The united effort of women in the East, combined with the moral influence of women in the West, would create homogeneous national institutions, she asserted. The family, the school, and the social morality upon which these institutions were based would everywhere be similar. Sectional and ethnic diversities would give way to national unity as the influence of women increased.

To make her image of a unified society more understandable to her audience, she explained that it was a Protestant parallel to the Catholic pattern of close interaction between social and religious forms. Protestant women should have the same social support for their religious and moral activities as Catholic nuns received from their society. She related the stories of many women she had known who were willing to sacrifice themselves to socially ameliorative efforts, but who had been rebuffed by public opinion and restricted to quiet domestic lives. "Had these ladies turned Catholic and offered their services to extend that church, they would instantly have found bishops, priests, Jesuits and all their subordinates at hand, to counsel and sustain; a strong *public sentiment* would have been created in their favor; while abundant funds would have been laid at their feet," she said.[6] Her plan envisioned a similar kind of cultural support for Protestant women. A web of interlocking social institutions, including the family, the school, and the church, would form a new cultural matrix within which women were central.

The ideological basis of Beecher's social theory was self-denial. The Catholic church's employment of self-denying women initially served as a model for her own plan. Yet she emphasized that her notion of self-denial was different from the Catholic one. The Catholics had "a selfish and ascetic self-denial, aiming mainly to save *self* by inflictions and losses," Catharine said, whereas she advocated self-denial not as the means of personal salvation, but as the means of social cohesion. The self was given over to the society. Expanding on the definition of virtue that she had evolved over the course of the last two decades, she said that "a universe of finite free agents" is held together only by acts of self-denial and that "*all* good" was created "immediately or remotely by *self-denial and self-sacrifice*."[7] Self-denial was an inclusive virtue that could be practiced by wealthy and poor, converted and unconverted, by persons of all ages and both sexes. As the ideological basis of a national morality it was especially congenial to Beecher since women could be both the embodiment and the chief instructors of self-denial. It made possible an expanded cultural space for women as the exemplars and the teachers of a national morality.

To support this cultural work for women Beecher advocated three corollary ideas, each of which pointed toward a more consolidated American society. First, she said, women should abolish class distinctions among themselves and form one united social group. Beecher had earlier defended class distinctions as a part of the natural order of God's universe, but such divisions were no longer endorsed in her public writings. This change in her views was prompted in part by a visit she made to Lowell, Massachusetts, where she went to look for teachers. Not believing the Lowell owners' claims that factory work was a means of self improvement for the women operatives, she concluded that women were deliberately exploited at Lowell and in New York City. "Work of all kinds is got from poor women, at prices that will not keep soul and body together," she wrote, "and then the articles thus made are sold for prices that give monstrous profits to the capitalist, who thus grows rich on the hard labors of our sex."[8] Rather than participate in this kind of class exploitation, Beecher suggested women should donate their services to the cause of education. Although they might still be poor, their economic sacrifice would transcend class lines and benefit the whole nation instead of a self-interested class of businessmen.

While economic factors oppressed working-class women, social custom suppressed upper-class women. "The customs and prejudices of society forbid" educated young women from engaging in socially useful employments. Their sufferings were just as keen as those of working-class women, she said, the only difference being that their spirits were starved instead of their bodies. "A little working of muslin and worsted, a little light reading, a little calling and shopping, and a great deal of the high stimulus of fashionable amusement, are all the aliment their starving spirits find," she wrote. "The influence and the principle of *caste*," she maintained, must cease to operate on both these groups. Her solution was to secure "a proper education for all classes, and make productive labor honorable, by having all classes engage in it."[9]

The specific labor Beecher endorsed for both groups was teaching. Working class women should leave the factories and seize the opportunity to go to the West as missionary teachers. Their places in the factories should be taken by men. Upper-class women, Catharine said, should do whatever they could to contribute to the "proper education" of American children. Whether by teaching themselves, or by raising funds, or by supervising schools in their community, all well-to-do women could do some productive labor for education. By their efforts, moreover, the public attitude toward the teaching profession could be changed. Teaching is regarded "as the most wearying drudgery, and few resort to it except from necessity," she said, but by elevating the teaching profession into a "true and noble" one, and by making it the special "profession of a woman," woman would be freed from the caste principles that suppressed them and enter into a new casteless, but elevated condition.[10] In effect she sought to eliminate the extremes of class identity and fortify a middle-class social order.

The second corollary to the new social prominence Beecher attributed to women was that of fostering the nation's social conscience. Young women teachers in the West would be in the vanguard of settlement, and from them the character of the place would take its shape. "Soon, in all parts of our country, in each neglected village, or new settlement, the Christian female teacher will quietly take her station, collecting the ignorant children around her, teaching them habits of neatness, order and thrift; opening the book of knowledge, inspiring the principles of morality, and awakening the hope of immortality," she said.[11] Beecher cited several examples of western settlement where the female teacher preceded the minister. Thus she asserted that a woman could be chiefly responsible for setting the moral tone of the community. A community could coalesce around women rather than the church.

The promotion of national unity was a third aspect of the new social responsibilities Beecher was defining for women. The special esteem in which American women were held meant that their united actions would have a nationwide effect. "It is the pride and honour of our country," she said, "that woman holds a commanding influence in the domestic and social circle, which is accorded to the sex in no other nation, and such as will make her wishes and efforts, if united for a benevolent and patriotic object, almost omnipotent." Women thus had the power to shape the character of the whole nation, and that character, she said, would be one of a united nation rather than a collection of sections.[12]

* * *

At the end of each address Catharine presented to her audience her plan for practical action. A committee of clergymen led by her brother-in-law, Calvin Stowe, would, as soon as sufficient funds were raised for a salary, "appoint one man who shall act as an agent," giving his full time to the organization. The committee would also appoint "a Board of Managers, consisting of men from each of the principal Protestant' denominations from each of the different sections of the country." In addition, local committees of women would raise funds "to aid in educating and locating missionary teachers." In the West such committees could aid in providing schools for those sent out. In both places the committees could publicize the cause. Lastly Beecher revealed how "every woman who feels an interest in the effort can contribute at least a small sum to promote it" by immediately purchasing her *Treatise on Domestic Economy* and her *Domestic Receipt Book,* since half the profits from the sale of these books was to be given to the cause.[13]

Catharine Beecher apparently misled her audience when she claimed that "the copyright interest in these two works is held by a board of gentlemen appointed for the purpose." Her original contract with Harper & Brothers, still preserved by Harper & Row, gave her full control of the profits and did not mention a "board of gentlemen." Her contract gave her 50 percent of the net profits, so she was correct in representing to her audience the fact that only half the price went to the publisher. But when she said that "Half the profits (after paying a moderate compensation to the author for the time and labour of preparing them, the amount to be decided by the above gentlemen) will be devoted to this object," she misrepresented the flow of power and profit between herself and the "gentlemen." For neither Stowe nor any of the other named Cincinnati clergymen would have been capable of questioning how she used the money that came to her from Harpers. She had a reputation in her family of being "clever" to deal with financially, and it was extremely unlikely that Calvin Stowe would have crossed swords with his sister-in-law on financial issues. Later, when a salaried agent was found for the organization, he received his funds from the money he himself raised, not from the profits from her books.

*   *   *

Beecher's tactics in presenting herself and her cause to the public made her an enormously successful publicist. She sent circulars signed by Calvin Stowe to county newspapers and small-town clergymen throughout the East and West, asking for the names of women who might be willing to serve as missionary teachers and for the names of towns and villages where such teachers would be welcomed. The Catholic analogy and the ideology of self-denial made her efforts newsworthy, and to make the work of county editors easier she dispatched articles, such as the one entitled "Education at the West—Sisters of Charity," for newspapers to print alongside Stowe's circular.[14] The primary targets for Catharine's fund-raising efforts were the local groups of church women she organized in every city and town she visited.[15] She asked each group to make at least a hundred-dollar donation, this being the amount necessary to train and locate one teacher.

Her efforts gained the endorsement of the most prominent American educators. Horace Mann, Henry Barnard, Thomas Burrowes, Samuel Lewis, and Gorham Abbot lent their support, and with each new endorsement by a national figure, her local fund-raising became more successful.[16] Beecher's tactic in each city was to plead her cause with the town's most eminent personage and, having gained his or her endorsement, to use it to build a substantial and active local committee. In this way she even drew into her cause those who traditionally opposed evangelical projects and especially opposed the Beecher family.

By the spring of 1846 Catharine Beecher had delivered her addresses in most of the major cities of the East. Everywhere she called upon women to "save" their country from ignorance and immorality, and everywhere women responded. In Boston the Ladies Society for Promoting Education at the West donated several thousand dollars over the course of the decade to Catharine Beecher and her cause, and in other cities similar groups of women were organized by her into active proponents of her ideas on women and education. She corresponded with these groups constantly, relating her recent advances in other cities and exhorting her followers on to greater efforts. In a typical five-week period early in 1846 Catharine spoke in Pittsburgh, Baltimore, Washington, D.C., Philadelphia, New York City, Troy, Albany, and Hartford. She retraced her steps often, sometimes staying only one night in a place—long enough to deliver a public speech, encourage her old supporters, and welcome new ones. She traveled like a candidate for political office, moving quickly from one city to another, thereby promoting a large amount of newspaper coverage of her arrivals and departures.[17]

*   *   *

In Albany in the spring of 1847 and in Hartford in the fall Beecher collected two groups of thirty-five young women for one month's training before they were sent to locations in the West. The local women's committees provided room and board for Catharine and her young women. Catharine lectured the prospective teachers on how to meet all the difficulties that were to face them in the West: how to overcome the lack of books and proper schoolrooms; how to train children to good moral habits "when all domestic and social influences tend to weaken such habits"; how to impart spiritual training "without giving occasion for sectarian jealousy and alarm"; and how to preserve their health "from the risks of climate and the dangers of overexertion and excessive care." Catharine also lectured on the ways in which they could influence the community outside the schoolroom. They learned how to teach "the laws of health by the aid of simple drawings on the blackboard so that the children could copy them on slates to take home and explain to their parents," and how to teach certain branches of "domestic economy" so that parents would "be willing to adopt these improvements." Most of all they learned how to be moral examples that the rest of the community could imitate.[18]

Most of the seventy young women were New Englanders; only three came from New York and one from Pennsylvania. More than half of them went to Illinois and Indiana, seven crossed the Mississippi into Iowa, and a few went to Wisconsin, Michigan, Kentucky, and Tennessee. Each of them was expected to act as "a new source of moral power" in her community, and the reports they made at the end of the year revealed how seriously they took this charge. All the teachers were obliged to repay the hundred dollars "lent" to them by the organization, and although few were able to do so in full, most of them returned some part of their very small salaries to Beecher's organization.[19]

The letters she received from these teachers testified to the effectiveness of her training and to the tenacity of purpose she instilled. One woman went West to join a constituency that had migrated from North Carolina, Tennessee, and Germany and was met with a log cabin classroom holding forty-five pupils ranging in age from six to eighteen, and a community of hostile parents. "They seem desirous to have their children educated, but they differed so much about almost every thing, that they could not build a school-house," she wrote Beecher.

> I was told, when I came, that they would not pay a teacher for more than three months in a year. At first, they were very suspicious, and watched me narrowly; but, through the blessing of my heavenly Father, I have gained their good will and confidence, so that they have provided me a good frame schoolhouse, with writing-desks and a blackboard, and they promise to support me all the year around.

Having proved herself in their eyes, she succeeded next in drawing both parents and children to a Sunday school. Then, because the nearest church was seven miles away and the people did not go to it, she persuaded them "to invite the nearest clergyman to preach" in her schoolhouse the next Sunday. This New England woman, though unused to frontier conditions, decided to stay on in the place even though she had to board "where there are eight children and the parents and only two rooms in the house," and she went without simple amenities such as candles and a place to bathe.[20]

*   *   *

Developments shaping the teaching profession at this precise moment made the field especially receptive to Catharine Beecher's view that it properly belonged to women. Although female teachers began to replace men in some eastern states in the 1830s, the utility of that shift was not apparent to most state and local boards of education until 1840. What had begun as an improvised economy measure had by then proved to be a pedagogic as well as a fiscal improvement, and as these obvious benefits were discovered by state and local boards of education from 1840 to 1880, women gradually replaced their male predecessors in the teaching profession. By 1888 63 percent of American teachers were women, and in cities women constituted 90 percent of the teaching force.[21]

Although it is impossible to measure completely Catharine Beecher's impact on the profession, her publicizing in behalf of women did at least facilitate an otherwise confused transition period in the nation's schools. For the traditionally higher value attached to male labor blinded many communities to the advantages of female teachers, and as late as 1850 the state of Indiana viewed the female teacher as the exception rather than the rule.[22] The West was, on the whole, slower to employ women as teachers, perhaps because it attracted ample numbers of ambitious men who, typically, would teach for a brief period or even a few years before locating more lucrative commercial employment.[23] These male teachers were usually paid twice as much as female teachers, and male teachers frequently brought fewer pedagogic talents to the job than did women. In New York, one of the earliest states to shift to women teachers, the state board of regents in 1838 still assumed that teachers should be male, and they failed to approve the governor's request that normal schools be attached to female academies because they concluded that men, rather than women, needed the normal training.[24] Therefore it was far from obvious to the American public that teaching was a woman's profession.

On the other hand, the shift to women teachers was well enough along by 1843 to provide a solid factual basis for Catharine Beecher's claims on their behalf. In Massachusetts, the first state to promote the employment of women as teachers, women outnumbered men three to two in 1837 and two to one in 1842.[25] Many school districts had since the 1820s routinely employed women to teach the summer session, although they believed men were needed to "manage" the older boys present at the winter school session. Some New York districts learned in the 1820s that they could, with the state subsidy of half a teacher's salary, employ a woman to teach full-time and thus not have to bear any of the cost themselves.[26] As a leading educator pointed out later in the century, "the effective reason" women were employed in schools was that they were "cheaper than men." If they had not been cheaper, "they would not have replaced nine-tenths of the men in American public schools."[27]

The need for such educational economies became more critical in the 1830s and 1840s, when immigration and internal migration increased the population of many areas, but did not immediately increase the tax base. By reducing the school costs by hiring women, a district could accommodate its larger numbers of children without taxing itself at a higher rate.[28]

Three basic assumptions were used to justify these lower salaries for women: women, unlike men, did not have to support a family; women were only working temporarily until they married; and the free workings of the economic marketplace determined cheaper salaries for women. Women do not "expect to accumulate much property by this occupation; if it affords them a respectable support and a situation where they can be useful, it is as much as they demand," wrote the state superintendent of Ohio in 1839. He therefore urged "those counties who are in the habit of paying men for instructing little children" to hire women since "females would do it for less than half the sum and generally much better than men can."[29]

Beecher exploited the short-term gains that these discriminatory practices brought to women, and her publicity on behalf of female teachers emphasized their willingness to work for less money. "To make education universal, it must be moderate in expense," she wrote in a petition to Congress in 1853 for free normal schools for female teachers, "and women can afford to teach for one-half, or even less, the salary which men would ask, because the female teacher has only to sustain herself; she does not look forward to the duty of supporting a family, should she marry; nor has she the ambition to amass a fortune." She also insisted that women's employment as teachers would not create a "celibate class" of women, but that their employment was only temporary, and would in fact prepare them to be better wives and mothers. By defining teaching as an extension of the duties of the home, she presented her idea in a form most likely to gain widespread public support. "It is ordained by infinite wisdom, that, as in the family, so in the social state, the interests of young children and of women are one and the same," she insisted.[30]

Since the profession had lower pay and status than most men qualified to teach could get elsewhere, since the economics of education called for even lower pay in the 1830s and 1840s, and since the schoolroom could be seen as functionally akin to the home, both public sentiment and economic facts supported Catharine Beecher's efforts to redefine the gender of the American teacher.

NOTES

1. Catharine Beecher [henceforth CB], *Treatise on Domestic Economy* (New York: Harper Brothers, 1842; reprinted annually until 1856). Sales of this and other domestic writings established Beecher's financial independence in the 1840s, although she never had enough money to create her own home.

2. CB, *Educational Reminiscences and Suggestions* (New York: J. B. Ford & Co., 1874), p. 101.

3. CB, "Memoranda," 3 October 1844 to 7 June 1845, Beecher-Stowe Collection, folder 316, Schlesinger Library, Radcliffe Institute for Advanced Study, Cambridge, Mass.

4. Beecher's success as a public speaker in the 1840s built on two decades of success as an educator and a writer. For her prior campaigns, see Kathryn Kish Sklar, *Catharine Beecher: A Study in American Domesticity* (New Haven: Yale University Press, 1973), pp. 151–67.

5. CB, *The Evils Suffered by American Women and Children* (New York: Harper & Bros., 1846), p. 29.

6. CB, *An Address to the Protestant Clergy of the United States* (New York: Harper & Bros., 1846), p. 29.

7. CB, *Address to the Protestant Clergy*, pp. 22–23.

8. CB, "Memoranda," 29 November to 4 December 1844; CB, *The Evils Suffered*, pp. 6–9.

9. CB, *The Evils Suffered*, pp. 11–14.

10. CB, *The Evils Suffered*, p. 11.

11. CB, *The Evils Suffered*, pp. 9–10.

12. CB, *The Evils Suffered*, p. 11.

13. CB, *The Duty of American Women to Their Country* (New York: Harper & Bros., 1845), pp. 112–31,

14. CB to Judge Lane, 26 July 1845, Ebenezer Lane Papers, Rutherford B. Hayes Library, Fremont, Ohio. CB undoubtedly knew that Elizabeth Seton had founded the first American religious community for women called "The Sisters of Charity" in 1810 and had soon thereafter opened the first parochial school free to children of all classes. Edward James et al., *Notable American Women, 1607–1950*, 3:265.

15. CB, *Reminiscences*, p. 115.

16. Samuel Lewis was the state superintendent of schools of Ohio; Gorham Abbot, the brother of Jacob Abbot, was the director of a fashionable school for girls in New York City. CB also appealed to Rufus Choate, then the director of the Smithsonian Institution, and Mrs. James

K. Polk, the nation's first lady, for their endorsements. See CB to The Hon. Rufus Choate, 29 August 1846, HBS Collection, Clifton Waller Barrett Library, University of Virginia; CB to Mrs. James K. Polk [1847], Hillhouse Family Papers, box 27, Sterling Memorial Library, Yale University.

17.   CB, "Memoranda," 21 March to 27 April 1846. Charles Foster, *An Errand of Mercy,* p. 136, describes the traditional support New England women gave to education. The first female organizations in the country were formed for such a purpose—specifically to support men studying for the ministry. Early in the nineteenth century these female "cent societies" maintained 20 per cent of the ministerial students in New England. CB therefore drew on an organizational structure and a charitable predisposition that had existed among New England women for at least a generation.

18.   William Slade, "Circular to the Friends of Popular Education in the United States," 15 May 1847. Increase Lapham Papers, State Historical Society of Wisconsin, Madison.

19.   *First Annual Report of the General Agent of the Board of National Popular Education* (Hartford, 1848), pp. 15, 22–25.

20.   CB, *The True Remedy for the Wrongs of Women,* pp. 163, 167.

21.   Woody, *History of Women's Education,* 1 : 499.

22.   Richard G. Boone, *A History of Education in Indiana.* p. 142.

23.   Katz, *Irony of Early School Reform,* pp. 57–58. Katz's evidence disproves the stereotype of the antebellum male teacher as a vacationing college student. His data suggest that teachers shifted to the ministry, commerce, and medicine. He concludes that "others may well have looked on teaching as a way both to stay alive and to establish a local reputation while waiting for the right business opportunity to appear." Paul Monroe, *Founding of the American Public School System,* 1 : 487: "In the newer settled regions of the Middle West men still predominated in the teaching profession throughout this period."

24.   Elsie Garland Hobson, "Educational Legislation and Administration in the State of New York from 1172 to 1850," *Supplementary Educational Monographs* 3, no. 1 (Chicago, 1918) : 75.

25.   Woody, *History of Women's Education,* 1 : 497.

26.   Hobson, "Educational Legislation," p. 66.

27.   A comparison of salary rates for a three- to four-month period near the end of the 1840s compiled from the above sources reveals these differentials:

State	Year	Men	Women
Michigan	1847	$12.87	$5.74
Indiana	1850	12.00	6.00
Massachusetts	1848	24.51	8.07
Maine	c. 1848	15.40	4.80
New York	c. 1848	15.95	6.99
Ohio	c. 1848	15.42	8.73

Henry Barnard was practically alone in protesting this discriminatory practice. See "Report to the Secretary of the Board," *Connecticut Common School Journal* 1, no. 13 (1839) : 163–64. Charles William Eliot, "Wise and Unwise Economy in Schools," *Atlantic Monthly* no. 35 (June 1875): 715, quoted in Katz, *Irony of Early School Reform,* p. 58.

28.   Katz, *Irony of Early School Reform,* pp. 56–58.

29.   Woody, *History of Women's Education,* 1 : 491.

30.   Petition appeared in *Godey's Lady's Book* (January 1853), pp. 176–177. CB wrote Horace Mann: "The great purpose of a woman's life—the happy superintendence of a family—is accomplished all the better and easier by preliminary teaching in school. All the power she may develop here will come in use there." CB to Horace Mann, in *Common School Journal* 5 [Boston, 1843] : 353.

15

Women and Indians on the Frontier

Glenda Riley

Interactions between white women and Native American men and women tell us a great deal about cultural patterns in both societies. In them we can see the distinctive quality of female culture within white society as well as the attractions Native American society held for white women. Glenda Riley shows us how white women enhanced their power in the new western territories by learning from and cooperating with Native Americans.

Because relations between whites and American Indians have not been examined in terms of gender, the assumption stands unchallenged that both white men and women played similar, if not identical, roles in their dealings with Indians. Once the issue of gender is introduced into the study of migration and settlement, however, it becomes apparent that men and women actually fulfilled different capacities in this and in almost every other facet of the westering experience. Both on the trail and in frontier settlements, men were charged with the care of the equipment and livestock, while women supervised the home and were responsible for children. Men who farmed produced the raw materials in their fields that their wives and daughters then converted into finished products in their houses or work places. Men who labored or managed businesses produced cash income instead of raw materials, yet they still depended upon women to function as domestic artisans.

Although men and women occasionally shared work or overlapping functions, the division of labor along the lines described was generally accepted. Applied to their associations with Indians, these labor assignments cast men into something of an adversary position with American Indians, while women played more of a collegial role. It was the men who were responsible for cutting paths into the Indians' domain. They pushed wagons, people, and stock over the trails; seized native hunting grounds; and fended off Indians who might choose to resist such incursions through pilferage or outright assault.

As a result, male migrants and settlers were wary of their opponents. They were constantly alert for any indication that their enemies were in the vicinity, and regular guards were mounted. It was primarily the men's respon-

Excerpted from Chapter 5 of *Women and Indians on the Frontier, 1825–1915,* by Glenda Riley (Albuquerque: University of New Mexico Press, 1984), pp. 167–84.

sibility to corral the wagons or to lie in the corners of fences to thwart attack. Moreover, men were committed to the success of these efforts because of their great desire to establish themselves in livelihoods in the West. They were also motivated by their firm belief in their own aggressive character and their equally firm convictions regarding the inferiority of their foes. . . .

Female migrants and settlers, on the other hand, did not share either the responsibilities or the bellicose way of thinking of their male counterparts. For one thing, in a large number of cases the decision to move westward was made by males. The enterprise itself was based on male desires and needs, with little thought for female wishes and concerns. A historian of western women, Lillian Schlissel, has argued that the westward move coincided perfectly with men's life cycles: it came at a time in their lives when they were "breaking away," that is, improving or bettering themselves. But for women the move was out of phase, for it usually disrupted their efforts to establish a home, produce children, and develop continuity for their families. Consequently, men's and women's accounts of the undertaking differed in predictable ways. Men focused on fighting, hunting, and conflict, while women concentrated upon family and domestic concerns, values, and other related matters.[1]

Whether as migrants or as settlers, women also differed from men in their primary responsibilities. In addition to child bearing and care, these duties centered around supplying food and clothing for their families. Therefore, women, like men, were dedicated to protecting themselves and their families from harm, but they were also constantly concerned with extracting vital resources for their families from the environment and its inhabitants.

Men too desired certain goods and services from American Indians. Grass, water, and route information were some of the commodities most commonly sought after, which men frequently attempted to wrest from the natives through cash payments, threats, or sheer pugnacity. In a typical action, the men of the Burrell party seized usage of an Indian-built bridge by brandishing their pistols at the American Indians who attempted to collect a modest toll.[2] But women, long taught to be soft and nurturing in their approach to problems and people, often derided their men for their aggressiveness. Women were usually dedicated to the success of their western venture because of their own involvement in it, the safety and survival of their families, or their own visions of frontier opportunity. Yet they did not necessarily support the means that men used to achieve that success. Steeped in the accepted female virtues of their era, these women frequently believed that "might" did not automatically make "right." . . . Thus, women tended to pursue a more gentle course than men in their dealings with native Americans.

As a consequence, women's sources portray American Indians as guides, assistants, and purveyors of provisions far more often than they describe them as enemies. According to Schlissel's study of 103 overland diaries, women, "having no special stake in asserting their bravery, having no special need to affirm their prowess . . . correct the historical record as they write of the daily exchanges by which the Indians were part of life of the road."[3] Women routinely bartered, traded, and entered into acts of mutual assistance. In other words, in their attempts to provide food, clothing, and other commodities for those people who depended upon them for succor, women often formed relationships for mutual support with Indians.

This is not meant to imply that women regularly allowed themselves to be pushed around or intimidated by intrusive Indians. On the contrary, numerous incidents involved newly confident women who resisted Indian demands that they deemed unreasonable. Women short-circuited native commands by actions that ranged from slapping their faces to brandishing empty pistols under their noses.[4] They also resorted to using a variety of threats. On one occasion, Susanna Ede evicted an Indian interloper from her kitchen by threatening to pour hot grease on him; in another incident, she raised a pot of boiling water to be thrown on the trespasser.[5] Still other women relied upon direct action. One woman simply tore her belongings out of the hands of trespassing American Indians.[6] Some of the truly assertive women depended on raw bravado to repel unwelcome requests. Lavinia Porter, for example, refused a demand for bread only to have bleeding scalps thrust at her to count and admire. When she refused to give ground, her would-be oppressor muttered "white squaw no fear" and departed.[7]

Some frontierswomen were even willing to engage in unfeminine, violent action when it was necessary to thwart natives. To protect stock from nearby Indians, Mary Burrell and Barsina French's mother took turns standing guard with the men.[8] An Arizona woman defended her family's horses and mules by spending a long night shooting at a band of Pima Indians from one end of the stable roof and then the other.[9] . . .

Apparently, some women were learning that their physical weakness was not as severe nor as debilitating as they had been led to believe. They also seemed quite willing to act in a martial fashion when they thought it was called for, even though they might decry such tactics as standard procedure.[10] These instances of aggressive action were, however, more often the exception than the rule. Women who recorded one or two such occurrences in their lives as migrants or settlers usually also noted many more occasions upon which they cooperated, traded, or had some other type of pleasant interaction with American Indians.[11]

Actually, the pattern that emerged in a great number of western women's accounts was one characterized by exchanges of goods and services between white women and native American men and women. Many frontierswomen overcame their anxiety to trade routinely items such as trinkets, clothing, and foodstuffs with Indians. Such trade occurred even during the years of intensified conflict during the 1860s and 1870s.[12] Both on the trail and in their new homes, women began to barter needles and thread, processed foods such as flour, articles of apparel, and trifles with natives, who usually offered fresh foods in return. Women's accounts frequently mentioned native American men and women bringing to them butter, eggs, potatoes, corn, pumpkins, melons, strawberries, blackberries, venison and other fresh meats, fish, and dried salmon.

The various types of food items supplied by Indians were often savored as a welcome relief from a diet of bread, bacon or salt pork, and beans. "We have so little change in our diet," Miriam Colt, a Kansas settler of the 1850s, wrote, "that almost anything is relished."[13] Similarly, California-bound Martha Moore considered some mountain trout that she purchased from an Indian to be "quite a treat." On another occasion, she was very pleased to have "procured a fine mess of fish."[14]

Many women also became interested in obtaining specialized Indian products and crafts for themselves. They grew skillful at bargaining for buffalo hides and robes, antelope and elk clothing, moccasins, baskets, and beadwork.[15] Army wife Cynthia Capron was particularly delighted with a watertight basket that she purchased for one dollar near Camp Wright in the 1860s.[16] Moccasins were probably the single most popular trade item, and some women even ordered them from native women.[17] Buffalo robes were also coveted, so much so that at least one woman agreed to surrender her shawl to obtain one.[18] Some of the other beautifully tanned skins, including beaver and otter, were carelessly used for rugs, a practice that women sometimes came to regret when these items were no longer widely available.[19] . . .

Women who engaged in trade with Indians soon learned, often to their amazement and occasionally to their dismay, that, in Catherine Haun's words, "the Indian is a financier of no mean ability." Bargains and good deals were not particularly easy to come by, for many natives had as strong a streak of Yankee cunning as the Yankees themselves. "Though you may, for the time congratulate yourself upon your own sagacity," Haun noted, "you'll be apt to realize a little later that you were not quite equal to the shrewd redman."[20] Katherine Dunlap, on her way to Montana in 1864, said that the Indians with whom she traded were so canny that they not only recognized the difference between "coin" and "greenbacks" but would only "take the latter at 50¢ on the dollar."[21]

Naturally, male migrants and settlers also traded with American Indians, but the types of goods involved were usually somewhat different from those purchased by women. Although men were also attracted by moccasins, buckskins, and buffalo hides, they generally spent more time on exchanges involving arms, ammunition, tobacco, horses, and other animals.[22] Men were generally judicious in distributing liquor or refused to do so at all.[23]

When they were part of an all-male expedition or settlement, many men found it necessary to purchase or swap food and clothing with the Indians. But when women were present they were not only primarily responsible for obtaining such items but commonly carried on the negotiations personally.[24] Apparently, as women's preconceptions concerning both themselves and

American Indians began to dissipate they were able to enter into business dealings with their once-dreaded enemies. In so doing, they fulfilled their function as providers of domestic goods. They also demonstrated their ability to practice a relatively gentle style in their contact with American Indians.

In addition to trading with Indians, both male and female migrants and settlers began to hire native men, women and children to perform a myriad of services for them. Men frequently employed, or even kidnapped, Indians to serve as guides who would lead them to the best trails and to grass and water.[25] To help them ford swollen rivers safely, they paid Indians cash or, more often, items such as shirts and caps or ammunition.[26] Occasionally, men even entrusted their stock to an individual Indian hired to act as a herder.[27] It was also not uncommon for men to pay natives "rewards" for locating "lost" stock, but it is impossible to determine whether this was simply a variation of the age-old protection racket.[28]

There was a good deal of complaining about the amounts of money or quantities of goods charged by American Indians for these services.[29] So many men viewed the idea of employing Indian helpers as little more than extortion that they shunned native guides, pilots, herders, and other workers entirely. Due to their belligerent attitude, such men often left a sharp taste of bitterness in their wake. And because they shunned assistance they frequently met with disaster.[30]

Women also began to hire natives to perform chores for them. Californian Mary Ackley employed some Paiute men to shovel, cut wood, draw water, and even wash clothes.[31] Other women, evidently relieved of some of their former anxieties, began inviting Indians into their homes as domestic helpers. Native men, women, and children performed household chores, such as washing dishes and clothes. Their female employers frequently commented that they did a good job or that they were "a great help," and they were paid for their labors with such commodities as sugar, salt, and bread.[32]

The most significant capacity in which women employed both Indian men and women was as nursemaids to their children.[33] This practice seems almost unbelievable, given the widespread fear that American Indians were lying in wait to pounce upon white children and carry them away as adoptees or as captives. Yet many mothers grew to trust Indians so thoroughly that they brought them not only into their homes but into their nurseries.

Interestingly enough, many of the women who engaged American Indian nurses did not appear to object to them teaching the children native customs, dialects, food preferences, and games. Nannie Alderson seemed delighted that her baby's "good and faithful" nurse carried the child on her back like a "papoose." She was pleased that the nurse crooned native songs to the baby, taught her a "squaw dance," made her pretty beaded moccasins, and followed the Indian custom of never spanking her.[34]

In addition, deep affection often developed between the children and their native caretakers as well as between the parents and the nurses. In one case, a young Puget Sound woman, who was raised by an Indian nurse during the 1850s, acquired a fondness for native food and gained some proficiency with her nurse's language. She also expressed a love for the woman that was overshadowed only by her feelings for her mother.[35] When her male Indian nurse died, Caroline Phelps said that her entire family felt his loss very much; her children cried for him "as much as though he had been a relative."[36] . . .

Rachel Wright, a settler in the Upper Napa Valley, claimed that the key to such favorable working relations with American Indians rested with the migrants and settlers themselves. Indians could be "an advantage rather than otherwise," she argued, "as they were not only willing but glad to work if they were left free, well treated and properly paid for their labor."[37] It was in this same spirit of gentleness and fairness that many frontierswomen entered into various types of social affairs with American Indians. Women began to visit them in their homes and to attend their celebrations and ceremonies. They formed close friendships with Indians, particularly with native women. And they occasionally married native men.

These relations between women and Indians were often characterized by warmth and affection. They shared time together inside each other's homes, a stage seldom achieved by male migrants or settlers. Although men visited native camps and villages, they typically joined the "braves" and "chiefs" around the fire to smoke the pipe together, to talk about land and politics, and to negotiate trades. They were often treated to meals prepared by the women of the family, and sometimes they were expected to admire the children, but men were not welcomed into the bosom of the Indians' homes and families as women were. Moreover, men did not regularly form close friendships with Indian males, as women did with Indian females. Furthermore, when they married native women it was often done with an element of necessity or exploitation. Such marriages were almost never legalized or solemnized according to white terms, as with marriages between white females and native males. When a white man did marry a native woman according to white law, it was a matter for comment. In one such case, Alice Baldwin wrote that the man involved was "the soul of honor," who "had the decent courage to marry her legally."[38] . . .

Thus, although both men and women conducted trade with Indians and employed them along the trail and in their new homes, they did not achieve the same degree of closeness with Native Americans. Men's accounts generally lacked the fond references to American Indian friends and neighbors that filled many women's writings as the time they spent on the frontier lengthened. Rather, men tended to remain in their adversary position to the Indians, while women tended to develop and expand their collegial role.

Relationships between women and American Indians often began with group visits to Indian camps. Even the women who had been at first very apprehensive about Native Americans described pleasant social time spent with them. "We often visited Indian camps," Allene Dunham maintained. "They always treated us to a piece of dried buffalo, or venison, or some other kind of meat."[39] Another woman on the way to Salem, Oregon in 1851 claimed that "if there were Indians we would go visiting their lodges and go around among them."[40]

While such occasions nourished cordiality on both sides, it was usually the more personal visits between white women and native women that fostered warm feelings. One trail woman of the 1850s who visited some Sioux women came away favorably impressed by both their hospitality and their skill with a needle.[41] Another female migrant of the 1860s recorded frequent and very genial social calls between her friends and "the Cherokee Ladies."[42] A Mormon woman added that the Indian women whom she visited were "really friendly." She remarked that they had enjoyed "quite a dish of conversation" together.[43] An Iowa settler of the 1870s explained that she grew up with friendly feelings toward the Indians who roamed the woods and camped in the fields around her home. She attributed this to the fact that her Aunt Liza had regularly taken her and her sister to a nearby native village, where the women had given them beads that they "treasured greatly."[44]

Pleasant contacts between white and native women often blossomed into deeper associations. Once army wife Alice Baldwin had invested some time in crimping and waving native women's hair she discovered that "thereafter the Indian women were my firm friends, and rendered me various favors and kindnesses." She commented perceptively that they were brought together by "feminine vanity and tastes," which she felt were "much the same the world over, no matter what the race or color."[45] . . .

Many other white and native women also exchanged bits of female knowledge, lore, and folk medicine with each other. For instance, Mormon migrant Eliza Roxey Snow learned about the sego root from native women, and she claimed that it "proved to be a nutritious, substantial article of food, and not unpalatable."[46] An Oklahoma woman recalled that she had acquired an extensive knowledge of "palatable and very healthful" greens and roots by accompanying Indian women on their gathering and digging expeditions into nearby woods.[47] Others learned how to use herb remedies or how to treat a rattlesnake bite with raw turkey meat.[48] White women were assisted in childbirth by Indian midwives, and often they received thoughtful and sometimes ornate gifts for their new babies. One California woman raved about the "beautiful baskets and elaborate moccasins worked with beads and feathers" that Indian women brought to her mother upon the occasion of the birth of her baby, the first white child to be born in that part of the country. Another remembered the Native American woman who had brought her persimmon bread and a papoose board that was intricately worked with beading and fringe.[49]

A representative case of this congenial and helpful exchange between white and native women was Leola Lehman, an Oklahoma settler who befriended Indian women. In turn, they visited her, bringing small presents to her, and gathered around in admiration when she displayed her new baby. As

Baldwin and other women mentioned, elements of female culture drew these women of different races into a close and easy bond. Lehman particularly liked one native woman who had come to see her because she thought that the transplanted white woman "might be lonesome." Lehman eventually came to "like and respect" this native woman and to regard her "as one of the best women she had ever known." She suggested that many such friendships between whites and natives were possible. However, whites must realize, she said, that American Indians were afraid of white people because they had heard terrifying stories about them. When she left the Indian region, Lehman wrote, "I was glad to be back among my own people but had learned to like the Indians. I was no longer afraid and understood that many of their ways that seemed strange to me were caused by fear of white people."[50] . . .

Women's friendships were . . . common . . . due to the crucial role played by female values in drawing together white and native women. They shared their interest in home, family, children, and domestic matters, and they were both committed to certain values, such as the ability to be open, nurturing, and supportive, which created a connection that was largely unavailable to the males of both cultures. It is unlikely, for example, that a native man would call upon a settler and tell him that he had come because he had thought the other might be lonely. An even more ridiculous picture emerges when one thinks of a settler partially disrobing to allow his new Indian friends to admire and assess his intimate apparel. Instead, males helped each other with weapons, stock, hunting, fighting, and similar activities that only infrequently resulted in the kind of mutuality and confidentiality that women so easily developed and shared.

It should be noted that frontierswomen almost never entered into close friendships with Indian males. They did, however, often find that their business and social relations with Indians generally, and with women particularly, fostered a sense of acceptance and admiration toward their male native acquaintances. As women overcame their anxieties and allowed themselves to know Indians, they soon realized that the natives were not as threatening as they had once appeared. Harriet Ward, for example, clearly contradicted her earlier negative attitudes when she wrote in her diary that her friends back home would "be surprised to see me writing so quietly in the wagon alone . . . with a great, wild looking Indian leaning his elbow on the wagon beside me, but I have not a single fear except that he may frighten the horses."[51] Women were often glad to see Indians arrive and sorry to see them leave. "We have parted with white folks that we did not regret so much," insisted one woman.[52] . . .

Most of these women, . . . were not reluctant to act upon their sentiments by actually visiting Indians and by attending native functions. Women did, for example, turn to Indian medical men for treatment for themselves or for other family members, and particularly for their children.[53] When her daughter's face was badly burned, Caroline Phelps called in a native doctor, who treated the child effectively.[54] In another case of Indian doctors treating settlers' ailments, a woman remarked that the Indians cared for her people "like a brother should treat a brother."[55] Women also aided Native Americans upon occasion. Nannie Alderson restored two "almost frozen" Indian men with a warm fire and a hearty meal.[56] . . .

When romantic love blossomed between a white woman and a native man, it often resulted in marriage. Since it is difficult for long-term affection to develop from occasional or superficial contact, it is not surprising that when intermarriage occurred it was usually the result of frequent contact based on mutual interests. In 1886, for example, a young New England woman of genteel family and demonstrated literary ability went to teach at the Great Sioux Reservation in the Dakota Territory. Here, Elaine Goodale came to see Indians as human beings, to respect their complex culture, and to like them as individuals. During her first five years among them, she wrote many articles and tracts about them and their problems. In 1891, she married a Sioux physician named Charles A. Eastman, with whom she shared a deep commitment toward helping the Sioux people adjust to a rapidly changing world. Together, the Eastmans wrote nine books, with Elaine continuing to write extensively about native American concerns.[57] That Elaine Goodale Eastman's decision to marry an American Indian was not unique among missionary women is supported by occasional and often passing references to other such instances in frontier accounts.[58]

Another situation that fostered marriages between white females and native males existed in Oklahoma during the 1880s, the 1890s, and the early 1900s. As large numbers of settlers took up land leases on Indian agencies, pushing into the region as "Sooners" in well-publicized land rushes, congenial associations often developed between whites and American Indians. These contacts, in turn, produced a large number of intermarriages. While reading through the hundreds of interviews with female settlers in Oklahoma during this era, one is struck by the recurrent references to intermarriages. A former Texas woman recalled, "I have two nieces who married Commanche Indians, one Clinton Red Elk, and one Buster Work-a-wam."[59] Other women mentioned that relatives, acquaintances, or they themselves had married native men.[60]

Oklahoma women chose a variety of Indian men as their mates. One woman explained that her husband was "a quarter-blood Choctaw Indian" who farmed near the Little Washita River.[61] Another woman said that she married a Cherokee who was a teacher trained at Tahlequah's male seminary.[62] Another chose as her husband "a full blood Chickasaw," an interpreter for the governor of the Chickasaw nation; she married him first under state law in 1892, and again under Indian law in 1897.[63]

Although the government fully recognized intermarriage by allowing the wives of native men to draw an allotment and payments made to blood Indians, there was some opposition to the idea from individual settlers.[64] Interviews with these Oklahoma women do not mention any objections being raised by other women, but they do call attention to male disapproval. One woman remembered that her father, a "one-half Cherokee," refused to prove a land claim because he thought it "a disgrace to be part Indian," and he would not publicly admit his background even to obtain a homestead.[65] Another woman spoke of her father's vehement objections to the possibility that any of his daughters would ever marry a Native American. Yet, in a curious twist of fate, after his sudden and tragic death, neighboring Indians were so kind to these women that, in the words of the interviewee, "my sister married a full blood and we have always been glad that she did."[66]

Unfortunately, current scholarship does not supply enough data or evidence to allow one to judge whether women and men were more, less, or equally accepting of the idea of marriages between white women and American Indian men. It might be hypothesized, however, that the female value system permitted relatively easy adjustment to the concept of intermarriage. Female values made it possible for women to enter into warm and comfortable situations with Indians in which intimate relationships could develop. In addition, because female ideals focused on home and family, women were not usually as dedicated as men to the eradication of Native Americans and the seizure of their property. Thus, it can be argued that it was at least possible that white women were more accepting of the idea of marriage between themselves and native men than were their white menfolk. . . .

. . . White women and white men developed quite dissimilar types of relationships between themselves and with American Indians. These differences in white female–American Indian and white male–native American contacts derived in large part from the roles and functions that women and men played in their dealings with Indians on the frontier. Because men were cast as aggressors and as land grabbers, they were pushed into an adversary role. Women, on the other hand, frequently had the opportunity—as procurers of food, clothing, and other domestic goods—to develop a collegial relationship with Indians in their mutual quest for survival.

NOTES

1. Lillian Schlissel, *Women's Diaries of the Westward Journey* (New York: Schocken Books, 1982), 14.

2. Mary Burrell, "Diary of a Journey Overland from Council Bluffs to Green Valley, California, 1854," Beinecke Collection, Yale University Library, New Haven, Conn.

3. Schlissel, *Women's Diaries*, 15. See also Helen E. Clark, "Diary" (1860), and Cara Whitemore Bell, "Journal, 1872–1876," both in the Denver Public Library, Denver, Colo., and Carol Fairbanks and Sara Brooks Sundberg, *Farm Women on the Prairie Frontier: A Sourcebook for Canada and the United States* (Metuchen, N.J.: The Scarecrow Press, 1983), 47–48.

4. Laura Ingalls Wilder, *The First Four Years* (New York: Harper & Row, 1971), 33; Eliza Ann Egbert, "Diary" (1852), Bancroft Library, Berkeley, Calif.

5. Barbara B. Zimmerman and Vernon Carstensen, eds., "Pioneer Woman in Southwestern Washington Territory: The Recollections of Susanna Maria Slover McFarland Price Ede," *Pacific Northwest Quarterly* 66–67, no. 4 (1976), 143, 147.

6. Bessie L. Lyon, "Hungry Indians," *Palimpsest* 9 (October 1928), 366.

7. Lavinia H. Porter, *By Ox Team to California: A Narrative of Crossing the Plains in 1860* (Oakland, Calif.: Oakland Enquirer Publishing Company, 1910), 56.

8. Burrell, "Diary"; Barsina French, "Journal of a Wagon Trip" (1867), Huntington Library, San Marino, Calif.

9. Christiane Fischer, "A Profile of Women in Arizona in Frontier Days," *Journal of the West* 16, no. 3 (July 1977), 43.

10. Porter, *By Ox Team to California,* 67, 79.

11. Burrell, "Diary"; Porter, *By Ox Team to California,* 34, 67.

12. Schlissel, *Women's Diaries,* 154.

13. Miriam D. Colt, *Went to Kansas; Being a Thrilling Account of an Ill-Fated Expedition* (Watertown, N.Y.: L. Ingalls & Co., 1862), 125.

14. Martha M. Moore, "Journal of a Trip to California in 1860," Beinecke Collection, Yale University Library, New Haven, Conn.

15. Fleming Fraker, Jr., ed., "To Pike's Peak by Ox Wagon: The Harriet A. Smith Day-Book," *Annals of Iowa* 35, no. 2 (Fall 1959), 138; Martha M. Morgan, *A Trip across the Plains in the Year 1849* (San Francisco: Printed at Pioneer Press, 1864), 7, 12, 15–16; Ellen McGowen Biddle, *Reminiscences of a Soldier's Wife* (Philadelphia: J. B. Lippincott Company, 1907), 83; Mrs. Edward Dyer, "Diary" (1860), Barker Texas Center, University of Texas, Austin.

16. Cynthia J. Capron, "Life in the Army," *Journal of the Illinois State Historical Society* 13, no. 3 (October 1920), 369.

17. Egbert, "Diary."

18. Mrs. B. G. Ferris, *The Mormons at Home* (New York: Dix & Edwards, 1856), 63.

19. Mary A. Hodgson, "The Life of a Pioneer Family" (1922), California State Library, Sacramento; Biddle, *Reminiscences,* 83.

20. Catherine M. Haun, "A Woman's Trip across the Plains, from Clinton, Iowa, to Sacramento, California, by Way of Salt Lake City" (1849), Huntington Library, San Marino, Calif.

21. Katherine Dunlap, "Journal" (1864), Bancroft Library, Berkeley, Calif.

22. Frink, *Journal,* 68, 77; Guill, "Overland Diary"; Kate Roberts Pelissier, "Reminiscences of a Pioneer Mother," *North Dakota History* 24 (July 1957), 131; Morgan, *Trip across the Plains,* 15–16; Washburn, "Journal"; Hopping, "Incidents of Pioneer Life"; Edwin Bryant, *What I Saw in California* (Minneapolis: Ross & Holmes, 1967), 166; Raymond W. Settle, ed., *The March of the Mounted Riflemen* (Glendale, Calif.: Arthur H. Clark, 1940), 223. . . .

23. John D. Unruh, *The Plains Across: The Overland Emigrants and the Trans-Mississippi West, 1840–1860* (Urbana: University of Illinois Press, 1979), 166.

24. Schlissel, *Women's Diaries,* 53.

25. Helen Carpenter, "Diary" (1856), Bancroft Library, Berkeley, Calif.: Unruh, *Plains Across,* 157; Frink, *Journal,* 72; Bunyard, "Diary," 121; French, "Journal"; Mrs. Nicholas Harrison Karchner, "Diary" (1862), California State Library, Sacramento.

26. Maggie Hall, "The Story of Maggie Hall," Bancroft Library, Berkeley, Calif.; Elizabeth L. Lord, *Reminiscences of Eastern Oregon* (Portland, Oreg.: Irwin-Hodgson Company, 1903), 68–69; Charlotte Stearns Pengra, "Diary" (1853), Huntington Library, San Marino, Calif.; Unruh, *Plains Across,* 157.

27. Abby E. Fulkerth, "Diary of Overland Journey of William L. Fulkerth and Wife from Iowa to California in 1863," Bancroft Library, Berkeley, Calif.; Unruh, *Plains Across,* 159; Lord, *Reminiscences,* 86.

28. Leo M. Kaiser and Priscilla Knuth, eds., "From Ithaca to Clatsop Plains: Miss Ketcham's Journal of Travel," pt. 1, *Oregon Historical Quarterly* 62, no. 3 (1961), 255; Unruh, *Plains Across,* 163; Caroline D. Budlong, *Memories: Pioneer Days in Oregon and Washington Territory* (Eugene, Oreg.: Pictures Press Printers, 1949), 4; J. William Barrett, II, ed., *The Overland Journal of Amos Piatt Josselyn* (Baltimore: Gateway Press, 1978), 20.

29. Mary Fetter Hite Sandford, "A Trip across the Plains" (1853), California State Library, Sacramento; French, "Journal"; Unruh, *Plains Across,* 158.

30. Unruh, *Plains Across,* 158.

31. Mary E. Ackley, *Crossing the Plains and Early Days in California* (San Francisco: Privately printed, 1928), 66.

32. Budiong, *Memories,* 38; Nannie T. Alderson, *A Bride Goes West* (Lincoln: University of Nebraska Press, 1969), 186; Fraker, "To Pike's Peak," 137; Hodgson, "Life of a Pioneer Family"; Albert L. Hurtado, "'Hardly a Farmhouse—A Kitchen without Them': Indian and White Households on the California Borderland Frontier in 1860," *Western Historical Quarterly* 14, no. 3 (July 1982), 245–70.

33. Alderson, *Bride Goes West,* 131; Caroline Phelps, "Diary" (1830–1860), Iowa State Historical Society, Iowa City.

34. Alderson, *Bride Goes West,* 132, 136.

35. Sarah McAllister Hartman, "Reminiscences of Early Days on Puget Sound, the Friendliness of the Local Indians, and Experiences during the Indian War of 1855" (n.d.), Beinecke Collection, Yale University Library, New Haven, Conn.

36. Phelps, "Diary."

37. Rachel E. Wright, "The Early Upper Napa Valley" (1928), Bancroft Library, Berkeley, Calif.

38. Robert C. and Eleanor R. Carriker, eds., *An Army Wife on the Frontier: The Memoirs of Alice Blackwood Baldwin, 1867–1877* (Salt Lake City: Tanner Trust Fund, University of Utah Library, 1975), 108.

39. E. Allene Dunham, *Across the Plains in a Covered Wagon* (Milton, Iowa: n.p., ca. 1920s), 7.

40. Mrs. H. T. Clarke, "A Young Woman's Sights on the Emigrant's Trail" (1878), Bancroft Library, Berkeley, Calif.

41. Lodisa Frizzell, *Across the Plains to California in 1852* (New York: New York Public Library, 1915), 25.

42. Malvina V. Manning, "Diary" (1862), Bancroft Library, Berkeley, Calif.

43. Ferris, *Mormons at Home*, 24.

44. Louise S. Gellhorn Boylan, "My Life Story: Reminiscence of German Settlers in Hardin County, 1867–1883," Iowa State Historical Society, Iowa City.

45. Carriker, *Army Wife*, 79, 99–100.

46. Eliza R. Snow, "Sketch of My Life" (1885), Bancroft Library, Berkeley, Calif.

47. Mollie Beaver, interview 9409, vol. 6, Indian-Pioneer Papers, University of Oklahoma, Norman.

48. Belle M. Yates, interview 12817, vol. 101, Indian-Pioneer Papers, University of Oklahoma, Norman; Bertha Brewer Plummer, interview 4833, vol. 72, Indian-Pioneer Papers, University of Oklahoma, Norman; Fannie Birdwell, interview 8360, vol. 8, Indian-Pioneer Papers, University of Oklahoma, Norman; Dan McAllister, "Pioneer Woman," *New Mexico Historical Review* 34, no. 3 (July 1959), 162.

49. Jean Webster, "The Myth of Hardship on the Oregon Trail," *Reed College Bulletin* 24 (January 1946), 37; Hodgson, "Life of a Pioneer Family"; Lorene Millhollen, interview 8957, vol. 63, Indian-Pioneer Papers, University of Oklahoma, Norman.

50. Leola Lehman, "Life in the Territories," *Chronicles of Oklahoma* 41 (Fall 1963), 373–75.

51. Ward G. DeWitt and Florence S. DeWitt, *Prairie Schooner Lady: The Journal of Harriet Sherrill Ward, 1853* (Los Angeles: Westernlore Press, 1959), 78.

52. Hopping, "Incidents of Pioneer Life"; Egbert, "Diary."

53. Nancy C. Pruitt, interview 7855, vol. 73, Indian-Pioneer Papers, University of Oklahoma, Norman.

54. Phelps, "Diary."

55. Hartman, "Reminiscences."

56. Alderson, *Bride Goes West*, 91.

57. Kay Graber, ed., *Sister to the Sioux: The Memoirs of Elaine Goodale Eastman* (Lincoln: University of Nebraska Press, 1978), xi–xii, 172–75.

58. Emily McCowen Horton, *My Scrap-book* (Seattle, Wash.: n.p., 1927), 17.

59. Barnes, interview 9735.

60. Mrs. William N. Moore, interview 7365, vol. 64; Emma Jean Ross Overstreet, interview 7240, vol. 68; Sarah Scott Phillips, interview 6251, vol. 71; Mrs. J. B. Antles, interview 4163, vol. 2; Harriet Gibbons Oakes, interview 12028, vol. 68; all in Indian-Pioneer Papers, University of Oklahoma, Norman.

61. Mrs. Bill Moncrief, interview 4189, vol. 64, Indian-Pioneer Papers, University of Oklahoma, Norman.

62. Sallie Butler, interview 7244, vol. 14, Indian-Pioneer Papers, University of Oklahoma, Norman.

63. Alice Parker, interview 4021, vol. 69, Indian-Pioneer Papers, University of Oklahoma, Norman.

64. Mary Ellen Williams, interview 6877, vol. 98, Indian-Pioneer Papers, University of Oklahoma, Norman.

65. Mrs. B. M. Austin, interview 9189, vol. 3, Indian-Pioneer Papers, University of Oklahoma, Norman.

66. Beaver, interview 9409.

16

Victorian Women and Domestic Life: Mary Todd Lincoln, Elizabeth Cady Stanton, and Harriet Beecher Stowe

Kathryn Kish Sklar

The most fundamental assertion of women's power in nineteenth-century America lay in the un-precedented control women exerted over their own bodies and the reproductive process. This article recounts how three women responded to the changes demographers call the "demographic transi-tion." That transition from high birth and death rates to low birth and death rates, which began around 1800 and was not completed until after 1930, potentially empowered women as wives, as mothers, and as persons. But by encouraging women to view their children as irreplaceable indi-viduals at a time when infant and childhood mortality still remained high, the demographic transition also made women feel the death of their children more keenly.

This essay explores themes in the private side of American life in the mid-nineteenth century. In particular it explores nineteenth-century family life from the female perspective, and studies the strategies women adopted in response to change in the domestic arena.

Historians have increasingly come to see the middle decades of the nineteenth century between 1830 and 1880 as sharing a common set of social and cultural assumptions called Victorianism. Daniel Howe has noted that not every American was a Victorian. "American Indians, recent arrivals from the peasant societies of Europe and Asia, and the Spanish-speaking inhabitants of lands taken from Mexico," had other cultural identities, as, to a significant degree, did Afro-Americans. The reign of American Victorianism extended primarily to white, English-speaking, Protestant members of the middle class—that entrepreneurially oriented, property-owning, and capital-investing group that emerged in the late eighteenth and early nineteenth centuries a little in advance of its modern companion, the industrial proletariat.[1]

Howe and other historians are interested in the Victorian period because it, more than any other, contains the social, economic, and cultural

Adapted from "Victorian Women and Domestic Life: Mary Todd Lincoln, Elizabeth Cady Stanton, and Harriet Beecher Stowe," by Kathryn Kish Sklar, Chapter 2 in *The Public and the Private Lincoln: Contemporary Perspectives*, Cullom Davis *et al.*, eds. (Carbondale and Edwardsville: Southern Illinois University Press, 1979). Courtesy of Cullom Davis and Sangamon State University.

"Joseph and Sarah Ann Emery," c. 1834. The New-York Historical Society.

transformations that are referred to collectively as "modernization." Victorian culture, Howe concludes, may be thought of as the culture that characterized English-speaking Americans during the climactic era of modernization when changes that had been taking shape more slowly before 1830 entered a period of accelerated development.

Profound changes in public life between 1830 and 1880 include the transportation and communication revolutions, the technologic culmination of the Industrial Revolution, and the abolition of slavery. Profound changes in family life include the widespread adoption of family limitation; the transfer of many domestic industries, such as spinning and weaving, from home to factory production; and the separation of public life and private life into two distinct spheres. Combined, these changes in family life constituted change in human history on the scale of the Neolithic Revolution.[2]

By the mid-nineteenth century when machine technology was recasting human work in unprecedented forms, human reproduction was already established on a new basis. This essay focuses on the first of these changes in Victorian families—the widespread adoption of family limitation. It illustrates how family limitation was integrated into the lives of three women who exemplify Victorian family planning and its various motivations: Harriet Beecher Stowe, Elizabeth Cady Stanton, and Mary Todd Lincoln. Each developed her own strategy toward, or response to, the conditions of mid-nineteenth-century family life, and each typified a strategy commonly found among her contemporaries. Harriet Beecher Stowe's strategy could be called that of "female domestic control," Elizabeth Cady Stanton's strategy that of "feminist domestic reform," and Mary Todd Lincoln's strategy that of "total commitment to husband and children." These three strategies represent the options most often pursued by Victorian women, and the contexts within which much of Victorian domestic life reverberated.

Harriet Beecher Stowe left behind graphic historical evidence of her private life through an exchange of letters with her husband, which were quoted extensively in Edmund Wilson's *Patriotic Gore*.[3] The exchange began in the summer of 1844 when Harriet had been married for eight years, was thirty-three years old, and had borne five children, two of whom were twins. That summer, as in subsequent ones, Calvin Stowe left his Cincinnati home to raise funds in New England for Lane Theological Seminary where he taught biblical history and where his salary depended upon his summertime fund-raising efforts. Harriet and Calvin agreed to state their grievances openly to one another in their summer letters, a common practice in evangelical correspondence which usually included a good dose of mutual criticism.

Harriet's grievances began with the drudgery of nineteenth-century housework: "I am sick of the smell of sour milk and sour meat, and sour everything, and then the clothes *will* not dry, and no wet thing does, and everything smells mouldy; and altogether I feel as if I never [want] to eat again."[4] Calvin's grievances began with Harriet's aversion to the drudgery of nineteenth-century housework: "By the way there is one other thing I will mention because it has often vexed and irritated me intolerably. I must clean the stable, wash the carriage, grease the wheels, black my boots, etc. etc. but you scorn to sweep the carriage, you must always call your servant to do it and not stoop yourself to so menial an act. This makes me mad, for you are not too good to do in your line what I am everyday obliged to do in mine."[5]

Harriet's grievances included being solely responsible for running her household. Except for her, she said: "You know that . . . my unfortunate household has no mainspring, for nobody feels any kind of responsibility to do a thing in time, place, or manner, except as I oversee it."[6] On this score

Calvin agreed: "You must manage all household matters in your own way—just as you would if I were dead, and you had never anything more to expect from me. Indeed, to all practical purposes I am dead for the present and know not when I shall live again."[7]

Harriet's grievances turned to the topic of her health: "As to my health, it gives me very little solicitude, although it is bad enough and daily growing worse. I feel no life, no energy, no appetite, or rather a growing distaste for food; in fact, I am becoming quite ethereal. . . . I suffer with sensible distress in the brain, as I have done more or less since my sickness last winter, a distress which some days takes from me all power of planning or executing anything."[8] While not challenging his wife's claims to the symptoms and prerogatives of an invalid, and while leaving his own symptoms unnamed, Calvin obscurely asserted that his own suffering had been greater than Harriet's: "I suffer amazingly every day. I hardly know what to make of it, unless it be the Lord's penance of our sin. You have suffered a great deal, but I doubt whether you have ever suffered as I have this summer."[9]

In addition to these everyday grievances, husband and wife discussed a larger problem in the summer of 1844—their sexual relationship. Calvin broached the topic by relating several recent instances of clerical disarray in the sexual arena, including the story of a fellow minister who "While half boozled [had] caught young ladies who were so unfortunate to meet him alone, and pawed them over in the most disgusting manner, and actually attempted to do them physical violence. This has been going on for years until it would be borne no longer, and now it all comes out against him, to the dishonor of religion, his own unspeakable shame and anguish, and the distress unutterable of his wife and children."[10] In connection with this "melancholy licentiousness" Calvin said he had "thought much of our domestic happiness," and in a paragraph packed with homesickness he drew both a parallel and a contrast between himself and his fallen colleagues.

> Though I have, as you well know, a most enthusiastic admiration of fresh, youthful female beauty; yet it never comes anywhere near the kind of feeling I have for you. With you, every desire I have, mental and physical, is completely satisfied and filled up, and leaves me nothing more to ask for. My enjoyment with you is not weakened by time nor blunted with age, and every reunion after separation is just as much of a honeymoon as was the first month after the wedding. Is not your own experience and observation a proof of what I say? . . . No man can love and respect his wife more than I do mine. Yet we are not happy as we might be.

Let us look at the place the summer of 1844 occupied in the sequence of Harriet Beecher Stowe's childbearing to see if we can understand better why she and Calvin were "not as happy" as they might have been, in spite of Calvin's testimony to their sexual compatibility. For that summer was not a time when Harriet wanted to relive her honeymoon, but a time when she was looking forward to what she considered a well-earned relief from childbearing. Such relief had not been possible for her mother, since most women who were married before 1800 bore children, in sickness and in health, regularly every two years from the time they married to the end of their childbearing years, or until their death, whichever came first. But limitation of childbearing was an option for Harriet—one she had considered long before the summer of 1844.

Harriet Beecher married Calvin Stowe in 1836 at the age of twenty-six after she had nearly ten years' experience supporting herself as a teacher. Nine months after their marriage—almost to the day—Harriet gave birth to twins. Then, a few months later she was pregnant again. At this point she was visited by her reform-minded older sister, Catharine Beecher, who later described Harriet's plight in a letter to another married sister: "Harriet has one baby put out for the winter, the other at home, and number three will be here the middle of January. Poor thing, she bears up wonderfully well and I hope will live through this first tug of matrimonial warfare, and then she says she shall not have any more *children, she knows for certain* for one while. Though how she found this out I cannot say, but she seems quite confident about it."[11]

The outcome of matrimonial warfare in the Stowe family during the next five years was the addition of two more babies, the second born in the summer of 1843. This second baby was sickly and languished in Harriet's arms all fall and winter while she herself suffered through a prolonged illness related, apparently, to the birth. A year later, in the summer of 1844, Harriet replied to Calvin's amorous letter and to his descriptions of clerical licentiousness dramatically and emphatically. Taking up the implicit threat contained in Calvin's admission of his "most enthusiastic admiration of fresh, youthful female beauty," but assuming that sexual infidelity was unjustified on any grounds, Harriet dramatized her horror at the possibility of Calvin's infidelity, but she did not respond in kind to his suggestions that marital love was better than burning.

> As I am gifted with a most horrible vivid imagination, in a moment I imagined—nay saw as in a vision all the distress and despair that would follow a fall on your part. I felt weak and sick—I took a book and lay down on the bed, but it pursued me like a nightmare—and something seemed to ask Is your husband any better seeming than so and so! I looked in the glass and my face which since spring has been something of the palest was so haggard that it frightened me. The illusion lasted a whole forenoon and then evaporated like a poisonous mist—but God knows how I pity those heart wrung women—wives worse than widows, who are called to lament that the grave has not covered their husband—the father of their children! Good and merciful God—why are such agonies reserved for the children of men![12]

Dwelling on the vividness, intensity, and even sublimity of her horror for a moment, Harriet continued: "I can conceive now of misery which in one night would change the hair to grey and shrivel the whole frame to prema-

ture decrepitude! misery to which all other agony is as a mocking sound!"
Then, with a brief reference to Calvin's sex, Harriet launched into a discussion of their marital love from her point of view.

> What terrible temptations lie in the way of your sex—till now I never realised it—
> for tho I did love you with an almost *insane* love before I married you I never knew
> yet or felt the pulsation which showed me I could be tempted in that way—there
> never was a moment when I felt anything by which you could have drawn me
> astray—for I loved you as I now love God—and I can conceive of no higher love;
> and as I have no passion, I have no jealousy. The most beautiful woman in the
> world could not make me jealous so long as she only *dazzled the senses.*

Calvin might declare his love for Harriet as "mental and physical," but Harriet made it clear to him that it was not for his body that she loved him. She
would admit to insanity before she would admit to sexual desire. In the
spring of 1845 Harriet left Calvin at home to manage the household as best
he could while she spent ten months at a Brattleboro, Vermont, water cure.
Almost immediately upon her return home, Calvin departed for fifteen
months of water cure himself.

From Brattleboro Harriet described to Calvin her analysis of their situation: "We have now come to a sort of crisis. If you and I do as we should for
five years to come the character of our three oldest children will be established. This is why I am willing to spend so much time and make such efforts
to have health. Oh, that God would give me these five years in full possession
of mind and body, that I may train my children as they should be trained."
Harriet may have related "full possession of mind and body" to the adoption
of "system and order" in family life, for she immediately continued: "I am
fully aware of the importance of system and order in a family. I know that
nothing can be done without it; it is the keystone, the *sine qua non*, and in regard to my children I place it next to piety."[13]

For six years from 1843 to 1849, Harriet Beecher Stowe avoided pregnancy. After bearing children in a pattern that resembled her mother's up to
the age of thirty-two, she enjoyed a long span of childlessness that was unknown to most women of her mother's generation, but quite common
among Harriet's contemporaries. Her mother, Roxana Beecher, gave birth to
nine children in seventeen years of marriage before she died at the age of
thirty-seven. Harriet bore five children in the first seven years of marriage,
none in the second six years of marriage, and two more at the end of her
childbearing years, in 1849 and 1850, when she was thirty-eight and thirty-nine.
She therefore omitted two to three children that her mother would not have
omitted, and in this time before artificial contraceptive techniques, she must
have relied largely on sexual abstinence.

How typical was the childbearing pattern of this distinguished nineteenth-century author who produced her most famous book the same year
she birthed her last baby?

The timing of Elizabeth Cady Stanton's children was very similar to that of Harriet Beecher Stowe's. She had three in the first five years of marriage, then, like Harriet, went six years without bearing children. It was toward the end of this interval between 1845 and 1851 that she began her campaign for woman's rights. Then, during the eight years from 1851 to 1859, she gave birth to four more babies, the last when she was forty-four years old.[14]

Harriet Beecher Stowe, Elizabeth Cady Stanton, and, as we will see, Mary Todd Lincoln were all participating in Victorian family planning—a phenomenon that had begun before they were born, and that had, by the time they were married between 1835 and 1845, become (for reasons that still elude historical explanation) a much-accelerated national trend, most emphatically felt in middle-class families, but affecting all economic groups, both urban and rural. Victorian families were deeply involved in what is called the "demographic transition"—a shift from the high birth and high death rates characteristic of traditional populations, to the low birth and low death rates characteristic of our modern population. More people lived longer, so the population as a whole grew rapidly, but fewer babies were born to individual women. Whereas the average number of children born to women who survived to age forty was seven to eight in 1800, in 1900 it was less than half that number and still falling rapidly.[15]

Up until about ten years ago historians attributed this reduction in family size to industrialization and urbanization. Thanks to the statistical techniques developed by French demographer Louis Henry in the 1950s, and the application of these techniques to American data, we have learned that the origins of modern family limitation predate significant industrialization and urbanization—in France by almost a century; in the United States by at least a generation. Many questions remain to be answered about the connections between economic and demographic change in the first half of the nineteenth century. But since we now know that family limitation was widespread throughout Victorian society before 1850, when industrialization and urbanization had barely begun, these latter forces no longer explain the emergence of marital fertility control. Robert Wells argues in "Family History and Demographic Transition" that family limitation was the result of "modern attitudes"—the belief that "the world is knowable and controllable" and that it serves one's own interests to plan one's life.[16]

Harriet Beecher Stowe's matrimonial warfare would seem to fall in this category of thinking, as did her strategy of asserting female control in the sexual arena. Invalidism and Victorian sexuality were not the only means Stowe used to control her circumstances rather than be controlled by them. In a letter to a close friend shortly after Catharine's visit in 1838, she described the full scope of her domestic self-assertion: "I have about three hours per day in writing, and if you see my name coming out everywhere you may be sure of one thing, that I *do* it *for the pay*. I have determined not to be a mere domestic slave without even the leisure to excel in my duties. I mean to have money enough to have my house kept in the best manner and yet to have time for reflection and that preparation for the education of my children which every mother needs. I have every prospect of succeeding in this plan."[17]

Harriet Beecher Stowe was a unique and gifted woman whose novel dramatizing the effects of slavery on family life made her more famous than representative among her contemporaries, but the general circumstances of her domestic life were widely shared. Another young mother living five hundred miles away in western New York, Elizabeth Cady Stanton, approached her domestic responsibilities with the same modern effort to plan and control the outcome. As Stanton described her response to motherhood in 1842 in her autobiography: "Having gone through the ordeal of bearing a child, I was determined if possible to keep him, so I read everything I could find on the subject."[18] One of the manuals Stanton might have come across in her search for pediatric guidance was Catharine Beecher's *Treatise on Domestic Economy*, first published in 1841, reprinted every year until 1856, and distributed nationally by Harper and Brothers. For Beecher's *Treatise*, the most important fact in a woman's life was not whether she was pious or loving, but whether she controlled her own life, for "there is nothing, which so distinctly marks the difference between weak and strong minds, as the fact, whether they control circumstances, or circumstances control them."[19]

Not passive submission to their biological identity nor fetching dependence on their husbands, but active control of their immediate life circumstances was the model Harriet's sister held out to her readers. Adopting a typical Victorian perspective, Beecher viewed motherhood as a qualitative rather than a quantitative activity, useful to society for the kind of child rather than the numbers of children it produced. In a chapter entitled "The Peculiar Responsibilities of American Women," she wrote: "The success of democratic institutions, as is conceded by all, depends upon the intellectual and moral character of the mass of the people. If they are intelligent and virtuous, democracy is a blessing; but if they are ignorant and wicked, it is only a curse. It is equally conceded, that the formation of the moral and intellectual character of the young is committed mainly to the female hand."[20] Beecher's view of the relationship between childhood and society was an essentially modern one. Rather than viewing society as a traditional set of established controls, and early childhood as a time when the will must be broken to conform to those controls, she saw society as an uncontrolled growth, except as it was regulated by the internalized values of "character" developed during early childhood. Seeing it possible to exert in early childhood an influence of lifelong personal and social significance, Victorians were far more sensitive than their ancestors had been to the importance of the right kind of mothering.

Qualitative motherhood and the elevated status it brought Victorian women could be the basis for initiating improvements in other aspects of female life. For Beecher it justified an appeal for the advance of female education. As her *Treatise* stated: "Are not the most responsible of all duties committed to the charge of woman? Is it not her profession to take care of mind, body, and soul? and that, too, at the most critical of all periods of existence? And is it not as much a matter of public concern, that she should be properly qualified for her duties, as that ministers, lawyers, and physicians, should be prepared for theirs? And is it not as important, to endow institutions which shall make a superior education accessible to all classes—for females, as much as for the other sex?"[21]

But for some Victorian women, qualitative motherhood and the female control and assertion we have seen Harriet Beecher Stowe exercise and Catharine Beecher advocate for women in the domestic arena, did not go far enough. Basic inequalities of status between men and women still intruded sharply into domestic life. Married women could not, without special legal efforts, own property, and their earnings belonged to their husbands. Responding to these and other limitations of nineteenth-century domesticity, Elizabeth Cady Stanton decided to do something about it in 1848. As she described her state of mind prior to organizing the first Woman's Rights Convention:

> The general discontent I felt with woman's portion as wife, mother, housekeeper, physician, and spiritual guide, the chaotic conditions into which everything fell without her constant supervision, and the wearied, anxious look of the majority of women impressed me with a strong feeling that some active measure should be taken. My experience at the World's Anti-Slavery Convention, all I had read of the legal status of women, and the oppression I saw everywhere, swept across my soul intensified now by many personal experiences . . . I could not see what to do or where to begin—my only thought was a public meeting for protest and discussion.[22]

While the growth of female autonomy, power, and control within the home was an important component of Victorian domesticity, one of the central tenets of Victorian family life—its separation from the public sphere—prohibited women from exercising outside the domestic world the influence they held within it. Thus the family world of Victorian women was half full or half empty, depending on how one looked at it—half full in providing the potential for the assertion of control over one's life, or half empty in denying to women the legal, political, and economic rights that men enjoyed. For Harriet Beecher Stowe it was half full and she worked to fill it more completely through her writings. For Elizabeth Cady Stanton it was half empty and would only be adequately filled when women were recognized legally and politically as people, rather than the "female relatives of people."[23]

While Harriet Beecher Stowe represents one common female response to the changing conditions of domestic life in taking the initiative to control and plan her life, and Stanton represents a reform strategy in response to the same conditions, Mary Todd Lincoln represents a strategy of total commitment to husband and children.

In her we see a slightly different and even more modern pattern of childbearing than we have seen in Stowe or Stanton. Lincoln's wife, like Calvin Stowe's, bore her first baby a neat nine months after marriage.[24] Mary Todd Lincoln, however, subsequently maintained what seems to have been a more controlled and more even spacing of her children than either Stowe or Stanton and she ceased bearing children altogether at a much earlier age than Harriet or Elizabeth. After an interval of nearly three years between her first and second child, Mary was not pregnant again until four years later when her second child, Edward, died and her third, Willie, was immediately conceived. After another interval of three years between her third and fourth births, Mary Lincoln ceased bearing children altogether when she was only thirty-five years old.

With babies born in 1843, 1846, 1850, and 1853, Mary Todd Lincoln gave less of her own life cycle to the reproductive life of the species than either Harriet Beecher Stowe or Elizabeth Cady Stanton. Mary Todd's mother had given birth regularly every other year after her marriage until she died from causes related to the birth of her seventh when Mary was six years old. Mary's stepmother followed the same traditional pattern, bearing ten children in all, with shorter intervals between births and continuing childbearing well beyond her mid-thirties. But Mary's pattern of childbearing was quite different.

Whereas family limitation for Stowe and Stanton was an on-again, off-again activity, concentrated in a six-year interval in the middle of their childbearing years, Mary Lincoln's family limitation seems to have begun soon after her first child was born, and to have gained momentum in 1847, the year after her second child was born and the year when Lincoln was first elected to Congress. Over the course of the eleven years between 1847 and 1858 when Mrs. Lincoln was twenty-nine to forty years old, she conceived only two children, although her mother's pattern would have produced five children in that length of time.

The greater effectiveness and longevity of fertility control in the Lincoln family seems to suggest the cooperation of husband and wife in the effort. Mary and Abraham Lincoln may exemplify a different kind of family-limitation motivation than the female initiative we saw with Harriet and Calvin Stowe. In many Victorian families, probably including the Lincolns, we can assume that husbands as well as wives viewed their economic betterment or professional advancement as more important than the biblical imperative to "be fruitful and multiply."

We might, indeed, see the bias toward sexual abstinence that Victorian sexual ideology promoted in women as a kind of "fail-safe" protection against the victory of instinct over economic self-interest, and as positive reinforcement for what was, in any case, a necessity of everyday life. In many families husbands and wives may have been in complete agreement about their priorities and have placed the husband's advancement high among these. This certainly seems to have been the case with Mary and Abraham Lincoln.

Nineteenth-century "togetherness" was nowhere better exemplified than in the Lincoln family. All the basic components were there. In their devotion to their children, both Mary and Abraham were making up for unhappy childhoods, loving their sons in ways that compensated for their own maternal deprivation, both having lost their mothers before they were ten years old. The Lincolns indulged their children notoriously, but they had other ambitions that limited the number of children they could raise with such devotion. Until he was elected to the U.S. Congress in 1847, Lincoln's career ambitions in law and politics meant that he was away from home as frequently as he was present, and after his election the Lincoln's home life was even more disrupted. But Mary Lincoln endorsed her husband's career ambitions and gave them top priority in their mutual family life. In 1860 the Lincoln home was an important political meeting ground. As Mrs. Lincoln wrote a friend: "This summer we have had immense crowds of strangers visiting us, and have had no time to be occupied with home affairs."[25]

Perhaps even more important than the terms on which Lincoln family life proceeded were those under which the marriage had begun. In contrast to Harriet Beecher and Elizabeth Cady, Mary Todd married against her family's wishes. Whereas Harriet and Elizabeth both married protégés of their fathers, and both bore their first child in their parents' home, Mary encountered considerable opposition to her marriage from her sister and brother-in-law, Elizabeth Todd Edwards and Ninian Wirt Edwards, who were her de facto guardians in Springfield. The Edwards did not try to hide their disapproval of a marriage they thought was beneath Mary Todd's social standing, and their attitude may have contributed to Lincoln's decision to break off the engagement in 1841. Mary bore her first child in Springfield's Globe Tavern, assisted by her husband rather than her sister, even though her sister lived within walking distance. Marrying for love against the wishes of her family, enduring poverty in early marriage after a wealthy upbringing, but never losing faith in the promise of her husband's career, Mary Lincoln's marriage was in many ways the very model of a nineteenth-century romantic love success story.

But Mary Lincoln's commitment to her husband and children generated trauma as well as joy in her life. One might go as far as to say that her psychological "untogetherness" was reciprocally related to the modern "togetherness" in her family life. With so much love invested in her children, she was spiritually broken with the death of four-year-old Edward in 1850; and although she was pregnant a month after Edward's death and replaced the child numerically immediately, qualitatively the child was irreplaceable to her. It was after Edward's death, when she was thirty-two years old, that she began to lose control of her life. According to the editors of Mrs. Lincoln's letters: "The humor and control that had sustained her in the past became increasingly submerged in fearfulness, self-indulgence, and in sudden outbursts of rage." Meanwhile Abraham Lincoln emerged from the crisis with a new spiritual strength. "The man who was by nature melancholy, solitary, and self-doubting would from then on gain in assurance and magnetism."[26]

The death of her second son, twelve-year-old William in 1862, drove Mary Lincoln across the boundary between this world and the spirit world. She began to see visions of Willie and Edward standing at the foot of her bed, and, after an incomplete recovery, she launched on a compulsive and disastrous effort to make up for her loss by buying clothes, jewels, and household furnishings she could not afford, accumulating twenty thousand dollars in personal debts Lincoln did not know about at the time of his death.[27]

Whereas Harriet Beecher Stowe and Elizabeth Cady Stanton participated in the active and extensive female subculture contained within Victorian society, Stowe through her writing and Stanton through her reform activities, Mary Lincoln's activities outside the domestic arena tended to reinforce the centrality of her husband in her life.

For Mary Todd Lincoln the doctrine of separate spheres did not apply. Her unladylike participation in the political arena, in the name of defending or advancing her husband's interests, earned her many enemies while she occupied the White House; but, for her, family life, political life, and social life were a single unit organized around her husband. There was a great deal of truth to her description of him as "lover—husband—father & *all all to me—truly my all.*"[28]

. . . Three years before her husband's assassination and nine years before the final blow of the death of eighteen-year-old Tad in 1871, Mary Lincoln wrote to a friend: "My question to myself is, 'Can life be endured?' "[29] In 1875 she was committed as a "lunatic" to a sanitarium for women in Batavia, Illinois, by her only living son, Robert.

Harriet Beecher Stowe, by contrast, after being very deeply shaken by the death of her eldest son at the age of nineteen in 1857, purged her despair and her fear for his afterlife in a novel set in the religious New England of her childhood, and through that novel moved from slavery to New England traditional life as the setting for her mature and best fiction. The interaction between Harriet's domestic life and her writing contained a built-in dynamic of growth, as through her writing she gained strength to endure family calamity, and through family loss she improved her writing.[30] Her 1858 novel, *The Minister's Wooing* (written after her son's sudden death), explored the similarities between Christ's love and a mother's love and concluded that her unconverted son could not be in hell because she (and therefore the Redeemer) loved him so much.

The contrast between Harriet Beecher Stowe and Mary Todd Lincoln is one between a Victorian woman who was able to build an autonomous self within the domestic arena and a woman who was not able to do so. The contrast between Stowe and Stanton is less marked, being between a Victorian wife and mother who was interested in portraying the private side of domestic life and therefore remained primarily a private person, and a Victorian wife and mother who wanted to portray and change the public policies governing domestic life and therefore grew into a public personage. Both women wrote at home, amid the play and interruptions of their children. Stanton, who after 1851 at the age of thirty-six began to spend a good deal of her life in public, bore four more children at the same time—two more than Harriet Stowe and four more than Mary Lincoln birthed after that age.

Stanton had help in sustaining this double commitment to family and public life. Indeed, one might say that after 1851 she lived in two marriages— one to Henry B. Stanton, one to Susan B. Anthony. Anthony came to visit Stanton often after they met in 1851, and their mutually supportive relationship formed the core of the woman's rights movement for almost fifty years. As Stanton described the relationship in her autobiography:

> We never met without issuing a pronunciamento on some question. In thought and sympathy we were one, and in the division of labor we exactly complemented each other. . . . We have indulged freely in criticism of each other when alone, and hotly contended whenever we have differed, but in our friendship of years there has never been the break of one hour. To the world we always seem to agree and uniformly reflect each other. Like husband and wife, each has the feeling that we must have no differences in public. Thus united at an early day we began to survey the state and nation, the future field of our labors.[31]

As Stanton described their equal division of domestic work: "We took turns on the domestic watchtowers, directing amusements, settling disputes, protecting the weak against the strong, and trying to secure equal rights to all in the home as well as the nation."

Scholars in American women's history have argued that "passionlessness" had positive effects on the lives of many Victorian women; that religion and female piety could serve as a basis for collective action in behalf of female interests; and that domesticity itself was not an empty set of prescriptions for idle women, but a vocation that complemented the career ambitions of nineteenth-century men.[32]

These three women have shown these modernizing trends in nineteenth-century family life. Each responded differently to the demands of qualitative motherhood, representing a common strategy found among her contemporaries. Stowe's strategy of female control in the domestic arena was a mainstream strategy shared by the "domestic feminism" of thousands, perhaps tens of thousands, of New England and New York women who joined the American Female Moral Reform Society between 1840 and 1860—an organization founded in the 1830s with the sole purpose of eliminating prostitution and the double sexual standard on which it was based.

Stanton's strategy of feminist domestic reform was less widespread than Stowe's brand of domestic feminism, but more radical. The title of Stanton and Anthony's first newspaper, *Revolution,* revealed this, while at the same time it reflected their appreciation of the difficulties involved in achieving their goal of full citizenship for women and the legal equality of the sexes.

Mary Lincoln's strategy of fulfilling her own personal ambition vicariously through husband and children was another mainstream strategy—one that enjoys continued popularity in the last quarter of the twentieth century. Women married to men with political careers still find it especially difficult to pursue autonomous life goals.

NOTES

1. Daniel Walker Howe, "American Victorianism as a Culture," *American Quarterly,* 27 (December 1975): 507–32.

2. The Neolithic Revolution, or the transition in the Near East from food gathering to food production, began after 9000 B.C. and was completed by 5500 B.C., when "farming and stock breeding were well established and the basic level of the effective village farming community had been achieved" (Carlo M. Cipolla, *The Economic History of World Population,* 6th ed. [Baltimore: Penguin Books, 1974] p. 19). Nineteenth-century family planning was a part of the second revolution in human population—the Demographic Transition, or the transition from relatively high birth and death rates to relatively low birth and death rates. Ansley J. Coale, "The History of the Human Population," *The Human Population* (New York: Scientific American Book, 1974), pp. 15–28.

3. Edmund Wilson, *Patriotic Gore: Studies in the Literature of the American Civil War* (New York: Oxford University Press, 1962), pp. 25–35. I am grateful to Louis Dabney for reminding me of these printed letters.

4. Annie Fields, ed., *Life and Letters of Harriet Beecher Stowe* (Cambridge, Mass.: Riverside Press; Boston, New York: Houghton Mifflin and Co., 1897), p. 110; Wilson, *Patriotic Gore,* p. 17, June 16, 1845.

5. Calvin Stowe to Harriet Beecher Stowe, September 30, 1844, Beecher-Stowe Collection, Schlesinger Library on the History of Women in America, Cambridge, Mass., folder 61.

6. Fields, *Life and Letters,* p. 110, June 16, 1845.

7. Wilson, *Patriotic Gore,* pp. 28–29, July 29, 1855. Summer correspondence between Harriet and Calvin Stowe continued for more than a decade to discuss the issues initially raised in 1844.

8. Fields, *Life and Letters,* p. 110, June 16, 1845.

9. Calvin Stowe to Harriet Beecher Stowe, September 30, 1844, Beecher-Stowe Collection, folder 61.

10. Calvin Stowe to Harriet Beecher Stowe, June 30, 1844, Beecher-Stowe Collection, folder 61.

11. Catharine Beecher to Mary Beecher Perkins, Fall 1837, Beecher-Stowe Collection, folder 17.

12. Harriet Beecher Stowe to Calvin Stowe, July 19, 1844, Beecher-Stowe Collection, folder 69.

13. Charles Edward Stowe, *Life of Harriet Beecher Stowe: Compiled from Her Letters and Journals* (Boston: Houghton, Mifflin & Co., 1889), p. 115. I am grateful to Rebecca Veach for pointing out this letter to me. Daniel Scott Smith, "Family Limitation, Sexual Control, and Domestic Feminism in Victorian America," *Feminist Studies* 1, nos. 3–4 (Winter–Spring 1973), discusses the extent to which family limitation fostered a new kind of personal autonomy among Victorian women.

14. Alma Lutz, "Elizabeth Cady Stanton," in Edward T. James et al., eds., *Notable American Women, 1607–1950: A Biographical Dictionary,* 3 vols. (Cambridge, Mass.: Harvard University Press, Belknap Press, 1971), 3:342–47.

15. Wilson H. Grabill, Clyde V. Kiser, and Pascal K. Whelpton, "A Long View," in Michael Gordon, ed., *The American Family in Social-Historical Perspective* (New York: St. Martin's Press, 1973), pp. 374–95, esp. 387.

16. Robert V. Wells, "Family History and Demographic Transition," *Journal of Social History* 9 (Fall 1975): 6.

17. Harriet Beecher Stowe to Mary Dutton, December 13, 1838, Mary Dutton-Beecher Letters, Bienecke Library, Yale University.

18. Elizabeth Cady Stanton, *Eighty Years and More: Reminiscences 1815–1897* (1898; reprint ed., New York: Shocken, 1971), p. 114.

19. Catharine Beecher. *A Treatise on Domestic Economy: For the Use of Young Ladies at Home and at School*, rev. ed. (Boston: Thomas H. Webb & Co., 1843), p. 160. See also Kathryn Kish Sklar, *Catharine Beecher: A Study in American Domesticity* (New Haven: Yale University Press, 1973), pp. 151–68.

20. Beecher, *A Treatise*, pp. 36–37.

21. Ibid., p. 52.

22. Stanton, *Eighty Years*, p. 148.

23. Aileen Kraditor, ed., *Up from the Pedestal: Selected Writings in the History of American Feminism* (New York: Quadrangle Books, 1968), Introduction, p. 8.

24. Justin G. Turner and Linda Levitt Turner, *Mary Todd Lincoln: Her Life and Letters* (New York: Alfred A. Knopf, 1972).

25. Ibid., p. 66.

26. Ibid., p. 41.

27. Turner and Turner, *Mary Todd Lincoln*, p. 237 and n., pp. 224–25, p. 355 and n.

28. Ibid., p. 534.

29. Turner and Turner, *Mary Todd Lincoln*, p. 128.

30. For a high critical estimate of Harriet Beecher Stowe's post-1857 fiction, see Alice Crozier, *The Novels of Harriet Beecher Stowe* (New York: Oxford University Press, 1969), pp. 85–151, and Henry F. May's "Introduction" to the John Harvard edition of *Oldtown Folks* (Cambridge, Mass.: Harvard University Press, 1966).

31. Stanton, *Eighty Years*, pp. 164, 166.

32. Carroll Smith-Rosenberg, "Beauty, the Beast and the Militant Woman: A Case Study in Sex Roles and Social Stress in Jacksonian America," *American Quarterly* 23 (1971): 562–84; Nancy F. Cott, *The Bonds of Womanhood: New England Women 1780–1820* (New Haven: Yale University Press, 1976).

17

Chinese Immigrant Women in Nineteenth-Century California

Lucie Cheng

Chinese immigration to California in the period 1849–1882 has commonly been viewed in terms of the male immigrant experience. Lucie Cheng traces the experiences of a forgotten group among the Chinese in California: women. Most commonly employed as prostitutes, Chinese women were enmeshed in an economy and social structure in which they were devalued in comparison to men. Comprising only 5 to 6 percent of the Chinese-American population in California, women rarely crossed the Pacific entirely of their own free will. Family considerations and unequal access to resources are particularly evident in the migration of Chinese women to California. The experience of Chinese women demonstrates the continuing influence of Old World traditions on immigrants in the United States.

The decades between 1850 and the turn of the century were the period of rapid development of the American West. Leading that development and to a large extent functioning as the core of the West was California, where the Gold Rush began in 1848. Once the discovery of gold became widely known, the population increased sharply and had to be fed, clothed, housed, and entertained. What characterized California in the mid-nineteenth century was its heterogeneous labor force, consisting of peoples from Europe, the Americas, and Asia, and individuals from diverse occupational backgrounds. Most of this population consisted of young men between the ages of 15 and 24. Although women were also part of the migration, their number was small. For example, in 1850 there were more than 12 men to every woman in California. The sexual imbalance and the youthfulness of the population had a number of consequences for the role of women in the development of California.

Despite the increase in population, the supply of labor lagged behind demand. The small number of women were therefore given more opportunities to participate in the labor force, and fewer restrictions were placed on them. Women were found in such occupations as mining and logging as well as teaching and nursing. Although some occupations were clearly dominated

Chinese Prostitute in San Francisco, c. 1890. Photo by Arnold Genthe. Library of Congress.

by men and other occupations were chiefly women's jobs, the range of options was wider than women could find on the economically more developed East Coast.

Services normally performed by women in the family were performed by women outside the family for the bachelor population. Most of these services were wage labor in the most backward sector of the economy. Domestic servants, laundresses, and prostitutes fell within this category and were the largest occupational groups among the female population.

Although natural resources and demographic factors defined the general pattern of women's work roles in nineteenth-century California, these factors alone do not shed light on the specific patterns exhibited by women from different national groups and different class backgrounds. For example, some of these groups, such as immigrant women from non–English-speaking countries, were precluded from certain occupations that required more fluent knowledge of the English language. In other words, though the general pattern of women's roles in developing California is more or less known, to date very little has been written about the particular functions of the women of any specific racial or national group.

We will discuss the major roles that Chinese immigrant women played during this period, describing their lives and experiences and relating them to the development of this frontier society.

The discovery of gold in 1848 along the Sacramento River brought thousands of immigrants to California. In San Francisco, where miners from nearby sites congregated during the winter and immigrants gathered before entering the mining areas, prostitution became a lucrative business. The demand for prostitution was met by women of varying racial and national origins, including Chinese women from Hong Kong, Canton, and its surrounding areas.[1]

During the first few years of the Gold Rush, Chinese prostitution in California was characterized by individual initiative and enterprise. Like their white counterparts, many Chinese prostitutes during this period were able to accumulate sufficient capital to leave the profession. Some of them returned to China as relatively affluent members of the business community; others remained in America and either continued in prostitution as madams or invested in other businesses. A second distinctive feature of this early period was that the Chinese prostitutes received white clients almost exclusively.

The first Chinese female resident in America was believed to be a domestic servant who arrived in San Francisco as a member of the Gillespie household in February 1848. The second arrival was said to be a 20-year-old prostitute, named Ah-choi, who landed in late 1848 or early 1849. She differed from her sisters of the later period of Chinese prostitution in one important respect: She was her own free agent and succeeded in accumulating enough money to own a brothel within two years.

Ah-choi's social background is not known.[2] Judging from the evidence that she could speak some English, had enough money to make the trip from Hong Kong to San Francisco, possessed jewelry and fancy clothes on arrival, and had the know-how to set up a business immediately afterward, it seems likely that she was already a fairly successful prostitute or even a madam in Hong Kong who catered to the foreign trade. Like her male countrymen, she took advantage of the opportunities provided by news of the discovery of gold.

During the first two years after gold was discovered in California, it was not unusual for a miner to wash or dig up 100 ounces of gold a day. Ah-choi was able to charge one ounce of gold or 16 dollars per visit and still attract a line of waiting customers a block long. This fee was not exorbitant; successful European prostitutes were known to have charged much more.[3] Almost all of Ah-choi's customers were non-Chinese. Ah-choi's income must have offset her expenses by a large margin because by 1850, just about two years after her arrival, she had made enough money to make trips to Hong Kong and

Canton and to import more Chinese women for her business. In 1852 she moved from her first place of business off Clay Street and opened up a larger house on Pike Street.[4]

Ah-choi was able to pay her passage to America; other free-agent prostitutes during this initial period emigrated under different circumstances. A popular social novel in the late Ch'ing dynasty contained a supposedly true story of a Cantonese prostitute who was brought to San Francisco by her American paramour when she was 18. After seven years she returned to Hong Kong with approximately 16,000 dollars, married a Chinese laborer and, because of her special knowledge of American trade, opened a store that sold only foreign goods.[5] While the details of this story may be suspect, it seems plausible that some women came to the Golden Hills as prostitutes and made enough money to open up businesses in America or China. The scarcity of women and the affluent condition of the men made it possible for prostitutes of different nationalities, mostly European, to amass a small fortune in a short period of time.

This period of free competition among owner-prostitutes did not last very long, and there were not many free agents, mostly because of the prohibitive cost of passage. In 1852, of the 11,794 Chinese in California, only 7 were women, 2 of these were independent prostitutes and 2 others were known to have been working for Ah-choi. Despite their small numbers, it was clear that a considerable sum of money could be made in the business. That prospect attracted Chinese entrepreneurs, who organized various aspects of the business.

By 1854 Chinese prostitution in San Francisco had become a highly organized institution under the control of Chinese men, and its network extended across the Pacific to Canton and Hong Kong. The persons chiefly responsible for this trade included the procurers who kidnapped, enticed, or bought the women; the importers who brought them into America; the brothel owners who lived by their exploitation; the Chinese thugs who collected fees for protecting them from other thugs; the white police and officials who collected money for keeping them from being arrested; and the white Chinatown property owners who leased their land and buildings for exorbitant rents.

As California gained its reputation as a fast-growing area, industries developed and labor was in demand. American businessmen had long been aware of the coolie trade that supplied indentured Chinese laborers to Australia, Peru, British West Indies, Cuba, and other countries, and some began to import Chinese laborers for mining, construction, and other physical work. But the majority of Chinese immigrants to California during the nineteenth century came not as coolie labor but by means of the credit-ticket system.[6] With the cooperation of the Chinese Six Companies, large numbers of Chinese laborers arrived, and when the first transcontinental railway was being built in the 1860s, more than 11,000 Chinese workers were recruited for the project. The Central Pacific Railroad as well as the many other feeder lines Chinese laborers helped to construct were vehicles for the dispersion of the Chinese population. Although San Francisco remained the county with the largest concentration of Chinese, by 1870 Chinese were found in every county of the state, and by 1880 their numbers in all but eight counties increased. While the total Chinese population in California increased from 34,933 in 1860 to 75,132 in 1880, the number of Chinese women only increased from 2,006 to 3,686. The tremendous increase of the Chinese male population without a corresponding increase in females provided a rare opportunity for the Chinese to accumulate money. While some Chinese businessmen set up small factories, shops, and restaurants, others organized as secret societies (tongs), established gambling joints and opium dens and developed the female trade.

There is no accurate count of Chinese prostitutes in California during the nineteenth century. But the manuscript population census from 1870 identified prostitution as an occupational category. If we juxtapose the census figures with those reported by Chinese and American observers, it is possible to derive some fairly credible estimates.[7] In 1870, among the 3,536 adult Chinese women in California, there were approximately 2,157 whose occupations were listed as prostitutes, and a majority of them (67 percent) were concentrated in San Francisco. By 1880, although the total number of Chinese women in California changed little, the number of prostitutes declined greatly. Among the 3,171 adult women, only 759 were listed as prostitutes. The decline is reflected even more sharply when we focus on San Francisco. Although 79 percent of the Chinese women in San Francisco were prostitutes in 1870, only 28 percent were so listed in 1880. Who were these women? How did they come? And what were their living conditions?

Like male Chinese laborers, who were first welcomed with open arms to California and then persecuted and excluded, the Chinese prostitutes faced similar treatment by the white population. This change in attitude is reflected in the accounts of nineteenth-century writers. Their works tended either to dwell on the exotic or to exaggerate the evil. Nevertheless, if selected cautiously and juxtaposed with other sources including those published in Chinese, these works can provide useful information in the construction of the history of Chinese prostitution.[8]

An examination of the available sources indicates that the most prevalent means of procurement were, in descending order, luring and kidnapping, contractual agreements, and sale.

Because of population pressure, class exploitation, and foreign imperialism, some areas in nineteenth-century China were so impoverished that many peasant families could not make ends meet even after a year's hard toil. To survive, a family, particularly in times of natural disaster and war, was frequently compelled to resort to mortgaging, infanticide, and the abandonment or selling of children. Female children were particularly vulnerable for both economic and social reasons. Since most productive labor was dependent on physical strength, female workers were less valuable than male ones. In any case, female labor would only contribute to the husbands' families. Furthermore, in patriarchal and patrilineal Chinese society, only males could carry on the ancestral line, and thus, it was always the girls in the family who were the first victims of extreme poverty.

One preferred solution for relieving the family of its female members was prostitution because it was remunerative: The family did not have to provide for the girl's upkeep and her sale or part of her earnings could help support the family. Parents sold their daughters and husbands sold their wives for various reasons, but the most fundamental one was survival—survival of the more "important" members of the family for the preservation and continuation of the lineage. Sometimes the parents sold their daughters in order to pay the bride price for a wife for their son. At other times daughters and wives were sold to pay a debt, and often they were given as mortgage security and became slaves through foreclosure. The Wells Fargo History Room in San Francisco contained a brief report of a Chinese man in California who sold his daughter in order to have the passage money to return to China. A number of prostitutes in San Francisco were originally orphans who were sold into brothels by their relatives. Young girls sold to masters or mistresses as *mooi-tzai* (domestic slaves) were often resold into brothels when they reached 12 years of age. Brothel owners in San Francisco often informed their agents in Canton and Hong Kong of an appropriate purchase price to ensure a large profit.

Sometimes the agents were not successful in getting enough females on the market to fulfill their orders. They would then send subagents into the rural districts to lure or kidnap girls and young women and forward the victims to the shipping ports. Quite frequently those individuals who did the luring were emigrants from the same communities who had returned temporarily for a visit. The baits used included promises of marriage, jobs, or education. . . .

Kidnapping and stealing young girls and women for purposes of prostitution was not uncommon in traditional China. Sometimes the victims were invited to see the big American steamer anchored at the docks, and while they were enjoying the tour, the boat would start on its way to San Francisco. More often, kidnapping was carried out by force, and the victims were frequently daughters of relatively well-to-do families. On an official visit to the United States in 1888, Chinese envoy Fu Yunlung composed a memorial that was inscribed on the gravestone of a Cantonese woman who had committed suicide after being kidnapped and sold into prostitution in San Francisco. . . .

Many brothels in San Francisco during this period seemed to have had an arrangement with their workers similar to that described as the Chinese contract coolie system that dominated early emigration to Cuba and Peru. They were brought in under a contract of body service for a specified time, usually four to five years, during which they received no wages, and if they succeeded in working out their terms of service, they could, theoretically, get out of the business.

After the women were landed in San Francisco, they were transported to Chinatown and housed in temporary quarters known as the *barracoons,* where they were displayed for bids. Except for a few women who were bought by the well-to-do Chinese as concubines, the rest ended up in brothels of various grades. While a small number were recruited to high-class dens where they would serve an exclusively Chinese clientele, the majority found themselves in brothels where, due to their comparatively low fees of 25 to 50 cents, they tended to attract white and Chinese customers. The latter type of prostitutes were often mistreated by their owners as well as by their customers. A few brothel owners, for example, occasionally beat some of them to death, and white men often forced them to engage in aberrant sexual acts, or, worse yet, occasionally shot them.[9]

Prostitutes of the highest grade lived in upstairs apartments in Chinatown and had a more or less long-term regular customer or customers. Very often the client was also the owner. It is not always accurate to characterize these women as prostitutes. Some may have been concubines and others may have lived in polyandry. They were often attractive and expensively adorned. While they may have appeared to be well treated, they were nevertheless chattels who could be sold by their masters at will. Essays and short stories written during the period tended to portray them as extremely vain. One story related the tale of a young man who labored day and night for three years in order to save 400 dollars to redeem his sister from a "humiliating and secret bondage." But the sister liked the life that she led with good dinners and pretty things and did not want to leave. She stole the money from her brother and bought a sealskin coat. The brother promised her owner that he would work hard for three more years to get the money again. As he left brokenhearted, she murmured: "Fool!"[10]

Most of the lower-grade prostitutes lived in the street-level compartments usually not larger than 4×6 feet and facing some dim alley. There were a few articles of furniture—a bamboo chair or two, a washbowl, and hard bunks or shelves covered with matting. The door usually held the only window in the room, and it was always covered with bars or a heavy screen, behind which the women, dressed in cotton tunics and trousers, could stand and call to passersby. The women were served two or three meals a day, the evening one usually consisting of a huge mound of rice and a stew of pork, mixed with hard-boiled eggs, liver, and kidneys.[11] The more fortunate ones were sometimes asked to entertain at parties given by tong leaders and Chinese merchants. They did not have regular wages, but instead were allowed to keep the jewelry, silk, and cash gifts given by their customers. This is perhaps why some prostitutes were able to send money to their parents in China. Although the amount is not known, it seems clear that some of the remittances that emigrant communities in Kwangtung received during the nineteenth and early twentieth centuries were from prostitutes in California.

The managers of the brothels, called "mothers" by the prostitutes, were not always the owners. Tong members who actually owned prostitutes often asked their wives or mistresses or an older prostitute to manage them. Normally half of the earnings of the prostitutes would go to the mothers and half to the owners.

Owners of brothels often also owned opium dens and gambling joints. Some prostitutes were addicted to opium and/or gambled excessively. The owners often loaned them money to feed their habits so that they would not only be dependent on the owners for these services, but they would also become more deeply indebted to them. From the point of view of many prostitutes, opium smoking was probably the only way they could find relief, and gambling the only avenue to an alternative life. Women who were desperate committed suicide by swallowing raw opium or drowning themselves in the bay.

The more fortunate ones were redeemed and married, mostly to Chinese workers. There did not seem to be the same stigma attached to prostitution among the Chinese masses as there was among whites. Part of the reason might be that prostitutes in China were generally not seen as "fallen women" or "degenerate women who craved for lust," but very often as filial daughters who obeyed the wishes of family. Although prostitution was definitely not considered an honored profession, particularly among the gentry, women who were able to get out of it were usually accepted in the working-class society.

Apparently quite a few women in San Francisco were able to leave the brothels, although not without struggle, and often at tremendous risk. Throughout the mid-nineteenth and the early twentieth centuries, reports of such instances abound. Typically, a woman would run away to the missions, the police stations, or to her lover, with the hired tong soldiers on her trail. They might succeed in kidnapping her directly or, failing that, resort to other methods. The tongs often utilized the American courts to get her back. They would file a charge of theft, claiming the woman had absconded with some clothes or jewelry. After the police had located the woman, the tong would hire white lawyers to pay her bail and then return her to the brothel.

When this maneuver was not effective, tongs would put up public announcements on Chinatown walls warning others who might assist her escape and offering rewards for her capture. If a specific man was known to have run away with her, the tongs would offer a reward for him, dead or alive. Such rewards sometimes could run into the thousands, depending on the value of the woman involved. Stories were told of cases where the man and woman would leave the area in disguise or hidden in wooden boxes and flee to another place. Some telegrams between Chinese men in Marysville, Downieville, San Francisco, and other places revealed that a network of search and return was in operation at least during the 1870s.[12] . . .

In order to prevent the woman from escaping, tongs were known to give the local police a retainer. Until 1877, a Special Police Force was engaged in a quasi-official capacity as peace officers in Chinatown. They received no set wages, but derived their incomes from the Chinese residents. At one point they were reported to be earning 1,000 dollars per month. They normally collected 50 cents a week from each prostitute and admitted that whenever there was a crackdown on prostitution, their income would be reduced.

If the prostitute did not succeed in escaping from the clutches of her exploiters, her life in the brothels probably would not last beyond four or five years. The length of a Chinese prostitute's working life in San Francisco did not seem to differ from that of other prostitutes in other large cities during this period. With a complete lack of medical care, many prostitutes became ill after a short time. The abundance of Chinese advertisements for a "secret formula" for curing syphilis and gonorrhea during this period testified to the prevalence of such illnesses. Although some doctors blamed the Chinese prostitutes for spreading the diseases to the white population, it was pointed out by other physicians that these illnesses were equally, if not more, prevalent among white prostitutes in San Francisco. Though they rarely led to death, these illnesses were often causes of sterility.

How much money did the average Chinese prostitute make for her owner during the length of her servitude? We have no direct information on this question. However, we can venture some estimates. The lowest grade of prostitute received 25 cents to 50 cents per customer. According to the literature on prostitution in general, an average full-time worker would receive at least four to ten customers per day. The contracts mentioned earlier bound the prostitute to at least four years of servitude and indicated that she would work 320 days per year. An absence of more than 15 days would subject her to a penalty of working one extra month. This means that at an average of 38 cents per customer and seven customers per day, a lower-grade prostitute would earn about 850 dollars per year and 3,404 dollars after four years of servitude. Since women in the inferior dens were kept at the subsistence level, the cost of maintaining them must not have exceeded 8 dollars per month or 96 dollars per year per person. Furthermore, the average capital outlay—that is, cancelled debt or the purchase price of a woman—usually amounted to an average of 530 dollars. These calculations indicate that the owner would begin to make a profit from the prostitute's labor in the first year of her service! Considering the average size of the brothel, which was about nine in 1870, this would give the owner a gross of 7,650 dollars per year. Subtracting rent and maintenance of the women, the owner would end up with an average of no less than 5,000 dollars. Even if we added other expenses, such as paying protection fees to the police and tax to the tongs, the profit the brothel owner received would still compare very favorably to the average income of other occupational pursuits that he or she might engage in, which was less than 500 dollars per year. These figures applied only to the lower grade of prostitutes; the higher grades would charge more for their services.

Although the majority of Chinese immigrant women in California in the 1860s and 1870s worked as prostitutes, others were scattered among different occupational groups including "keeping house," a designation used by census takers primarily as the occupation of unemployed housewives. For instance, in 1870, of the approximately 3,536 Chinese adult women, 21 percent were recorded to be "keeping house." As mentioned before, the largest employed group was prostitutes, accounting for 61 percent of all women. The remaining 18 percent were distributed among a variety of occupations, none of which can be labeled white collar.

By 1880, a number of trends seem evident. As indicated in Table 1, there were some changes in the first ten largest occupations from 1860 to 1880. But the changes did not signify a tendency toward upward mobility among Chinese women. The occupations remained largely the same except in different rank order. To a considerable extent, these changes in rank order can be related to the changes in economic development and the resulting population movement of Chinese women.

When the method of mining changed from placer mining to mechanized mining, and the organization of production changed from small independent miners to capitalist mining companies, the number of independent Chinese miners dwindled, and the Chinese along with other laborers were re-

TABLE 1 Occupations of Immigrant Chinese Women

1860	1870	1880
Prostitute	Prostitute	Keeping house
Wife or possible wife	Keeping house	Prostitute
Laundress	Servant	Seamstress
Miner	Laundress	Servant
Servant	Seamstress	Laundress
Laborer	Miner	Cook
Seamstress	Housekeeper	Needlework
Housekeeper	Fisherman	Entertainer (actor, theatrical performer)
Cook	Shoe binder	Laborer
Gardener	Cook	Miner
Lodging house operator	Laborer	Lodging house operator

Source: Compiled from the manuscript population censuses of California, 1860, 1870, and 1880.

cruited to work for mining companies. Among them were a small number of women, whose numbers declined with the development of mining technology. Specifically, the number of Chinese women engaged in mining dropped from 63 in 1860 to 29 in 1870 and to 11 in 1880, or from third place to fifth and then to ninth place. This pattern of decline reflected not only the changing mode of production but also the persecution and subsequent departure of Chinese workers from the mines into railroad building and other pursuits. This relationship is corroborated by the fact that among the small number of female laborers in 1880, a majority were identified as railroad laborers, the first time that this designation appeared in the manuscript population census. These female railroad workers, between the ages of 24 and 40, were found rooming together near Truckee. Additional evidence of the relationship is provided by the increase in the proportion of Chinese women in San Francisco. While in 1880, more than half of the Chinese women were found living in San Francisco, only one-third resided there in 1860.

If we compare the occupational distribution of Chinese women with that of all California women during the same period, we find that the former were not represented in the white-collar occupations like nursing and teaching, occupations that ranked among the top ten for California women as a whole. Their concentration in the least-esteemed occupations reflected the lack of employment opportunities for Chinese women, not only in relation to Chinese men but also in relation to white women.

The second trend in occupational change during this period was the increase in the number of housewives. While the total number of Chinese adult women decreased somewhat, those designated as keeping house doubled from 753 (21 percent) in 1870 to 1,445 (46 percent) in 1880. Most of this increase occurred outside of San Francisco County.

It is necessary to point out that keeping house was only one of the roles performed by Chinese married women, many of whom were also wage workers or worked in small family-operated businesses. A few married women even worked as prostitutes. The designation keeping house was given only to women who were not performing household functions for pay, and who reported no other occupations. Among all married women in 1880, about 72 percent were classified as such.

The increase of married women during this period cannot be explained by new immigration alone, since the total number of women in California actually declined and it is unlikely that a large number of prostitutes went back to China while wives came. The partriarchal family system in China, the successive restrictions placed on immigration by United States authorities, the racial hostility against the Chinese all combined to retard the immigration of Chinese women. Therefore, it is very likely that a proportion of the married women in 1880 were former prostitutes.

The traditional Chinese family of three generations in one household was apparently not transplanted into California. We found no complete three-generational families in the 1880 records. Occasionally a grandfather was found living with his son's family, but such phenomena were extremely rare. More typically, the family structure included a married couple, the husband about 14 years older than the wife, and no child. The average age of wives was as high as 30.2, and the lowest recorded was 16. . . . One expression of racial hostility in the late nineteenth century was the fear that there would soon be a permanent yellow population in California. Given the facts that the average number of children per Chinese family was only 0.70 and the average age of Chinese wives was over 30, many were nearing the end of their reproductive cycle, and given the declining number of female immigrants in 1880, such fear seemed more like hysteria.

Family size was obviously related to the class status of the male head of household. Although the average family size among workers was 2.4, that among the merchants and business owners was 4.1. Some families of the petit bourgeoisie had as many as 9 persons.

The life of a Chinese businessman's wife was quite different from that of a laborer's. Although both were likely to have come from Canton, the merchant's wife was usually of middle-class background and the laborer's wife was more often the offspring of a peasant family. The former lived in seclusion, generally upstairs from her husband's place of business. Her quarters were usually furnished with Chinese tables and chairs and decorated with Chinese ornaments. Until she gave birth to a child, she was unlikely to be seen in public places. Sui Seen Far, a Eurasian woman writing in the nineteenth century, described the social life of these Chinese women in the following passage:

> Now and then the women visit one another; and when they are met together, there is such a clattering of tongues one would almost think they were American women. They laugh at the most commonplace remark and scream at the smallest trifle; they examine one another's dresses and hair, talk about their husbands, their babies, their food; squabble over little matters and make up again; they dine on bowls of rice, minced chicken, bamboo shoots and a dessert of candied fruits.[13]

Since well-to-do families had house servants, their women did not have to perform daily maintenance chores such as cooking, laundering, and cleaning. They usually filled their leisure time with needlework to be used as presents for distant relatives or as ornaments on caps for husbands and children.

These descriptions applied only to less than 1 percent of Chinese married women. The rest led a much less comfortable life. Although many of the women married to the less prosperous Chinese had two sets of responsibilities, one related to a job outside the home, the other related to being a wife, most were not employed and were identified as keeping house. But it would be grossly incorrect to conclude that most wives did not work. It was with good reason that wives were often given the occupational designation keeping house if they were not wage earners. For those households where a woman was so designated, a study of the number of residents per household revealed that at least 20 percent of the households had boarders or lodgers. In some households, the number of boarders reached 38, although 2 or 3 seemed to be the most common. Under these circumstances, the work of the housewife must have been considerable and no less trying than a job outside the home. Furthermore, housewives of small businessmen who could not afford to hire servants often helped out in the business without being recorded. It was also highly probable that many women did piecework at home for subcontractors but did not report these activities to the census taker.

Even if she were "just a housewife," her life could not have been an easy one. Food had to be cooked, clothes mended and laundered, rooms cleaned, and children tended. Many married women made clothing and cloth shoes for their families.

The third observation that can be made from Table 1 is the rise in the number of Chinese women engaged in wage labor. Despite the significant decrease of women recorded as prostitutes, they remained the largest occupational group aside from keeping house, comprising 24 percent of the total of Chinese women in 1880. The sewing trade, including occupations such as seamstress, tailoress, and dressmaker, jumped to the second largest place in the rank order of employment, rising from 36 (1 percent) in 1870 to 192 (5 percent) in 1880. Actually, the number of Chinese women engaged in sewing for pay must have been more. The San Francisco *Alta* reported that one Chinese official estimated about 764 women depended on sewing for their livelihood. As would be expected, sewing was predominantly an urban pursuit. Unlike the increase of women who kept house, which took place mainly away from San Francisco, the growth in the sewing occupation was exclusively a San Francisco phenomenon. Even then, Chinese women engaged in the sewing trade were outnumbered by Chinese men at a 10 to 1 ratio. It was not until the twentieth century that Chinese women took this occupation over from the men.

Except for their occupational distribution there is very little information concerning the Chinese female wage earner in nineteenth-century California. The seamstress might be either married or unmarried. If unmarried she tended to live together with other seamstresses. Most of the married seamstresses were widows or women whose husbands were in similar lines of business, such as tailoring. Regardless of their marital status, they tended to work at home, receiving their work from Chinese subcontractors. Contemporary writers told of their working from dawn till late at night in exchange for very low wages. It was reported that few sewing factories paid women the standard wage of 2 dollars per day; most paid much less. The California State Bureau of Labor Statistics claimed that women normally received only 50 cents per day for sewing and repairing clothing. This was the chief reason that the report gave for the prevalence of white prostitution.

The female Chinese servant was mostly found in white families. If she were married, her husband would most likely be found working for the same family. The husband was often the cook and his wife the domestic who cared for the household. Her duties included cleaning, washing, and caring for children. Often she was asked to sew or mend for the family also. A nineteenth-century writer reported such a woman being made a spectacle by the white children, who charged visitors 5 cents for a look at her.

Sometimes Chinese servants were also found in well-to-do Chinese families. Some were older women in their late 40s or 50s who, as the census indicates, might be widowed or former prostitutes.[14] But many of these female servants were young and single, often in their early teens. Some might have been brought by the families from China and were held for an indefinite period of time. Others, like prostitutes, were bought from poor families in China. . . . Although we find such female child domestics in California, there is no evidence that a similar situation existed for male children. This difference again is attributable to both economic and social factors. Female children more than male ones were sacrificed for the survival of the family. And because owners of female child domestics could always look forward to selling the girl when she came of age, they could benefit not only from her service as a servant but also from her sale as a commodity.

California in the mid-nineteenth century was a fast-developing frontier society. The sexual imbalance and the youthfulness of the male population had particular consequences for women. Although demographic factors delimited the general forms of women's participation in this development, racial hostility, cultural traditions, and internal class structure fostered the particular roles that Chinese immigrant women fulfilled. The racial, sexual, and class biases of most nineteenth-century writers have left an image of Chinese women as either degenerates by nature or helpless robots. White observers tended to emphasize the exotic or the evil, and Chinese writers tried to counter with exaltations of a few upper-class or highly educated women. Hidden from history are the experiences of the majority of early Chinese immigrant women, who tried to survive within a complex structure characterized by racial antagonism, sexual oppression, and class exploitation. This essay is only the beginning in uncovering their history.

NOTES

1. The following discussion on Chinese prostitution is a brief summary of the author's paper, "Free, Enslaved, and Indentured Workers in 19th-Century America: The Case of Chinese Prostitution," *Signs* (1979).

2. However, there is a great deal written about her. See, for example, Herbert Asbury, *The Barbary Coast,* Alfred A. Knopf, New York, 1933; Charles Dobie, *San Francisco's Chinatown,* Doubleday, New York, 1964; C. Y. Lee, *Days of the Tong Wars,* Ballantine, New York, 1974; and Wu Shang-ying, *Mei-guo Hua-qiao bai-nian ji-shi,* Hong Kong, 1954. Many of the details in these works are contradictory.

3. For example, one European prostitute in the West was reported to have charged 1,000 dollars per night in the 1850s. See Dee Brown, *Women of the Wild West*, Pan, London, 1975, p. 70.

4. Curt Gentry, *Madames of San Francisco*, Doubleday, New York, 1964, pp. 50–60.

5. Wu Yan-ren, *Er-shi-nien mu-du guai xian-zhuang*, n.p., 1903.

6. Thomas Chinn, *A History of the Chinese in California*, Chinese Historical Society, San Francisco, 1969.

7. Unless otherwise noted, all numbers and demographic characteristics concerning Chinese women in California during the nineteenth century are computed from the U.S. Manuscript Population Census for California for 1860, 1870, and 1880. The 1890 census was destroyed in a fire.

8. In addition to the titles cited in footnote 2, see also California Senate Report on Chinese Immigration, 1878; San Francisco Board of Supervisors Special Committee Report on Chinatown, 1885; U.S. Congress Joint Special Committee to Investigate Chinese Immigration Report, 1877.

9. *The Golden Hills News*, July 29, 1854 (in Chinese).

10. Sui Seen Far, "Lin John," *Land of Sunshine*, 10 (1899), 76–77.

11. Dobie, *San Francisco's Chinatown*, p. 243.

12. *California Chinese Chatter*, Dressler, San Francisco, 1927.

13. Sui Seen Far, "The Chinese Woman in America," *Land of Sunshine*, 6 (January 1897), 62.

14. Dorothy Gray, *Women of the West*, Les Femmes, Millbrae, Calif., 1976, p. 69.

18

Reproductive Control and Conflict in the Nineteenth Century

Janet Farrell Brodie

In the following article, adapted from her book-length study, Contraception and Abortion in Nineteenth-Century America, *Janet Farrell Brodie considers the ways that nineteenth-century American women controlled reproduction and analyzes the writings of advocates and opponents of contraception and abortion. She shows how opponents of abortion mounted a "carefully orchestrated campaign" that criminalized contraception and abortion, driving their medical practitioners underground. Only with the Supreme Court decision,* Roe v. Wade, *in 1973, would women in the United States regain legal access to contraception and abortion.*

The ancient contraceptive practice of coitus interruptus took on new meaning in nineteenth-century America. It became increasingly well known and openly discussed, and it appears to have been widely practiced well into the twentieth century. Its growing public visibility can be seen in the number of synonyms it garnered, from the derogatory "conjugal onanism," "marital masturbation," and "coitus imperfecti," to the more benign "withdrawal," "the pullback," "the drawback," "the method of retraction," "incomplete coition," or simply "the way." Lecturing and writing on health, marriage, and sex in antebellum America, William Andrus Alcott expected audiences to understand his references to a reproductive control method that was "a species of self-denial on the part of the husband, which though it should be in its essential form like that of Onan, would be without his particular form of guilt."[1] This was "withdrawal." In 1831, Robert Dale Owen, son of the founder of New Harmony in Indiana and a pioneer in publicizing reproductive control, described a Quaker couple who had been married for twenty years. They had six children and claimed that they would have had twelve if they had not practiced withdrawal.[2]

Couples in these case studies who discussed the need for spacing or preventing any further pregnancies whatsoever cited motivations that were primarily health concerns—a wife's or couple's fears about a wife's health, fears about a husband's overwork—and, secondarily, financial concerns. The late-eighteenth-century Quaker couple was greatly pleased to have only six children, but couples in the 1860s and 1870s found two children in four years or two children in seven years too many.

Coitus interruptus, for all its seeming simplicity, was not a uniform contraceptive technique. Historians have paid too little attention to the varia-

MADAME RESTELL.

☞FEMALE PHYSICIAN, is happy in complying with the solicitations of the numerous importunities of those who have tested the efficacy and success of her medicines, as being so especially adapted to female complaints.

Their known celebrity in the Female Hospitals of Vienna and Paris, where they have been altogether adopted as well as their adoption in this country, to the exclusion of the many and deleterious compounds heretofore palmed upon their notice, is ample evidence of the estimation in which they are held to make any lengthened advertisements superfluous: it is sufficient to say that her celebrated 'FEMALE MONTHLY PILLS,' now acknowledged by the medical fraternity to be the only safe, mild and efficient remedy to be depended upon in long standing cases of Suppression, Irregularity or stoppage of those functions of nature, the neglect of which is the source of such deplorable defects on the female frame, dizziness in the head, disturbed sleep, sallow complexion, and the innumerable frightful effects which sooner or later terminate in incurable consumption.

The married, it is desired necessary to state, must under some circumstances abstain from their use, for reasons contained in the full directions when and how to be used accompanying each box. Price $1.

Females laboring under weakness, debility, fluoral bas, often so destructive and undermining to the health, will obtain instant relief by the use of these Pills.

PREVENTIVE POWDERS, for married ladies in delicate health, the adoption of which has been the means of preserving many an affectionate wife and fond mother from an early and premature grave. Prices $5.00 a package. Their nature is most fully explained in a pamphlet entitled 'Suggestions to the Married.' which can be obtained free of expense, at the office, where ladies will find one of their own sex, conversant with their indisposition, in attendance.

FEMALE MEDICAL OFFICE, No. 7 Essex street, Boston. Office hours from 8 A.M. to 8 P. M.

Philadelphia Office, No 7 South Seventh street.

Principal Office, No 148 Greenwich street New York.

Abortifacient advertisement, Boston Daily Times, *Jan. 2, 1845.*

tions. Historians also disagree about whether withdrawal is one of those simple folk contraceptives that individuals can invent easily on their own or whether it needs special circumstances to be learned.[3] In Victorian America some said they had "invented" withdrawal, much like the young man who, after his marriage in the 1820s, wrote to Robert Dale Owen explaining that he had used withdrawal successfully for seven years to improve his economic circumstances and his health before having a family. He had learned about it, he claimed, when "withdrawal presented itself to my mind."[4] In the 1930s a white tenant farm woman in Appalachia told a WPA interviewer that withdrawal was easy to understand: "If you don't want butter, pull the dasher out in time."[5]

Others needed instruction. Owen described the visit to his New York newspaper office in the early 1830s of a man who lived "west of the mountains." He had used withdrawal successfully for nearly eight years after the birth of three children. Owen asked if his neighbors also found it effective, but his visitor had not thought it prudent "to speak with any but his own relations on the subject, one or two of whom, he knew had profited by his advice and afterwards expressed to him their gratitude for the important information."[6] Such reticence apparently did not bother an Upstate New York farm woman, Calista Hall, who wrote to her husband, Pliny, in 1849 to reassure him she was not pregnant, to commend him for using withdrawal so effectively, and to suggest that he instruct a friend or relative in its advantages: "The old maid came at the appointed time. . . . I do think you are a very *careful* man. You must take Mr. Stewart out one side and learn him."[7]

The publication in 1831 of Owen's pamphlet *Moral Physiology* made it easier to learn about withdrawal. It was concise and plainly written, without the many euphemisms and metaphors that cloaked so many discussions. . . . In its many editions and through its many imitators and competitors, Owen's tract put coitus interrupts in the culture. Almost all contraceptive advice literature from the 1830s through the 1880s gave explicit or tacit recognition to coitus interrupts. Much of it disparaged withdrawal because it competed with other methods such as douching, condoms, rhythm, or abortion, which they themselves were touting, but few ignored it.

Twentieth-century studies of the effectiveness of various contraceptive methods show that, under optimal conditions, coitus interruptus can be quite reliable but also that there is great variation in success rates.[8] It ranks in some studies as more effective than douching and nearly equal to spermicidal suppositories, contraceptive jelly, and condoms.[9] Its reliability depends on the care with which withdrawal is practiced—no sperm at all may be left in or near the vagina, even on the external labia, because sperm move quickly and can fertilize an ovum within minutes. Knowledge of sperm mobility grew only slowly in the last century.

Partial withdrawal, that is, ejaculation as far as possible from the cervix but possibly still in the vagina, appears to have been as widely known as complete withdrawal both in Europe and in America. Because it required less concentration from men, it may have been more widely practiced . . .

When people believed, as many did in earlier centuries, that conception occurred only if a woman experienced orgasm or if the sperm were thrown forcefully against the cervix, partial withdrawal appeared a logical method. But by the mid nineteenth century, new theories about how sperm reached the ovum (by their own motility, by absorbant vessels in the vaginal lining) convinced some that partial withdrawal could not work.[10] Yet well-established ideas and practices change slowly, and, apparently—or why were there so many continuing warnings against it?—at least some Americans continued to rely on partial withdrawal. . . .

Withdrawal of any degree fell into increasing disfavor as time went on, and medical professionals, promoters of reproductive control, and the middle class public began to raise doubts about it, or worse. Medical opponents claimed that withdrawal caused in men "general debility of brain and brawn," "tubercula foci" in the prostate and seminal vesicles, and symptoms like gonorrhea; and, in women, hysteria, degeneration of the womb, neuralgias, and a host of "local and constitutional disorders."[11]

Physicians frequently commented negatively on coitus interruptus. In 1876, Nicholas Francis Cooke, a physician and birth control critic, wrote *Satan in Society: A Plea for Social Purity. A Discussion of the True Rights of Woman, Marital and Social* chiefly "to stigmatize . . . conjugal onanism," which he deplored as a "deeply rooted vice . . . a national curse, a reason for the widespread moral degradation and a powerful reason for the decline of the native population."[12] . . .

Some physicians late in the century reported that withdrawal caused psychological disorders. A Philadelphia doctor who had advised a delicate female patient who was about to be married not to have children immediately and her husband-to-be to practice withdrawal, reported that the couple had no children for three years and the wife had become healthy and robust, but the husband "nervously affected" and "rendered delicate."[13] . . .

Yet the public may well have paid scant attention to the negative onslaught. The remark of a farmer in pre–World War I Germany (where withdrawal and postcoital douching were the most common forms of contraception among the working class) may be equally applicable to nineteenth-century Americans. Asked if he believed medical reports that withdrawal is harmful, the farmer replied no, "otherwise everybody would be sick."[14] Annie Besant wrote in her pamphlet *The Law of Population* in 1878 that although doctors said that withdrawal might be injurious to women, its universal practice by the French attested to its safety.[15]

Dislike of withdrawal became more openly expressed over the course of the century as other contraceptive and abortive options emerged in the commercialization of reproductive control. Men, in particular, began to express complaints about it more openly, centering on how difficult coitus interruptus was to practice and how much it lessened their sexual pleasure. . . .

When Gilbert Vale, Owen's fellow freethinker, published an edition of *Moral Physiology* in 1858, adding his own publisher's notes at the end, he said that withdrawal was difficult for any but mature men in "the decline of life." Younger men could not be expected to have sufficient control to practice withdrawal and so should use condoms or rely on partial withdrawal, followed by the wife's douching. The pirated edition of *Moral Physiology* put out in 1846 by the unknown "physician" Ralph Glover, too, played on the discontent, commenting, "How frequently do we hear the mothers say, I have all the family I want and am determined to have not more children if I can prevent it; but alas: she has not the power when the partner of her bosom loses the self-control of his passions.[16] . . .

Women had their own reasons for disliking withdrawal. A woman had to have great confidence in her sexual partner's reliability, self-control, good will, and judgment. This dependence was not satisfactory for many women. A man's reliance on coitus interruptus might actually have increased a woman's level of anxiety because a man who became more confident about his ability to "pull back" effectively may have become less willing to be abstinent or to be overruled in the timing and frequency of sexual intercourse. Still, family-limitation critic Nicholas Francis Cooke was lamenting in 1876 that a husband who practices coitus interruptus is "eulogized by his wife and applauded by her friends."[17] . . .

Unlike men, women did not leave a record of complaints about withdrawal's interference with their sexual pleasure, but it can hardly, one assumes, have had any other effect. And fears that the pullback would not be in time can only have increased their anxiety. Nevertheless, husbands and doctors occasionally blamed wives for making their husbands practice withdrawal. L. Bolton Bangs, a physician opposed to contraception, wrote in 1893 that his male patients felt anger and disgust toward their wives at the moment of withdrawal. Other historians have seen the practice of withdrawal as an example of the increasing power of women within marriage. Daniel Scott Smith's well-known article "Family Limitation, Sexual Control, and Domestic Feminism in Victorian America" argues that women in mid-nineteenth-century America gained considerable power within marriage to control the timing and frequency of sexual intercourse and thereby to control reproduction.[18] . . .

In what may be viewed as another variant of withdrawal in that it, too, involved a man's control of ejaculation during the sexual act, coitus reservatus was known and practiced by some in nineteenth-century America. Coitus reservatus (prolonged coition with no emission of semen and with gradual loss of the erection while the penis is still in the vagina) is an ancient sexual practice, but Americans believed that it was invented in the 1840s by John Humphrey Noyes, the leader of a New York communitarian group, the

Oneida Perfectionists.[19] Noyes, who called the practice "male continence," explained that he invented it after his wife, Harriet, suffered six pregnancies but only one live birth in the eight years after they were married in 1838. He promised Harriet she would never again have to suffer the pain and anguish of childbirth even if they had to sleep apart. Worried by such a prospect, he "studied the subject of sexual intercourse in connection with my matrimonial experience and discovered the principle of male continence."[20] This then became the way conception was prevented at the Oneida Community, which from 1848 until the mid 1870s proved to be the longest-lasting, most publicized, and most financially successful of all the nineteenth-century American experiments in communal living. It apparently worked remarkably well, for there were only thirty-one accidental pregnancies from 1848 to 1869, although the community grew from some eighty-seven to 219 by 1874. To Noyes, for whom the method was as much a spiritual as a contraceptive practice, its advantages were manifold: it preserved men's health by preventing the loss of semen; it freed women from "the curses of involuntary and undesirable procreation," a freedom that, he believed, would promote happier relations between the sexes and happier maternity for women, who now regarded childbearing as a burden and a curse. Above all, it enabled both men and women to enjoy sexual intercourse.[21]

Male continence was probably never widely practiced in the United States except at Oneida, but it received considerable publicity and was far from unknown. Noyes first described it in a chapter of his book *The Bible Argument* in 1848.[22] In 1866 the Perfectionists decided that American society would benefit from a wider knowledge of male continence, so Noyes published as a four-page leaflet a letter he has written to a young medical student who requested detailed information on how the community controlled reproduction. They mailed the leaflet, *Male Continence; or, Self-Control in Sexual Intercourse. A Letter of Inquiry Answered by John Humphrey Noyes,* only in response to specific requests for information, but even so it went through four editions. In 1872 rather than issue a fifth edition, Noyes revised and enlarged the leaflet, adding twenty pages on the history of his discovery of male continence. This he published in 1877, and it was sold by general booksellers and agents. Ezra Heywood, who stood trial and served a jail term for breaking the laws against dispersing birth control information by selling his own book, *Cupid's Yokes*—an antimarriage tract—and Russell Thacher Trall's *Sexual Physiology,* sold *Male Continence* without any trouble.[23]

In some years over two hundred visitors a month passed through the Oneida Community, and all had access to freely given information about its beliefs and practices. The community's newspaper, the *Oneida Circular,* with a weekly circulation of two thousand in the 1860s, discussed male continence in its columns. Later birth control publicists included discussions of it in their books,[24] and critics of fertility intervention disparaged it. John Harvey Kellogg's *Plain Facts for Old and Young,* in 1880, labeled male continence "double masturbation" and warned readers that it was as destructive to health as with-drawal.[25] Members of the Boston Gynaecological Society in 1871 discussed "the pathological results of conjugal fraud as practiced in so disgusting a manner at the so-called Oneida Community."[26]

THE RIGHT TO DECIDE: EARLY SPOKESWOMEN

Before the 1860s there is little direct evidence that female lecturers dissemi-nated contraceptive or abortive information. The most important of those who did do so was probably Mary Gove Nichols, whose public and private life, like that of Frances Wright, was full of sexual paradox. Mary Gove was intel-lectually curious and upwardly mobile, but at a young age married, unhap-pily, a dour Quaker, Hiram Gove. She secretly read medical textbooks and taught herself the rudiments of medicine and the water cure. Six years of in-creasing marital misery and five pregnancies later (all but one ending either in miscarriage or stillbirth), Mary and Hiram Gove left their New Hampshire farm and moved, in 1837, to Lynn, Massachusetts, where Mary supported the family by operating a boarding school run on the dietary principles of Sylvester Graham, supplementing this income by lectures on physiology and hygiene.[27] Her lectures, in turn, brought her to the attention of the American Physiological Society (founded in 1837 in Boston by William Andrus Alcott and Sylvester Graham).

Because some women attending the first lectures of the American Physi-ological Society were embarrassed to be in an audience with men, the society decided to hire separate speakers for men and women and create the Ladies Physiological Society. Mary Gove came to Boston in September 1837 and began to lecture on diet, dress, menstrual difficulties, and the dangers of female mas-turbation, sometimes to audiences of more than four hundred women.[28] So successful were these lectures that she continued throughout New England and as far south as Philadelphia and New York, speaking on "sanitary educa-tion," "the laws of life and health," the evils of wearing corsets, the problems of masturbation in girls' boarding schools, and, most radically of all, on the phys-ical and emotional problems resulting from "indissoluble marriage." Desper-ately unhappy in her own marriage, she spent as much time away from her husband as possible, but he would not grant her a divorce. In 1842 she left him, but feared that he would never allow her to see their daughter and that he would continue to claim her financial earnings. Even though she was immersed in itinerant lecturing, consulting lawyers about her marital rights, and in poor health, she still found time in 1842 to publish some of her lectures as a book, *Lectures to Women on Anatomy and Physiology*.[29] If the book mirrored her lectures (as the title implies), then she did not speak on reproduction except to lament the prevailing ignorance among women on the subject of their bodies, but the book may have omitted such comments. Some of her lectures were given separately to married and unmarried women.[30] Her lectures scandalized some because of her comments on masturbation (the topic alone was shocking) and her references to her own (clothed) body to demonstrate anatomical points. She consulted a favorite cousin, the writer John Neal, whether he thought it proper to speak before men and women on the evils of "tight lacing," but added, "I think I have a *right* to speak on proper subjects in a proper manner before a mixed audience."[31] New York newspaper editor James Gordon Bennett denounced her, but the *Boston Medical and Surgical Reporter* commended her book and her lectures, noting that "useful knowledge becomes a woman, let it embrace whatever department it may," and adding that there is "nothing objectionable or indelicate for one woman to tell another those important facts . . . in a country where ladies have been too negligent of the laws of health, and sometimes apparently proud of being profoundly ignorant of the mechanism of themselves."[32]

Mary Gove supported herself (and her husband, though separated) as a water-cure physician in a series of hydropathic resorts, in Brattleboro, Vermont, Lebanon Springs, New York, and then at the establishment of Joel Shew in New York City, and finally in 1846 at her own water-cure boardinghouse on Tenth Street in Manhattan. In 1847 she met Thomas Low Nichols, a young itinerant novelist and journalist who had studied medicine at Dartmouth College and was absorbed in the theories of John Humphrey Noyes, Josiah Warren, and Charles Fourier. They married the following year when her husband, also wanting to remarry, finally granted a divorce.[33]

In the 1850s Mary and Thomas Gove Nichols became active New York water-cure practitioners and lecturers and writers on sexuality, marriage, and reproductive control. They operated a Reform Bookstore at 65 Walker Street in Manhattan, from which they sold their literature and advertised their services. Mary Gove Nichols probably influenced her new husband in these directions, for only after their marriage did he show any interest in many of the subjects they subsequently wrote about. Both lectured to large mixed audiences, but she specialized in intimate talks to small groups of women. They wrote and lectured on the benefits of the water cure, especially its aid in ameliorating the dangers and pains of pregnancy and childbirth,[34] and advocated easier divorce, women's property rights, and, above all, women's sexual rights. She had long believed that a woman had the right to determine if and when she would bear children and to choose who would father them. When Mary Gove Nichols and Thomas Low Nichols published such views they were branded "free lovers" by critics, although they emphasized the dangers of excessive sexuality, women's rights to *refuse* sex, and the legalized "prostitution" created by contemporary marriage laws.

The book *Esoteric Anthropology* appeared in 1853. Although Thomas Low Nichols is credited as its sole author, the wording of the text—especially the opinions about contraception and abortion—suggests that Mary Gove Nichols wrote parts.[35] In any case, both probably shared its views and may have expressed them in their lectures and, almost certainly, in their private consultations. *Esoteric Anthropology* boldly argued a position she had long held: "If a woman has any right in this world it is the right to herself; and if there is anything in this world she has a right to decide, it is who shall be the father of her children. She has an equal right to decide whether she will have children and to choose the time for having them."[36] . . .

Esoteric Anthropology suggested how women and men could achieve reproductive control, discussing a variety of methods, among them abstinence (it is "unhealthy and unnatural" but "easily done by most women and by many men"), and rhythm ("in ordinary cases . . . conception can only take place when connection is had a day or two before or ten, or for safety's sake, say sixteen days after menstruation"); complete withdrawal; use of a soft sponge "to cover the upper vagina over the mouth of the womb"; use of condoms or other "delicate coverings of the whole penis"; and "pressing upon the urethra to prevent emission of the semen," effectual but harmful. Above all, it advised an "immediate, very deep, thorough" douche—an "immediate injection of cold water by the vagina-syringe" to "kill and wash away zoosperms." Douching was, after all, an important part of the water cure. . . . *Esoteric Anthropology* included advice about the simplest and least dangerous abortion method, and warnings about the most dangerous techniques. The reformist physician Elizabeth Blackwell in 1853 noted with asperity in a letter to her sister Emily, who was studying medicine in Edinburgh, that "the Nichols set is spreading their detestable doctrines of abortion and prostitution under spiritual and scientific guise—they are placing agents with the advertisements of their books at the doors of the conventions now being held here, worded in the most specious and attractive manner." In her published autobiography, Blackwell changed the wording of these remarks slightly and referred not by name to the Nicholses but to "an active set of people," whose "detestable doctrines of abortion and prostitution" were now the "detestable doctrine of 'free love.'"[37]

Another lecturer, Paulina Kellogg Wright Davis, an antislavery and woman's rights activist in the 1830s, became active in health reform after her husband's death. From 1845 to 1849 she toured throughout the East and the Midwest speaking to audiences of women on health reform, anatomy, and physiology. Following the precedent established by Mary Gove Nichols, she used a manikin to illustrate her lectures; but unlikely Nichols, she did not publish them. . . .

Harriot K. Hunt, another antebellum lecturer, practiced medicine in Boston for more than forty years, trained by a husband-and-wife team of homeopathic physicians, though she was repeatedly denied entry to the Harvard Medical School. One of the best known and most outspoken of the first generation of women physicians and a fervent participant in the early woman's rights movement, Hunt had contact with an unusually wide range of women, from those in Charlestown, Massachusetts, who joined her "Ladies

Physiological Society" in 1843 to those in a working class district in Boston before whom she gave free public lectures in 1849. . . . Earlier, in Lynn, she had boarded at Mary Gove's house "for a day or two every month," finding affinity with the water-cure practitioner: "Her deep interest in anatomy and physiology drew me to her."[38]

Hunt severely criticized doctors for conducting physical examinations of their female patients, calling them "skeptics who lived sensually and "contaminated their patients" with examinations "too often unnecessary."[39] She was obviously thinking about what she called "abuses of the marriage relation" and believed that women needed more control over a husband's sensuality. Investigating this complex issue, she visited a Shaker community in the late 1840s but found Shaker celibacy too extreme a response to the problems of fertility and sexuality.

*   *   *

General topics connected to reproductive control, such as the need for wives to have control of marital sexuality or to determine the timing and frequency of sexual intercourse, would, no doubt, have been easier than more explicit ones for women lecturers to raise. The rhythm method might well have been discussed without discomfort because of its seeming "naturalness." Withdrawal, on the other hand, might not have been, though it could have come up in connection with comments on menstruation or with recommendations for sexual abstinence. So, too, women lecturers may have found it relatively comfortable to refer to medicinal and hygienic douching or the use of vaginal suppositories or the vaginal sponge rather than measures men might take to avoid insemination of their wives. The freedom of women to speak publicly on sexual matters was greatly enhanced by the woman's rights movement that itself was stimulated by the war-time struggle for emancipation and racial equality.

*   *   *

ABORTION AS A BUSINESS

Folk remedies for abortion and superstitions about abortion survived essentially unchanged over many centuries. Older abortion methods continued to be available throughout the nineteenth century, but practices were changing. From the 1840s on, the selling of abortive products became a commercial business. Abortion was more openly discussed and increasingly available from sources that seemed scientific, modern, and professional.

Many women continued in the decades after 1840 to bring about abortion in their homes through use of the pills, fluid extracts, and medicinal oils that were nonpublicly marketed with such suggestive names as the "Female Regulator," "Periodical Drops," "Uterine Regulator," and "Woman's Friend." Ely Van de Warker, a Syracuse, New York, gynecologist who studied American abortion methods, noted that "every schoolgirl knows the meaning of these terms." Anyone who did not could have learned others from the printed labels on the drug containers. The label on Graves Pills for Amenorrhea was typical: "These pills have been approved by the Ecole de Medecine, fully sanctioned by the M.R.C.S. of London, Edinburgh, Dublin, as a never-failing remedy for producing the catamenial or monthly flow. Though perfectly harmless to the most delicate, yet ladies are earnestly requested not to mistake their condition [if pregnant] as MISCARRIAGE WOULD CERTAINLY ENSUE."[40] . . .

Most abortifacients were sold as pills or as fluid extracts in which one ingredient predominated, usually aloes or black hellebore. The pills often were combinations of aloes, hellebore, powdered savin, ergot, iron, and solid extracts of tansy and rue. The instructions on the pill bottles told women to supplement the doses by drinking tansy tea twice daily until the "obstruction" was removed. The fluid extracts were most commonly oils of savin, tansy, or rue dissolved in alcohol and improved in taste by wintergreen.[41] . . .

These medicines were often effective, though they also posed considerable risk and, at times, acute danger to a woman's life.[42] Ely Van de Warker concluded that "female pills" often worked as abortives because women took them in dangerously copious amounts without regard for their general health. He believed that the extensiveness of the trade in commercial abortion drugs and the relative rarity of publicized fatalities indicated a degree of effectiveness: "I know many married women who have gone years without the birth of mature children, who resort habitually to some one of the many advertised nostrums with as much confidence of 'coming around' as if they repaired to the shop of the professional abortionist."[43] . . .

In medical journals of the second half of the nineteenth century, physicians discussed the uses patients had made of catheters, speculua, and uterine sounds (a type of uterine probe).[44] The president of the Gynaecological Society of Boston said, in 1871, that "the populace seem to have the idea that Simpson's sound was designed to produce abortion," and in the 1890s a physician in the middle of a discussion with his medical peers about the dangers of coitus interruptus observed that he had advised a male patient who did not want additional children to stop using withdrawal because it was affecting his health; the patient managed to avoid an increase in his family because, the doctor implied, his wife was handy in the "occasional passing of a sound."[45]

Abortion instruments, like drugs, were readily available through the mails or from a variety of retail establishments, particularly drugstores, and wholesale druggists' catalogues carried a considerable variety of styles and models in uterine sounds and dilators. Newspapers regularly carried advertisements for abortion-inducing drugs.

In June 1870, Frank Leslie's *Day's Doings,* a racy New York newspaper carrying sensationalist articles and theatrical and sporting news, carried advertisements for seven medicines with language some women no doubt associated with abortion, including "Madame Van Buskirk's Regulating Medicine," "Dr. Richau's Female Remedy," and "Dr. Harrison's Female Antidote . . . certain to have the desired effect in twenty-four hours without any injurious results."[46] By mid century there was a growing number of "professional" abortionists, and not only in large cities, as W.M. Smith, a physician in the small farming town of Atkinson, Illinois (population 300), noted in 1874:

> I know three married women, respectable ones, who are notorious for giving instructions to their younger sisters as to the modus operandi of 'coming around.' After the failure of tansy, savin, ergot, cotton root, lifting, rough trotting horses, etc., a knitting needle is the stand by. One old doctor near here was so obliging as to furnish a wire with a handle, to one of his patients, which did the work for her, after which she passed it to one of her neighbors, who succeeded in destroying the foetus and nearly so herself.[47]

Smith estimated that his town had one abortion for every ten live births. He was opposed to abortion but expressed sympathy for women who needed some means of controlling reproduction, suggesting, ambiguously, that women use "bromide of potassium"—probably meaning a douche.

Urban women, in particular, and those with access to transportation to urban areas found highly desirable anonymity and the comfort of a supposedly safer, more modern abortion from the services of a newly visible entrepreneur: the "professional" abortionist.

The term "female physician" was frequently a euphemism for abortionist by mid century, a time when respectable women midwives found their role and power increasingly circumscribed by a medical profession intent on establishing its own professional identity. When Elizabeth Blackwell first tried to establish a medical practice in New York City in the 1850s she was denied rental at the first few boardinghouses she approached because landlords mistook her for an abortionist. This assumption was particularly galling to Blackwell, who abhorred abortion, and she described with scorn the flags midwives hung from their windows as wordless advertisements of their services.[48] . . .

In the cities of New England and of the Middle Atlantic states women could find a variety of offices, clinics, and boardinghouses offering lying-in services and illicit abortions. Although we do not know with any certainty who operated these establishments or even how many there were, contemporary observers believed that many were operated by women who had been trained as midwives in Europe.[49] . . .

Of all the nineteenth-century abortionists, Ann Trow Lohman (1812–1877) is the best documented. Better known as "Madame Restell," she ran a lucrative mail-order business and abortion service in New York City from the 1840s through the 1870s.[50] . . . Shortly after her marriage, Ann Trow Lohman adopted the alias "Madame Restell" and went into the abortion and contraceptives business, advertising her services and products in newspapers and hiring agents to distribute circulars along the eastern seaboard. Historian James C. Mohr notes that she had branch agencies in Boston and Philadelphia in the 1840s, and an 1846 article in the *Police Gazette* suggested that "Madame Costello," another female physician advertising abortifacient pills, was an agent of Restell's.[51] . . .

It did not take "Madame Restell" long to gain notoriety and a fortune. She appeared in the 1844 novel by Thomas Low Nichols, *The Lady in Black: A Story of New York Life, Morals, and Manners,* about the "tangled mass of vice and virtue" in New York City. . . . Lohman (Restell) was indicted and tried a number of times between 1841 and 1878, charged variously with performing abortions, manslaughter, and with running illegal adoption services for infants born in her establishment. One 1847 case tells a good deal about her practice: she was charged with second-degree manslaughter for producing an abortion on one Maria Bodine after quickening of the fetus. After a seventeen-day trial, reported in the sensationalist New York press. . . . Restell was convicted and sentenced to a year in prison on Blackwell's Island. The young woman obtaining the abortion was an unmarried servant who had been having regular sexual relations for two years with her employer, a widowed cotton manufacturer in Walden, New York. When she found herself pregnant in the spring of 1846, she took a boat down the Hudson to New York to stay with a married sister, and when she was nearly six months pregnant she called on Madame Restell. The price was five dollars for an examination, from one to five dollars for a box of pills, and one hundred dollars for "operating." Restell asked her whether her "beau" were employed and would help pay for the operation. When the girl returned several weeks later with seventy-five dollars from her lover, Restell induced an abortion by rupturing the amniotic sac and prescribing pills to cause uterine contractions. After several days in bed in a private room, the girl went home. Restell gave her money for the boat fare, told her how to alleviate her milk-swollen breasts, and advised her to come back for a private carriage if approached by the police. Although contemporary critics saw Restell as an avaricious quack, such details of her practice, ironically brought out at the trial by the prosecution, suggest compassion and competence as well as business shrewdness.

*　*　*

As reproductive control became commercialized after 1850, and as some women became increasingly able to assert a degree of independent control over their fertility through contraception and abortion, the deep ambivalences with which many Americans regarded such changes came increasingly into play. In the second half of the nineteenth century diverse groups emerged to try to restore American "social purity," and one of the issues they focused on was restricting sexual freedom and control of reproduction. Often historians have studied the campaigns against abortion and contraception as separate phenomena[52] but the two movements shared important similarities in the opponents' motivations, in the imagery and symbolism of their public campaigns, and in the consequences. Both crusades were led by energetic, driven men; both were backed by professional organizations of white, middle class, native-born men—and women, as well—who had assumed the role of custodians of the public good. All branches of government were their allies; their goals were won through enactments of federal and state legislation and sustained by judicial decisions that criminalized contraception and abortion, both of which had in earlier decades been legal.

AFTER TWO CENTURIES OF LEGALITY, REPRODUCTIVE CONTROL BECOMES A FELONY

In the second half of the nineteenth century, state laws altered two hundred years of American custom and public policy toward abortion. In some states it became illegal to obtain an abortion at any stage of pregnancy: abortionists began to face charges of second-degree homicide or manslaughter and women seeking abortions faced criminal prosecution.[53] Some but not all states made an exception if an official physician performed the abortion to save a woman's life.

For two centuries in America, abortion had been treated according to common law tradition in which abortions before "quickening"—fetal movement—were not punishable, and those procured later, after quickening, might be high misdemeanors if the woman died, but not felonies.[54] Some states began criminal code revisions in the 1830s and 1840s and included in those revisions statutes against abortion. The thrust of the new laws was twofold: to regulate those who could legally give abortions and to punish unlawful abortionists. In some states—Connecticut, Missouri, Illinois—abortion restrictions came in the form of tighter laws against the use of poisons. Only in New York was there a foretaste of the more stringent antiabortion laws to come. The New York law, passed in 1829, prohibited anyone, including a doctor, from attempting abortion at any period of pregnancy except to save a woman's life.

Between 1840 and 1860 the new statutory restrictions on abortion were challenged in nine state supreme courts, seven of which had upheld the common law tradition and ruled that an abortion before quickening was not a criminal offense.[55] Even after 1860 abortion cases were hard to prosecute: prosecutors found it difficult to obtain convictions, especially if there was any doubt about whether quickening of the fetus had occurred, or if common law traditions covering evidence and criminal defendants' rights appeared to have been violated by the prosecution or the police.[56] Juries continued to treat the prequickening distinction as significant, and of course it was difficult to prove that quickening had or had not occurred. . . .

From the 1860s through the 1880s, however, states passed a new wave of restrictive abortion legislation.[57] Hugh S. Pomeroy, a Boston physician opposed to reproductive control, compiled information in 1888 about state laws on the subject. He concluded that there was still considerable confusion over whether "destruction of the infant" before quickening was a common law offense, although he cited two states—Pennsylvania and North Carolina—which unambiguously declared it a misdemeanor, eight states—California, Connecticut, Indiana, New Hampshire, New York, Wisconsin, Wyoming, and the Dakota Territory—which made the abortion-seeking woman criminally liable, and five states—Kentucky, New Jersey, Oregon, South Carolina, Texas—and the District of Columbia which had not yet passed any law regulating abortion. Laws in eight states—California, Indiana, Kansas, Massachusetts, Michigan, Nebraska, New York, and Ohio—forbade the advertisement of abortion-inducing drugs, and Illinois, Indiana, and Michigan outlawed advertisements for medicines for women if the language was ambiguous, such as "caution to the married."[58] Loopholes in earlier laws were now gradually eliminated so that, for example, individuals charged with violating the law could no longer claim that the medicine would not have induced abortion.

The most general result of this welter of conflicting and confusing state statutes was to drive abortion underground, making it far more difficult, expensive, and dangerous to obtain—a criminalization that lasted until the 1960s, when sixteen states liberalized their laws, and until 1973, when the U.S. Supreme Court ruled in *Roe v. Wade* that a woman has a fundamental right to decide, without governmental interference, whether to have an abortion in the first three months. Even in the *Roe* decision, however, the Court upheld the right of the state to restrict abortion once fetal viability was determined, unless a woman's life was at stake.

In addition to the changing legal status of abortion, federal and state laws passed in the 1870s and 1880s made it a felony to mail any products or information about contraception or abortion. Between the 1860s and the 1880s activist opponents secured legislation that made contraceptive literature "obscene" and attempts to disseminate information about contraception felonies. In the closing days of its third session in March 1873, the forty-second Congress, embattled and excoriated by the Credit Mobilier scandal (Union Pacific Railroad executives diverted funds into a separate company and bribed investigating congressmen and other politicians) passed what came to be called "the Comstock Law"—named for Anthony Comstock, a self-appointed vice hunter, a sponsor of the bill, and its zealous enforcer in the following decades. The stated purpose of the new law was to tighten loopholes in earlier legislation prohibiting the interstate trade in obscene literature and materials. But in one crucial departure from earlier laws, the long list of items prohibited from the mail, from private mail carriers, and from importation included "any article whatever for the prevention of conception, or for causing unlawful abortion." For the first time in U.S. history the federal government declared the dissemination of information about contraception and abortion to be illegal. State laws that followed went beyond the federal statute, punishing the receivers as well as the senders of information and in some cases making the actual practices of contraception and abortion illegal. Control of women's reproductive behavior now had the force of law. . . .

By 1885 twenty-four state legislatures had passed "little Comstock laws" modeled on the federal statute or on a more stringent New York obscenity law passed shortly after the federal statute. Because of the federal precedent, the existing obscenity laws of the other states had begun to be interpreted as prohibiting reproductive control itself.[59] Some state laws went considerably further than the federal law. Fourteen—Colorado, Indiana, Iowa, Massachusetts, Minnesota, Mississippi, Missouri, Montana, Nevada, New Jersey, New York, Pennsylvania, Washington, and Wyoming—sought to make even private conversations illegal by prohibiting the verbal transmission of information about contraception or abortion; eleven states—Colorado, Indiana, Iowa, Minnesota, Mississippi, New Jersey, New York, North Dakota, Ohio, Pennsylvania, and Wyoming—made it a criminal offense to possess instructions for the prevention of conception; the state of Colorado forbade anyone to bring contraceptive knowledge into the state; four states—Colorado, Idaho, Iowa, and Oklahoma—authorized the search for and seizure of contraceptive instructions. Connecticut—and only Connecticut—outlawed the act itself of controlling conception; this is why, in 1965, the Griswold case was brought in Connecticut: defense lawyers chose its law as the most extreme violation of women's sexual freedom.[60] . . .

The laws were upheld and even strengthened by court cases. In *U.S. v. Foote* in 1876 the court ruled that "a written slip of paper" giving prohibited information about contraception was a "notice" within the meaning of the law even if it had been sent in reply to a letter asking for information. In *U.S. v. Bott* in 1873 the defendant was found guilty of sending an advertisement even though the prohibited article was not at the designated place. In *Bates v. U.S.* in 1881 the defendant was guilty even though he had not actually deposited the pills in the mail himself and even though they "would not *alone* prevent conception or procure abortion."[61] Although in an 1892 case a Milwaukee judge chastized Comstock for his entrapment methods and in an 1897 case a judge ruled that a whole book and not just the passages deemed obscene had to be admitted as evidence, the Comstock laws were not mitigated by court decisions until the 1930s and were not overturned until a series of U.S. Supreme Court decisions in the 1960s and 1970s. . . .

The stronger antiabortion legislation of the second half of the nineteenth century was the result of a carefully orchestrated campaign organized and led by a few physicians in the nascent American Medical Association. Behind the obscenity laws were "social purity" reformers and their organizers. In the drives against both contraception and abortion, the determined will of zealous individuals gave focus and energy to large public crusades.

NOTES

1. Alcott, *The Physiology of Marriage* (1866), p. 190.
2. Owen, *Moral Physiology* (1858), Appendix to 5th ed., p. 80.
3. Joan M. Jensen, *Loosening the Bonds: Mid-Atlantic Farm Women, 1750–1850* (New Haven: Yale University Press, 1986), p. 28, notes that historians are mystified by how withdrawal was learned and transmitted. She is incorrect, however, that this was the practice among the Oneida Perfectionists. Their method, "coitus reservatus," was different (requiring that a man never come to orgasm but gradually lose tumescence while inside a woman). For arguments that withdrawal was "close to being a self-evident method of contraception," see John T. Noonan, Jr., *Contraception: A History of Its Treatment by the Catholic Theologians and Canonists* (Cambridge: Harvard University Press, 1965), p. 10, while P. P. A. Biller, "Birth-Control in the West in the Thirteenth and Early Fourteenth Centuries," *Past and Present: A Journal of Historical Studies* 94 (1982): 5–7, argues that it was well understood in the medieval West from the twelfth century on. Orest Ranum and Patricia Ranum, eds., "Introduction," *Popular Attitudes toward Birth Control in Pre-Industrial France and England* (New York: Harper Torchbooks, Harper & Row, 1972), p. 6., argue that couples did not know withdrawal in the Middle Ages. M. K. Hopkins, "Contraception in the Roman Empire," *Comparative Studies in Society and History* 8 (1965–66): 124–51, argues that withdrawal needed to be learned.
4. Owen, *Moral Physiology* (1858), p. 78. Charles Knowlton, *Fruits of Philosophy* (Philadelphia, 1839), p. 8, made a similar comment about how easily people could think up withdrawal for themselves. Rebutting his critics who said that knowledge of "checks" would lead to illegitimate sex. Knowlton argued that if a couple had already become so "familiar" as to douche to prevent conception "they would practice the 'way' or drawback . . . [even] if no such book as this had ever been written."
5. Margaret Jarman Hagood, *Mothers of the South* (New York: Norton, c. 1939: rpt. ed. 1977), p. 123.
6. Owen, *Moral Physiology* (London, 1842), p. 38.
7. Quoted in Degler, *At Odds,* p. 211.
8. Studies of the effectiveness of individual birth control methods employ estimates of the number of pregnancies which would result if one hundred women used the method for one year. The base line is the estimate that with no birth control whatsoever eighty to ninety of the one hundred women would become pregnant in the first three to four months. In some contemporary studies, couples relying solely on withdrawal had only five to ten pregnancies per 100 woman years, while in others the failure rate was thirty-eight. Anna L. Southam, "Contraceptive Methods: Use, Safety, and Effectiveness," in *Family Planning and Population Programs: A Review of World Developments,* ed. Bernard Berelson (Chicago: University of Chicago Press, 1966).
9. See Robert W. Kistner, *Gynecology, Principles and Practice,* 2d ed. (Chicago: Year Book Medical Publishers, 1971), p. 676, and Christopher Tietze, "The Use-Effectiveness of Contraceptive Methods," in *Research in Family Planning,* ed. Clyde V. Kiser (Princeton: Princeton University Press, 1962), p. 362.
10. William Potts DeWees, *A Compendious System of Midwifery . . . ,* 12th ed. (Philadelphia: Blanchard and Lea, 1853), p. 42. Nichols, *Esoteric Anthropology* (1853), pp. 171, 173, argued that pregnancy could result from semen left anywhere in the vagina; Soule, *Science of Reproduction and Reproductive Control* (1856), p. 64, noted that "withdrawal of the penis before emission" was a "sure prevention" as long as not even the smallest particle of semen got into the vagina.
11. Letter to the editor from "X.Y.Z.," [Philadelphia] *Medical and Surgical Reporter* 59 (1888): 600; W. R. D. Blackwood, letter to the editor, [Philadelphia] *Medical and Surgical Reporter* 59 (1888); 698; Thomas E. McArdle, "The Physical Evils Arising from the Prevention of Conception," *American Journal of Obstetrics and Diseases of Women and Children* 21 (1888): 934–37; S. G. Moses, "Marital Masturbation," [St. Louis] *Courier of Medicine* 8 (1882); 168–73.
12. Cooke, *Satan in Society* (1876), p. 146.

13. Letter to the editor from "X.Y.Z.": 600; Blount, *A Talk to Mothers,* no pagination.
14. Quoted in R. P. Neuman, "Working Class Birth Control in Wilhelmine Germany," *Comparative Studies in Society and History* 20 (1978): 419. Annie Besant, *The Law of Population: Its Consequences and Its Bearing Upon Human Conduct and Morals* (1878), p. 33, noted that although French doctors believed that withdrawal might be harmful to women, its universal practice in France attested otherwise.
15. Besant, *The Law of Population* (1878), p. 33.
16. [Glover], *Owen's Moral Physiology* (1846), p. 115.
17. Cooke, *Satan in Society* (1870), p. 146.
18. Bangs, "Some Effects of `Withdrawal,'" p. 119. Daniel Scott Smith, "Family Limitation, Sexual Control, and Domestic Feminism in Victorian America," in *Clio's Consciousness Raised: New Perspectives on the History of Women,* ed. Mary S. Hartman and Lois Banner (New York: Harper & Row, 1974), pp. 130–32.
19. References to coitus reservatus among twelfth- through fifteenth-century Catholic theologians are in Noonan, *Contraception,* pp. 296, 336–38, 447. The Oneida Community has been well studied. Maren Lockwood Carden, *Oneida: Utopian Community to Modern Corporation* (Baltimore: Johns Hopkins Press, 1969); Louis J. Kern, *An Ordered Love: Sex Roles and Sexuality in Victorian Utopias: The Shakers, the Mormons, and the Oneida Community* (Chapel Hill: University of North Carolina Press, 1981).
20. John Humphrey Noyes, *Male Continence* (1872), p. 10.
21. Noyes, *Male Continence,* p. 24.
22. John Humphrey Noyes, *The Bible Argument* (Oneida, N.Y.: The author, 1848). This had several editions but was out of print by 1872. Noyes reprinted all the essential points in the book except the chapter on male continence in his *Strange Cults and Utopias of Nineteenth Century America* (Philadelphia: J. B. Lippincott, 1870; rpt. ed., *History of American Socialisms,* New York: Dover, 1966).
23. See Sidney Ditzion, *Marriage, Morals, and Sex in America: A History of Ideas,* expanded ed. with a new chapter by the author (New York: W. W. Norton, 1953), p. 172.
24. See Foote, *Plain Home Talk* (1873), pp. 376–78, quoting Noyes, *Male Continence;* Alice Bunker Stockham, *Karezza: Ethics of Marriage* (1897), pp. 22–23, 120.
25. Kellogg, *Plain Facts for Old and Young,* chapter "Prevention of Conception."
26. Society Proceedings, *Journal of the Gynaecological Society of Boston* 4 (1871): 290.
27. Mary Sargeant Nichols [Mary Gove Nichols], *Mary Lyndon; or, Revelations of a Life: An Autobiography* (New York: Stringer and Townsend, 1855).
28. See Hebbel E. Hoff, "The Centenary of the First American Physiological Society Founded at Boston by William A. Alcott and Sylvester Graham," *Bulletin of the History of Medicine* 5 (1937): 687–734.
29. Mary S. Gove [Mary Gove Nichols], *Lectures to Women on Anatomy and Physiology with an Appendix on Water Cure* (New York: Harper, 1846). This is a reissue of an 1842 book with the appendix added.
30. See John B. Blake, "Mary G. Nichols, Prophetess of Health," *Proceedings* [of the American Philosophical Society] 106 (1962): 219–34.
31. Irving T. Richards, "Mary Gove Nichols and John Neal," *New England Quarterly* 7 (1934); 335–55. Blake, "Mary Gove Nichols," notes that she was denounced by some Quakers and by some newspapers that said that her lectures were obscene although Blake does not identify them.
32. No author, "Lectures to Ladies on Anatomy and Physiology," *Boston Medical and Surgical Journal* 26 (1842): 97–98. Grace Adams, *The Mad Forties* (New York: Harper, 1942), p. 20, cites Bennett's disapproval.
33. See Bertha-Monica Stearns, "Two Forgotten New England Reformers," *New England Quarterly* 6 (1933): 59–84. *The National Union Catalog of Pre-1956 Imprints* lists several of Nichols's novels from the 1840s: *The Lady in Black, Ellen Ramsay, Raffle for a Wife.*
34. Mary S. Gove Nichols, *Experience in Water-Cure* (New York: Fowlers & Wells, 1850), a twenty-five-cent pamphlet. There is information on their views in the short-lived *Nichols' Journal of Health, Water-Cure, and Human Progress* (1853–ca.1858).
35. Nichols, *Esoteric Anthropology* (1853), pp. 163–64, discusses female ovaries using the pronoun "we": "while zoosperms are formed by millions . . . we have but one or two, or in rare cases, three to five, ova perfected once a month."

36. Nichols, *Esoteric Anthropology* (1853), p. 151; page 192 noted that the "surgical" method of abortion was simplest and least dangerous.

37. Elizabeth Blackwell to Emily Blackwell, [August] 1853, in the Blackwell Family Papers, Library of Congress; Elizabeth Blackwell, *Pioneer Work* (1985), p. 162.

38. Hunt, *Glances and Glimpses*, pp. 139–140.

39. Quoted in Ann Douglas Wood, " 'The Fashionable Diseases': Women's Complaints and Their Treatment in Nineteenth-Century America," in *Women and Health in America*, ed. Leavitt, p. 231.

40. "Criminal Abortion," *Druggists Circular* 2 (1858): 139.

41. Van de Warker, "Abortion from Medication. Part II of The Detection of Criminal Abortion," *Journal of the Gynecological Society of Boston* 5 (1871): 229–45; pt. 1, vol. 4 (1871): 292–305; Van de Warker, "The Criminal Use of Proprietary or Advertised Nostrums," *New York Medical Journal* 17 (1873): 23–35.

42. Edward Shorter, *A Short History of Women's Bodies* (New York: Basic Books, 1982), pp. 184–88, discusses abortifacients.

43. Van de Warker, "The Criminal Use of Proprietary . . . Nostrums," p. 23.

44. See George W. Gay, "A Case of Criminal Abortion," *Boston Medical and Surgical Journal*, n.s. 9 (1872); 151–52; "The Causation of Sudden Death during the Induction of Criminal Abortion," *Journal of the Gynaecological Society of Boston* 2 (1870): 283–89; "Dr. Baxter," "Case of Abortion Procured by Violence," *American Medical Recorder* 8 (1825): 461–62.

45. Quoted in "The Liability of Physicians to a False Charge of Abortion," *Journal of the Gynaecological Society of Boston* 4 (1871): 348–49. See also L. Bolton Bangs, "Some of the Effects of 'Withdrawal'," *Transactions of the New York Academy of Medicine*, 2d ser. 9 (1893): 122.

46. *Day's Doings*, June 1870.

47. W. M. Smith, Letter to the editor, "The Prevalence of Abortion," *Medical and Surgical Reporter* 33 (1875): 259.

48. Elizabeth Blackwell to Emily Blackwell, 1851–56, Blackwell Family Papers; Ishbel Ross, *Child of Destiny* (New York: n.p., 1944), p. 87, attributes Blackwell's decision to become a doctor to her abhorrence of abortion.

49. James Dabney McCabe, *Lights and Shadows of New York Life* (Philadelphia: National Publishing Co., 1872; facsimile rpt., London: Deutsch, 1971), pp. 618–30, "Child Murder," discusses European-trained midwives operating lying-in institutes.

50. The sources differ on the details of Restell's life. Seymour Mandelbaum's entry on her in *Notable American Women* is the most authoritative to date. There is some information in [no author], *Wonderful Trial of Caroline Lohman, Alias Restell*, 3d ed. (New York: National Police Gazette [1847]), editorial. "Madame Restell and Some of Her Dupes," [New York] *Medical and Surgical Reporter* (1846), pp. 158–65, and James Dabney McCabe, *Lights and Shadows of New York Life* (London: Deutsch, 1971; facsimile of 1st ed., Philadelphia: National Publishing Co., 1872), pp. 618–30.

51. James C. Mohr, *Abortion in America: The Origins and Evolution of National Policy* (New York: Oxford University Press, 1978), p. 48. See also the article "Restell the Female Abortionist," *Police Gazette*, 21 February 1846.

52. Several studies see connections between the nineteenth-century opposition to abortion and contraception: Michael Grossberg, *Governing the Hearth: Law and the Family in Nineteenth-Century America* (Chapel Hill: University of North Carolina Press, 1985), pp. 155–95; Linda Gordon, *Woman's Body, Woman's Right: A Social History of Birth Control in America* (New York: Grossman, 1976), chaps. 1, 3, 6; James Reed, *From Private Vice to Public Virtue: The Birth Control Movement and American Society since 1830* (New York: Basic Books, 1978), pp. 34–45. For extended analyses of one or the other oppositional impulse, see: James C. Mohr, *Abortion in America: The Origins and Evolution of National Policy, 1800–1900* (New York: Oxford University Press, 1978); John Paull Harper, " 'Be Fruitful and Multiply': The Reaction to Family Limitation in Nineteenth-Century America" (Ph.D. diss., Columbia University, 1975); David J. Pivar, *Purity Crusade, Sexual Morality, and Social Control, 1868–1900* (Westport, Conn.: Greenwood Press, 1973); Carroll Smith-Rosenberg, "The Abortion Movement and the AMA, 1850–1880," in her *Disorderly Conduct: Visions of Gender in Victorian America* (New York: A. Knopf, 1985).

53. The legal history of abortion is in Lawrence Lader, *Abortion* (New York: Bobbs-Merrill, 1966). Also Kristin Luker, *Abortion and the Politics of Motherhood* (Berkeley: University of California Press, 1984), p. 15.

54. See Harper, " 'Be Fruitful and Multiply,' " chap. 2.

55. See Smith-Rosenberg, "The Abortion Movement," p. 219.

56. See Grossberg, *Governing the Hearth,* pp. 178–79.

57. Mohr, *Abortion in America,* identifies three phases to the antiabortion laws, the third, from the 1860s to the 1880s, the most stringent. Harper, " 'Be Fruitful and Multiply,' " isolates the 1840s as the decade of hardening against abortion. Smith-Rosenberg, *Disorderly Conduct,* discusses the 1840s to 1880s as a single period.

58. See Hugh S. Pomeroy, *The Ethics of Marriage* (New York: Funk & Wagnalls, 1888), app.

59. See Mary Ware Dennett, *Birth Control Laws: Shall We Keep Them, Change Them, or Abolish Them?* (New York: Da Capo Press, 1970; Copyright 1926), pp. 10–15; C. Thomas Dienes, *Law, Politics, and Birth Control* (Urbana: University of Illinois Press, 1972), p. 40.

60. See Harriette M. Dilla, "Appendix No. 1," pp. 268–70, in Dennett, *Birth Control Laws.* Dennett, pp. 10–28, notes that in no other country was contraceptive information classified with "penalized indecency."

61. U.S. Code *Annotations,* 18, sec. 1461. Other cases summarized in this section include rulings that the public record does not have to record the exact language or titles of obscene works, that postmarks are presumptive proof of deposit in the U.S. mail, and that it is immaterial to show that obscene passages are common to other literature.

Selected Links to U.S. Women's History Resource Materials on the World Wide Web, 1600–1880

In recent years a wide array of primary documents and secondary accounts in American women's history has been mounted on the World Wide Web, readily accessible for use by teachers and students. What follows is a selective listing of materials chosen because of their relevance to issues raised in the readings in *Women and Power in American History,* Volume 1. Items on the "Women and Social Movements" website at Binghamton include discussion questions. You can go beyond what is recommended here by using search engines to locate additional materials related to the readings in this book.

To access the materials listed below, go to the web address noted with the description of each website. In addition, we are maintaining a Worldwide Web site, http://chswg.binghamton.edu/publication.htm, where you will be able to link to a regularly-updated version of this list of related websites. If URLs for sites change after the publication of this edition, the correct URLs will be found at this website. If new web-based materials appear that relate closely to this reader, descriptions of those materials and URLs will be added to this website. Using the website is the best way for you to access the most current web materials relating to the articles in this reader.

Pocahontas and Powhatan Links
URL: http://members.tripod.com/~AlanCheshire/index-15.html

This website offers a large number of links of varying quality and reliability. Examine the first group of links associated with Pocahontas and Powhatan in light of the analysis offered by Kathleen M. Brown in the article, "The Anglo-Algonquian Gender Frontier." This particular group of links permits readers to consider the interplay of history and memory and to think about how views of the interrelations between Euro-Americans and Algonquins of the Powhatan Confederacy have changed over the centuries and how those views reflect the vantage points of subsequent artists and writers. Particularly worth considering are the perspectives offered on the Pocahontas myth as expressed by representatives of the Renape Powhatan Nation (today's New Jersey descendants of the Virginia Algonquin nation) and the analysis of the recent Disney treatment offered by David Morenus in "The Real Pocahontas."

Anne Hutchinson: "The Examination of Anne Hutchinson at the Court at Newtown"
URL: http://classweb.uchicago.edu/Civilization/American/Supp135/Hutchinson.html

This 18-page document provides a transcript of Anne Hutchinson's two-day examination by Massachusetts Bay Governor John Winthrop and other assistants and ministers at Newtown, a document cited several times by Lyle Koehler in his article, "The Weaker Sex as Religious Rebel." The examination was full of lively exchanges between Hutchinson and her ministerial accusers. In the end Governor Winthrop put the question of her banishment to a vote and then sentenced her to be "banished from out of our jurisdiction as being a woman not fit for our society."

"Africans in America," a PBS website accompanying a six-hour documentary film of the same title.
URL: http://pbs.bilkent.edu.tr/wgbh/aia/

This extensive website includes historical documents and historians' commentaries on African-American history between 1450 and 1865. The first of its four sections, "The Terrible Transformation, 1450–1750," explores the origins and institutionalization of slavery in the British southern mainland colonies, and offers numerous connections to the analysis offered by Allan Kulikoff in his article, "The Beginnings of the Afro-American Family in Maryland."

Jonathan Edwards, "Sinners in the Hands of an Angry God, 1741"
URL: http://classweb.uchicago.edu/Civilization/Supp135/Edwardssinners.html

This famous sermon by Jonathan Edwards at the height of the Great Awakening in the mid-eighteenth-century Connecticut Valley highlights new Lockean ideas about the importance of human experience in religious life. Rather than presenting theological arguments, it engaged the emotions. Edwards figured prominently in the Hawley-Root fornication proceedings in Northampton discussed by Kathryn Sklar in her article, "Culture Versus Economics."

Women in the American Revolution
URL: http://womhist.binghamton.edu/amrev/doclist.htm

This site depicts the vigorous support given to the Revolutionary cause by the members of the Ladies Association of Philadelphia. It demonstrates the ways that American women drew on their traditional activities to contribute to opposition to Great Britain, thus complementing "'Daughters of Liberty': Religious Women in Revolutionary New England," by Laurel Thatcher Ulrich.

Martha Ballard, the Maine midwife, at the DoHistory website
URL: http://www.dohistory.org/

This website reproduces the diary kept by Maine midwife Martha Ballard between 1785 and 1812 and numerous other historical documents that Laurel Thatcher Ulrich used to write her Pulitzer-Prize-winning history, *The Midwife's Tale.* The sources highlight issues related to childbirth and midwifery and relations between men and women in northern New England in the early national period. Case studies of particular incidents permit users to follow Ulrich's keen detective work with the documents to arrive at understandings that are not self-evident at the outset.

Lowell Mill Women: "Uses of Liberty Rhetoric among
Lowell Mill Girls"
URL: http://www.library.csi.cuny.edu/dept/americanstudies/
lavender/start.html

Professor Catherine Lavender, at the College of Staten Island, has assembled an interesting group of images and primary documents focusing on the "ways nineteenth-century women used 'liberty rhetoric' to argue for changes in their worlds." The resources at this website explore, in turn, the Revolutionary tradition, women in Lowell, and the 1848 Declaration of Sentiments adopted at Seneca Falls. From the site's home page, click on the Lowell section and examine the primary sources assembled there in relation to the argument made by Thomas Dublin in the article, "Women, Work, and Protest in the Early Lowell Mills."

Harriet A Jacobs: *Incidents in the Life of a Slave Girl Written*
by Herself, **1861**
URL: http://xroads.virginia.edu/~HYPER/JACOBS/hjhome.htm

This website provides an online edition of a notable slave memoir written by the escaped slave Harriet Jacobs, edited by the abolitionist Lydia Maria Child and published in 1861. Unlike the slave women on large plantations described by Deborah Gray White in her article, "Female Slaves: Sex Roles and Status in the Antebellum South," Jacobs was an urban house slave whose first mistress was the half-sister of her slave grandmother. Until the death of her mistress the young Jacobs had been sheltered from the harshest elements of slavery. Her life as a house slave, however, soon exposed her to some of the worst abuses of slavery and she became the mistress of a white neighbor rather than submit to being the concubine of her master. Jacobs's narrative confirms White's argument concerning the importance of family to slave women and shows a slave woman's agency even under the constraints of unfreedom.

Angelina Grimké: Speech at Pennsylvania Hall, Philadelphia, May 1838
URL: http://www.pbs.org/wgbh/aia/part4/4h2939t.html

After the Massachusetts tour in the spring and summer of 1837 on behalf of abolition, Angelina Grimké spoke in public for the last time in May
1838 at Pennsylvania Hall in Philadelphia. While she spoke, the hall was attacked by a hostile mob estimated at about 10,000 men who threw stones,
broke windows, and disrupted the proceedings inside. That night the mob
burned the Hall to the ground. This online document provides the text of
Angelina's speech transcribed by a person in the audience at the time and
printed shortly afterward. Interruptions by the mob are noted in the tran-
scription. For an account of the women's exit from the Hall before the mob
torched the building, see Kathryn Kish Sklar, *Florence Kelley and the Nation's
Work*, pp. 18–19. This speech provides a rich example of the rhetoric that
Angelina Grimké probably employed in the Massachusetts campaign treated
by Kathryn Kish Sklar in "Women's Rights Emerges within the Antislavery
Movement."

Early Women's Rights: "Votes for Women" exhibit, Huntington Library
URL: http://www.huntington.org/vfw

This fine online exhibit traces the women's rights movement from
Seneca Falls in 1848 to the passage of the nineteenth amendment in 1920.
Numerous portions of the exhibit will be of interest to students of U.S.
Women's History. Three pages offer particularly valuable information on
the emergence and the development of the early women's rights movement
between the years of the Grimké sisters' speeches in 1837 and 1869, the
year of the founding of two national women's rights organizations. See:

http://www.huntington.org/vfw/orgpub/declarations/decsentiments.
html, the text of the Declaration of Sentiments adopted at Seneca Falls in
July 1848.
http://www.huntington.org/vfw/orgpub/resolutions/, a listing of
major resolutions adopted at women's rights conventions between 1848 and
1875 with links to online texts of the resolutions.
http://www.huntington.org/vfw/orgpub/schism/, a chart depicting
the differences between the two major national women's rights organizations
founded in 1869.

**Female Moral Reform: "What Was the Appeal of Moral Reform
to Antebellum Northern Women?"**
URL: http://womhist.binghamton.edu/fmrs/doclist.htm

Daniel Wright has collected documents that explore the appeal of the
moral reform movement, in which women banded together to reshape gen-

der relations in the 1830s and 1840s. They complement Caroll Smith-Rosenberg's article, "Beauty, the Beast, and the Militant Woman," showing the extensive presence of the movement at the village level as well as in the cities that Smith-Rosenberg analyzes.

Catharine Beecher: A Letter to Mary Lyon, 17 November 1844
URL: http://clio.fivecolleges.edu/mhc/lyon/a/2/ff22/441117/02.htm

The archives and special collections of the University of Massachusetts, Amherst College, Smith College, Hampshire College, and Mount Holyoke College have joined together to sponsor the Five College Archives Digital Archives Project. The project has digitized significant portions of numerous manuscript collections from their respective holdings. Included in these online resources is the Mary Lyon Collection at Mount Holyoke College, with letters from the educational reformer Catharine Beecher. In one letter Beecher outlined her plans to draw on Protestant women as teachers in the West, a project discussed in detail by Kathryn Sklar in her article, "Catharine Beecher Promotes Women's Entrance into the Teaching Profession."

Harriet Beecher Stowe: Her Work, Her Life
URL: http://xroads.virginia.edu/~MA97/riedy/hbs.html#HER

This brief examination of the life and work of Harriet Beecher Stowe is part of an online project of the American Studies Department at the University of Virginia entitled "Mothers in Uncle Tom's America." After reading the brief quote at the outset from one of Harriet Beecher Stowe's letters, read the three additional letters that appear in the section "Her Life" further down on the page. How do the letters underscore the argument that Kathryn Sklar makes about Stowe's efforts at birth control in her article, "Victorian Women and Domestic Life?"

Freedman's Aid: How Did White Women Aid Former Slaves during and after the Civil War and What Obstacles Did They Face?
URL: http://womhist.binghamton.edu/aid/doclist.htm

Carol Faulkner has collected documents that explore gender conflict within the Freedman's Aid movement during the Civil War and Reconstruction. In these years, northern white women volunteered to assist freedmen and women and sought to mobilize the federal government in support of these efforts. With private assistance and through the Freedmen's Bureau, these women taught in schools, dispensed charity, ran employment bureaus, and assisted migration. This project tells the story of their efforts and the conflicts that arose with male reformers whose chief priority was to end freedpeople's dependence on others.

Helen Lefkowitz Horowitz, "Victoria Woodhull, Anthony Comstock, and Conflict over Sex in the United States in the 1870s"
URL: http://www.historycooperative.org/journals/jah/87.2/ horowitz.html

This online article appeared in the September 2000 issue of the *Journal of American History* and offers a thoughtful complement to the article, "Reproductive Control and Conflict in the Nineteenth Century," by Janet Farrell Brodie. Horowitz explores the conflict between sex reformer Victoria Woodhull and the federal morals agent, Anthony Comstock. She places the 1872 trial of Woodhull and other legal cases during the 1870s within a broader set of cultural frameworks that she argues shaped representations of sexuality in the United States in the nineteenth century. The article offers concrete examples of the changing legal treatment of abortion and contraception that Brodie delineates.

Suggestions for Further Reading

ALLGOR, CATHERINE. *Parlor Politics: In Which the Ladies of Washington Help Build a City and a Government*. Charlottesville: University Press of Virginia, 2000.

ANDERSON, BONNIE S. *Joyous Greetings: The First International Women's Movement, 1830–1860*. New York: Oxford University Press, 2000.

ARMITAGE, SUSAN and ELIZABETH JAMESON, eds. *The Women's West*. Norman: University of Oklahoma Press, 1987.

BAKER, PAULA. "The Domestication of Politics: Women in American Political Society, 1780–1920," *American Historical Review* 89 (June 1984): 620–47.

BLEWETT, MARY. *Men, Women, and Work: Class, Gender, and Protest in the New England Shoe Industry, 1789–1910*. Urbana: University of Illinois Press, 1988.

BLOCH, RUTH. "The Gendered Meanings of Virtue in Revolutionary America," *Signs* 13 (1987): 37–58.

BREKUS, CATHERINE A. *Female Preaching in America: Strangers and Pilgrims, 1740–1845*. Chapel Hill: University of North Carolina Press, 1998.

BRODIE, JANET FARRELL. *Contraception and Abortion in Nineteenth-Century America*. Ithaca, N.Y.: Cornell University Press, 1994.

BROWN, KATHLEEN M. *Good Wives, Nasty Wenches and Anxious Patriarchs: Gender, Race, and Power in Colonial Virginia*. Chapel Hill: University of North Carolina Press, 1996.

BYNUM, VICTORIA E. *Unruly Women: The Politics of Social and Sexual Control in the Old South*. Chapel Hill: University of North Carolina Press, 1992.

CHAMBERS-SCHILLER, LEE VIRGINIA. *Liberty, A Better Husband: Single Women in America, the Generations of 1780–1840*. New Haven, Conn.: Yale University Press, 1984.

CLEARY, PATRICIA. *Elizabeth Murray: A Woman's Pursuit of Independence in Eighteenth-Century America*. Amherst: University of Massachusetts Press, 2000.

COTT, NANCY. "Eighteenth-Century Family and Social Life Revealed in Massachusetts Divorce Records," *Journal of Social History* 10 (Fall 1976): 20–43.

———. "Passionlessness: An Interpretation of Victorian Sexual Ideology, 1790–1850," *Signs* 4 (1978): 219–36.

———. *The Bonds of Womanhood: "Woman's Sphere" in New England, 1780–1835*. New Haven, Conn.: Yale University Press, 1977.

DEGLER, CARL. *At Odds: Women and the Family in America from the Revolution to the Present*. New York: Oxford University Press, 1980.

D'EMILIO, JOHN and ESTELLE FREEDMAN. *Intimate Matters: A History of Sexuality in America*. New York: Harper and Row, 1988.

DEMOS, JOHN. *A Little Commonwealth: Family Life in Plymouth Colony*. New York: Oxford University Press, 1970.

DINER, HASIA. *Erin's Daughters in America: Irish Immigrant Women in the Late Nineteenth Century*. Baltimore: Johns Hopkins University Press, 1983.

DUBLIN, THOMAS. *Farm to Factory: Women's Letters, 1830–1860*, second ed. New York: Columbia University Press, 1993.

———. *Transforming Women's Work: New England Lives in the Industrial Revolution*. Ithaca, N.Y.: Cornell University Press, 1994.

———. *Women at Work: The Transformation of Work and Community in Lowell, Massachusetts, 1826–1860*. New York: Columbia University Press, 1979.

DUBOIS, ELLEN CAROL. *Feminism and Suffrage: The Emergence of an Independent Women's Movement in America, 1848–1869*. Ithaca, N.Y.: Cornell University Press, 1978.

DUDDEN, FAY. *Serving Women: Household Service in 19th Century America*. Middletown, Conn: Wesleyan University Press, 1983.

DUNN, MARY MAPLES, "Women of Light," in Carol Berkin and Mary Beth Norton, eds. *Women of America: A History*. Boston: Houghton Mifflin, 1979, pp. 114–138.

FARAGHER, JOHN. *Women and Men on the Overland Trail.* New Haven, Conn.: Yale University Press, 1981.

FAUST, DREW GILPIN. *Mothers of Invention: Women of the Slaveholding South in the American Civil War.* Chapel Hill: University of North Carolina Press, 1996.

FLEXNER, ELEANOR. *Century of Struggle: The Woman's Rights Movement in the United States,* enlarged ed. Cambridge, Mass.: Harvard University Press, 1996; originally published in 1959.

FOX-GENOVESE, ELIZABETH. *Within the Plantation Household: Black and White Women of the Old South.* Chapel Hill: University of North Carolina Press, 1988.

GIESBERG, JUDITH ANN. *Civil War Sisterhood: The U.S. Sanitary Commission and Women's Politics in Transtion.* Boston: Northeastern University Press, 2000.

GOLDMAN, KARLA. *Beyond the Synagogue Gallery: Finding a Place for Women in American Judaism.* Cambridge, Mass.: Harvard University Press, 2000.

GORDON, ANN D., ed. *The Selected Papers of Elizabeth Cady Stanton and Susan B. Anthony,* volumes 1 and 2. New Brunswick, N.J.: Rutgers University Press, 1997 and 2000.

GORDON, LINDA. *Woman's Body, Woman's Right: Birth Control in America.* New York: Penguin, 1977.

GUTMAN, HERBERT, *The Black Family in Slavery and Freedom, 1750–1925.* New York: Pantheon, 1976.

HARDESTY, NANCY A. *Your Daughters Shall Prophesy: Revivalism and Feminism in the Age of Finney.* Brooklyn, N.Y.: Carlson, 1991.

HEWITT, NANCY. *Women's Activism and Social Change: Rochester, New York, 1820–1870.* Ithaca, N.Y.: Cornell University Press, 1984.

HODES, NANCY. *White Women, Black Men: Illicit Sex in the Nineteenth-Century South.* New Haven, Conn.: Yale University Press, 1997.

ISENBERG, NANCY. *Sex and Citizenship in Antebellum America.* Chapel Hill: University of North Carolina Press, 1998.

JAMES, JANET WILSON, ed. *Women in American Religion.* Philadelphia: University of Pennsylvania Press, 1980.

JEFFREY, JULIE ROY. *Frontier Women: The Trans-Mississippi West.* New York: Hill and Wang, 1979.

JENSEN, JOAN M. *Loosening the Bonds: Mid-Atlantic Farm Women, 1750–1850.* New Haven, Conn.: Yale University Press, 1986.

JONES, JACQUELYN. *Labor of Love, Labor of Sorrow: Black Women, Work and the Family, from Slavery to the Present.* New York: Vintage, 1985.

———. *Soldiers of Light and Love: Northern Teachers and Georgia Blacks, 1865–1873.* Chapel Hill: University of North Carolina Press, 1980.

KARLSEN, CAROL. *The Devil in the Shape of a Woman: Witchcraft in Colonial New England.* New York: Norton, 1987.

KATZMAN, DAVID. *Seven Days a Week: Women and Domestic Service in Industrial America.* Urbana: University of Illinois Press, 1978.

KERBER, LINDA. *No Constitutional Right to Be Ladies: Women and the Obligations of Citizenship.* New York: Hill and Wang, 1998.

———. *Women of the Republic: Intellect and Ideology in Revolutionary America.* Chapel Hill: University of North Carolina Press, 1980.

KESSLER-HARRIS, ALICE. *Out to Work: A History of Wage-Earning Women in the United States.* New York: Oxford University Press, 1982.

KOEHLER, LYLE. *A Search for Power: The "Weaker Sex" in 17th Century New England.* Urbana: University of Illinois Press, 1980.

KULIKOFF, ALLAN. *Tobacco and Slaves: The Development of Southern Cultures in the Chesapeake, 1680–1800.* Chapel Hill: University of North Carolina Press, 1986.

LEACH, WILLIAM. *True Love and Perfect Union: The Feminist Reform of Sex and Society.* New York: Basic Books, 1980.

LEAVITT, JUDITH W., ed. *Women and Health in America: Historical Readings.* Madison: University of Wisconsin Press, 1984.

LEBSOCK, SUZANNE, *The Free Women of Petersburg: Status and Culture in a Southern Town, 1784–1860.* New York: Norton, 1984.

LEONARD, ELIZABETH D. *Yankee Women: Gender Battles in the Civil War.* New York: Norton, 1994.

LERNER, GERDA. *The Creation of Patriarchy.* New York: Oxford University Press, 1986.

———. *The Grimké Sisters from South Carolina.* New York: Schocken, 1967.

MCCURRY, STEPHANIE. *Masters of Small Worlds: Yeoman Households, Gender Relations, and the Political Culture of the Antebellum South Carolina Low Country.* New York: Oxford University Press, 1997.

McFADDEN, MARGARET H. *Golden Cables of Sympathy: The Transatlantic Sources of Nineteenth-Century Feminism.* Lexington: University Press of Kentucky, 1999.
MELDER, KEITH. *Beginnings of Sisterhood: The American Woman's Rights Movement, 1800–1850.* New York: Schocken, 1977.
MOHR, JAMES. *Abortion in America: The Origins and Evolution of National Policy, 1800–1900.* New York: Oxford University Press, 1979.
NORTON, MARY BETH. *Founding Mothers and Fathers: Gendered Power and the Forming of American Society.* New York: Knopf, 1996.
————. *Liberty's Daughters: The Revolutionary Experience of American Women, 1750–1800.* Boston: Little, Brown, 1980.
PLANE, ANN MARIE. *Colonial Intimacies: Indian Marriage in Early New England.* Ithaca, N.Y.: Cornell University Press, 2000.
RILEY, GLENDA GATES. *Women and Indians on the Frontier, 1825–1915.* Albuquerque: University of New Mexico Press, 1984.
ROBERTSON, STACEY M. *Parker Pillsbury: Radical Abolitionist, Male Feminist.* Ithaca, N.Y.: Cornell University Press, 2000.
RYAN, MARY P. *Cradle of the Middle Class: The Family in Oneida County, New York, 1790–1865.* Cambridge: Cambridge University Press, 1981.
————. *Women in Public: Between Banners and Ballots, 1825–1880.* Baltimore: Johns Hopkins University Press, 1990.
SALMON, MARYLYNN. *Women and the Law of Property in Early America.* Chapel Hill: University of North Carolina Press, 1986.
SCHLISSEL, LILLIAN. *Women's Diaries of the Westward Journey.* New York: Schocken, 1982.
SCHWALM, LESLIE A. *A Hard Fight for We: Women's Transition from Slavery to Freedom in South Carolina.* Urbana: University of Illinois, 1997.
SHAMMAS, CAROLE. "Black Women's Work and the Evolution of Plantation Society in Virginia," *Labor History* 26 (1985): 5–28.
SIZER, LYDE CULLEN. *The Political Work of Northern Women Writers and the Civil War, 1850–1872.* Chapel Hill: University of North Carolina Press, 2000.
SKLAR, KATHRYN KISH. *Catharine Beecher: A Study in American Domesticity.* New York: Norton, 1973.
————. *Women's Rights Emerges within the Antislavery Movement, 1830–1870.* Boston: Bedford Books, 2000.
SMITH, DANIEL SCOTT. "Family Limitation, Sexual Control, and Domestic Feminism in Victorian America," *Feminist Studies* 1 (Winter-Spring 1973): 40–57.
SMITH-ROSENBERG, CARROLL. "The Female World of Love and Ritual: Relations Between Women in Nineteenth-Century America," *Signs* 1 (1975): 1–29.
————. *Disorderly Conduct: Visions of Gender in Victorian America.* New York: Knopf, 1985.
SOLOMON, BARBARA MILLER. *In the Company of Educated Women: A History of Women and Higher Education in America.* New Haven, Conn.: Yale University Press, 1985.
SPRUILL, JULIA CHERRY. *Women's Life and Work in the Southern Colonies.* New York: Norton, 1983; originally published in 1938.
STANLEY, AMY DRU. *From Bondage to Contract: Wage Labor, Marriage, and the Market in the Age of Slave Emancipation.* New York: Cambridge University Press, 1998.
STANSELL, CHRISTINE. *City of Women: Sex and Class in New York, 1789–1860.* New York: Knopf, 1986.
STERLING, DOROTHY, ed. *We Are Your Sisters: Black Women in the 19th Century.* New York: Norton, 1984.
STEVENSON, BRENDA E. *Life in Black and White: Family and Community in the Slave South.* New York: Oxford University Press, 1996.
ULRICH, LAUREL THATCHER. *Good Wives: Image and Reality in the Lives of Women in Northern New England, 1650–1750.* New York: Oxford University Press, 1982.
————. *A Midwife's Tale: The Life of Martha Ballard, Based on Her Diary, 1785–1812.* New York: Knopf, 1990.
WEINER, LYNN. *From Working Girl to Working Mother: The Female Labor Force in the United States, 1820–1980.* Chapel Hill: University of North Carolina Press, 1985.
WHITE, DEBORAH GRAY. *Ar'n't I a Woman?: Female Slaves in the Plantation South.* New York: Norton, 1985.

Photo Credits

Index

of Chinese immigrants, 251
family limitation, 4–6, 80
outside marriage, 38, 50n14, 51n19,
  58, 74–76, 79, 90n24, 163
white women and, 4, 51n24, 230–31
See also Abortion; Birth control; Demographic transition
Finney, Charles, 191

Garrison, William Lloyd, 171–72, 174
Great Awakening, *see* Religious revivals
Grimké, Angelina, 5, 167–84, 202,
  277–78
Grimké, Sarah, 5, 167–72, 184, 197–98,
  202

Hawley, Elisha, 76–78
Hawley, Joseph, 76–79, 81–88
Homosocial relationships, women, *see*
  Women's relationships
Hutchinson, Anne, 23–23, 275–76

Immigration
  Africans as slaves, 57–58, 68
  British, 9–10, 35–40
  Chinese, 240–45, 249–50
  German, 122, 133
  Irish, 122, 132–36
Indentured servitude
  and British immigrants, 35–36
  and Chinese immigrants, 245–46
  and extramarital pregnancy, 38,
    50n14, 51n19
  and family structure, 39–40, 44, 47
  and labor contracts, 37
  and marriage patterns, 35, 39, 46,
    52n38, 53n56
  and premarital pregnancy, 39, 46–47
  and sex ratio, 35–47
Irish
  in Ireland, 9, 13, 20n1
  in United States, 122, 132–36

Jacobs, Harriet, 277

Kinship networks
  in colonial Maryland, 36, 44, 47
  among slaves, 57, 59–60, 64–68, 156,
    162

Labor movement
  and hours of labor, 145, 150–52

ideology of, 117–18, 123, 125
male control of, 124
strikes and women, 124–25, 142,
  146–49
See also Strikes; Ten Hour Movement;
  Women's labor organizations
The Liberator, 171, 173
Lincoln, Mary Todd, 227, 233–35
Lowell Female Labor Reform Associa-
  tion, *see* Women's labor organiza-
  tions
Lowell Offering, 142, 444
Lynn Cordwainers' Society, *see* Women's
  labor organizations
Lyon, Mary, 279

Marriage
  age at, 39, 46, 48, 80
  in colonial Maryland, 35, 38–39,
    44–48
  and indentured service, 35, 38–39
  cross-race, 70n9, 218, 221–22
  polyandry, 44–45, 246
  polygyny, 57, 69n6
  slaves and, 162
  See also Common law
McDowall, John, 189–92, 194–95
Midwifery, 27, 80, 83, 158–59, 266
Modernization, 225–26
Mortality
  child, 40, 235–36
  in colonial Maryland, 35, 37, 44,
    47–48
  infant, 3, 40
  maternal, 40
Motherhood
  among slaves, 57–58, 67–68, 162–63,
    165
  maternal societies, 173
  and Victorianism, 6
  and female moral reform, 188
  and single women, 38, 50n14, 73–75,
    77, 81–82, 85
Mott, Lucretia, 171, 173–74, 178, 196
Moynihan Report, 154

Native Americans
  Algonquian, 9–10
  and barter with whites, 18–19, 215,
    217
  Cherokee removal, 175
  education of, 98

Sewing, 45, 130, 158–59, 196
Sex ratio
  and slaves, 7, 57, 59, 69
  of Chinese immigrants, 7, 240, 243–44, 253
  of Euroamericans, 35–37, 58
  in shoe industry, 122
Sexual division of labor, 11–15, 94, 117–25, 145–52, 160, 213–14
Sexual double standard, 74–75, 81–85, 188, 192–93, 195, 237
Shoemaking
  change from home to factory, 7, 122–25
  introduction of sewing machine, 121
  and sexual division of labor, 117–25
  shoebinding, 107, 119–25
  strike of 1860, 122–25
  See also Sex ratio
Slave codes (Virginia), 5
Slavery, 277
  and breakup of families, 59–63, 68, 163, 277
  and family life, 56–57, 59, 62, 64–67, 162–64
  marriage within, 57, 162–63
  and men's work, 157, 162
  resistance by slaves, 65, 68–69, 71n36, 72n37, 169
  and status of women, 160–61
  and women's work, 157–59, 162
  See also Fertility; Kinship networks; Motherhood; Sex ratio
Smith, John, 12, 15, 17–18
Social purity movement, see Comstock laws
Spinning
  meetings, 7, 94–101
  mills, 96, 106
  and poor relief, 96
Stanton, Elizabeth Cady, 198, 227, 232–34, 237
Stowe, Harriet Beecher
  beliefs about childraising, 230
  family limitation practice, 227, 279
  relationship with husband, 227–30
  teaching career, 174, 229
  work as writer, 231–32, 236
Strikes
  in textile industry, 142, 146–49
  in shoemaking, 122–25

  women's participation in, 122–25, 142, 146–49

Teaching
  Catharine Beecher and, 117, 202–11
  and education of women, 208
  feminization of, 209–11
  and westward migration, 206, 209
  women's wages in, 210, 212n27
Ten Hour Movement, 145, 150–52
Textile production
  in households, 46, 102n14, 108–09, 115n13, 130
  at Lowell, 3, 7, 142–43, 145–52, 205

Victorianism, 74, 88, 225, 233, 237
Voice of Industry, 150

Weld, Theodore, 176, 182–83
Wheelwright, John, 28
Willard, Emma, 197
Williams, Roger, 24, 28
Winthrop, John, 27, 29, 275–76
Woman suffrage, 5, 184
Women as health care providers
  abortionists, 256, 266–67
  herbalists, 219
  homeopaths, 263–64
  midwives, 27, 80, 158–59
  Native American, 219–20
  physicians, 97, 159, 261–64, 266
  water cure, 262
Women and law
  religion and, 87–88
  and reproduction, 75
  property ownership, 41–43, 45, 48–49, 233, 261–62
  and sexual double standard, 88, 195
  See also Common law
Women as producers
  African-American women, 7, 157–63
  of goods for market, 7, 11, 45, 77, 87, 94, 102n14, 104–14, 119–21, 130
  household production, 11, 45–46, 77, 87, 94–101, 104, 130
  Native American women, 12, 216
Women ministers, 171, 177
Women's voluntarism, 92–101
Women's relationships
  among slaves, 159–62, 165
  class and, 127–38
  homosocial, 3, 142–45, 152

Women's relationships (*cont.*)
   See also Cross-race interactions
Women's Rights Conventions, Seneca
   Falls (1848), 5, 8, 182–83, 233,
   237, 278
Women's labor organizations
   Factory Girls' Association, 149
   Lowell Female Labor Reform Associ-
      ation, 150–51
   Lynn Cordwainers, 121
   Manchester Female Labor Reform
      Association, 151
Women's rights movement, 182–85,
   196–98, 278
   See also Antislavery; Female moral re-
      form societies
Women's waged work
   and communities of women, 140–52
   and outwork, 104–14
   and sexual division of labor, 118–25

   in factories, 7, 121–25, 130, 140–43,
      145, 205
   and life cycle, 111–12
   married women, 109, 112, 118–21,
      125
   men's control of, 119–20, 122
   role of technology, 107, 119–21, 123,
      140
   shoemaking and, 107, 119–21
   single women, 109–11, 114n5, 122,
      123–25, 127, 129–36, 138, 249
   wages, 106, 109–10, 112–13, 119,
      122–23, 130, 138n6, 147–48,
      153n21, 196, 210, 212n27, 252
   women's control of, 107–08, 111,
      113, 125, 242–43
   See also Domestic service; Outwork;
      Shoemaking; Strikes; Teaching;
      Textile industry
Woodhull, Victoria, 280